Routledge Revivals

Kierkegaard's Authorship

First published in English in 1968, *Kierkegaard's Authorship* begins with a brief account of the life and meaning of Kierkegaard and concludes with the brief treatment of his relation to multifaceted existentialism. By reviewing the total authorship and by making available much of the fruit of widespread research, this work throws into relief Kierkegaard's central purposes and makes it possible to avoid some of the dubious interpretations which have grown out of more narrowly selective study.

This critical introduction and guide is especially important because Kierkegaard's style was deliberately indirect and distorted and even more because half of the works are actually antagonistic to Kierkegaard's own views. By the pseudonymous works he intended to lead into truth through a process of frustration, provoking the reader into existence. In another sense, the body of the book is also a biography for, in a degree perhaps without parallel in world history, the library which he created was his deed and life. This is an important read for scholars and researchers of Philosophy specially existentialism.

Kierkegaard's Authorship
A Guide to the Writings of Kierkegaard

George E. Arbaugh and George B. Arbaugh

First published in 1968
by George Allen & Unwin Ltd.

This edition first published in 2024 by Routledge
4 Park Square, Milton Park, Abingdon, Oxon, OX14 4RN

and by Routledge
605 Third Avenue, New York, NY 10017

Routledge is an imprint of the Taylor & Francis Group, an informa business

© George Allen & Unwin Ltd., 1968

All rights reserved. No part of this book may be reprinted or reproduced or utilised in any form or by any electronic, mechanical, or other means, now known or hereafter invented, including photocopying and recording, or in any information storage or retrieval system, without permission in writing from the publishers.

Publisher's Note
The publisher has gone to great lengths to ensure the quality of this reprint but points out that some imperfections in the original copies may be apparent.

Disclaimer
The publisher has made every effort to trace copyright holders and welcomes correspondence from those they have been unable to contact.

A Library of Congress record exists under LCCN:

ISBN: 978-1-032-64344-1 (hbk)
ISBN: 978-1-032-64356-4 (ebk)
ISBN: 978-1-032-64354-0 (pbk)

Book DOI 10.4324/9781032643564

KIERKEGAARD'S AUTHORSHIP

A Guide to the Writings of Kierkegaard

BY

GEORGE E. ARBAUGH

and

GEORGE B. ARBAUGH

'Such books are mirrors: when an ape peers into them, no apostle can be looking out.' (Lichtenberg. Quoted as motto for The Banquet in *Stages on Life's Way*.)

London
GEORGE ALLEN & UNWIN LTD
RUSKIN HOUSE   MUSEUM STREET

FIRST PUBLISHED IN 1968

This book is copyright under the Berne Convention. Apart from any fair dealing for the purposes of private study, research, criticism or review, as permitted under the Copyright Act, 1956, no portion may be reproduced by any process without written permission. Inquiries should be made to the publishers.

© George Allen & Unwin Ltd., 1968

PRINTED IN GREAT BRITAIN
in 11 on 12 point Plantin
BY UNWIN BROTHERS LTD
WOKING AND LONDON

ACKNOWLEDGEMENTS

For permission to make extended quotations from the writings of Kierkegaard the authors wish to thank the following publishers and copyright holders:

Princeton University Press: *Stages on Life's Way*, trans. by W. Lowrie, copyright, 1940, by Princeton University Press; *Concluding Unscientific Postscript*, trans. by D. F. Swenson and W. Lowrie, copyright, 1941, by Princeton University Press; *Fear and Trembling*, trans. by W. Lowrie, copyright, 1941, by Princeton University Press; *Sickness Unto Death*, trans. by W. Lowrie, copyright, 1941, by Princeton University Press; *Either/Or*, Vol. I, trans. by D. F. Swenson and L. M. Swenson, copyright, 1944, by Princeton University Press, rev. by H. A. Johnson, copyright © 1959 (by Doubleday & Co., Inc.) held by Princeton University Press; *Either/Or*, Vol. II, trans. by W. Lowrie, copyright, 1944, by Princeton University Press, rev. by H. A. Johnson, copyright © 1959, by Doubleday & Co., Inc.; *For Self-Examination*, trans. by W. Lowrie, copyright, 1944, by Princeton University Press; *Training in Christianity*, trans. by W. Lowrie, copyright, 1944, by Princeton University Press; *Concept of Dread*, trans. by W. Lowrie, copyright, 1944, by Princeton University Press; *Attack Upon Christendom*, trans. by W. Lowrie, copyright, 1944, by Princeton University Press; *On Authority and Revelation*, trans. by W. Lowrie, copyright, 1955, by Princeton University Press; *Philosophical Fragments* (2nd ed., 1962), orig. transl. by D. Swenson, new Introduction and Commentary by N. Thulstrup, revised transl. by H. V. Hong, copyright © 1936, 1962, by Princeton University Press.

Augsburg Publishing House: *Thoughts on Crucial Situations in Human Life*, trans. by D. F. Swenson, copyright, 1941, by Augsburg Publishing House; *Edifying Discourses*, four volumes, trans. by D. F. Swenson and L. M. Swenson, copyright, 1943–46, by Augsburg Publishing House; *The Gospel of Suffering*, trans. by D. F. Swenson and L. M. Swenson, copyright, 1948, by Augsburg Publishing House.

Harper and Row: *The Point of View for My Work as an Author*, trans. by W. Lowrie, copyright © 1962, by Harper & Brothers; *Purity of Heart is to Will One Thing*, trans. by D. V. Steere, copyright, 1938, 1948, by Harper & Row; *Works of Love*, trans. by Howard and Edna Hong, copyright © 1962, by Howard Hong; *The Present Age*, trans. by A. Dru and W. Lowrie, published by Oxford University Press, 1940, and by Harper & Row, 1962, translation © 1962, by Alexander Dru; *The Concept of Irony*, trans. by L. M. Capel, © in the English translation, William Collins Sons & Co. Ltd., London and Harper & Row, 1965.

Philosophical Library: *Diary of Søren Kierkegaard*, trans. by G. M. Andersen, ed. by P. P. Rohde, copyright, 1960, by Philosophical Library, Inc.

Stanford University Press (Stanford) and A. & C. Black Ltd. (London):

Johannes Climacus, or De Omnibus Dubitandum Est, trans. by T. H. Croxall, copyright, 1958, by A. & C. Black Ltd.

Lee M. Hollander: *Selections from the Writings of Kierkegaard,* trans. by L. M. Hollander, published by Doubleday & Co., copyright © 1960, by Lee M. Hollander.

Alexander Dru: *The Journals of Søren Kierkegaard,* edited and trans. by A. Dru, published by Oxford University Press, 1958.

Howard A. Johnson: *Christian Discourses,* trans. by W. Lowrie, published by Oxford University Press, 1939.

The authors also express appreciation to the following publishers for permission to quote from the works indicated:

Augsburg Publishing House: *Kierkegaard's Way to the Truth,* by G. Malantschuk, trans. by M. Michelsen, copyright © 1963 by Augsburg Publishing House; *Lectures on the Religious Thought of Søren Kierkegaard,* by Eduard Geismar, copyright 1937 by Augsburg Publishing House; *Something About Kierkegaard,* by David F. Swenson, copyright 1945 by Augsburg Publishing House.

E. P. Dutton & Co., Inc., *Introduction to Kierkegaard,* by R. Jolivet, trans. by W. H. Barber, 1951.

George Allen & Unwin Ltd: *Faith and Logic,* ed. Basil Mitchell, © George Allen & Unwin Ltd., 1958.

Harcourt, Brace & World: *The Cocktail Party,* by T. S. Eliot, copyright 1950 by T. S. Eliot.

Presbyterian and Reformed Publishing Company: *Kierkegaard,* by S. U. Zuidema, trans. by D. H. Freeman, copyright 1960 by Presbyterian and Reformed Publishing Co.

The Devin-Adair Company: *Journey Through Dread,* by Arland Ussher, copyright 1955 by Arland Ussher.

The University of Chicago Press: *The Prayers of Kierkegaard,* ed. P. D. LeFevre, © 1956 by the University of Chicago.

The Westminster Press: *Meditations From Kierkegaard,* trans. and ed. by T. H. Croxall, copyright 1955 by W. L. Jenkins.

Sheed & Ward: *Kierkegaard as Theologian,* by Louis Dupré, © Sheed and Ward, Inc., 1963.

Pantheon Books, a Division of Random House, Incorporated: *Sören Kierkegaard,* by J. Hohlenberg, trans. by T. H. Croxall, copyright 1954 by Pantheon Books, Inc.

James Nisbet and Company Ltd: *Glimpses and Impressions of Kierkegaard,* by T. H. Croxall, © James Nisbet & Co. Ltd., 1959.

Harper & Row: *Kierkegaard,* by Walter Lowrie, New Material Copyright © 1962 by Lee M. Capel; *Sören Kierkegaard, The Last Years,* © Ronald Gregor Smith, 1965.

Alfred A. Knopf, Incorporated: *Markings,* by Dag Hammarskjöld, trans. by Leif Sjöberg and W. H. Auden. Translation copyright © 1964 by Alfred A. Knopf, Inc., and Faber and Faber Ltd.

PREFACE

What common man—or uncommon man—can muster the courage to read a hundred books of the vast Kierkegaard literature? When a man has written about thirty-five books, together with an equal body of unpublished manuscripts, and when others have written even more about him, it may be asked why another title should be added to the rapidly growing list. The answer is partially disclosed in the question. A guide to this great library is needed.

There is a unique peril in writing *about* the Kierkegaard authorship. Kierkegaard would have been outraged at people studying about him or his writings. Quite appropriately, he wanted people to learn *from* the writings, or more precisely to learn *about themselves* from the writings, using the authorship as a mirror. Yet it is true that unless one knows something —indeed a good deal—about S.K. and his authorship it is virtually impossible to learn from them. In this complexity scholarly criticism is a necessity, but it must place in prominence the author's purpose and technique.

There are splendid biographical studies of this amazing Christian-philosopher-artist-existentialist. There are penetrating critical studies and commentaries of great worth. Nevertheless, for one who would like quickly and meaningfully to find his way into this literature there is no good guide. To an extent Kierkegaard's own *Point of View* might be used, but it is very brief and is more a personal apologia than a guide to the literature.

Worse still, without a guide, how does one interpret and orient himself within so subtle and complex a production? Here is an author who has been so misunderstood as to have his passionate religious earnestness taken for irreligion. Unfortunately he did invite the grossest misunderstanding, as perhaps no other author did. For example, he wrote half of his works under diverse and carefully chosen pseudonyms, and was subsequently so misunderstood as to have the fact taken for a symptom of multiple or dissociated personality. To grasp the significance of these works one must know that the pseudonymous 'authors' and actors on this dramatic stage all have precise but different meanings and functions. Some of them represent views antithetical to those of Kierkegaard himself, so that 'their' writings lead to Kierkegaard only by contradicting him, or, rather, by his contradicting them. Other pseudonyms are close to him, are on the way to becoming him, or his ideal, but lack decisiveness and perhaps, in a measure, clarity. One of them (Anti-Climacus) is so close to S.K. that he is even more Kierkegaardian than Kierkegaard himself; he stands where Kierkegaard would like to be.

Kierkegaard is often discouragingly difficult. At times he is so dialectical that even his abstruse and dialectical arch-enemy Hegel would have had difficulty in following his train of thought. As an example, consider this statement from *Sickness Unto Death*: 'The self is a relation which relates itself to its own self, or it is that in the relation (which accounts for it) that the relation relates itself to its own self; the self is not the relation but (consists in the fact) that the relation relates itself to its own self.' (P. 17) Fortunately, much of Kierkegaard is nothing like this, and reads beautifully. Unfortunately, such passages are not infrequent and when they do occur they often conceal crucial and, in themselves, quite transparent thoughts. The technical difficulties in interpretation are magnified by occasional deliberate mystification, so that only the '*true reader*' (and no aesthetic profligate) should be able to follow the trend of thought. Moreover, there is also a confusing involvement with the technical jargon and modes of thought of the age. The net result is that despite great public interest and excellent scholarly research, Kierkegaard and his work remain subtle and perplexing.

One might even dare to suggest that a guide to the Kierkegaard literature is needed because there are so many guides which involve fundamental distortion. For example, it is most unhappy that people should see Kierkegaard in the mirror of

PREFACE

a Sartre or Jaspers. More reasonably, such thinkers might be interpreted in the light of their intellectual progenitors.

It is to be noted that the following pages are intended to furnish, not primarily a study of Kierkegaard, but a guide to the literature. Further, it is not intended to enter in great depth the technical problems of interpretation, but to give a relatively simple and—we hope—inviting introduction to all the works, so that anyone can discover readily and quickly what to expect and where to read.

The review of S.K.'s works will be chronological. There are admittedly perils in this. There is no intention of implying that the first works written by Kierkegaard are to be read first or that those written last are most important. On the other hand, the time scheme does have the advantage of demonstrating growth and changes in the authorship. The attempt will be made to give the sort of cross-reference which will make selective reading relatively practical.

A brief comment is needed concerning primary sources. Happily the *Works* (*Samlede Vaerker*) of Kierkegaard, which had become rare, appeared in a new edition in 1964. Volumes are listed by Roman numerals and pages by Arabic. The twenty volumes of unpublished *Papers* (*Papirer*), which are quite rare, include his journals, notebooks and uncompleted writings. References to them list the volume in Roman numerals, adding 'A' for journal, 'B' for manuscripts, and 'C' for notes, and the specific entry in Arabic. A page reference is added if needed. For further explanation regarding the *Papers* and *Journals*, see the treatment of the *Journals* in section 52 below. In addition to the *Works* and *Papers*, the *Letters and Documents* of Kierkegaard quite recently have been published: *Breve og Aktstykker vedrøende Søren Kierkegaard*. Ed. Niels Thulstrup, I–II. Copenhagen: Munksgaard, 1953, 1954. The reader is referred also to the bibliographical references in Walter Lowrie, *Kierkegaard* (New York: Harper & Brothers, 1962) and *A Kierkegaard Critique*, ed. by H. Johnson and N. Thulstrup (New York: Harper & Brothers, 1962). Wherever possible quotations are taken from the published translation. The edition referred to will be that indicated in the treatment of the given work. Acknowledgements for assistance in translation appear in connection with the texts involved.

CONTENTS

PREFACE		*page* 9
I. THE MEANING OF KIERKEGAARD		17
II. THE AESTHETIC LITERATURE		40
1. From the Papers of One Still Living		43
2. The Concept of Irony		47
3. 'Either'—Volume One of Either/Or		59
4. 'Or'—Volume Two of Either/Or		76
5. Two Edifying Discourses		90
a. The Expectation of Faith		
b. Every Good and Perfect Gift is from Above		
6. Repetition		94
7. Fear and Trembling		105
8. Three Edifying Discourses		117
a. Love shall cover a Multitude of Sins		
b. Love shall cover a Multitude of Sins		
c. Strengthened in the Inner Man		
9. Johannes Climacus, Or De Omnibus Dubitandum Est		119
10. Four Edifying Discourses		124
a. The Lord Gave, and the Lord hath taken Away		
b. Every Good and Perfect Gift is from Above		
c. Every Good and Perfect Gift is from Above		
d. To Acquire one's Soul in Patience		
11. Two Edifying Discourses		126
a. To Preserve one's Soul in Patience		
b. Patient in Expectation		
12. Three Edifying Discourses		128
a. Remember now Thy Creator in the Days of Thy Youth		
b. The Expectation of an Eternal Happiness		
13. Philosophical Fragments or a Fragment of Philosophy		131
14. The Concept of Dread		158
15. Prefaces		171
16. Four Edifying Discourses		173
a. Man's Need of God Constitutes His Highest Perfection		
b. The Thorn in the Flesh		
c. Against Cowardice		
d. The Righteous Man Strives in Prayer with God and Conquers—in that God Conquers		
17. Thoughts on Crucial Situations in Human Life		177
a. A Confessional Service		
b. On the Occasion of a Wedding		
c. At the Side of a Grave		

18. Stages on Life's Way	page 183
19. Concluding Unscientific Postscript	197

III. THE CHRISTIAN WRITINGS — 227

20. On Authority and Revelation: The Book on Adler	230
21. On the Difference between a Genius and an Apostle	236
22. A Literary Review	236
23. The Present Age	236
24. Edifying Discourses in Various Spirits	240
25. Purity of Heart is to Will one Thing	241
26. The Lilies of the Field	245
27. The Gospel of Suffering	248
28. Works of Love	258
29. The Dialectic of Ethical and Ethico-Religious Communication	272
30. Christian Discourses	275
31. The Crisis and a Crisis in the Life of an Actress	282
32. The Lilies of the Field and the Birds of the Air	285
33. Two Ethico-Religious Treatises	288
a. Has a Man the Right to let Himself be put to Death For the Truth?	
b. On the Difference between a Genius and an Apostle	
34. The Sickness unto Death	295
35. The High Priest—The Publican—The Woman that was a Sinner	310
36. The Point of View	312
37. Armed Neutrality	314
38. The Individual	315
39. My activity as a Writer	320
40. Training in Christianity	322
41. Reply to Theophilus Nicolaus (Faith and Paradox)	333
42. An Edifying Discourse. The Woman that was a Sinner	337
43. Two Discourses at the Communion on Fridays	339
a. But to whom little is Forgiven, the Same Loveth Little	
b. Love Covers the Multitude of Sins	
44. For Self-Examination Commended to This Age	341
45. Judge for Yourselves	347
46. Attack upon 'Christendom'	352
47. Articles in *The Fatherland*	357
48. This Has to be Said; So Be it Now Said	360
49. The Instant	362
50. What Christ's Judgment is about Official Christianity	374
51. The Unchangeableness of God. A Discourse	376

CONTENTS

IV. MISCELLANEOUS WRITINGS *page* 379
   52. The Journals of Kierkegaard 379
   53. Newspaper Articles 384
   54. Meditations from Kierkegaard 387
   55. The Prayers of Kierkegaard 390

V. KIERKEGAARD AND EXISTENTIALISM 394

NOTES 413

INDEX 425

CHAPTER I

THE MEANING OF KIERKEGAARD

The twentieth century is marked by anxiety and even by anguish, and perhaps no voice speaks to these more pertinently and provocatively than Kierkegaard. At the heart of our generation's anxiety and turbulence is the issue of choice, freedom and commitment or purpose. This is illustrated in the Marxist-Western conflict, in racial struggles, and in youth's disenchantment and alienation. Aristotle was not the first philosopher who tried to identify the defensible meaning and significance of freedom, nor will Sartre be the last. Among all the reflective minds which have probed the legitimate and illegitimate notions of human freedom, none has given it more microscopic scrutiny or more imaginative accounting than Kierkegaard. He does not impose dogmatic formulae but proposes a descriptive morphology. Thus he finds a difference between a merely 'aesthetic' and egocentric morality and a universal ethic. He compares a mere interest in *things* with a concern for one's *self*. He even questions the possibility of a true 'choice' of pleasure, instead viewing the 'choice of despair' as the only authentic commitment, and contrasts this with an interest in the pleasurable. The forms of possible decision, their presuppositions, their varying authenticity and their involvement of pathos and passion are spelled out in a manner which is of equal interest to social reformers, philosophers, psychologists, and persons with a special religious concern. In the main, Kierkegaard does not offer conclusions—and never easy solutions—but he does offer a brilliant analysis of the varied ways in which struggling men are trying to lead free and meaningful lives.

Who was Søren Kierkegaard?
A poet capable of both beautiful language and refined sensitivity;

The man who fathered existentialism, including, in a measure, Sartre and other atheistic existentialists;

A psychologist who would have a permanent place in history, if for no other reason, because of his vivid psychological categories;

A humorist whose unfailing wit was sometimes gay, often sharp, and who even considered the place of humour in metaphysics;

A tragic lover who broke his engagement and poured forth a literary flood discussing the love affair as a 'psychological experiment', but who inwardly used the tragedy as an occasion for religious earnestness;

An iconoclast who lampooned the clergy for making a good living off the blood of Christ and who denounced the 'church' for pretending to be essential Christianity, yet who now exerts an enormous influence on Christian thought;

The great critic of Hegel, who ridiculed this 'philosopher of history' as one who wrote about the past as if it had never happened, of ourselves as if we were already dead, of the future as if it were necessary, and of all things as if they did not concern him in the least;

An eccentric, who suffered in melancholy, but who nevertheless found occasion for joy in experiences where others find only sorrow, and who used every problem as occasion for seeking and illuminating truth;

A passionately earnest Christian who denounced the church for making Christ an interesting and noble figure, rather than acknowledging that he is a Paradox, to be responded to as a contemporary, with either faith or offence;

All this—and very much more.

In this study only the briefest review of the life and personality of Kierkegaard is needed. The story has been told many times.[1] A variety of factors helped make him an eccentric man, fearful of fire, sensitive to beauty, given to excessive charity, fond of hot baths, and outwardly gay but inwardly depressed.[2] He was a frail man, dying at the age of forty-two, seemingly of a paralysis of the spine. He had a slight deformity, a crooked back, which he thought resulted from a fall in childhood, but which may have been congenital. He had frail, spindly legs, a large head and prominent nose, but eyes which were beautiful and brilliant. His voice was weak, but nevertheless was wonderfully expressive.[3] Kierkegaard's appearance, although not unpleasant, attracted some attention and lent itself to the cruel caricatures which appeared in a popular journal, *The Corsair*. The physical infirmity profoundly distressed Kierkegaard and he referred to it as a 'thorn in the flesh'.* It seems likely that his bodily limitation made him hypersensitive and helped produce the irritability and bitterness which manifested themselves in his last years. Almost certainly it affected his theory of suffering and his religious views. Yet he was not broken by personal problems but used them as a means to spiritual insight and growth.[4]

As if physical disability were not a sufficient trial, Kierkegaard suffered equally and perhaps more from a strange and powerful parental influence. The father forced a gloomy religious outlook on the home, making Christ's sufferings a source of misery even to a little child, who, as he later reflected on it, felt that he had been insanely brought up. Yet S.K. loved and respected his father, to whom he dedicated many of his writings, and in time he came to feel that this old man had been of untold blessing by personally demonstrating the power of love working through and transforming suffering.

It would be gross misrepresentation to suggest that the gloomy aspects of the life of Kierkegaard were fully or accurately representative of it. Even the strange walks in which the old man would take the little boy *about the living room* rather than the park, were, by virtue of their imaginative and sparkling dialogue and their precise descriptive comments, a marvellous if fantastic introduction to a life of keen perceptive observation of persons and circumstance. These walks carried father and son in fantasy

---

* This was not *the* 'thorn in the flesh' which instead is identified as sorrow on account of his father's sin and his own broken engagement. (*Papirer*, XI[1] A 484.) He insisted that, even with the aid of his journals, no one would ever ferret out the mysteries of his life (*Journals*, 431), and, although some mysteries have been brought to light, it is doubtless true that in important respects S.K. will forever remain a mystery. It is also clear that in part the reason for his secretiveness was his 'God-relationship' which he thought should concern the private person and not the public. (*Point of View*, p. 9.)

through both Copenhagen and wonderland, and exerted a tremendous influence on S.K.'s story-telling and his nicety of description. Not only Søren, but his father and the entire household, were marked by wit, lighthearted play, and a genteel and relatively happy life, so that it came as a great surprise to those who were closest to Søren to learn that behind the façade of gaiety, humour and tenderness he carried a deep burden of sorrow. Regarding this duality of existence—internal suffering and outward gaiety—Kierkegaard's critic, Arland Ussher, observes that throughout his life S.K. lived as 'a man about town, yet led the most exciting inner life ever recorded'.[5] S.K. was a wonderful conversationalist. He loved to visit with people of all ages and all circumstances, and was known everywhere for both his lively manner and his thoughtfulness of others.[6] While his liveliness was often charming, it was also at times contentious, involving a remarkable style of humour which won admiration more than friends. This helped drive him to despair and the lively manner became in turn a means of concealing loneliness, sorrow and gentleness.[7]

As a university student Kierkegaard had a tragic experience which he referred to as a 'great earthquake'. He discovered that the father whom he revered as a model of piety was actually suffering the torment of feeling that he was a lost soul for having once cursed God, when as a child he had suffered from hunger, cold and loneliness. Further, S.K. learned that his father had married S.K.'s mother, the housekeeper, out of necessity, not long after the death of his first wife. The father was convinced that his sin had brought doom upon the entire family, so that it would be obliterated, and that he should be obliged to see all of his seven children die before him. Seeing this expectation seemingly confirmed by the sudden deaths of most of his brothers and sisters, S.K. himself accepted this strange sense of family guilt and doom, but reacted in rebelliousness against the father, and, in a measure, against God. He then regarded Christianity as a 'radical cure', to be put off as long as possible,[8] an attitude somewhat reminiscent of that of St Augustine who prayed for purity but not so soon as to spoil his life of pleasure. S.K. had no doubt as to the truth of Christianity, but was in a state of anguish and rebellion over its seeming judgment and severity. This had to do particularly with his understanding of its relationship to the sins of his father, whose 'faith' seemed more an inward despair than a confident trust. The outcome of this was that Søren lived apart from his father and for a time conducted himself in a reckless and despairing manner.

On May 19, 1838, young Kierkegaard gained a religious recovery, and also a reconciliation with his father. He quickly completed his protracted theological studies, but in the meantime another event occurred which changed the entire course of his life. Although feeling that melancholy made him unfit for marriage, he fell in love with a beautiful and sensitive girl, Regine Olsen.[9] No sooner had they become engaged than he concluded that he would only bring suffering upon her. In the anguish of this thought, and in an attempt to break the engagement without hurting her—as well as in an effort to comprehend the pathos of his own life—he embarked upon a career of publication which is without parallel in history. Love letters in the form of philosophical treatises were followed by Christian writings in which he sought to find the meaning of life for himself, and for any other needy man. His lonely writing desk became his real world of social existence.*

The later events of the life of Kierkegaard will be so fully set forth in the review of his writings that they need only bare mention here. There were two major subsequent crises. The first was a conflict with an unworthy journal in which S.K. sought, at the cost of great personal suffering, to defend the integrity of Denmark's leading people. The second was his attack on the established church which he charged with worldliness.

An important question now asks itself: Is it possible to inquire for the (single) meaning of a man who had such an astonishing number of highly coloured meanings? In spite of such evidence as that just cited and in spite of the thrust of the question, it is still true that there is a single meaning in Kierkegaard. In fact, he

---

* There is a significant element of truth in Regis Jolivet's suggestion that when S.K. was in animated dialogue with companions he was actually in melancholy solitude, but that in the quiet of his room he was no longer solitary but living in a world peopled by actors more real than living persons. Accordingly, he could say, 'Therefore I love thee, thou quiet hour of spiritual exercise in my chamber...' (*Stages on Life's Way*, p. 307.) Cf. R. Jolivet, *Introduction to Kierkegaard*, pp. 24 f., 29.

possessed a unified existence to a far greater extent than is true of most men. His one pervading meaning is found in his *existence as a Christian*. This concern is the magnetic centre around which all other aspects of his thought, life, bitter controversy, and work revolve; by which they are held in position; and from which they derive their final importance.

These statements should not be construed as implying that Kierkegaard's thought never changed. Indeed, his plans were fluid and grew or were modified by the flow of circumstance. His visit to the opera, a journey to Berlin, his falling in love, the ousting of a heretic from his pulpit, public ridicule, a moment at the moody, silent sea or in the recesssses of a forest, his own crippled body, and the sins of his father—all such matters became occasions for S.K. to reflect, pray, see things in a new way, and write another book. Even S.K.'s relationship to Christianity changed, as he moved from a somewhat negative relation, through one of intellectual concern for and defence of faith, and towards an eventual passionate commitment.[10] Kierkegaard's childhood relationship to Christianity was an ambivalent mixture of dread and attraction. In his period of university study he retained an intellectual curiosity about Christianity and he understood it well but was repelled by it even though still adhering to it. He then held it to be in conflict with philosophy, and more particularly he resented the demands upon him which it seemed to make. Thus, later on, when he described Christ as the occasion or possibility of both offence and faith, he was vividly expressing his own personal experience. Yet most important for our understanding is the fact that before the authorship commenced Søren Kierkegaard had completed his return to Christianity and had resolved upon a life of religious dedication, a life henceforth unqualified by ambivalence or compromise.

In spite of such growth and change, Kierkegaard's unity of thought and purpose remains far greater and much less accidental than with most men. The great diversities of his writing (even in a single book including a romantic diary, excursions in metaphysics, criticism of opera, and reflection on a family outing) represent the most deliberate planning. The strange literary structures were intended to produce specific effects, and in particular to startle the reader into self-examination. Singleness of purpose is expressed within a diversity of interests and a rich artistry of form which cannot be less than the quality of genius. The psychoanalytic charge that the many-faceted writings are brilliant projections of maladjustments is not without foundation. Yet Louis Dupré is surely correct in holding that personal problems were only the condition or occasion for S.K.'s discovery of Christianity, which from then on determined his life and thought.[11]

Kierkegaard's single theme is commonly broken by interpreters into two phases, the one involving the concept of existence and the other that of Christian revelation as *paradox*. For S.K. these are interlocking ideas. In fact, it is paradox on which existence rests. If God could be rationally understood, then man would not need to passionately exist; he could be an unconcerned spectator. However, when God approaches man in a manner which cannot be logically understood and which transforms revelations into a kind of hiddenness it follows that man must respond existentially, i.e. with lowliness and passion. Unlike Kierkegaard, later thinkers have separated the two ideas so that two main streams of thought issue from Kierkegaard, the one existential and philosophical, largely ignoring paradox; and the other dialectical and theological, and attending for the most part to the concept of paradox. For the moment it will be helpful to view the two ideas separately, but with the reminder and warning that for S.K. they are interwoven. Existentialism is a philosophy of life, sensing life's daring and perilous adventure, 'in the climate of Einstein, Picasso and Freud',[12] but Kierkegaard sees the adventure as an encounter with God.

Existence might be defined as the kind of being which a true human individual would attain. By a spiritual commitment which is an act of will one should realize his proper nature. Merely being a member of 'the race' does not guarantee that one will possess existence. Sometimes it is assumed that to be a man means for one to assimilate food, engage in reproduction, and in general to be a biological success. However, such an understanding applies to a fruit fly or a horse but not to a man. S.K. believed that if a man merely repeats the customary acts of the species he will be a radical failure as a human individual. Either he will be little more than an animal obeying instinct and being merely another instance of the species; or else he will exercise his will in choosing something less than human, thus evidencing his autonomy but in such fashion as to violate his nature. To truly exist is not to be a mere Cartesian 'thinking thing', but is to morally act by willing to transform imagined possibles into concrete actualities, and to willingly repeat one's value commitments. Far from separating the self from the objective world, Kierkegaard treated it as inescapably bound up with the world. The world is the arena in which the self is confronted by alternatives, and by them the self is called upon to take a decisive stand.

Kierkegaard's emphasis on the self-determined uniqueness of the individual does not eliminate the notion of a prescriptive pattern. In fact, in contrast to many later existentialists, he insisted upon *essence* quite as much as on existence. Contrary to a common definition of existentialism, as the doctrine that existence precedes essence, S.K. insisted that the goal of existence is for man to seek and acquire the essence which God has in one sense already given him. This cannot be casually done but requires spiritual patience and resolution. In responsible freedom man must exist in fear and trembling before God, yet this is not the dreadful freedom of a Sartre who suggests that man must 'make himself' with no pattern to follow. Existence has objective meaning; the pattern is set by God. Ultimately, to exist is to live one's life before God, taking into account one's involvement with both time and eternity. Since passing time brings evanescent glories, changing perils and dilemmas, existence is never simply secure. It calls for a 'repetition' or continual reacquirement of responsible selfhood.

The relation between actual existence and proper human nature was of course not noted for the first time by Kierkegaard. That the nature or whatness of an object (as humanness, mermaidness or centaurness) must be distinguished from its concrete existence (actual or imaginary) was recognized by a long line of thinkers, including Kant, Duns Scotus, Aquinas and Aristotle. As Kant points out, a hundred actual dollars are not in any way different in *essence* (meaning or nature) from imaginary dollars. It seems equally obvious that from an *essence* (e.g. the concept of a red swan or purple man) nothing whatsoever follows as to the actual existence of such a thing. There are many problems involved in the relation of existence and essence and Kierkegaard takes clear stands relating to them.* He holds that to exist is to exemplify (or fail to exemplify) an essence, a proper human nature, which nature subsists prior to and independent of any actual existing. On the one hand, this involves a clear repudiation of an idealistic ontology as represented by Hegel or Neoplatonism, where essence necessarily unfolds into existence and where existence is a kind of natural unfolding or fulfilment of essence. S.K. further rejects the idealistic assumption that greater perfection in the idea implies anything about its concrete reality. If a fly exists it does so as absolutely as a god and its existence is no less likely because of its less impressive nature. It was the tendency of Hegel's evolutionary conception of Being to reduce freely existing individuals to determined moments in the career of the Absolute which particularly evoked S.K.'s protest. On the other hand, if a proper human nature does not necessitate an actual human existence, neither does the existing human being—as Sartre suggests—live without meaning, creating his nature by his free choices. Man's essence is present in the plan of God prior to human existence, but man has freedom to accept or reject (but not escape from) it. Existence is conditioned by an ideal essence, a standard in the mind of God. If man is to exist properly then he must choose this pattern of being.

Such an account of existence is decidedly voluntaristic, with emphasis on value awareness, emotion, and choice. Existence cannot be primarily intellectual because the intellect may occupy itself with conjuring up all sorts of imaginations and bare possibilities which have no real status. Further, even when the intellect does comprehend reality it may do so with such unconcern and detachment that the awareness is more like a photographic sensitivity than a living self. To be human is to be concerned—ultimately not with any finite thing but with absolute Being.

Existence as defined by Kierkegaard is not otherworldly, in

* Far from being a 'radical existentialist', S.K. is in many regards an essentialist. He holds that wherever an object comes into existence there must be an essence, else it would have no meaning, whatness or nature. That which comes into existence remains unchanged in the transition from possibility to actuality, whereas an existence is obviously subject to change. Thus existence is exemplification of essence. Nevertheless, S.K. will not tolerate a merger of the two which would permit the notion that existence is an unfolding of essence, or the notion that existence is characterized by degrees of being. Cf. Michael Wyschogrod, *Kierkegaard and Heidegger*, London: Routledge & Kegan Paul Ltd. (1954), pp. 15 ff.

spite of its focus on ultimate Being and the eternal. Indeed, his individualism is a determined earthly humanism, but he insists that only the solitary individual, with the eternal as its touchstone, is authentically human and that only such individuals can compose a proper human society. He repudiates the tempting assumption that participation in a high civilization makes one richly human. There is instead a danger of progressive dehumanization within the very framework of an advancing civilization. In *Sickness Unto Death* S.K. satirizes the man who really has no meaningful self and who is in such stupor as not even to be aware of that fact. The easily shattered mask of personhood which civilization fosters is intimated in the following lines from T. S. Eliot's play, *The Cocktail Party*, where it is pointed out that unwittingly one may be little more than the outer shell of a human being.

> 'When you've dressed for a party
> And are going downstairs, with everything about you
> Arranged to support you in the role you have chosen,
> Then sometimes, when you come to the bottom step
> There is one step more than your feet expected
> And you come down with a jolt. Just for a moment
> You have the experience of being an object
> At the mercy of a malevolent staircase...
>
> 'There's a loss of personality;
> Or rather, you've lost touch with the person
> You thought you were. You no longer feel quite human.
> You're suddenly reduced to the status of an object—
> A living object, but no longer a person.'[13]

Kierkegaard's understanding of existence had a profound effect on his literary style and endeavour. Even though he wished to reveal the inherent limitations of the aesthetic and even the ethical way of life, he had no desire to logically coerce people into relinquishing them, or to provide them with a dispassionate conviction of the inadequacy of these spheres. In the matter of a life stance, not objectivity but subjectivity is truth. To exist is not calmly to know even the truth *about* existence, but to exercise one's freedom, to be cognizant of the risks, and in integrity to stand for something. Kierkegaard's 'persuading' of the reader therefore had to be subtle, indirect, Socratic. Instead of objectively arguing the faults of the aesthetic life he furnished a showcase of experience, hoping that the reader would then select wisely for himself. Neither is S.K. given to luring the reader away from the aesthetic by displaying its glaring faults. He wanted men to perceive it at its best and then despair of it for what it actually is. He sought, often with brilliant success, to demonstrate the rich qualities of such aesthetic forms as music, opera, poetry, comedy, drama and tragedy. He even pointed to the inclusion of a rudimentary morality and an aspirational religiosity in the aesthetic.

The ethical life, which as a way of life S.K. had personally transcended at the beginning of his authorship, was similarly glorified by him at the same time that he sought to point out its inherent limitations. He portrayed it as a special and unique category within the larger family of 'moral' qualities, marked by both the nobility and the pathos of responsibility to the eternal. Yet it is revealing that his moral exemplar, Judge William of *Either/Or* and of *Stages*, is no heroic figure but a slightly simple and superficial if earnest man. Plainly, S.K. emphatically avoids the careless identification of Christianity with moral integrity, with poetic wistfulness, or even with 'religion'. By making the categories clear he prods the reader into making his own choice from among them.

If existence is one aspect of Kierkegaard's central theme, Christianity—particularly under the concept of paradox—is the other. Not only do such notables as Karl Barth, Emil Brunner, Gustaf Aulen and Paul Tillich follow this impulse, but the whole stream of contemporary theology revolves about this tormenting point. However, since for S.K. existence before the God-man is not one among various kinds of existence, but is the one authentic existence, it follows that Christianity must be comprehended within the total framework of life. Christian existence is the culmination of three successive stages wherein, hopefully, one moves from an aesthetic, through an ethical, to a religious way of life. To comprehend Christianity is also to understand the stages. S. U. Zuidema suggests that there is a reminiscence of Hegel's dialectic in the suggestion that each stage includes the preceding (lower) stage in a higher synthesis,[14] but the central thesis of the stages is anti-Hegelian in that if there is any movement from stage to stage it is never by natural evolution but by free choice. An aesthete is anyone living for the various pleasures of the *moment*. The ethical man is one who lives energetically in obedience to duty, in the constancy of continuous resolve through *time*; he seeks to develop the secure value of personal moral character. The religious man is one who despairs of aesthetic pleasure and self-won character, who risks all and secures the *eternal* by faith.

Broadly conceived, the three stages which culminate in Christianity describe all possible modes of existence. They are so articulated, with level upon level within them, as to neatly identify almost every conceivable type of personality, and every possibility for the spirit. In a sense, all of them, even the apparently non-religious modes of existence, manifest in some fashion the influence of God. Thus the aesthetic includes a religious intimation in its sense of wonder. Correspondingly, the ethical rests on a quasi-religious consciousness of the moral law as the will of God and contains a second, more advanced, religiosity in the form of godly repentance arising as an acknowledgment of the debacle of the moral endeavour.[15] That which nevertheless marks the ethical as still merely ethical and not truly religious is its attitude of self-assurance, such confidence as that of the reputed Pharisee regarding his ability to fulfil the law. Consequently, man enters the doorway to the truly religious (Christian) sphere only when he senses the pathos of his endeavour and understands that God's grace rather than man's self-assertion offers the solution.[16] Judaism and Christianity are thus reasonable examples of the ethical and the religious stages respectively.

In a technical sense there is a manner in which the stages may be either increased in number or diminished. On the one hand, S.K. suggests that irony may be added as a kind of intermediate state between the aesthetic and ethical, and another transitional phase of experience, viz. humour, between the ethical and the religious. If we include these intermediate stages, then the total possible modes of existence might loosely be designated as Epicurean, ironic, Stoic (or Judaic); humorous, and Christian.*

---

* Humour, as S.K. conceives it, is not pleasantry. It is essentially derisive, a moment of unmasking. It is a sense of the comical over pretension. Humour

On the other hand, the number of stages threatens to reduce to two. In Kierkegaard's view, the aesthetic, well defined as it is, appears almost as a pseudo form, because the aesthete deals with reality more in imagination than in the genuine action which for S.K. is requisite for existence. Aesthetic awareness, as, for example, in one's reading a novel, does not help a man so much to enter into reality as to merely (non-existentially) contemplate it.[17]

The aesthetic stage seems to express the outlook of romanticism by which S.K. was considerably influenced. It stands for spontaneous vitality, with no primary concern for duty or for Christian grace. The ethical sets aside this 'immediacy' or spontaneity of the aesthetic. It is the life of the good citizen, the responsible married man, dutiful in his labours. It manifests a Kantian consciousness of universal duty, but with Hegelian objectivity and optimism, having neither an awareness of the pathos of the moral life, nor of the burden of sin. Whereas the aesthete lacks lawful objectivity, and whereas the ethical man lacks personalized subjectivity in his obedience to law, the religious attitude is a second immediacy. It recovers the inwardness of the aesthetic, blending this with a consciousness of the objective normativeness of religion, but in both instances transformed and in a fashion transcended in a God-relationship marked by forgiveness. It makes man an exception to the law and glorifies faith rather than self-expression.

A critically important but commonly misunderstood point regarding the stages is that in S.K.'s thought each is a philosophy of life, not a kind of experience. The aesthetic is a distinct kind of value commitment. Morality is another. Still more important, the religious is not another sphere reconciling these, or added on to life's other values; it is a unique God-relation, involving love, repentance and faith. It dethrones the aesthetic and ethical, even if in so doing it restores their concerns to modest but legitimate

mocks the supposed godliness of the geese who look heavenward but are content to waddle. However, humour is not necessarily the derision which the Christian heaps on the pseudo-Christian. More naturally it is the awareness of the folly of self-betrayal on the part of those who know a more glorious way but can do no more than whimsically bemoan their lack of commitment to it. Unlike the aesthete who sees evil and suffering as tragic cosmic accidents, the humorist knows that they are of inward origin, yet will not take them seriously. The Christian repents but the humorist only laughs at evil. (*Postscript*, pp. 400–2.) Regarding irony as an intermediate stage, see the treatment of *Irony*. On S.K.'s role as humorist, see *Postscript*, p. 528.

roles. Consequently, the stages do not represent a comparative 'scaling' of values. Although there is a sense in which the aesthetic appears as the lowliest of values, S.K. does not treat it as a value among values but as a *way of existing*, excluding other ways, so that it makes pretence of being the life goal. A view of the good life which will not tolerate rivals or even acknowledge others cannot be placed among them as one value in a comparative system. This is what S.K. portrays in the aesthetic and ethical modes as philosophies of life. There remains, in his judgment, only one legitimate *way* of existing, the religious. That the aesthetic and ethical forms of *awareness* are preserved within the religious in no sense means that the aesthetic and ethical philosophies of life are in some measure reconstituted and preserved in it.

Strictly speaking, Kierkegaard does not mean to say that Christian existence is literally a 'stage' on life's way—even the final stage—because this would suggest a regular or necessary movement through a series of steps. In his *Postscript* he corrected this impression by changing the term from 'stages' to 'spheres' of existence. (Pp. 144 *et al.*) A man ought to move upwards from sphere to sphere. However, he may choose to remain in the aesthetic life of pleasure and externality, dwarfing himself by never becoming morally earnest. Or, a man may become a moralist, but, even though failing in his moral striving, may fail to turn to Christianity and its redemptive grace. It is even possible to move, as S.K. himself did, rather quickly from the aesthetic to the religious, with no dallying in the ethical. In any movement from sphere to sphere the change does not come about by growth or evolution (Hegelian 'mediation'). It is instead a responsible act, in freedom, a kind of 'leap' in which the previous sphere is cast behind. Thus one is *either* aesthetic, *or* ethical, *or* religious, the lines of separation of the spheres being quite hard and fast.

In each major transition of life the role of the eternal is decisive. What lifts one from the aesthetic to the ethical is the challenge of the eternal which makes man conscious of the time-eternity complexity of his life and demands a choice. Again, it is the breaking in of the eternal which lifts one from the ethical to the religious sphere because a mere sense of moral guilt cannot make one religious. Only the eternal can make man conscious of sin as constituting *opposition to God*, thus giving an absolute perception of ethical failure.

Upon entering Christian existence one does not leave behind the qualities of aesthetic and moral experience, even though abandoning the aesthetic and the ethical ways of life. Instead these contents are redeemed so that full human existence is found in the religious sphere. Thus, for the moralist (and for the religious man) the aesthetic awareness still furnishes the raw content of experience but is given a new and more adequate order and a goal. Likewise the religious life incorporates ethical consciousness even though it transcends the goals of the latter, for which reason it would be impossible to become a Christian without having been morally earnest.[18] Because of such intertwining of experience, S.K. at times spoke of the 'ethico-religious', as in his unpublished 'Dialectic of...Communication'. Morality remains for him the very nature of responsibility to divine governance, a responsibility which is as valid in the God-relationship marked by forgiveness (Christianity) as under the God-relationship of creation and law (morality). This sense of the ethical as being incorporated within the religious is particularly prominent in the great *Postscript*.

There are enormously important consequences of this interlocking of the stages. The properly religious person does not mystically transcend the ethical, as for example in Buddhism, nor does he transcend awareness of and interest in the sensory qualities of experience as in ascetic Hinduism. Instead, he recognizes that religion guarantees the fulfilment or self-identity of such personhood as the moral man sought but could not attain. That the religious life likewise incorporates the aesthetic and cannot be simply ascetic, S.K. illustrates by means of marriage: 'All the beauty of the pagan erotic has validity also in Christianity, in so far as it can be combined with marriage'.[19] Christian existence avoids the failings of the ethical and aesthetic spheres without simply abandoning the values inherent in them, and it provides the completion which in them could not be attained.

In this connection, transcendent Christianity must also define its relationship to the immanent natural religion which emerges within the aesthetic and ethical spheres. As the aesthetic and ethical are never abandoned as qualities of experience, so the Christian is not to unqualifiedly reject natural religion. There is an obvious peril in this assimilation in that the Christian may confusedly revert to an aesthetic religiosity where 'wonder' alternates with the inescapable rationality which is already present in aesthetic awareness and which dissipates wonder; or, to an ethical religion of God-given law. Yet the natural human religiosity, first of wonder and second of duty furnishes the content which, although transcended by Christianity, still gives empirical meaning to the transcendent. Although it is the role of Christianity to offer fulfilment to the natural religious quest, yet this fulfilment is not a simple additional gift, like precious gold which had been sought but could not be found. Instead, strangely, Christianity first heightens one's natural religious need, expands it to the infinite point, then blends this need with joy over a revealed heavenly assurance. To be Christian is to be 'upon seventy thousand fathoms of water and yet to be joyful'.[20]

A critically important point in Kierkegaard's understanding of Christianity which, oddly, seems not to have been noted by the Kierkegaard scholars, is the matter of his dual, related and equally violent protests against the neglect of temporality on the one hand and eternality on the other. His strident complaint in his last writings, as is only too well known, is against worldly unconcern with the eternal, an unconcern astonishingly common among even 'religious' people. Equally familiar is the protest against Hegel in the earlier literature. What is overlooked is that the raging attack on Hegel is precisely a denunciation of such absorption in the eternal as to result in neglect of the temporality of existence. If everything is *sub specie aeternitatis*, even one's sleeping and blowing his nose, then, says S.K., such a one is not a human being. To exist is not to have the order of logic or the immutability of heaven. It is to become oneself by a continuing series of ethical choices in which the eternal is grasped (incarnate) within the straining experience of time. When S.K.'s bitter outcries against worldliness grate on sensibility, the reader must bear in mind his equally raucous denunciation of the betrayal of temporal and earthly existence by the focus on an Hegelian eternity. Existence is thus a precise concept, an unstable blending of earth and heaven, forever threatened by fevered spirits. The two polarizations, worldliness at the one extreme and other-worldliness at the other, are—in either case—despair, sin, and sickness unto death. Against them Kierkegaard waged unremitting war.[21]

To be fully precise, it should be noted that existence is not a simple blending or merger of time and eternity. Man is *in time*, and true existence is his orienting himself to the eternal within the temporal. Man cannot simply comprehend the eternal because it remains strictly transcendent, and even in its most adequate manifestation (Christian) it is paradox. Yet temporal man encounters the absolute by experiencing its claim upon him, its call to integrity. At this point, S.K.'s departure from Socratic (or Platonic) idealism is dramatic. Socrates seemed to think of man's connection with the eternal as being in the past, something now hidden within the soul and therefore recoverable by earnest contemplation. Kierkegaard thinks that the eternal lays hold upon a man, from without, as a responsibility for the *future*, and a promise to be accepted. While S.K. is not a gnostic or a legalist, neither is he a mystic; neither through rational cognition nor mystic contemplation, but through earnest commitment is true existence realized. In the *Postscript* it is proposed that the man who in inward honesty commits himself to objective error (as a false god) is existentially closer to the truth than the man who knows the objective truth but lacks commitment to it. In the former case there is at least the integrity stemming from obedience to the claim of the eternal, even though that claim is poorly comprehended, while in the latter instance there is no movement whatsoever towards proper personhood.

The concept of man as synthesis of temporal and eternal, or of finite and infinite, has many applications, and even furnishes the background for the theory of stages. The aesthetic existence is best understood not with reference to art or beauty, but as man's desire for the fully *temporal* life in the world, whereas the ethical and the religious stages represent a yearning for the eternal and transworldly, yet incorporating the earthly order in its domain. The fact that the ethical and the religious are both concerned with the eternal explains why there is only one basis either/or of decision. To be ethical is to be obedient to divine imperatives; morality is the sphere of the universal and changeless to which man ought to be obedient. Christianity is likewise the sphere of the absolute, but pertains to grace rather than law. It offers fulfilment through unqualified divine love for the failing and despairing man.

We cannot conclude these comments on the synthesis of time and eternity without considering the accusation that Kierkegaard betrayed his own principles by abandoning time and the world in an overwhelming concern for eternity and heaven. It is true that he began his life work with a remarkably sensitive account of the kind of worldly existence which charms most people and moved progressively in the direction of severe ideal requirements, until at last he seemed to be advocating celibacy and the end of the human race. One might say, not altogether whimsically, that S.K.'s standards kept getting better and better until they were utterly terrible—from the standpoint of a humanity which delighted in waltzing, socializing and reproducing.

One inviting interpretation is that S.K. may very well not have intended to describe a practicable way of life but only to define with crystal clarity the essential meaning of humanness (and of the Kingdom of God within which alone it is entirely conceiveable). This appears to reflect Christ's manner, who, for example, proposed that one let the dead bury the corpses, and gave equally impracticable injunctions for discipleship. To the rich young man he said that the way to be a disciple was to give away all that he had to the poor—a rule which, universally applied, would turn every man into a giver, leaving no receivers. In S.K.'s insistence on the need for honesty and repentance rather than transformation of life there seems to be a close parallel. If one wants to know the nature of the good it can only be by identifying absolute but unrealizable standards. The nature of discipleship must be defined even if there are and indeed can be no true disciples. It appears that S.K.'s primary concern was with identification of a criterion, a standard whereby it is possible to identify one as an 'individual', as an aesthete, an ethical man, a naturally religious man, or a Christian. He left it to the reader to try to apply the yardstick. The minimum essential which S.K. wanted was agreement on the instrument of measurement.

If the implication here is that there are no genuine Christians but only the unattainable model, elsewhere S.K. suggests that every man can be a Christian.[22] This suggests that S.K.'s concern is for identifying an authentic Christian *quality* of life which is only feebly and variably present in 'becoming' Christians. Whatever the real thought was—and it is likely that it remained incompletely formulated—it does appear that the Christian life, as S.K. defines it, is not stated as a programme of action but as an illumination for quickening conscience, arousing penitence and fostering faith. Christian ideality is not an ethic but a disclosure of the nature of the godly. It bisects earthly existence and is behaviourly conceivable (as to turn the other cheek or to enter a monastery) but it cannot be expanded into a workable social order. S.K. seems to have thought of monasticism not as a desirable goal but as an illuminating standard whereby the family man can judge his life. So too Kierkegaard may well have thought of celibacy not as a concrete goal but as a clue to the concept of solitariness before God whereby true individuality can be brought into marriage.

There are some critics who have deplored Kierkegaard's failure to develop a social action programme out of his inward ethic. Nevertheless, his position is a stalwart one which insists that the one absolute imperative is clarity on fundamental principles, not tinkering with society. In this regard S.K. may well belong in the company of Socrates, and also of Plato whose Republic is not so much a blueprint of an improved society as an attempt at determining what true virtue would be like if it could be attained.

Søren Kierkegaard belongs, increasingly, to the twentieth century, even though he directed his keen analytical powers and acid pen quite specifically to a bitter attack upon his own 'age'. It is the very incisiveness of his insight into the life of his own age and people which makes him a prophetic figure for a later generation, experiencing the fulfilment of the impulses at issue in his time. Kierkegaard saw himself at a crossroads in the course of civilization. Through a thousand years of Christendom men had been admitting their sinfulness and the limits of their creaturely knowledge, but these admissions were becoming empty words. S.K. sensed the undetected loss of religious categories; he anticipated growing secularism which would replace the consciousness of sin with a psychological concept of maladjustment. He understood that the coming age would deny, first, that God can be known, and second, that anything can have meaning which cannot be empirically apprehended.* For S.K. as for Nietzsche it is neither scientific truth nor refinement of culture, but only the spiritual rebirth of the individual which can heal the sickness of modern man.

For the sickness, Kierkegaard offers a cure. Basically, what he sought to do was to exhibit and restore faith, and identify faith's object, viz. the transcendent, which man initially encounters as 'the limit' to reason. It is a kind of Christian 'Socratic ignorance' which he champions. He insists on admitting that there are *limits* to knowledge, that reality is larger than human apprehension, and yet that this cognitively Unknown is no mere void but a meaningful intruder in human experience. Only by admitting the transcendent can one do justice to existence, as only the transcendent could furnish the 'eternal' values to which S.K. dares to refer. Without the transcendent, man falls into a 'dissolute pantheism', an egotistic and pathetic humanism, which can find no higher norm or deity than society or the state (Hegel). It is this loss of transcendent orientation which leads men to prostrate themselves before the wooden-footed and gilded idol of society, and eventuates in loss of character.

Søren Kierkegaard is our contemporary. Where, then, does he stand in our world? Of all things ironical, he not only has his *public*, even though he despised a 'public' as a faceless crowd; more, he has a coterie of publics, each with its own cravings and bias.

Just as Kierkegaard wrote *The Point of View*, and other works, to compel the public to recognize that he did have a single message, so, too, if he were living now he would surely write another guide to his authorship in order to compel readers to face him honestly. He would assuredly resent his admiring publics, e.g. the anti-intellectualists who sense in him an affinity in view of his separation of logic and reality. Yet it cannot be too emphatically asserted that he is not, as has been proposed, one of the great irrationalists.

* Traits of the twentieth-century mood which appear in S.K. are cited by M. Chaning Pearce. He included a tortured and divided consciousness, loathing for dead formula and its professors, priests and officialdom, fear of imprisonment of the self, delight in self-transcendence gained through danger, lust for life, anxiety and a sense of impending catastrophe, suspicion of optimistic humanism and culture. (*The Terrible Crystal*, London: Kegan Paul, Trench, Trubner & Co. (1940), p. 19.)

Analytical philosophers would approve of S.K.'s denunciation of speculative idealism, yet their own attitude would be unacceptable to him, for unlike them he is frankly metaphysical. The sophisticated person may delight in S.K.'s biting sarcasm and irony, but might well himself be despised by this earnest man for lack of earnestness. Irreligionists have glorified in S.K.'s scathing attack on the clergy and on hypocritical churchianity, yet ignore the crucial fact that he carried out this attack in behalf of authentic Christianity. Religious conservatives have welcomed S.K.'s illumination of gospel, law, and grace, of the categories of Christian experience, and of the genuine meaning of the person of Christ—freed of the false trappings of piety, yet they might well cringe before his denunciation of dogmatic orthodoxy. Those with wavering faith have seized on Kierkegaard as a means for restoring to Christian thought a rational respectability—but strangely, for they have seized on a man who with Nietzsche insisted on the foolishness of the gospel.

In order to better grasp the singleness of meaning of Kierkegaard, perhaps it is helpful to recognize some of the different images of him. Professors are one public. A goodly number of them regard Kierkegaard as a strange, fringe phenomenon, nevertheless at least worthy as a topic for learned lecture and discourse. The outcome is that this earnest soul, this 'hart panting after the water brooks', comes to be treated by professors as another phlegmatic professor, or as one more reflective and dialectical mind. The plain truth is that S.K. was not an academician, either by vocation or by mood, and he was brutally caustic about professorial reasoning.* He wryly complained that the 'Professor' would eventually inherit his writings, and suggested that even this complaint itself would eventually become the 'subject of a lecture'.[23] The bright note in all this is that, in spite of the pedantic picking of meat from the bones, a large, discerning and in some ways useful body of interpretative literature about Kierkegaard is steadily growing.

Churchmen have become a second public. They tend to be disciples, and are inclined to *use* Kierkegaard for their own

---

* S.K. was particularly incensed by the theological professors who 'in tranquil security' had a pleasant life, thanks to Christ's sweating blood and his cries of forsakenness. Cf. *Papirer*, XI[1] A 374.

purposes. Yet it is likely that he would attack them as vigorously as he did the churchmen of his own day, commenting again on how institution-minded preachers make a fat living 'off the blood of Christ'. In particular, he would resent anyone's using his writings as a means of defending Christianity. In *The Sickness Unto Death* he made his stand clear. Whoever invented the notion of defending Christianity is *de facto* Judas No. 2; he also betrays with a kiss. Presumably anyone who transforms S.K. into a defender of Christianity is Judas No. 2 once removed. S.K. certainly does not defend Christianity but rather seeks to define its message, and then, for the purpose of eliciting decision, to exhibit the Christian life with startling and unavoidable clarity. The human task is not to defend God but to respond to God's dramatic confrontation.

The aesthetically minded are a third major public. They wish to cast Kierkegaard in the role of a poet, ignoring the point that for him a true poet does not glorify his art, and more specifically ignoring the fact that S.K. was intent on showing the preparatory and pathetic nature of poetic and aesthetic experience. Nevertheless, S.K. did commonly exhibit great artistry, and, although it would have grieved him, many will be charmed by the tones of his voice and not by the words which he sings. To judge him at the aesthetic level alone is to disregard the fact that he viewed this level as preliminary, pointing to something beyond itself. His belief was that the ultimate outcome of the aesthetic life is boredom, due to the inevitable failure of any object to permanently satisfy the inward life.

Those interested in existentialism constitute a fourth public, since Kierkegaard was probably the chief initiator of this philosophical school. He set out to rediscover that central reality which philosophers from Descartes to Hume seemed to be in the process of losing, even while searching for it, viz. the human self. For a David Hume, the only reality which seemed to survive critical inspection was the world, or more precisely the raw stuff given by the senses—a bundle of impressions. Kierkegaard objected that such analysis ignores the real self. The *subject* is that reality to which an object is an object; but more than that it is that unique being which transcends the moment of such awareness by recalling its past and by striving towards its future. Past, present and future are meaningless apart from one another. Existence is not a mere act of knowing but an act of will in the temporal duration. It is only by voluntary repetition of oneself that one gains true selfhood, a self-identity which is never grasped in terms of mere contents of consciousness which in themselves are always in process of change.

Finally it is to be noted that the openness of our century to existential thought does not mean that Kierkegaard's genuine message is particularly welcome. There is a common tendency to stop with the existential mood of pathos and despair, and its glorification of the autonomous individual, rather than to move on to religious faith. The modern man who longed for freedom and welfare has found them, and discovers that he can scarcely endure them, registering his distress by a readiness to accept totalitarianism on the one hand and by a movement towards suicide or debauchery on the other. The new man is quite free but is now ready to listen to voices which explore the sense in which freedom is dreadful. Here he is prone to end his journey through dread, and his resistance to Christianity perhaps justifies the shrewdness by which Kierkegaard slyly and only indirectly sought to insinuate the Christian message into secular wisdom and sophistry.

CHAPTER II

THE AESTHETIC LITERATURE

The writings to be treated in this section are those of a period, the first major one of Kierkegaard's productivity, and are commonly designated 'aesthetic'. It must be confessed that there is a certain awkwardness in this name. The literature of the first period (1838 to 1856) includes some works predominantly philosophical, some religious, and some ethical, in addition to the extensive writings which are specifically aesthetic. Nevertheless, for the most part, all of these works fit into a neat pattern, being intended to aesthetically attract the reader, to awaken him to his true situation, and to prompt him to consider the Christian answer to his problems.

The writings of this period are eminently Socratic, evidencing an affinity between S.K. and the great Greek moral philosopher and manifesting the evocative-provocative character of the Socratic thought. 'Socrates always kept talking merely about food and drink—but in reality he was constantly talking and thinking about the Infinite', whereas others prattled about the Infinite and selfishly thought about food and money. So, in the aesthetic literature, S.K. writes in glowing terms of life in the world, but his sights are on the Eternal. It was the ironic art of both men to charm people by focusing on the interesting, while slyly and indirectly introducing the matters of infinite importance.[1]

There is a sense in which even the religious discourses of this period are 'aesthetic'. They are not sermons which proclaim divine truth, nor are they theological treatises. Rather, they are—usually in the form of edifying discourses—religiously oriented psychological reflections, treating man's need, existence, youth, joy—all in relationship to God. These writings root in the common graces

THE AESTHETIC LITERATURE

and sorrows of life but point beyond them. In a later period S.K. wrote his 'Christian' discourses, which start with God instead of with man, but in this first period the aim is (aesthetically) to awaken interest in things of the spirit rather than to specifically direct one to Christianity. In addition to their own aesthetic (naturally grounded) interest, the edifying discourses are often designed to provide answers, some very specific, to the questions around which S.K.'s great aesthetic treatises revolve. Indeed, the discourses were commonly made to 'accompany' the aesthetic treatises, even to the date of publication.

There is a strange and at times almost irritating art in this literature. Philosophy and theology are put in diaries, novels, aphorisms, letters, psychological experiments, tipsy banquet speeches, studies of the opera, and the like. Yet it is not the art but the artfulness which is astonishing, exciting and disturbing. In sheer irony, in one instance, S.K. deliberately misleads his reader through an entire book (*Repetition*) to see if the reader will have sufficient integrity of character to follow through to the grave issues at its end. He writes under pseudonyms, each one with its own dramatic personality expressing its own brand of mockery, all of which is intended by shrewd half-truths to confirm a 'pagan' reader in his evil, but at the same time serve as a remarkable prod to conscience for any who has eyes to see and spirit to attend.

The pseudonyms are remarkable actors, and Kierkegaard, who loved the theatre, here created his own 'marionette theatre', each actor an elaborately developed personality.[2] To the objection that an actor turned author may deceive people by his point of view, Kierkegaard's characteristic retort is that hopefully a pseudonym may be able to '"deceive" a person into the truth'.[3] There is one sense, however, in which the pseudonyms are not realistic actors. Since they are to exemplify *types* they are not permitted to act on impulse, as figures in a novel might do; they must express precisely the characters which they typify.[4] Thus the seducer is an unqualified seducer, the aesthete strictly an aesthete, and every role is played with resolution.

Obviously the pseudonyms were more than pure literary devices. By objectifying one of his own potentialities and forcing such a fictional character to move to its inexorable outcomes, S.K.

not only helped others to honestly face their possibilities, but was also more readily able to detach himself from and cast aside his own temptations and lesser inclinations. What is critically important is that for him these alternative points of view are indeed cast aside. In what may appear to be a dramatic overstatement, yet which contains an essential truth, he insists that 'not a single word' of any of the pseudonyms is his own; 'I have no opinion about these works except as a third person, no knowledge of their meaning except as a reader, not the remotest private relation to them...'[5] It might have been more accurate for S.K. to say that the pseudonyms employ his reasoning and reflect his feelings but not his conclusions or value commitments.

If to the twentieth-century reader Kierkegaard's pseudonymity seems overly extended it might be noted that in a measure he was following the literary custom of his age. More fundamentally, however, he was trying by this means to compel the reader to discover the necessity for every man to say 'I', i.e. to discard the façades of impersonal roles and eventually to declare, 'Here I stand'. Kierkegaard suggests that a poet might be allowed to utter any nonsense and an actor to portray any obscenity if only he does it well, with the hope that this will provide the reader or observer with the inescapable and awesome responsibility of forthright response.[6] In this manner it is evident that the pseudonyms manifest a basic existentialist concern. If truth is not merely an idea to be comprehended but the choice of an authentic (for S.K. Christian) way of life, then one can understand why Kierkegaard could not instruct his readers by providing them with objective information. Rather he felt obliged by means of his strange and at times appalling 'authors' to provocatively demonstrate for men the rival modes of existence which they themselves must choose to lead or not lead. If the only way to gain ethico-religious truth is by living it out or existing in it, then a textbook account of it is of little help. On the other hand, in watching Hamlet one may acquire an understanding of Hamlet's pathos. This explains S.K.'s creation of the dramatic characters, although it also points to a special peril in objectively reviewing the aesthetic literature; knowing the plot of Hamlet is no substitute for watching the prince waver and suffer. A final consequence of the view that 'existence' itself is the ideal goal of instruction is that S.K. felt obliged not to merely entertain the reader but also to reveal plainly the heavy price in suffering which the Christian must pay for the good.

Most of the pseudonymous figures are inferior in character to Kierkegaard. Two of them he regarded as more spiritual than himself. In addition to Anti-Climacus, the author of *Training in Christianity*, there is H.H. who, in *Two Minor...Treatises*, is concerned with apostleship and martyrdom. Both of these 'authors' represent a kind of Christian witness which S.K. regarded as being definitely excluded for himself.

For rightly comprehending the literature one must therefore be sure to ask when he is reading the real Kierkegaard. S.K.'s more famous writings are not *his* works, if we are to believe his bold assertion: 'In the pseudonymous works there is not a single word which is mine'.[7] If this assertion fails to penetrate the subtlety and diversity within the person of the artist and fails to adequately analyse the nature of his imaginative literary creation, yet it does remind one that the aesthetic writings are intended to be a dramatic and startling provocation and neither a direct persuasion of the reader nor an accurate representation of their author. Since the pseudonymous 'authors' are so unlike one another and often so unlike Kierkegaard himself, the reader is urged in each case to fix in mind who the 'author' of a pseudonymous work is and then carefully to weigh the problem of the manner in which this fictional character expresses the meaning or purpose of Søren Kierkegaard himself.

1. FROM THE PAPERS OF ONE STILL LIVING

From the Papers of One Still Living. Published *against* his will by S. Kierkegaard [S.K.'s own statement]. September 7, 1838. Not translated. In Vaerker, Vol. I. The authors are indebted to Paul David Johnson for a manuscript translation.

Kierkegaard is famous for a poetic, lyrical style and for pungent writing, and even *From the Papers of One Still Living* has been characterized as 'highly tooled prose'.[8] However, in spite of passages with fine literary form, its utterance is frequently extraordinarily complex. Indeed, because of its ponderous and obscure passages, it was humorously suggested by some of S.K.'s contemporaries that only the author and the person whom it attacked had read it through.[9]

This essay constitutes an attack on Denmark's famous storyteller, Hans Christian Andersen, yet it is chiefly important because already here it is evident that Kierkegaard had attained his own goal of a philosophy of life. Surprisingly and unhappily the essay begins with neither Andersen nor S.K.'s philosophy but with Hegel and the laboured point that some novels are like Hegel in that they 'begin with nothing'. The involvement of Hegel may in part have been a polite nod to this lordly figure, but S.K. also wanted to appeal to Hegel's sense of historical continuity and normal social growth ('evolution') in a protest against the rash and revolutionary mood of the age, in particular as it tended to occupy itself with political issues. The relation of these matters to the book's central theme is obviously tenuous.

One intriguing point about this essay is its strange title. It reflects Kierkegaard's surprise that he was still living, since he shared his father's strange feeling that like five others of his seven brothers and sisters, he was doomed to die young, because of the father's sins.* Søren, remarkably like his father, was vivacious, witty, given to amusing stories, dutiful, gentle, and profoundly reflective, but inwardly afflicted with a deep melancholy, generally hidden from relatives and friends alike.[10] The title of this work is one of the manifestations of that sombre side of his life.

Three points of concern emerge in this work, the attack on Andersen, a theory of the novel, and S.K.'s theory of 'the individual'. These three are here stated in order of their prominence, but undoubtedly in inverse order of their importance. The concept of the individual, perhaps S.K.'s central doctrine, is here evident in a tentative and preliminary form. The individual is a spiritually self-reliant person who is not dependent upon circumstances, still less broken by them, and who manifests personal integrity in his realization of basic purposes. In particular, S.K. is outraged by Andersen's self-pity and his contention that it is an unhappy environment which transforms a genius into a pitiful wretch.

* See below, the closing treatment of *Stages*.

THE AESTHETIC LITERATURE

S.K. replies that it is false vanity in both Andersen and the hero of his novel, *Only a Fiddler*, which leads to this cowardly outlook. 'Genius,' says Kierkegaard, 'is not a candle which is blown out by the wind, but a fire which the storm causes to flare up.'

The implicit philosophy of life is the position that proper existence is not a mere set of experiences nor even a set of convictions ('theses'), but a 'transubstantiation of experience, an inviolable certainty in self wrested from all empiricism'. In anticipation of the subsequently developed concept of existence as 'repetition', S.K. points out that to be an authentic person requires a constant struggle to prevent life from slipping away from one; a person must lead 'its particular expressions back into himself once more'. This process of self-becoming does not guarantee that all of life's incidents can be easily accepted or fitted into a purposeful whole, but it does mean that the person has attained an illumination which serves as the key for the understanding and living of life's strenuosities.[11]

Kierkegaard's view of the self-sustained individual furnishes the core of his theory of the novel as literature. Whereas in Andersen's novel the author does little more than project his own emotional problems and maladjustment, the true novel must express a philosophy of life and a confidence won through experience. This can be no mere fixed idea, as that of impending doom for the good and the great, for such a spirit—manifested by Andersen—is only a weakness in the face of trial and fails to demonstrate or vindicate any principle whatsoever. A philosophy of life must be the real theme of a novel and shape its direction, surviving all else, even when its hero dies. In contrast, says S.K., all that survives at the end of *Only a Fiddler* is the author's sigh.

Kierkegaard acknowledges a certain lyrical quality in Andersen, but says the poetic elements are undigested, badly appropriated, and misused. In addition, there is a lack of an epic quality, together with a variety of specialized deficiencies, a list of which is of importance to the student of Andersen rather than to the student of Kierkegaard. However, it is the lack of basic integrity in Andersen and the resulting lack of a philosophy of life which are the chief points of criticism, for S.K. thinks they make it impossible to furnish the novel with any proper unity. The hero of the novel is in fact a mirror of the author. 'What goes to wrack and ruin in Andersen's novel is not a genius, but a sorry wretch who, Andersen assures us, is a genius.'[12]

From the Papers points to a violent personal clash between Kierkegaard and Hans Christian Andersen, and discloses both a less happy side of the great story-teller's personality than the readers of fairy tales would like, and at the same time a contentious spirit in Kierkegaard. These two authors, together with other gifted young men, had shared the busy social life of Copenhagen and had enjoyed the invigorating literary table talk of the coffee houses. Far from having a lonely existence, S.K. was a very sociable person, with many friends as well as relatives with whom he had the happiest of relations. For many of the notables of Copenhagen, and very particularly for S.K., the streets, parks, coffee houses and the beautiful strand were like a large reception room.[13] In his social interchange, the wit and brilliant dialectic which in part S.K. had learned by imitating his father were in full play, but often with a destructive spirit. He was ready to attack anyone's point of view, seemingly out of sheer love of contradiction.[14] In this way, as was revealed by a novel of the time, *Moods and Conditions* by Henrik Hertz, Andersen and S.K. came into violent conflict. S.K. despised Andersen's pretentious ambitions and hiding of his personal weakness and 'inner emptiness' behind colourful pictures. Accordingly, in his essay he charges that Andersen has only the possibilities but not the actuality of a personality, that he has no philosophy of life to exemplify, and that 'the same joyless battle which Andersen himself fights in his life is now repeated in his art'. Outraged at being called an unfinished poetic creation, Andersen in bitterness satirized S.K. in *The Shoes of Fortune*, where S.K. was made to appear as a sharp-beaked, destructive and conceited parrot.[15] Further, S.K. was obliged to sit in the Royal Theatre and hear Andersen's play, *En Comoedie i det Grønne*, mock him. In the latter an actor recited with painful humour tortuous passages from S.K.'s own essay.[16]

THE AESTHETIC LITERATURE

2. THE CONCEPT OF IRONY

The Concept of Irony with Constant Reference to Socrates. September 16, 1841. Dissertation for the Master's degree (equivalent to Ph.D.). Translated with an introduction and notes by Lee M. Capel. New York: Harper & Row (1965).

This rather large book, of considerable significance for all of Kierkegaard's authorship, was written in Danish in spite of the fact that Latin was usually required. S.K. observed that to write in Latin about romanticism—which he here discusses—would be like describing a circle with squares. (P. 30) Although some of the views expressed here were soon abandoned, *Irony* set the pattern for subsequent writings by its masterful and at times lyrical style, its humour and satire. Because of its subtlety the dissertation has often been misunderstood. In particular, it has commonly been viewed as a youthful Hegelian writing, whereas actually it is an ironic attack on both Hegelianism and romanticism, each being made to overwhelm the other.[17] From the literary standpoint the book is rich with allusions to philosophic and general sources, and is a surprising accomplishment in view of the fact that it was written during the agonizing period just prior to the author's breaking of his engagement to Regine Olsen.

There was a background in Kierkegaard's personality for his intense interest in irony. His youth had been marked by a display of gaiety, partly employed as a means of concealing a profound melancholy, a pretence which has an affinity to irony although involving actual concealment which is not the case in irony. In the dissertation it was the irony of Socrates which most captured his imagination and in it there is constant reference to Socrates, although more immediately the goal is a critique of the literature of German romanticism.

Readers familiar with Socrates may find it strange to find him portrayed here as an ironist. To many the *maieutic* method of Socrates would seem more basic, the method whereby (as a midwife) he helped truth to be born in a soul. S.K. rather stresses the aspect of irony (pretended ignorance or pretence of the opposite state from the truth). Thus Socrates pretended to be ignorant in order to show the 'wise' that they were not really wise, just as Kierkegaard eventually pretended that he was not Christian in order to demonstrate to professed Christians that they were hypocrites.* Irony, as here presented, is more a quality of the person than of his manner of expression. In Socrates it is his attack on the superficial civilization of the age, yet offering no solution for the defect. Irony is 'ignorance' which challenges but offers no answers. It is infinite negativity. Socrates is seen to possess no truth and to only negatively prepare the way for truth by demolishing the false opinions of others. Such a Socrates would not even know the purposes he served. S.K. acknowledges, however, that this deficiency in Socrates has the benefit of avoiding indoctrination and of teaching by challenging the learner.

In agreement with Hegel, S.K. here sees the significance of Socrates in his seeking to identify the rights of the individual as opposed to the state, even at the expense of the proper claims of society. Like Hegel, S.K. argues that true virtue is manifested only within the state. Later on, with a growing stress on individuality and an awakening to the perils of the social mass, he branded the views expressed here as nonsense. He then viewed the state as evil (although obviously serving a necessary purpose) in that it exhibits human egoism on a large scale, passing off collective greed and 'injustice in a grand style' as justice.[18] Even the irony of Socrates is dealt with rather critically in this work, for it suggested that Socrates' pretence of ignorance and his endless questioning meant that he really had no significant and positive message to give.

In addition to its major focus on Socrates, the dissertation offers an ambivalent treatment of German romanticism. In a far greater degree than casual reading might suggest, the dissertation shares the outlook and evidences the influence of romanticism's protest against stolid respectability. S.K.'s own mood rooted in his despairing rebellion against his father and his father's pietism, and reflects his consequent indulgence in an aesthetic mode of life. In his *Journals* he railed against respectability and its exemplars: 'For them the most important thing is to be a useful member of

---

* The parallelism is not precise. In a sense Socrates was not ironical; he *did* lack the wisdom for which he longed. It was the critics of Socrates who lived in pretence, although not having an 'ironical' spirit. It might be argued that it is S.K. more than Socrates who is ironical in that S.K. was a Christian when he pretended not to be, although only a 'becoming' Christian.

the state, and to air their opinions in the club of an evening; they have never felt homesickness for something unknown and far away.... The bourgeois' love of God begins when vegetable life is most active, when the hands are comfortably folded on the stomach....[19] The dissertation joins in romanticism's satire of the unimaginative, phlegmatic and custom-ridden life of the contemporary world. It protests that everyone insensitively follows custom, whether in a proposal of marriage, a country revel on a midsummer's day, a saying of prayers, or retiring faithfully at ten o'clock. To such existence, monotonous, spiritless, and matter of fact, romanticism brings a breath of fresh air. 'The forest breathes easy, the birds sing, the beautiful princess surrounds herself with suitors, the woods echo the sound of hunting horns and baying hounds, the meadows shed fragrance, poetry and song tear themselves loose from nature...' (Pp. 318 f.)

The influence of romanticism will partially explain a perplexing feature of S.K.'s subsequent conception of the moral life. He came to define it as dutiful conformity to universal principle, but he viewed this as an overly-confident moral stance and even a complacent self-deception. This not only expresses genuine Christian despair of self-righteousness, but also romanticism's irritation with the bourgeois morality. Perhaps lacking something of romanticism's tolerance, S.K. yet expressed its contempt of moral stodginess when he viewed the stoic's pretence of a good life as a façade which covers concealed sin, a guilt which perhaps only psychoanalysis can ferret out, and which cries out for penitence and redemption. In the dreams of romanticism we find one of the sources of Kierkegaard's great stress on ideality as one of the poles of life, existence being a synthesis of ideality and reality.

In view of the affinity with romanticism, it is the more impressive that *Irony* makes a bitter attack upon it. There is nothing but dreams to be found in romanticism. There is neither true vision of the eternal nor firm rooting in temporal reality. The dreams of the romantic poet hang suspended, serving as a substitute for reality but making no proper contribution to it. Neither do they bring the soul into the presence of God. This position will be elaborated below.

There are two matters first treated in *Irony* but developing in the entire Kierkegaard authorship which ought now to be given special attention. The one is the role of irony in S.K.'s system of thought. The other is the changing role of Socrates in S.K.'s outlook. Regarding the latter, it was not long before the evolving concept of existence called for a revision of judgment, to the extent that the sage of Athens became his supreme ideal and model, representing concern for values and personal decisiveness. In the *Fragments* and *Postscript* Socrates is no longer a relentless inquirer who disillusions others without knowing where he is going. He becomes a person who possesses truth and who is motivated by ethical passion in his exercise of inwardness.[20] With this sharp change in judgment, S.K. commented with some bitterness: 'Influenced as I was by Hegel..., there is a place in my dissertation where I could not help showing it up as an imperfection in Socrates that he had no eye for Totality but, numerically, only saw Individuals. Oh, what a Hegelian fool I was.'[21]

In this new perspective Kierkegaard identified himself so emphatically with his Greek mentor that he has come to be thought of as the Danish Socrates, and indeed he viewed himself in such a role. Above all he saw Socrates as manifesting the need for decisiveness on the part of the solitary individual. Whereas it was the manner of the Hegelians to find something of truth in opposite points of view and seek a synthesis of opposites, Socrates symbolized the need for clear and uncompromising stands on matters of truth and falsehood. The personal consequence, as Socrates reported it, was that some of his pupils wished to bite him for having 'deprived them of a darling folly'.

Swenson cites a number of Socratic elements in Kierkegaard, including a concern for moral philosophy, insistence on concreteness, the maieutic method, an instrumental and pragmatic use of thought for practical ends rather than as a mere means of speculation, and a polemical concern with the contemporary society.[22] There remains, of course, a profound contrast in substantive matters between Kierkegaard and Socrates. The Greek philosopher sought contact with the eternal by the recovery (recollection) of it as an immanent but obscure presence in the seeker. His Danish counterpart sought recovery of the eternal (lost by sin) through personal response to the confrontation by a transcendent power, which power remains itself even though it approaches man within the realm of the commonplace.

The concept of irony is the second important matter introduced in the dissertation which deserves prefatory comment in the light of its later development. Unfortunately, S.K.'s connotation for irony is not always the same. In his late journals he seemed to regard it as signifying a situation contrary to what might reasonably be expected. Thus he thought it ironical that by the exalted gift of speech man degrades himself below the animals—'for a chatterbox is truly a lower category than a dumb creature'.[23] On the other hand, elaborated into an actual way of life, irony came to play a permanent and strategic role in Kierkegaard's general theory of existence. In the latter instance, irony seems to pertain to the caustic awareness of an untenable existential condition, without, however, involving the Socratic element of pretence. S.K. recognized only three basic spheres of existence, and then identified two transitional steps between them. In the *Postscript* irony is the border zone between the aesthetic sphere and the ethical, whereas humour stands between the ethical and the religious.[24] Irony is there portrayed as transitional in that it is an attack on the grossness and externality of the aesthetic life which loses itself in immediacy, yet it only looks wistfully in the direction of the ethical life without actually moving into it.

The intermediate experience between the ethical life and the religious, humour, is fully informed about the pathos and the debacle of the moral life. Thus, like irony, humour senses the failure of the lower stage but does not commit itself to faith as God's way of redeeming evil. Instead, with a sense of pain, the humorist laughs or smiles at human folly, but does so reflectively rather than existentially. He has despaired of the folly of man's protestations, but with no hope of religious recovery.[25]

The Concept of Irony is divided into two parts, the first dealing with Socrates as an 'ironist' and the second with the concept of irony *per se*. Part One, a bulky unit, treats first the rival classical interpretations of Socrates as background for S.K.'s interpretation of the ancient philosopher; second attempts to validate this hypothesis by reference to the actual life of Socrates; and third argues that Socrates by necessity took such a role in relation to decadent Hellenic civilization. The sweep moves thus from *possibility*, through *actuality*, to historical *necessity*.

Chapter One is an erudite and discerning but somewhat disturbing treatment of Socrates, suggesting that his entire significance is as an ironist. It is not argued that this interpretation is inescapable, but that it is a possible hypothesis which solves many problems. For the contemporary student, it is perhaps more important that in this manner the hypothesis throws the concept of irony itself into bold relief.

Kierkegaard holds that the Socratic (earlier) dialogues of Plato are throughout ironic, ending with negative results, as in the *Protagoras* where Socrates ends by arguing that virtue can be taught and Protagoras denying it, each having thus exchanged places with the other. (Pp. 91–98) This general thesis is argued with great skill, although the material also lends itself to other interpretations, such as that of Alexandre Koyré. Koyré maintains that the dialogues end with *implicit* conclusions, which properly are to be drawn by the reader. The latter is to complete the dialogue himself if he has the intelligence and moral character essential for the purpose.[26] It is interesting that Marjorie Grene, so often insensitive to what Kierkegaard is about, nevertheless notes his 'uncanny directness' and his 'tremendous power' of insight in dealing with the Platonic dialogues. The outcome is that in the spirit of Socrates he escapes, in her judgment, from the completely unreal 'self' of either empirical atomism or rationalistic fabrication. He is said to grasp the 'inner feeling' of experience much as Socrates, who is reported in the Phaedrus to have sensed within himself both the perplexing hints of a monster stranger than Typhon, and also of a spirit of a gentler sort.[27]

Several of the dialogues are subjected to careful analysis. The *Symposium*, it is argued, is ironic in that it first makes love 'the substantial element in life' but then negates this by reducing love to empty longing, a desire for that which is not in any sense possessed. (P. 100) The dialogue then seeks to recover something of significance for love by making Socrates an exemplification of it. This, however, also ends in nothingness because the quality in Socrates which charms those who love him is not a positive trait; it is nothing other than his irony, which, in its mocking quality is both enchanting and painful. 'The ironist is a vampire who has sucked the blood out of her lover and fanned him with coolness, lulled him to sleep and tormented him with turbulent dreams.' (P. 86)

As the *Symposium* longs to *possess* love but destroys its meaning, so the *Phaedo* desires to *lose* the bodily existence and issues in a formless immortality which has no predicates and is 'as tedious as the eternal number one'. Life fades away in the 'reverberations of a dying echo'. It is striking that already in this preliminary work Kierkegaard insists that the world-renunciation of Platonic idealism ends in unhappy negativism and loses all meaning, whereas Christianity's view that 'life essentially consists of dying' is a *moral* view which understands that the sinful earthly life must perish but also sees it ennobled, so that a new life arises as the old life crumbles away. The protest against otherworldliness is as impressive as is the Christian hope. Indeed, the Christian's seeking to die to *sin in the world* is declared to be a healthiness which 'rescues the soul from the snares of relativity', whereas a mystical or otherworldly philosopher's wanting to die to the world is a sickness which cannot 'tolerate the absolute except in the form of nothingness'. This longing for death is itself ironic in that the concern is not to overcome the fear of death by means of moral enthusiasm but to rid oneself of all delusions and of every excessive emotion. (Pp. 108-15)

What is it for Socrates to be ironical? Xenophon made the hero of Greek philosophy too earthly, not genuinely concerned about the good and the beautiful but only about the useful and serviceable. Yet Xenophon correctly understood that Socrates could not abandon the world for the sake of sheer ideality. Plato, on the other hand, recognized ideality in Socrates but overstated it, changing it from an aspiration to an objective idea. Strangely, Aristophanes in his mocking play, the *Clouds*, captured some of the truths of both Xenophon and Plato. He showed Socrates comically suspended between heaven and earth in a basket, ideally hovering above the earth but unable to reach heaven. (Pp. 157-67) This is the nature of irony, to oscillate 'between the ideal self and the empirical self', negating all worldly inadequacies, yet, unable to reach the divine, issuing in a stuporous nothingness.

Having reviewed irony as a possible hypothesis for understanding the early Platonic dialogues, in the next chapter S.K.

presents the 'conception made actual'. This does not offer an alternative hypothesis to the images given by Plato, Xenophon and Aristophanes but the actual image as presented by the conduct of Socrates under the influence of his famous 'diamon' or guiding spirit.

Charged with rejecting the gods of Athens, Socrates defended his piety by an appeal to the religious prompting of the daimon. Kierkegaard protests that Socrates actually did not follow either the public religion of the state nor the oracle (which had to do with personal affairs). In other words, the daimon was grossly individualistic, and placed Socrates above the state and in defiance of it, even though indeed it was not pure subjective conscience but was, as Hegel had noted, vaguely 'intermediate between the externality of the oracle and the pure inwardness of mind'. (P. 191) The divine voice which Socrates heard was supremely ironic in that it furnished only negations, preventing Socrates from giving assent, and leaving him without knowledge. In this way Socrates destroyed false (finite) religion but had no true and absolute religion with which to replace it.

The charge that Socrates corrupted youth likewise embodied a truth, says Kierkegaard, in that he awakened in them a spirit of criticism which broke down the loyalty of the individual as a citizen and stirred up longings which, however, Socrates was unable to satisfy. In this relationship as in others irony permeated everything. The wisdom which the master gave his pupils was negativism. His defence was that he should be instructed and not punished if he was in error. His proposal was that he be rewarded for his 'crime', or be permitted to pay a small fine of money, which money he did not desire anyway (the penalty thus negating itself). Yet in this mockery and negation Socrates did at least arrive at the idea of the true good, the beautiful and the true, if not in positive form, at least as limits or negations for the half-truths and qualified values which he despised. (P. 221)

Having treated the concept of irony as possible and then as actual, Kierkegaard next characterizes it as necessary, from the historical standpoint. This is the theme of Chapter III. Greece, with her dangerous cult of subjectivity, had been seduced by the Sophists who professed to know everything but who had so little genuine respect for truth that they made it serve momentary purposes, distorted it to win a case in court, and ended by holding that *everything* is true. A 'radical cure' was *necessary*. 'Truth demanded a silence before again lifting up its voice, and it was Socrates who should occasion this silence.' (P. 232) If the Sophists knew everything, he knew nothing, and this cleansing negation made him, for the moment, an historically momentous 'hero'. Yet his deed was one of irony, for his wisdom was ignorance and it was only as a gadfly that he was a gift of the gods. Like the Law which prepares for the gospel by condemning man, so Socrates prepared for universal truth by sweeping away puny misconceptions by negativity. Negativity was infinite at least in the sense of longing for the universal and rejecting all the finite truths and inadequate values which masqueraded as eternal and absolute.

In the Supplement to Part One, Kierkegaard briefly comments on the concept of Socratic irony as it relates to Hegel who, in S.K.'s judgment, does focus notably on large issues. He protests against the way in which Hegel leaves important (but dogmatic) remarks carelessly strewn about, like a 'commanding general in world history' who has no more time for particulars 'than the regal glance'. (P. 244) Yet he feels that in the main Hegel's position agrees with his own. Socrates is the founder of moral philosophy in that he talked with men about the beautiful and good, stripping from them their impoverished values and half-truths as he ferried them naked to ideal infinity. (P. 255) However, S.K. believes Hegel erred in thinking that Socrates reached the shore where the positive and absolute truth and beauty could be possessed. Hegel saw this in Socratic glorification of obedience to universal law, but S.K. insists that this veneration of law actually is an inconsistency. Socrates has forgotten that law is not universal but is only a part of the established state (not the Idea of the state) which in individual conscience he had opposed and transcended. (P. 252) Although S.K., perhaps in ironic tribute, refers to his view of Socrates as a 'modification' of Hegel's position, the difference between them is monumental in that Socratic irony is, according to S.K., a pathetic *negative* infinity, leaving no positive message.

In Part Two which is a mere fourth of the treatise, Kierkegaard turns from Socrates as an exemplification of irony to the concept of irony itself, at the same time seeking to demonstrate that the concept was fully exhibited in Socrates but appeared in deformed character in German romanticism. For clarity, a contrast is made between the many forms of *ironic* speech and true irony. Ironic speech says the opposite of what is intended, but only with the purpose of mocking some single feature of experience. Thus an anonymous author might ironically 'induce some crowing rooster, who would so dearly love to lay an egg, to allow the paternity to be imputed to him'. (P. 269) But such irony is only a minor negation; it mocks or overwhelms only some single species of existence. The true irony is not in such fashion finite or restricted in application; it is '*infinite* absolute negativity', which destroys 'the whole given actuality of a certain time and situation'. Its massive negativity is not the result of little cumulative battles but is a cancellation of all being outside the self, a repudiation of its validity. Then the cancellation issues in the countless skirmishes. (P. 271)

Turning to recent philosophy and literature, Kierkegaard whimsically notes that modern philosophy has been 'like a man who has his spectacles on but goes on searching for them'. (P. 289) The more it tried to find the ego 'the more emaciated it [the ego] became'. Fichte tried to recover the ego by asserting its self-identity, but his 'ego' became devoid of content. The romanticists seized on the lordliness of the ego to justify the wilfulness and eccentricity of a self, unlike Fichte overlooking the fact that it is a metaphysical self rather than an adolescent worldly self with which one should be concerned. This led to the onslaughts by Schlegel and Tieck against their world order. With no sense of validity in a culture, they viewed every culture as—for the moment —of equal value, regarded all religions as 'equally good', and no philosophy as better than another. More cautiously, Hegel rightly found a genuine if limited validity in each development, even though only within its proper locus in history. (P. 295) For the romantic ironist whatever is rejected is not repudiated in order to replace it with something better or truer, but because the ironist has abandoned the very principle of objective validity by which the temporal may be judged. (P. 300) The romantic image of the self, without norms other than shifting moods, feelings, and dramatic sense, poetically and playfully produces itself and its world. This is the aestheticism which in subsequent writing came under S.K.'s own dreadful ironic attack.

THE AESTHETIC LITERATURE

The treatment of Schlegel's notorious *Lucinde* is of particular interest. S.K. holds that romanticism was justified in making such protests against the drab virtue which makes love 'as tame, well-behaved, sluggish and apathetic, as utilitarian and serviceable as any other domesticated animal, in short, as unerotic as possible'. (P. 303) Yet he makes a devastating attack on *Lucinde*. Its difficulty is not merely that it is obscene but that it offers no solutions for the recognized evils. If prosaic morality denies freedom, Schlegel's aestheticism does likewise, letting man be a slave to inward caprice. It dehumanizes the self, confining it to mere images reflected from glassy mirrors, images of a vegetative stupor. (P. 311) True freedom is impossible for a self which has no real self-identity or continuity. 'Boredom is the only continuity the ironist has.' (P. 301)

The outcome is that irony is defended, but only as a mastered moment. So it appears in a true poet, a Shakespeare or Goethe, for whom the aesthetic production is simply a moment over which the poet is master. For romanticism, on the contrary, the poetic production is master over the poet, making him feel infatuation (or disgust) with it. In this case the essence is obliterated by what should be only a phenomenon of the essence. (Pp. 336 ff.)

In a sense the entire authorship of Kierkegaard is anticipated in *Irony*, in his distinction—here relatively undeveloped—between the wise and noble Socrates who is an epitome of humanity at its best—and the person of Jesus representing divine disclosure, the transcendent and not the humanistic. At this time of writing S.K. was still to a considerable extent under the influence of Hegel. His break with Hegel was progressive. It became dramatically evident in *Fear and Trembling* where Christianity is shown to involve (how far from Kant as well) a suspension of the ethical as constituting the very quality of faith. Abraham's faith might have required him to commit the sin of human sacrifice and the murder of his own son. To this extent is religion removed from being a mere echo of the ethical. Unlike tragic heroes who obey universal principles even at the cost of personal suffering, Abraham placed religion mysteriously above the universal principles of ethics. Perhaps Socrates had prompted Kierkegaard, in the Euthyphro (if to the contrary in the *Crito*), to call universality in question. Whereas Euthyphro—in Plato's dialogue by that name—prosecutes his own father for a crime, Socrates responds with the objection that the universal moral rules are not so infallible (or at least so infallibly known) as to require this. Piety, he says, cannot be reduced to legal performance.

In view of Kierkegaard's profound emphasis on man's temporality, as contrasted with the eternal, one might suppose that by its very nature the ethical life ends in a pathos caused by finitude. Yet this is not the meaning. The reason that the moral life ends in failure is rebellion, not natural limitation. Perhaps it is in the moral earnestness of Judaism as nowhere else that the pathos of morality becomes definitive. 'It was already a deep irony against the world when the Law, after having proclaimed the commandments, added the promise: if you obey these, you shall be happy, for it soon became apparent that mankind was unable to fulfil the Law, hence a happiness attaching itself to this condition became rather more than hypothetical.'*

Socrates, Kierkegaard's idol, does not bring sin to attention. However, like Abraham, he does try to set aside the absolutism of conventional moral rules for an absolutism of eternal values, in his case marked by the voice of conscience rather than the mandate of God. Unsatisfied with the customary principles of conduct which are imposed by society and are doomed to relativity, he sought by means of 'recollection' and reason to discover an absolute standard. Thus by truly knowing oneself, Socrates felt that man might discover the purposes of God for him.

---

* P. 279 f. In view of Judaism's assumptions of the possibility of obeying God's law and of the righteous man receiving blessing, S.K. came to define Judaism as an expectation for help in this life, so that suffering ceases. In contrast, Christianity despairs of fulfilling the law, and therefore expects suffering in this life, with the fulfilment of salvation in eternity. (*Papirer*, XI^1 A 496.)

3. 'EITHER'—VOLUME ONE OF EITHER/OR

Either/Or. A Fragment of Life. By Victor Eremita. February 20, 1843. Vol. I translated by David F. and Lillian Marvin Swenson; Vol. II translated by Walter Lowrie. Princeton: Princeton University Press, 1944. New edition with translation and notes revised; together with a foreword by Howard A. Johnson. Garden City: Doubleday, 1959; Anchor paperback A 181 a–b. (Page references are to the Anchor edition.)

Almost unbelievably, this two-volume work is a love letter, written to make the sweetheart believe that the lover was a scoundrel, in order that she would willingly reject him rather than grieve over her loss of him. S.K. broke his engagement to Regine Olsen, convinced that marriage to him could only bring her misery. She pleaded pitifully with him not to desert her. In despair, S.K. was tempted to commit suicide and finally shaped a fantastic plan to make himself repulsive in Regine's sight. In Volume One he portrayed himself as a spiritually bankrupt person. In the second volume he appeared in a very different light by showing how one can struggle for integrity. Regine did understand that, in a sense, the work was written for her, but did not grasp the full significance of it. For the cultured people of Denmark these volumes were a demonstration of the genius of Kierkegaard and they were the starting point of a vast authorship.

Because *Either/Or* is indeed a love letter, with a special message for Regine, yet also a book written for any who will read, it has certain peculiarities. In it Kierkegaard certainly cannot freely say what he longs to say. Even the message for Regine is not unambiguous, for beneath the suggestions of his less than honourable character are intimations that he is anything but the scoundrel he pretends to be. Indeed he suggests that he is utterly faithful but cannot marry because of his secret sorrows, and that Regine must reconcile herself to their parting even though the matter remains something of a mystery to her. Accordingly, S.K. presents picture-personalities, one after another, as drawn from opera or literature, each suggesting some unique kind of explanation for the tragic relationship, yet even more hinting that none of them are adequate answers. In effect, he seems to be asking Regine whether she can truly believe him to be an aesthetic cad (portrayed in 'Either') or an ethical man of prosaic duty (portrayed in 'Or'). The latter she can hardly believe, and the former she must not believe. S.K. thought of revealing the deeper and more important religious exceptionality of his life,[28] but could not so openly bare his soul. Regine must therefore remain in a state of uncertainty but hopefully of neither bitterness and despair on the one hand, nor of unrealistic hope on the other. S.K.'s intent is to reveal enough of his inner thoughts to keep her from despising or hating him, yet to disguise himself sufficiently as a detached aesthete to prevent her from trying to possessively regain or protect him. He attempts to make her realize that she is not like any of the 'brides of sorrow' whom he here describes, persons who were literally betrayed. Yet if such a terrible misunderstanding of his motives must be prevented, the full tragic truth of his life must—partly for her own happiness—remain a mystery.

Obviously, *Either/Or* was more than a love letter. While it intended to help Regine face the crisis of her life—in S.K.'s judgment essentially a spiritual one—it aimed to help every reader face his spiritual existence. To accomplish this, S.K. was led far beyond presenting a moral or even a religious plea. In fact, *Either/Or* became a great philosophical treatise, containing the uthor's first attack on Hegel and the latter's spiritually misleading notions.* S.K. had gone to Berlin to hear Schelling's criticism of Hegel but to his bitter disappointment found no light there and developed his own critique. That *Either/Or* heralded a new (unsystematic) philosophy was not evident to its first readers, and it is not evident to a casual reader today. All this, however, would be precisely to S.K.'s satisfaction because he did not wish to found a 'counter-System' to that of Hegel. Rather he wished to compel people to forget the System—and systematizing itself—which were then very much in vogue in Denmark, and to face the one reality which is intimately known to every man, viz. his own existence. In fact, Kierkegaard himself argued that the merit of *Either/Or* is precisely that it does not lead to a conclusion (something philosophical or cognitive) but transforms 'everything into inwardness', in such a way that the reader is compelled to choose

---

* See Appendix at the end of this unit in regard to the attack on Hegel.

his own style of life.* Unfortunately to the author's distress, most readers missed the underlying philosophy of existence.

The nature of human existence is the central concept which is here explored and which becomes the theme of the entire authorship. There are eventually charted in grand outline three stages of existence, viz. the aesthetic, ethical and religious—the first two being the subject matter of the two volumes of *Either/Or*. Are there no other kinds of human existence than these three? Inasmuch as the genuine aesthete is a person conscious of an ethical alternative to his way of life (probably also with a religious foundation), Kierkegaard takes note of great numbers of people—unnamed by him—whom we might call 'sub-aesthetes'. Their blundering sordidness makes them virtually unconscious of any either/or of value decision. To be so nearly spiritless is no innocent animal-like unawareness of duty; it is a condition which they have chosen, for men are not born spiritless.[29] Once too dissolute to sense the frustration of their nobler possibilities and therefore unable even to experience true despair, the 'sub-aesthetes' plod from folly to folly. In a sense they pitifully outlive themselves, in a state of perdition. (II, pp. 161, 172) Do such people 'exist' humanly? S.K. barely alludes to these creatures who are almost unconscious of their potentiality, and is clearly not interested in portraying their sub-aesthetic state of existence. In so far as they in any measure share in human existence they are aesthetic. The point is that they have almost lost contact with the realm of freedom, self-determination, and values which are constitutive of human existence.

At the other extreme, is there no higher or supplemental category of existence, e.g. the cognitive, the intuitive or the mystical? S.K. denies it. To be a person is to *care* about things, in particular to be concerned about one's self. For this reason, S.K. says that 'passion [as faith, feeling, love] is the culmination of existence'.[30] A crude analogy will make clear why it is that a cognitive self is not an authentic human self. A computer can

* I, p. xi. The astonishing style and varied literary qualities of the authorship should not be construed as a basis for making S.K. essentially a literary figure ('poet' is his own term) rather than a philosophic mind. Indeed, he wrote in such livelier forms rather than in textbook style in order to compel the reflective mind to avoid losing itself in abstractions and to realize the gravity of its personal undertakings.

store and process 'knowledge' remarkably well, but it is not a person because it is neutral to the value or significance of any of the material it deals with. S.K. obviously understands that there are kinds of mentality, as that of animals, which do not involve 'existence'.[31] Possible mystical experience likewise would not constitute 'existence' because it too would involve no value commitments. Proper human life is not found in tranquil insight or bliss, but in the responsible and strenuous choice of values, above all in the choice of one's proper self regardless of the buffetings and allurements of experience.[32]

Either/Or is a complex and mystifying work, edited by the pseudonymous Victor (victorious) Eremita (religious recluse or solitary individual). It consists of remarkably diverse yet truly unified papers, put in carefully planned order. The papers were purportedly found by Victor and written by other fictional persons. The first volume, supposedly written largely by a young man designated 'A', who appears as an utterly sophisticated but melancholy aesthete, was intended to show the inevitable pathos of pleasure-seeking. The second volume consists of moral persuasions addressed to this young man by a sober but kindly judge. In it S.K. plainly intended to lead in the direction of a dedicated moral life. It seems that by the relative incoherence of the parts of the first volume, there was suggested an incoherent quality in the life of pleasure. In contrast, the second volume, with its moral emphasis, has more of unity and of quietness of spirit, but perhaps also less of genius. It is also, probably by deliberate intent, less interesting.

Some persons unfamiliar with Kierkegaard's literary style have so misunderstood him as to trace his pseudonyms to some aberration of personality. In actuality, each pseudonym is planned as a dramatic character, an actor with a personality and a point of view. F. J. Billeskov Jansen points out that *Either/Or* is thus actually a philosophical novel, developed with dramatic genius, yet considerably influenced by Goethe's *Wilhelm Meister*, in which by a variety of literary devices, 'the history of a man and the formulation of a doctrine merge into one'.*

A key feature for the understanding of *Either/Or* is S.K.'s

---

* F. J. Billeskov Jansen, 'The Literary Art of Kierkegaard', *A Kierkegaard Critique*, ed. by H. Johnson and N. Thulstrup, p. 12 f. The pseudonyms sustained use of 'indirect communication'. He wants to set Christianity before people but knows that they would 'put their fingers in their ears' if he were to speak directly about it. Therefore he writes of what people are always interested in, i.e. pleasure, and more particularly, of the erotic. S.K. had just been personally schooled in indirect communication, when he tried to make Regine believe him a scoundrel in order not to hurt her by revealing the sad perplexities of his life. The pseudonyms, standing somewhat detached from the personality of the author, offer one important means for such communication. Each presents its own brand of seductive allurement and stands as a dramatic symbol of it. It is in keeping with this chosen style of communication that *Either/Or* consists of such varied and provocative elements as the Diapsalmata (fragmentary, poetic ejaculations), the famous 'Diary of the Seducer' (in which S.K. pretends that he toyed with Regine's heartstrings), and a long and brilliant, if controversial, essay on the sensuous character of music as symbolized by Mozart's *Don Juan*. One poignant passage in the Diapsalmata will suggest not only the pathos of the aesthetic (its real intent), but also S.K.'s own suffering through misunderstanding: 'What is a poet? A poet is an unhappy being whose heart is torn by secret sufferings, but whose lips are so strangely formed that when the sighs and the cries escape them, they sound like beautiful music.... And men crowd about the poet and say to him: "Sing for us soon again..."' (P. 19) Thus the tragic, sometimes boring, but always pathetic character of the aesthetic life is vividly portrayed for the reader, not by an admonishing critic who might put the wary reader on the defensive, but by the sophisticated if disillusioned pleasure-seeker himself.

Volume One, to be reviewed in this section, dramatically and definitively portrays the aesthetic way of life. The aesthete is a

were more than pure literary devices. By objectifying one of his potentialities and forcing this fictional character to move to its inexorable outcomes, S.K. not only helped others to honestly face their possibilities but was also more readily able to cast aside his own temptations and partialities. But that S.K. does reject the extreme points of view he skilfully but pseudonymously portrays is critically important. He asserts that not 'a single word' of any of the pseudonyms is his own. (*Postscript*, p. 551.) It might have been more accurate for S.K. to say that the pseudonyms employ his reasoning and feelings but not his conclusions or value commitments.

refined hedonist who throws off restraint in a restless search for satisfaction. He tends to manifest both sentimental charm and sophisticated intellectuality. His hedonism may be so refined that the object of his enjoyment is his own reflective experience of enjoyment. (P. 301) Its concern is pleasure more than beauty or art, and personal *interest* even more than sheer pleasure. With an aesthetic attitude one is caught up in the various attractive experiences of the moment, in a state of 'immediacy' which does not reach beyond itself. What is actually pursued may be wealth, honour, pleasure, health, or self-expression, yet none of them lead to a significant moral consciousness or prove to offer a genuine hope of happiness.

Such a style of life does not mean that the refined aesthete is totally devoid of moral awareness. He is conscious of morality as a possibility, but is unwilling to commit himself. Such morality as the aesthete possesses may even give a wistful intimation of the eternal, as in the feeling of lovers that they ought to make vows of eternal love.[33] The aesthete may even use moral principles, seeing them as accessories to satisfaction in life, and perhaps even in themselves interesting details on this stage of existence. Yet he does not actually live within ethical or religious categories, and can only vaguely understand these as possibilities. He is not yet a true self because he lacks chosen purpose. Even his pleasures are not so much goals to which he is committed as interests to which he is passively attracted. His attitude towards the call of duty is hopeless indifference rather than defiance. (II, pp. 225 ff.) The aesthete is then swept along in the process of change in which his pleasures are caught. Hoping for permanence, but looking for it in objects and fleeting experiences rather than in the self, he is doomed to despair.

As the aesthete is not totally devoid of moral consciousness, so too he is not totally devoid of religion. The thought of God superintending life for the satisfaction of everyone is itself a gratifying notion. Further, religion can be interesting. Its music is inspiring and not all sermons are dull. Moreover, it affords endless possibilities for socializing. Yet in religion as in morals, the aesthete remains uncommitted and detached. He finds various possibilities interesting but chooses none of them with finality. Existence remains an endless *possibility*, and the aesthete's difficulty is that he fails to transform possibility into actual experience. He is in despair of becoming a true self, trying instead to make adjustment by tinkering with the environment. He is still in a state of 'immediacy' whereby he responds in rather animalistic fashion to the environment.

It is distinctive of the aesthetic life that it is chaotic and ill-proportioned, somehow meaningless in spite of endless intimation of meaning. (I, p. 24) Its springs of pleasure run dry. 'Vainly I seek to plunge myself into the boundless sea of joy; it cannot sustain me, or rather, I cannot sustain myself.' (I, p. 40) The shortcomings of reality give a kind of compensating amusement. That a man can guide his love so as to marry an heiress or can be pious by communing once a year occasions laughter, but it is bitter laughter. (I, p. 33) The aesthete resembles Hegel in a peculiar way, 'mediating' (obliterating) distinctions and alternative ways of life, not speculatively however, but in a 'higher madness'. (II p. 174)

Because the aesthete passively responds to the object which captures his attention and thereby rules him, rather than asserting himself, the choice which lies before him is not between good and evil (as for the moral man) but between choosing and not choosing. Ultimately, the only possible movement towards salvation is for the aesthete to accept and commit himself to the despair which issues from indecisiveness. Despair is at least a relating of oneself to oneself (one's true self), a facing of oneself, even if it is also a confession of hopelessness in this relationship. (II, p. 172) S.K.'s point that despair is the first step towards recovery cannot well be understood apart from the then popular romanticism, which ranged from ecstatic pantheism at one extreme to an exhibition of 'despair' over one's sorry lot within the 'divine' universe at the other. S.K. means to say that in such emotional indulgence what is needed is for the sentimentalist to really despair, honestly recognizing the hopelessness of his existence. This will focus attention on his eternal significance and the need for finding a way of realizing it.

'Either' opens with the 'Diapsalmata', brilliant aphorisms which are at times reminiscent of the proverbs of Nietzsche. Perhaps the most beautiful, steeped in poignancy, is the definition of a poet, mentioned above. Another utterance which points to the coupling of pleasure and pathos is the following: 'There are well-known insects which die in the moment of fecundation. So it is with all joy; life's supreme and richest moment of pleasure is coupled with death.' Another, even less hopeful: 'I prefer to talk with children, for it is still possible to hope that they may become rational beings. But those who have already become so—good Lord!' The initial aesthetic hope, sometimes gay but often ironic, finally issues in complete despair: 'Life has become a bitter drink to me, and yet I must take it like medicine, slowly, drop by drop.' (I, pp. 20, 19, 25) While the lyrical jests and cries of the aesthete are in part an unburdening of Kierkegaard's own moods, it is far more significant that they stand severely judged by him. To readily understand the entire work, one might read *Either/Or* backwards, beginning with its religious 'ultimatum' in the second volume. Then it becomes evident that the outcries of the opening Diapsalmata, despite their vividness and poetry, are the expressions of a lost soul. S.K.'s own judgment of the matter is found in his appraisal of the two pseudonymous authors of *Either/Or*. He thinks the aesthetic author far more intellectually clever but lacking the incorruptibility and maturity of the judge.

Why does Kierkegaard give such great prominence to anguish? Many answers of a psychological nature have been offered, including his inborn melancholy, somewhat unhappy childhood, and particularly his disillusionment over the discovery of his father's sins, but these answers—although not pointless—are too easy. Dark forebodings are in truth not a small part of humanity's common experience, and S.K. with his ample share of sorrows and his perceptiveness was keenly aware of them. 'How was the chain made with which the Fenris wolf was bound? It was wrought from the sound of a cat's paws walking over the ground, from women's beards, from the roots of rocks, from the nerves of bears, from the breath of fishes, and the spittle of birds. And thus I, too, am bound in a chain formed of dark imaginings...' (I, p. 33) It would thus be a grave mistake to identify Kierkegaard's melancholy simply with consciousness of sin. More than that, it reflects a profound spiritual hunger. S.K. made this clear when he wrote that the terrible thing about the 'spiritual incapacity' from which he suffered was that it was a spiritual passion which was so 'formless' that he did not even know what it was for which he yearned.[34] Such expressions do reflect the personal sufferings of a poetic soul, but for the incisive mind of Kierkegaard personal melancholy becomes the stimulus for an objective psychological study of human experience, and a doctrine of pathos. Existential despair, he concludes, is no chance disillusionment; it is the mark of futility in a human life which seeks nothing more than evanescent enjoyment and passing diversions to give it meaning and stability. The movement to despair represents the discovery of one's enslavement by pleasure and thus prepares the way for freedom and responsibility. However, such conclusions lie beneath the surface and are not explicitly argued for in this volume.

From the Diapsalmata S.K. turns to music, the most immediate of enjoyments, as contrasted with such pleasures as are sought by scheming and calculation. In music the aesthetic appears in its most elemental form, as the sheer delight of natural human existence. As a medium of feeling music is said to manifest an effervescent, passionate, on-rushing immediacy. By 'immediacy' is meant a natural valuational response to the world—or even to fantasy—without any alteration resulting from reflective choice. It seems to avoid the problems of boredom, frustration, and change, but only at the price of selflessness. Music furnishes essential aesthetic content for experience. Every art except music —poetry for example—employs a medium of symbols. In music the lyric is not a representation. It is the 'immediate stage' of the erotic. Music is spiritually (but perhaps blindly) generated; it 'is force, life, movement, constant unrest, perpetual succession; but this unrest...does not enrich it, it...storms uninterruptedly forward as in a single breath.' (I, p. 70) Music is neither good nor evil, but, as of all aesthetic contents, one must finally despair of music in order to seek the good and the holy.

Operatic figures are here subjected to brilliant if rather speculative analysis. The Page in *Figaro* is taken by Kierkegaard to represent the initial stage of awakening sensuality, a kind of dream state, as yet without a specific object of desire and involving a melancholy foreboding which is related to 'dread' (cf. *Concept of Dread*). Papageno in *The Magic Flute* symbolizes the second stage in which desire quickens so that it finds actual objects of longing.

These vanish in a moment, however, so that their disappearing is the only treasure which desire can cling to. (I, p. 78 f.)

It is Don Juan who represents the culmination of the aesthetic awareness. In him aestheticism takes the form of demoniacal intensity. There was a double fascination for Kierkegaard in this Mozart opera. First, the music delighted him, and second, the Don Juan myth seemed pointedly to symbolize the sensuous. Music and myth, he thought, were here perfectly blended. According to S.K., Don Juan was not so much a person but sensuousness itself personified, i.e. the life of feeling. He cannot be a real person since he literally loves not many but all, and thus is the epitome of an ideal extreme of the aesthetic life, i.e. complete absorption in the experience of the moment. Therefore, neither is he a lover nor a seducer, but an embodiment of the immediate non-moral mood of love. In the medieval mythical mountain of Venus, 'there sound only the voice of elemental passion, the play of appetites, the wild shouts of intoxication, it exists solely for pleasure in eternal tumult. The first-born of this kingdom is Don Juan'. (I, p. 88) In dread he dances lightly over the abyss in a lust for life which would perish if he paused for reflection in the tumult. The dancing music of the violins portrays this. Such experience is not evil because it is pre-ethical. The important implication is that, far from trying to make music (or any art) moral, or religious, S.K. understands art as a morally neutral expression of feeling. At the same time he insists that art has its natural limits and its unavoidable pathos, to be resolved only in religion. Religion itself turns to art for means of expression even though recognizing that the art thus borrowed must still be judged by aesthetic standards.

The next four units of 'Either' may be thought of as dramatic treatments of tragedy in its varied forms, all conceived as outcomes of the aesthetic life and as moving in the direction of despair. Despair is not only the culmination of the aesthetic life but it is also the beginning of its redemption. To truly despair is to make a choice in the form of an ethical decision, whereby one chooses himself 'in his eternal validity'. (II, p. 215) Mere despair is of no value in itself; what is of value is to choose oneself as despairing. Then, even though he is in despair, he at least possesses an abiding self rather than being utterly subject to the tides of changing vicissitudes. To choose oneself is to recognize eternal norms and validity for one's responsible value decisions, even while one grieves over his helplessness. Choosing oneself in despair is thus a kind of spiritual birth whereby the choice between good and evil can acquire significance. (II, p. 172) However, this is only the initiation of the corrective, for when the penitent aesthete becomes an earnest moralist he then finds his way to the good blocked by the new pathos, a very different ethical despair. The truly tragic person, as indicated in *Fear and Trembling* (pp. 72, 122) is a hero, a 'knight of infinite resignation', who with moral courage renounces everything and finds the cleansing which comes by integrity. Yet he lacks the victoriousness of faith which redeems and restores rather than annihilates; the tragic hero's sorrow is as deep as is the joy of the knight of faith.[35]

Unforgettable delineations of aesthetic despair follow in the 'Shadowgraphs', which are treatments of such heroines of grief as Margaret in *Faust*, and in the strange 'enthusiastic address' about 'The Unhappiest Man', whose grave, when opened, was found to be empty, suggesting that the unhappiest man is yet to be found. Addressing him, 'A' writes: 'May no secret sympathy suspect your lonely pain'. 'Lest even the memory of him should make another unhappy,' the ironic wish is expressed that he may have an early death and no human remembrance. (I, p. 228)

Another section, 'First Love', reviews a comedy by that name, and gives one more affirmation of the frivolous and deceptive nature of the aesthetic. Comedy is actually tragedy in clowns' clothing. How sentimentally precious first love is taken to be! Every lover passes himself off in this character; even a widower and a widow with their five children make rapturous assurances to each other that this is their first love! (I, p. 252) Thus the deceit of sensuousness may infect the proper married couple as readily as the seducer or the seduced.

A remarkably profound portion of the treatment of tragedy is 'The Ancient Tragical Motif as Reflected in the Modern', and the attached 'Shadowgraphs' mentioned above. Perhaps the chief point is that grief has a 'crafty character' which eludes understanding. The brides of sorrow in the 'Shadowgraphs' suffer in being betrayed, yet remain unconvinced of their own innocence.

A faint intimation of a religious resolution of grief appears in the suggestion that in a higher consecration of grief the wounded souls may receive a 'measure of relief'. (P. 213) In these essays S.K. recaptures the ancient understanding of tragedy as the performing of a deed which must be adjudged guilty and must be punished, yet with the performer of the deed being really blameless. What he wants to show, in part, is that in Hegel's thought there is no place for the category of tragedy because either the actor is viewed by Hegel as the creator of his own destiny so that what happens is an evil deed *committed by him* rather than a tragedy befalling him, or else he is merely a single *instance of the world spirit*, in which case there is properly neither tragedy nor evil. Genuine tragedy and evil are virtually eliminated by Hegel through his rejection of mystery and his subsumption of all of existence under rational categories.

S.K.'s commitment to a Christian perspective leads him to oppose this Hegelian 'mediation' and enables him to appreciate Greek tragedy and its catharsis. Also, he views the appearance of Christ as in a certain sense 'the deepest tragedy'. (I, p. 140) Blameless though he is, Christ is judged and punished and his suffering provides a kind of infinite catharsis for the paradoxically irrational and impersonal guilt of original sin. It is also this deepening of the concept of tragedy and the greater inwardness which it is given in Christianity which enabled S.K. to comprehend his own suffering. He himself is an Antigone who experiences the catharsis. A pronounced change which occurs is that the tragic hero himself can now be healed, and not merely the spectators as at a Greek play.

Pierre Mesnard has argued that tragedy is nevertheless not the proper concept under which Kierkegaard is to be understood. His argument is that S.K.'s sense of the tragic degenerated into a persecution complex in which he finally turned into a shouting reformer, seeking to portray himself as a Christ-like sufferer.[36] The true message of Kierkegaard, argues Mesnard, is instead in the theory of the stages of existence, with his own proper role being that of an anonymous maieutic persuader who suffers 'anguish' (but not tragedy) by virtue of his very activity of persuasion, an anguish which is relieved by humour. Mesnard's brilliant hypothesis has difficulties. The insistence that one category only (anguish, but not tragedy) should be employed in interpreting Kierkegaard is difficult to reconcile with the varied roles which Kierkegaard actually assumes. The complaint that S.K. came to view Christ's mission as like his own overlooks his profound sense of unlikeness to Christ in being a follower. Finally, it is unlikely that S.K. intended to remain indefinitely in the anonymity of a maieutic persuader. A tragic sense of life may well have been implicit from the outset, and not without some appropriateness.

The portrayal of the aesthetic in Volume One begins with such unreflective enjoyment as the experience of music and comes to an end in coldly calculating schemes of seduction. Between them stands a whimsical (and grim) little essay on 'The Rotation Method'. If pleasures forever slip out of one's grasp is it possible by shrewdness to preserve one's joy in life? This is the question which the essay ironically answers.

Boredom is the great problem for the aesthete. A life of pleasure at its richest grows wearisome. Whom he marries today he divorces tomorrow. To escape the misery of mere boredom, one can —like a farmer rotating his crops—try by shrewdness to inject novelty into his waning pleasures, but it is ultimately to no avail. To be safe one will not marry, nor have a friend—how friends tyrannize us! Or, if one does marry, he had better promise not 'until death do us part', but perhaps until Easter; that would be far safer. (I, p. 291 f.) So the aesthete tries to avoid problems by avoiding choices. He ends in despair because by avoiding choices he has no personal reality but instead only glittering possibilities.

Boredom marks a transition from the child's level where simple pain and pleasure are the motivators, to a mature level of experience where interest is cultivated as an escape from ennui. When pleasures grow dull the aesthete tries to cling to the pleasure principle by seeking to sharpen and refine his appetite. If, accordingly, satisfaction be redefined as the *interesting*, not only pleasure but even pain and ugliness may satisfy. Indeed, the tragic—as demonstrated in the theatre or in literature—may be less boring than that which is superficially pleasant. This kind of awareness represents the ultimate in the aesthetic way of life.

The rotation of pleasure is inventive and shrewd, and by it the aesthete hopes to gain an artistic and truly satisfying life. However, fruitful artistry begins only when the hope has been cast aside, because genuine hope clings to a 'heavenly inheritance' rather than a succession of passing charms. (I, p. 288) The aesthetic selections of new sensual satisfactions are not genuine choices, but are yieldings to pressures from without. They lack 'the baptism of the will which lifts up the choice into the ethical'. (II, p. 173) S.K. does not intend to characterize the aesthetic life as a crude hedonism, and it is therefore not subject to Plato's contemptuous criticism that if pleasure is all that counts then it is immaterial whether it is a man or a dog-faced baboon that experiences it. The aesthete, as S.K. views the matter, is human and his pleasures are rationally conceived and structured. However, even in a redefined hedonism, man is still not making genuine choices or finding meaning in life, but is only responding to preferred pleasures.

The closing third of the volume, the famous and strange 'Diary of the Seducer', applies the theory of rotation. This subtle work, despite its title, manifests a delicacy of feeling and imagination. Its subject (Johannes) is not a seducer in the ordinary sense. He is an intellectual sophisticate who plans a careful campaign for arousing—without any actual romantic advances—the interest and devotion of a charming girl named Cordelia. First there is an engagement, but the seducer succeeds in persuading her to break the engagement and to experience love's delights 'in freedom'. After this he immediately casts her aside. 'I do not wish to be reminded of my relation to her; she has lost her fragrance.' (P. 439) The astonishing amount of reflection in the 'diary' points up the fact that the aesthetic life is *human* existence. It equally demonstrates the fact that reflection and sophistication are not sufficient to provide genuine existence, which requires absolute standards which issue from God. As James Collins phrases it, 'Kierkegaard agrees with Socrates that the unexamined life is not worth living, but he adds that some ways of conducting the self-examination of one's life are worth more than others'.[37] Seduction not only violates the person of the seduced, but also brings despair to the seducer in that his love vanishes as soon as the amorous conquest is finished. Aesthetic eroticism is always a seeking, but never an attaining of the goal; it is doomed to cancellation and a new search at the very moment of seeming fulfilment.

Some of the shrewdest psychological reflections and some of the most lyrical prose of the entire Kierkegaard authorship appear in the Diary. A wry example of the former is this pronouncement: 'What does a young girl fear? Intellectuality. Why? Because it constitutes a negation of her whole feminine existence.' (P. 358) An illustration of the latter is this reference to woman's beauty: '...the roguish glance, the wistful eye, the pensive head, the exuberant spirits, the quiet sadness, the deep foreboding, the brooding melancholy, the earthly homesickness, the unbaptized movements..., the earthly modesty, the angelic purity, the secret blush..., the inexplicable sighs, the willowy form, the soft outlines, the luxuriant bosom, the swelling hips, the tiny foot, the dainty hand'. (P. 423) Here the aesthetic experience is antithetical to that of Schopenhauer who could see in woman's beauty nothing more than sexual allurement.

The pronounced emphasis on despair in Volume One and on rigorous duty in Volume Two may give the erroneous implication that *Either/Or* is gravely sombre. Actually, the mood is often gay, light, playful and whimsical. An example is the plan of Johannes to write a book entitled, 'Contribution to the Theory of the Kiss' (in *Diary of the Seducer*): 'It is quite remarkable that no such work on this subject exists...I am able to offer several suggestions immediately. The perfect kiss requires a man and a girl as the participants. A kiss between men is tasteless, or—what is worse is distasteful. Next, I believe a kiss comes nearer to the idea when a man kisses a girl than when a girl kisses a man. When in the course of years there has come about an indifference in this relation, then the kiss has lost its significance. This is true about the domestic kiss of marriage with which married people, apparently in lieu of a napkin, dab each other's lips...' (I, p. 411)

Despite its occasional light-hearted and frequently amusing interludes, the total impact of *Either/Or* is undeniably serious. The perspectives of Volume One move progressively from the impulsive sensuality of Don Juan to the seducer's coldly reflective and calculating quest for pleasure. Yet the outcome of the aesthetic life is always the same—a passionate search for worldly satisfactions which, unhallowed by dedication, leaves a hollow void which tempts one to bitterness. The hedonic rule, 'satisfy yourself', if left unqualified by moral concerns, leads to a melancholy debauchery rather aptly illustrated by the Roman emperor Nero. (II, pp. 188 ff.) It is in view of these facts that S.K.'s aesthetes are so sophisticated and—by and large—restrained. On the other hand, he wants to show what the aesthetic life can be at its best. Further, like Epicurus, he recognizes that only such a hedonist can long remain a hedonist. A sex fiend or debauched person soon loses the pleasure which he seeks, and perhaps loses his life as well.

Yet one might object that there surely exist noble examples of the aesthetic life, sensitive artists who have nothing to do with vulgar bunglers and drunken revellers. Judge William agrees heartily but drives home a painful point, viz. that the difference between the noble artist and the drunken reveller is 'something unessential' since the 'noble' artist too has no higher aim in life than pleasure. If, on the other hand, the artist should seek by his art to serve moral goals, he is no longer an aesthete but an aesthetically talented ethical man. (II, p. 184) In that case, his moral purpose does not override or reject the artistic impulse. To the contrary, it frees it from the jerky movements which carry the aesthete nowhere because the latter follows every impulse and moves in all directions.[38] The conclusion is that aesthetic interest is an essential and good ingredient in existence, but neither a proper nor rewarding goal for it.

APPENDIX: REACTION TO HEGEL

The doctrine of choice pinpoints the issue in Hegel which disturbed Kierkegaard. He satirized Hegel's monism whereby opposites had appeared not as true opposites but as complementary phases of a single dialectical process. Theoretically, the denial of polar opposites seems to lead towards a pantheistic identification of God and man and towards the practical consequences of indecisiveness. 'If you marry you will regret it; if you do not marry you will also regret it...' (I, p. 37) Fearing such neutralism, S.K. argues against Hegelian mediation and for the acknowledgment of

THE AESTHETIC LITERATURE

true logical contradictories and real ethical alternatives. He insisted that whatever is real excludes its opposite and can never be synthesized with it. What seemed particularly insidious in mediation was that it was a contemplative act, not a dynamic resolving of a conflict. It was a passive *awareness* that in the grand perspective there is a place for everything, so that one seems to be relieved of strenuous duty by immersing oneself in supposedly philosophic understanding. Kierkegaard's term 'the leap' can best be understood in this regard. This term, used to represent movement from one value stage to another, has irritated some people by its supposed disregard for circumstance and growth. Actually, it is a reasonable reminder that when a person moves from one place to another, particularly from one set of values to another, he is not externally pushed into the new position, nor does he naturally evolve into it, nor fall or slide into the new stand. He must act.

A second and related doctrine which emerges is that of freedom. A remarkable existential conversion of the Socratic 'Know thyself' appears. In place of it man is bidden, 'Choose thyself'. The self which becomes known is known not as a product of necessity; indeed, if it were necessary then no 'self' would exist. To be a self is to freely stand for something. Thus self-knowledge presupposes commitment. 'Choose thyself' must precede 'Know thyself'. A system of logic is possible, but a system of reality in which free persons are involved is nonsense because systems are possible only where there is necessity. (II, p. 263)

An ontological feature of opposition to Hegel is found in S.K.'s insistence that one kind of reality is apprehended immediately, viz. the self itself in its decision-making. This is not arrived at by speculation but is the reality from which speculation starts and about which it may reflect. Expressing a kind of voluntarism, this thought also contradicts Hume's notion that experience gives nothing but a bundle of impressions. The decisive self is the most elemental fact of experience.

What incensed Kierkegaard above all was Hegel's destruction of Christianity from within by a process of interpretation and assimilation. Christian language continued in use but as merely symbolic of philosophic truth. S.K. despised the willingness to use Christian language while falsifying its meaning. In Denmark it was H. L. Martensen who had made Hegelianism the dominant mode of thought, trying through it to reconcile orthodox Christianity and rationalism. Actually, Martensen *used* Hegelianism in the interest of Christianity, but the end result appeared to be an inauthentic Hegelianism and a confused understanding of Christianity. It may be noted that similar tendencies in the twentieth century, such as theologies which delete the paradoxical from the person of Christ and attempt to assimilate him into humanistic culture, fall under the same Kierkegaardian assault.

Kierkegaard's revolt against Hegel seems more cautious in *Either/Or* than in later works. In *Philosophical Fragments*, written not long after *Either/Or*, he insisted that merely by coming into being an event proved that it was not logically necessary—otherwise it would already have been. In *Either/Or* however, S.K. still acknowledged 'with reverence' the achievements of the age (Hegel) and even allowed that philosophy might properly view history under the category of necessity. Indeed, history is *not*, according to *Either/Or*, simply the free actions of free men, for every person has a 'dual existence', of ethical freedom and of necessity. Necessity is not merely the force of circumstance but also the way in which one's action 'passes into the order of things which sustains the whole of existence'. (II, p. 178) Yet in spite of this seemingly inconsistent bow to Hegel, the entire thrust of *Either/Or* is found in the insistence that, whatever may be true for the abstract philosopher who views history contemplatively, personal existence is not essentially contemplative, and is therefore not philosophical. It is decision-making in acts of freedom whereby one posits himself. (II, pp. 174 ff.)

4. 'OR'—VOLUME TWO OF EITHER/OR

Either/Or. Volume II. See the item at the head of the treatment of Volume One for data on publication. (Page references are to the Anchor edition.)

Against the uncommitted life of pleasure, Volume Two urges duty and responsibility. It repudiates the wishful supposition of the

THE AESTHETIC LITERATURE

aesthetic life that man can attain his life's dreams and goals without the aid of moral strenuosity. In many respects this volume more nearly reflects Kierkegaard's own views than was true of the first volume. Its labyrinthine attack on the life of pleasure must not be underrated, nor even obscured by the later and more famous attack on hypocrisy in the church. If S.K. were living in the twentieth century he would perhaps drop for the moment his 'attack on Christendom' and turn his acid pen again to the devotees of sensuality, in order to compel them to realize the despair to which they inexorably move. Nevertheless, even by the time he wrote it, 'Or' represented a position which S.K. had already transcended by moving into the religious sphere. Accordingly, he apparently deliberately made it dull, in a sympathetic parody on the somewhat superficial moralist, lacking in rigorous self-understanding and religious depth.

The beginner in Kierkegaard is in danger of grossly misunderstanding the concept of the 'ethical' because of the subtlety and distinctiveness of S.K.'s categories. The initial definition of the ethical (as for Hegel) is to be *autonomous*, ruled from within, to have inwardness; whereas the aesthetic life is marked by externality, being ruled by things and one's interest in them.

This definition is nevertheless too simple. The deeper meaning of the ethical relates to the central thesis (cf. *Sickness Unto Death*) that man is a mixture of temporal and eternal. To be aesthetic is to give over one's life to the temporal and the temporary. To be ethical is to be concerned with the eternal and with what it requires in one's choices and deeds. The ethical, since it is founded on the eternal, has an implicit religious significance, even though this fact may be totally misunderstood by the self-righteous man. Judge William, the 'author', makes it clear that it is not ordinary morality with which he is concerned. Even the aesthetic or worldly man has his moral code; he cannot escape this because as a human being he is involved in choices which relate to self-fulfilment and social life. Indeed, although the ethical is qualitatively distinct from the aesthetic, it nevertheless is naturally situated within aesthetic experience and emerges from it in remarkably deceptive simplicity. Thus when man is faced with the problem of rival pleasures, and particularly of pleasures for which one must patiently strive and wait, there almost inevitably emerges the implicit *moral* question of a higher good, and also the moral issue of the constancy of the self. Nevertheless, the ethical life-stance is not a simple result of the emergence of moral consciousness *per se*, but is the kind of existence which man has when he consciously chooses to transform universal moral principles into his own fixed values and standards. To be 'ethical' is thus much more than to be moral in the usual sense of that term; it consists in accepting one's responsibilities *under the sovereignty of God*. 'The heavens part, as it were, and the I chooses itself—or rather, receives itself.' (II, p. 181)

In this manner Kierkegaard sets personal self-realization in the frame of duty rather in that of artistic self-determination, and of the eternal rather than of wise temporal choices. It is not consciousness of and respect for the many practical duties of life which make a man ethical, but the fact that he looks through the window of duty with such an intense gaze that he feels assured of 'the eternal validity of his being'. Duty, which is universal, is to be appropriated as one's own. Thus self-realization is not a mere self-creation but is a 'synthesis of the universal and the particular', resting on the fact that man can attain his own stature only by standing before God. (II, pp. 270 f., 268) Here the aesthetic is incorporated in the ethical but it is given a relative status rather than being the absolute goal of existence. (II, p. 182)

It follows that what men are accustomed to call morality is pre-ethical and belongs more to the aesthetic stage of existence. The point is that most morality is relative and is a natural outgrowth of temporal life, whereas the true ethical imperative comes as an absolute principle, representing the transcendent. The ethical at times even seems to involve what one might call, in Kierkegaard's language, a 'teleological suspension of the moral'. The ethical imperative for Socrates and the divine imperative for Abraham (cf. *Fear and Trembling*) require them to violate or transcend the ordinary morality which represents earthly existence at its impoverished best. That this absolute imperative comes from God (the Transcendent) also makes it religious, but as yet with nothing of the Christian significance of grace which reaches out to sustain the ethical man who finds himself fallen and broken. It is obvious that the full significance of the aesthetic as a rebellion against the Christian (eternal), as well as the full significance of the ethical and religious categories are not possible apart from Christianity.

Judge William, the central figure of 'Or', exemplifies a whole way of life—happiness in work, a love of life, responsibility as a citizen, delight in the native tongue and nation, happy acceptance of friendship and of the normal round of daily existence. He is the complete antithesis of the rebellious self-seeking aesthete portrayed in Volume One.

Judge William selects, as his chief exemplification of the responsible life, the relationship of marriage. If the ponderous argument appears laboured, at least certain points should be recognized. As love had provided an excellent illustration of aesthetic interest, so marriage affords unique opportunity to show the transforming nature of ethical life as it deals with identical contents of existence. Ethics makes it clear that love ought not be a mere experience of passion, but should be transformed by accepting it as a gift of God and a holy task. Judge William understands perfectly well that the glory of marriage is not to be located in the culinary arts, in providing an heir to continue the family name, or in the comforts of the fireside. Therefore, he will not tolerate merely aesthetic (and less than aesthetic) defences of marriage, which instead must have no lesser justification than the will of God. (II, p. 89)

Marriage is defended as an example of the moral life. Through it S.K. was reflecting profoundly on the nature of all human existence. Here he wanted to portray existence as duty rather than pleasure-seeking, and married love merely furnished a most dramatic example. In a world full of poetized romance, of sex and seduction, of flirtation and divorce, he wanted to show that all such ways of living are choice-less and ultimately self-defeating substitutes for dutiful marriage. What more compelling demonstration, drawn from all of humanity's experience (or from his own) could he have found than this example of the need to rise above passionate *interest* to disciplined duty? His point is that it is the quality of the eternal which distinguishes love from lust—giving a promise of the everlasting. Yet this promise is related to an earthly passion. It has no sure guarantee and it is true here as elsewhere that the eternal is concealed in this very revealment.

(II, p. 21) To a biologist who urged collegiate 'human animals' to engage in pre-marital sexual relations, S.K. would reply that it is not even possible to be a 'human animal'. The most accomplished aesthete cannot escape a sense of futility over undisciplined life, nor can he escape the challenge of genuine self-realization.

Judge William defends marriage against the monk (or mystic) with force equal to that directed against the irresponsible aesthete. If the monk loved 'being a man' as he should then he would confess the impoverishment of his life as contrasted to the beauty, normality and greatness of men who live according to the natural order. Man is not built for eternity but is precisely a mixture of eternal and temporal. The imperative need is to welcome the prompting of God within the finite life. It is very important that here S.K. positively rules out the temptation to renounce the world, in spite of the fact that the motif of renunciation grows prominently in his last writings. (II, p. 333) It may also be added that there was a strange irony and pathos in the fact that S.K. was describing the glory of marriage—indeed, the very duty of man to marry—at the exact time when he was suffering the anguish of a broken love.

The elemental philosophical issues in this work are indeed closely intertwined with S.K.'s romantic problems. While this may complicate interpretation, it is not inappropriate for a writer who maintains that truth is to be found in inwardness to draw upon his profound personal experience in order to illuminate truth. Like Socrates, Kierkegaard was insistent on finding an answer to the question, 'What is man?' and, also like him, he found the answer not in what man knows but in how he lives with values—love, work and marriage, trust and forgiveness. Existential truth, not surprisingly, roots in existence. An author's love, marriage, and faith are not irrelevant to his theory of existence.

David Swenson has called attention to the anomaly that many recent philosophers have denied the significance of moral values except as arbitrary desires, have approached values only through an analysis of conventional language and social custom, but nevertheless have remained enormously concerned with finding wives who meet their own standards of excellence.[39] In contrast, S.K. had no difficulty in finding an appropriate bride, but he found the requirements of marriage to be so exalted that he had to regard

THE AESTHETIC LITERATURE

himself as a sorrowful exception to the universal validity and normativeness of marriage. Proper existence normally requires the opposite of what he was able to do, i.e. live by divinely given norms rooted in human nature. In spite of the questioning of transcendently grounded values on the part of positivistic philosophers, there is a remarkable affinity between Kierkegaard and contemporary empiricism. The transcendent is never known *qua* transcendent, says S.K., yet it is intimated by the absolute quality of certain basic experiences. Man cannot be content with finite meanings, yet he possesses the absolute only in expectation of it. For this reason existence must be a tension and a striving for the eternal.

Just as marriage is 'before God', so too a man's work can properly be appreciated only if it is viewed before God. It too is an expression of 'man's perfection'. (II, p. 287) The consequence is that work does not exist for the sake of external reward. Whereas a mere aesthete is prone to view it as slavery or drudgery, work should be a joyful element in the good life, contributing to personal growth. (II, p. 290)

Judge William is at times long-winded and in many instances seems occupied with the obvious, but his arguments conceal the image of a tortured soul. As a youth, Kierkegaard had rebelled against Christianity's moral requirements, not by choosing evil but by avoiding—in a sophisticated quest for rich experiences—the very issue of good versus evil. Judge William is thus the personification of S.K.'s own conscience, seeking to demonstrate the fact that by avoiding the choice between good and evil one has really already chosen evil. The voice of conscience deplores the very use of 'either/or' by the aesthete, the youthful 'A' of Volume One. 'You will perceive,' Judge William addresses him, 'how essentially my view of choice differs from yours (if you can properly be said to have any view), for yours differs precisely in the fact that it prevents you from choosing.' (II, p. 168) The implication is that the trifler never does commit himself to anything; he only talks about choice, and in the meantime lives a life of pleasure which is neither deliberately good nor evil. Therefore, significantly, the fundamental either/or is not a choice between good and evil. Surprisingly, it is suggested: 'As soon as one can get a man to stand at the crossways in such a position that there is no recourse but to choose, he will choose the right.' (II, p. 172) Moral choice is not of one thing as opposed to another; it is instead an absolute as opposed to a relative choice, whereby one concerns himself about his eternal worth. But, one might inquire, is any person who commits himself bound to choose correctly? Yes, *if* he really chooses, but he can submit again to the lure of the aesthetic which is then neither a true 'choice' of the aesthetic nor an 'ethical choice' but is instead sin. (II, p. 172)

It is implicit in these facts that *Either/Or* does not present alternative possible choices, such as pleasure versus morality. If ever one comes to a choice, its direction is already set. One cannot truly choose the aesthetic. 'The act of choosing is essentially a proper and stringent expression of the ethical.' (II, p. 170) The actual either/or is the option of languishing indecisively in pleasure, which can lead to despair, or, becoming decisive.

The notion that if one chooses he will choose the good might suggest that Kierkegaard is accepting a kind of ethical determinism. To the contrary, he understands the necessity of careful and clear judgment in finding one's path among rival claimants to the title of 'right'. However, he feels that the *existential* problem is the danger of evasion. If only one will commit himself to the good he will somehow manage to find it, and, in any event, the existential goal of personal integrity is secured by the effort itself. The danger is that of postponing the moral decision. 'In making a choice it is not so much a question of choosing the right as of the energy, the earnestness, the pathos with which one chooses... Therefore even if a man were to choose the wrong, he will nevertheless discover precisely by reason of the energy with which he chose, that he has chosen the wrong.' (II, p. 171) Wyschogrod suggests, dubiously, that S.K. is more concerned about the 'how' (the decisiveness) of choice than about the 'what' or content.[40] Actually, for S.K., it is critically important that the *right* choice be made, but he holds that unless there be genuine commitment there is no hope of correctly perceiving and attaining the right. The 'how' is the means to the 'what'.

Strangely, ethical choice involves two kinds of movement, free self-development and obedient fulfilment of divine purpose. First, the person is realized only by his own self-determination. Self-identity comes into existence by the very act of choice. Second, the self which is chosen does somehow already exist, for a person does not create himself but only chooses himself. 'He repents himself back into himself, back into the family, into the race, until he finds himself in God.' (II, p. 219) Becoming oneself is thus both an admission of sin and a rejection of sin.

Ethical choice seems to have much the same function in Kierkegaard as in Greek eudaemonism. Yet the nature of the ethical self-realization as interpreted by Judge William is very different for it culminates in repentance, and rests upon the despair in which the life of pleasure ends. (II, p. 245) Despair cannot be escaped and should be freely accepted as the doom inescapably attached to moth-like fluttering about a luring flame. Repentance is the moral acknowledgment of this despair as one turns from desire to duty. Clearly, the ethical category has a large 'religious' element in it, just as the aesthetic experience contains a wistful acknowledgment of moral and religious values. The ethical man recognizes that the moral law is a divine imperative. Further, in penitence he makes confession which is a kind of religious act, but he continues to live under the ethical category in that he is still confident of his ability to do better and to obey. The proud Greek idealistic ethic misleads one by omitting the very starting point for becoming oneself, i.e. the confession that before God one has not been able to choose oneself. (II, p. 217)

It is quite important that, for Kierkegaard, duty does not rob experience of beauty; the ethical incorporates and enriches aesthetic experience. Thus, married (dutiful) love has unique aesthetic value. A maiden may be charming, but a wife and mother grows in beauty. Accordingly, the aesthetic experience is not in itself evil; it is neither good nor bad, but furnishes content which one can use in his self-realization. Natural accomplishment, as the art of the poet, is legitimate and important but it must be freed from vanity and pride by making it obedient to the ethical impulse. 'Talent is beautiful only when it is transfigured as a call, and existence is beautiful only when everyone has a call.' (II, p. 298) What this signifies is that only the ethical man can successfully live a pleasurable life, doing so by overcoming the self-destructive tendency of pleasure-seeking and by holding it in a subordinate position to higher values. What is more, that artistry of life which the aesthete sought but lost because he had no moorings, not only is possible for the ethicist; it is essential. The good man is singular, with no one else like him, but 'in such a way that he is also the universal man' engaged in a true art of living. (II, p. 261) However, S.K. grants that this ideal of an artistically created life, when put into practice, involves monumental difficulties. A person in fact tends to confuse the traditions and biases of his group with truly universal duties, and even tends to overlook the special requirements of his own life by virtue of the emphasis on the universal.

Even the ethical life has its pathos for it is marked by man's failure to attain his goals. Whereas the pathos of the aesthetic is inability to find any permanently satisfying externality, the pathos of the moral life is despair over failure to become one's proper self. *Either/Or* thus moves in the direction of the religious (third) sphere of existence; yet it moves chiefly towards the realm of a merely immanent religion, which is implicit in and grows out of the ethical experience.

The earnest man may taste of disillusionment in a variety of ways, through errors of moral judgment, personal failure in measuring up to ideals, or even conflicts between individual conscience and public morality. Thus there is a tragic web of circumstance which drives the moral man to despair. The very complexity and perplexity of the world of rival duties over-taxes his ethical wisdom. Worse, however, is inward failure. Purity is to will *one* thing, to be single-minded, but man is forever floundering in duplicity. Perhaps most perplexing of all is the apparent conflict between the universal moral principle, which is never really cancelled, and the unique needs and responsibilities of the individual which do not fit easily into this general pattern and may clash with it.

It may well be that these diverse grounds for ethical despair indicate some ambiguity in Kierkegaard's understanding of the ethical. Ambivalently, the ethical is man's 'highest task', yet is a 'dangerous science'.[41] In any event, S.K. mentions two basic deficiencies in the ethical life—first, inability to deal with exceptional cases (being strictly universal), and moral impotence because of sin. These two unrelated themes are not brought into any systematic conjunction.

The despair which issues from the deficiency of the ethical

THE AESTHETIC LITERATURE

life—deepening with the growing awareness of that deficiency—is not merely negative. If one does not taste of this bitterness then he has not understood the nobility and beauty which life ought to hold. To come to despair is, from the positive standpoint, to be cognizant of the good which however desired cannot be personally grasped. Therefore, ideally, despair is the stepping stone to trust in God's saving power. (II, p. 213) S.K. characterizes such despair as repentance, indeed as an 'overdose' of repentance, although it relates primarily to a sense of inadequacy for the future rather than to past failure. (II, pp. 148 f., 210 f.) 'His [S.K.'s] moral pathos is a raging conflagration that will not be extinguished. It is safeguarded from sentimentalism on the one hand and priggishness on the other by an omnipresent and equally proportioned sense of humour that never lets him forget his own personal relativity.'[42] The solution of ethical despair can only be found in a person-to-person relation between God and the penitent, at a new level of existence, viz. faith.

Great caution must be employed in interpreting ethical despair, lest it be confused with a sense of social and moral despair. Kierkegaard agrees with Luther that a kind of civic righteousness is possible for the natural man. Indeed, it is only before God that man is absolutely guilty. Oddly, S.K. might agree with Lin Yutang's one-time satirical comment that Christianity tries to convince man that he is sinful in order to make him appreciate his salvation. Moreover, he would also agree that the conviction of sinfulness cannot be rationally achieved, because for S.K. *absolute* guilt before God is not equivalent to obvious social impropriety. It is as much a paradox (grasped only by faith) as is the paradox of reconciliation in Christ.[43] That the widow's mite is as great as the largest gift is not true at the bank but only with God who lifts the believer out of relativities.[44] Thus it was that the noble young man turned away in sorrow and guilt when Jesus imposed absolute requirements upon him in place of the relative morality which he had honourably pursued.[45] In this light, while the more profound ethical consciousness is an awareness of duty to God (yet remaining human *duty* rather than religion which is a God-relationship), it is only when the burden of the absolute issues in guilt that the ethical consciousness completes itself in pathos.[46]

Volume II comes to a decisive culmination in its closing unit, reported as a sermon by a country pastor, such as S.K. aspired to become. The use of a sermon might lead one to suppose that here a third, religious stage is introduced. To the contrary, the sermon intensifies the moral way of life by leading the moral man to repentance, the final form of ethical consciousness. God is indeed introduced because it is only before God, i.e. when one is measured by absolute rather than relative standards, that it becomes evident to a man that he is always guilty, that he cannot blame circumstances for his predicament, and that, like the widow's mite which was an absolute gift of love, so too the littlest sin is absolute sin. Thus the concern here is still ethical and God is introduced only to deepen the gravity of the moral crisis. The moral man who had begun with hopeful striving is now made to end with a realization of guilt in relation to that moral law which is the law of God. The sermon's theme, appropriately, is that in God's sight man is always in the wrong. To give added weight to this final message it is entitled 'Ultimatum'. On the other hand, the severe message is also one of assurance as to the ways of God. Kierkegaard asks whether anyone could really wish to have his own misshapen view replace the wisdom and judgment of God. 'Could you wish that that beautiful law which for thousands of years has supported the race...might burst?' (II, p. 356) It is noteworthy that, like the Diary of the Seducer, the sermon is presented as the work of another party. It is in fact written by one pseudonym, presented by a second, and edited by a third. Hohlenberg is presumably correct in holding that this triple anonymity is to make it clear that the work is far removed from S.K.'s own point of view; indeed, it is three times removed! In this instance, S.K. had already transcended the ethical view of Judge William and had entered the religious life.[47]

Perhaps the question whether repentance may not be viewed as a form of religious consciousness should be pursued in greater depth. For S.K., the answer remains negative; *Either/Or* 'goes no further than the ethical'. (II, p. xxi) Repentance is only ethical and not religious because the ethical man, although sorrowful over his failings, does not thereby put his trust in God. Repentance is man's own final and honest response to personal failure. The religious state, in contrast, is marked by a divine act, a divine

THE AESTHETIC LITERATURE

atonement which man accepts but certainly does not achieve by means of his faith. Repentance is a final negative element in the unsuccessful human quest for the eternal.[48] The ethical life does indeed have the foundation in God mentioned above because, for Kierkegaard as for Kant, a moral command implies a giver of the law, and thus it gains the weight of the eternal and a sense of the holy. Yet the moral man's basic relationship is to the law and not to God.*

Judge William, although the champion of the ethical life, has not himself arrived at the ultimate existential understanding of this mode. While S.K. never rejects the concept of the law of God as a moral universal, he makes it more deeply personal than does Judge William. In particular, he repudiates the Hegelian objectivity which supposes that this universal principle is readily discernible in world history. It is instead in the inwardness of radical subjectivity, with uniqueness of personal duty, if also universality, that the full meaning of the ethical emerges.[49] The reason for this treatise stopping short of the religious stage is that to have openly treated these would have been too clear a baring of S.K.'s heart. Duty, in the religious mode of life as he construed it for his circumstances, called for him to be an exception to the universal rule, e.g. to give up marriage, but S.K. dared not here plainly state how and why he felt called upon to be such an exception.

It may be said that *Either/Or* prepares for the religious stage, though it does not introduce it. Repentance is the ultimate form of the ethical, yet it can not heal the sickness or bestow purity of heart. To move into the religious sphere there is presupposed a divine redemptive act and a positive 'leap' of faith on the part of man. The failure of the ethical suggests the need for this leap but

---

* S.K. agrees with Kant that we dare not take a simply phenomenal view of the moral self. We must act as if under universal moral law and under the lordship of God. However, S.K. is less timid than Kant. Not only must we live 'as if' under a divine law; the moral law is literally the will of God. Where Kant tries to view the moral law as rational in nature, springing autonomously from human nature, S.K. objects that this would leave man in 'lawlessness or experimentation'. If a man is a law unto himself his principles are no more dependable than his desires. There can be no true moral law without a law giver. (*Journals*, 1041.) Indeed, Kantian autonomianism makes untenable assumptions about the rights and dignity of the standard human ego, assumptions which are severely set aside by God's law, which not only gives a heteronomous law but also discloses man's guilt in relation to it. (*Ibid.*)

cannot produce it. Repentance cannot break the sinful enslavement to finite ends, but it can bring one to truth and to a readiness for grace. Thus despair over self-realization prepares for the leap of faith in which the believer, at last completely honest about his helplessness, chooses himself 'absolutely'.

Just as moving from the aesthetic stage to the ethical meant moving from indecisive pursuit of interests to resolute moral choice, so the move from the ethical to the religious is a movement from reliance on self to reliance on God, and despair to faith. Because it prepares the way for this proper movement, Kierkegaard thinks it a 'blessed thought' that *before God* man is always in the wrong. Such a thought makes it clear that the moral man as well as the aesthete is in need of divine grace. The moral man's problem originates in the fact that his duty to the universal law of God tends to be set aside in the interest of relative purposes. The problem is not the impossibility of a proper relation between absolute and relative, for properly they can fit together. The moral man's pathos is sin; he refuses to give to both absolute and relative that which is their due. Indeed, the very essence of sin is to cut short one's allegiance to the absolute and eternal because of concern with earthly and temporal ends.

How can it be that there are three radically separated stages of life but only one either/or? The implicit answer is that there is only one basic *choice* to be made, i.e. the eternal—first manifest in its immanent ethical form. One scarcely chooses the aesthetic but only dallies within it. On the other hand, the ethical life can be entered only by firm choice, in consciousness of a divine imperative. One cannot yield to it for mere reward or punishment; that would be to reduce it to a matter of aesthetic satisfactions. By choice of the ethical one places himself under the sovereignty of God, even though he fails in obedience to the sovereign will. In an odd sense, it is scarcely true that man can be said to choose the religious even though it and the ethical are akin. At least, one cannot effectually choose the religious, but rather, having once expressed one's proper self by accepting the responsibility of the eternal, and having once discovered the pathos of the ethical, the religious is entered when one responds in faith to God's assistance.

THE AESTHETIC LITERATURE

One specialized concept which is involved in the notion of existence is a new doctrine of time. Already in the second part of *Either/Or* S.K. initiates his attack on the static concept of time in which the 'now' alone is real, the past only a 'no-longer-now' and the future a 'not-yet-now'.[50] More in line with philosophers who start with *duration* as a basic presupposition than with those who think of time as a succession of discrete instants, S.K. insists that past, present and future are meaningless—with reference to man—apart from their involvement with one another (and, eventually, apart from their involvement with the eternal). He finds this demonstrated by the durational constancy of Christian experience: 'If I would represent a hero who conquers kingdoms and lands, he can very well be represented in the now, but a cross-bearer who every day takes up his cross cannot be represented either in poetry or in art, because the point is that he does it every day...Courage can very well be concentrated in the now, but not patience, precisely for the reason that patience strives with time.' (II, p. 138) The general thought is that the aesthetic is marked by momentariness, with nothing which endures. Such time is related to chatter whereas eternity is 'sheer haste and intensive' and aims at transforming character.[51] Thus eternity breaks into ethical and religious existence, giving the constancy which is an image of the eternal. The spiritual task is to grasp the eternal in time. Moral decision is threatened by lack of decisiveness; it cannot be postponed. Failing to be decisive not only removes the *either/or* but also causes one to lose his opportunity for selfhood. (II, p. 167) This doctrine, which was to be subsequently developed by the existential philosopher Heidegger, was more fully developed in *Concept of Dread*, and very particularly in *Repetition*.

5. TWO EDIFYING DISCOURSES

> *Two Edifying Discourses.* By S. Kierkegaard. May 16, 1843. Translated by David F. and Lillian Marvin Swenson in *Edifying Discourses*, Minneapolis: Augsburg Publishing House, 1943, 1962 (volumes reduced from four to two in 1962 edition). Also included in *Edifying Discourses, A Selection*, ed. by Paul L. Holmer. New York: Harper & Brothers, 1958, Harper TB 32. (Page references are to Vol. I of 1943 edition.)

There is a startling challenge in this title, even though it is obscured by the familiar language of piety. In a world which supposes that man's great need is for international peace, economic opportunity or political equality, S.K. puts his most crucial thought in 'edifying discourses'. He is convinced that the great need is not for what can be accomplished by scientific technology or political action but for the 'edification' (building up) of a self, a task in which each must rigorously engage by himself.[52]

This tiny volume of discourses was intended to 'accompany' *Either/Or*. Herein lies a critically important fact and a need for correcting an almost invariable misunderstanding. The common error is the assumption that *Either/Or* is the masterpiece (it soon became very popular and famous) and that the discourses are only pious asides in the style of the age, or at least are much less important. That they are small means that they go directly to the point. That they are religious means that they deal with S.K.'s primary concern, a fact in part indicated by their being published under Kierkegaard's own name. The aesthetic works were intended to raise problems and the discourses were intended to solve them. However, it appeared that people preferred to be entertained rather than edified. Sorrowfully, S.K. reported: 'I held out *Either/Or* to the world in my left hand, and in my right hand the *Two Edifying Discourses*; but all, or as good as all, grasped with their right what I held in my left'.[53]

These two discourses and the subsequent sixteen with which they were eventually assembled, were made to 'accompany' and in a sense correct, or at least complement, the aesthetic works which appeared pseudonymously at the same time. Yet like the aesthetic works, they are somewhat preparatory, not 'fully' Christian, if yet impressively Christian. They avoid the transcendent themes (as atonement and paradox) which were later developed. In them is manifested a kind of natural religiosity out of which the more distinctively Christian themes could emerge. In the *Postscript* S.K. identified this natural religiosity as 'religion A' in contrast to paradoxical Christianity which is 'religion B'. Religion A is not viewed as false but as a more subjective and immanent or natural awareness of the holy, possibly including an awareness of transcendent Christianity.

Kierkegaard made two important distinctions concerning these writings. First, the discourses are not sermons. They merely plead for reflection; and they are not preached with the authority he associated with the apostles and to a lesser extent (at least in his early period) with the ordained clergy. However, this point is dubious because S.K. also used the term 'discourse' to refer to a sermon which he preached, apparently with some sense of authority. Second, S.K. distinguished the 'edifying' discourses from 'Christian' discourses which more positively and specifically introduced Christian themes, and also from 'godly' discourses which were more like sermons in emphatically rejecting poetic reflection and boldly giving Biblical proclamation and commandment. In general the Christian and godly discourses come somewhat later in the authorship but the three types are quite intermingled and the distinctions are not precise.*

The first meditation, 'The Expectation of Faith', finds solace in the future by means of the eternal. Man's peering through the future towards the eternal is not escapism but instead a mark of human nobility. 'If there were neither past nor future, then would man be enslaved like the beasts, his head bent towards the earth, his soul ensnared in the service of the moment.' (P. 18) Like the

* It has been suggested that the reason for S.K.'s reference to his sermons as 'discourses' was to call attention to the weakness of the 'sermons' of his time. This seems improbable in view of his insistence on authority for preaching. Yet it is true that in S.K.'s discourses there are implicit criticisms of customary sermons. Their fault was that they only edified, gave reflection, and toyed with pretty sentiment. They failed to speak with a voice of authority as a witness for Christ and they failed to call upon the hearer to follow in discipleship—or else acknowledge his separation from Christ. Cf. Hermann Diem, 'Kierkegaard's Bequest to Theology', *A Kierkegaard Critique*, ed. by H. Johnson and N. Thulstrup, pp. 258 ff.

sailor on the restless sea where waves are forever being born and dying, and who must look to the eternal stars for faithful guidance, so the man of faith finds guidance in the eternal.

This discourse attacks the aesthetic problem of boredom (Vol. I of *Either/Or*) resulting from reliance on small and insecure satisfactions, doing so by introducing the quality of the eternal into the flux of experience. For Kierkegaard himself and for Regine this would seem to mean that under God and only by his grace might there be a repetition, a renewal of their relationship coupled with authentic self-hood.[54] The future can have a frightening indeterminate quality. We make wishes for our loved ones, but what wish can we safely make for them? Shall we wish for them wealth, health, power, or marriage? Any such gift can bring tragedy, and, if the moral of *Either/Or* is to be respected, all aesthetic concern with the temporal is overshadowed with the threat of tedium. A secure future is gained only through the eternal which is grasped by faith. Faith does not seek after particular finite goals but only desires the blessedness of fellowship with God. Faith is a passion *for the eternal*, not for what the eternal can bestow; it does not use God. Therefore, faith is no mere substitute for, or preliminary step leading to knowledge. It is the victorious apprehension of the transcendent God, who is beyond knowledge. It is a passion which by its infinitude becomes a communion with the infinite. Doubt also is a 'cunning' passion, not an intellectual quandary, and by its anxiety it robs life of peace. Yet doubt can become the instrument of the eternal, consuming itself by its own acids, and generating the concern which eventuates in faith. (Pp. 21, 26, 30)

Echoes of Socrates permeate the discourse. Although faith is not philosophic wisdom, S.K. agrees with Socrates that truth cannot be communicated, but can be awakened. By his witness the religious person can only remind the unbeliever that if he lacks faith it is because he himself has failed to respond. (P. 17) Whereas the aesthete eventually gives way to despair, the believer says 'I expect victory', not, however, on the ground of evident probability but by an act of will which trusts the inscrutable power of heaven. 'It is still beautiful that God will not thus appear to me in the visible things; we were separated in order to meet again.' (P. 30) Bare expectation is itself victory, and it arises out of an awakened subjectivity.

THE AESTHETIC LITERATURE

Since it is God who makes faith available to all, faith is an unfailing good—unless one rejects it. Faith, here broadly conceived rather than in specific Christian terms, is responsiveness to the eternal; yet it is also a dynamic expression of the self which chooses to reach beyond the boredom and frustration of existence to the promise of the eternal.

The second discourse, 'Every Good and Perfect Gift is from Above', faces the problem of moral pathos (implicit in Vol. II of *Either/Or*). It indicates that the ethical life may be doomed to brokenness and frustration, yet insists that God can use the evil for good. A man can make every effort, pray early and late for God's blessing, only to be denied his most earnest desire. Nevertheless, God's denial of the prayer is not an injustice; the denial too can be a perfect gift which compensates with faith and love for what is denied. Indeed, every circumstance of life becomes a good and perfect gift if it is received with thanksgiving. The human fault is that men fail to reflect on what constitutes a good and perfect gift, and identify it with the satisfaction of one or another temporal desire. Even wrongs (which remain wrong) and tragedies (which do not cease to be tragic) should be received with thanksgiving since God can use them for his purposes.

In this thought of omnipotent but often inscrutable providence the pathos of *Either/Or* is redeemed—not in either the aesthetic or the ethical—but in the religious way of life. For broken love, under which S.K. was suffering, the import is that the personal tragedy must be seen as somehow redeemed by the sovereign power of God. The object of man's pitiful prayer may not be granted but God changes him who prays. It is then not the quality of the divine gift which leads one to recognize that it is from above. Rather, when one understands in faith that from above come all manner of, and only, good gifts, then he can give thanks even for his sufferings, punishment, and for blessings which the Lord has taken away. (P. 54)

This discourse is quite important in that it introduces a theme which was to become a chief point of focus in S.K.'s later thought, namely the acceptance of suffering as a gift of God. In this discourse suffering retains a basic element of mystery; the thought is that somehow in spite of its obvious evil, it can still somehow be God's gift, and that since He gives nothing but good gifts.

Subsequently, Kierkegaard tended to ignore the element of mystery in this unhappy gift. His formula of explanation for suffering was never entirely systematic but it included two major themes. On the one hand, it is the consequence of sin. On the other hand, more or less apart from this, it is a consequence of the lure of the eternal within temporal existence; it is a testing to which God subjects the believer in order to see if he will still be faithful when he seems to be forsaken by God.[55] The blessedness of the God-given suffering is that it is intended to destroy man's selfish will and to cause man to die to the world as he is lured by the eternal.[56] In this later development suffering is no longer viewed as a perplexing intrusion in the life of the Christian but rather as the distinctive quality of his life.

Finally, if the discourses are taken to represent the religious stage of life, caution must be given not to fit them too tidily into a structured tri-partite system. Throughout the whole literature there occurs an amazing interweaving of form and content—from lyrical parable to metaphysical argument, and from the aesthetic interest to religious faith. The 'religious' experience described here must not be thought of as a neatly defined third in a naturally unfolding series of life stages. Further, there is no necessary movement from aesthetic to ethical, or from ethical to religious. One's movement can be from the aesthetic to religious, i.e. from pleasure to grace, with no long striving in the intermediate ethical stage. This was actually S.K.'s own experience, and it might even be argued that he moved first from the religious stage (in childhood) to the aesthetic, and back to the religious without ever being fixedly involved in the ethical as a distinct category.

6. REPETITION

> *Repetition.* An Essay in Experimental Psychology. By Constantine Constantius. October 16, 1843. Translated by Walter Lowrie. Princeton: Princeton University Press, 1941. New York: Harper & Row, 1964; Torchbook paperback TB 117. (Page references are to the Torchbook edition.)

This fantastic and profound work is one of a second series of love letters written from Berlin, and is outrageously although not

THE AESTHETIC LITERATURE

obviously autobiographical. It is a charming book, full of humour and satire, but showing a somewhat less pleasing side of Kierkegaard's personality. In it he blames Regine for causing him such suffering by her very faithfulness and devotion to him. (P. 46) By means of *Either/Or* Kierkegaard had tried—somewhat half-heartedly—to make himself repulsive to Regine and bring her to a religious healing. However, at church on Easter, 1843, instead of showing disgust towards him or ignoring him she nodded to him. Again in an agony of despair he quickly fled for the second time to Berlin. Dropping the philosophical treatise (*Johannes Climacus*) on which he was working and which in fact he never completed he poured out his heart and his wisdom in *Fear and Trembling*, in *Repetition*, and in *Three Edifying Discourses*.

By means of all these works, Kierkegaard hoped to make it clear to Regine that in spite of his love for her he could not marry. Undoubtedly there were varied reasons in back of this decision, particularly his melancholy, but also a sense of guilt, and a consciousness of a unique religious mission which prevented him from binding himself closely to any person. All of this was coupled with the dual convictions that in marriage there must be no hidden secrets, and yet that it was unthinkable to impose upon Regine all his secret problems, most particularly his consciousness of the sins of his father.* In spite of all this, Kierkegaard apparently was daring to wonder if there were not still a possibility of a 'repetition' of his love and of its consummation in marriage.

In *Repetition* S.K. picked up again some of the concepts

---

* Cf. *Either/Or*, II, p. 119. In addition to the problem of disclosing his father's sin and his sense of involvement in the father's guilt, S.K. seems to have been hindered from marriage by a feeling that sexual desire is sinful, a feeling apparently inculcated in him by his father during childhood as a means of preventing the child from repeating the father's sins. S.K. understood intellectually that this was a mistake in parental guidance but never escaped from the feeling and in later life increasingly gave it an ascetic justification. (*Journals*, 539.) The truly remarkable, melancholy, poetic personality of Kierkegaard has evoked endless reflection and the most diverse explanatory hypotheses, in some cases more fantastic than the data interpreted. One of the most sensitive, but not thereby more certain, interpretations is that of Eduard Geismar which suggests a completely untypical form of manic-depressive personality, not however manifesting alternating moods but a synthesis of exaltation and melancholy, enriched by complete intellectual gifts. (E. Geismar, *Lectures on...Kierkegaard*, pp. 6–8.) In the judgment of the authors a far more likely interpretation would recognize S.K. as maladjusted, neurotic, but certainly not psychotic.

particularly that of repetition itself, which he had been developing in *Johannes Climacus*. Casual observation might seem to show that the flux of the world infects even the self, thus undermining the essential unity of personhood. However, by repetition, S.K. argued, one can escape from an unstable momentary existence and gain enduring reality. This continuity of the self with itself is gained by the continual re-commitment of the new self to the ideals of the former self. Without such commitment the past would indeed be simply dead and the future a hollow dream. By chosen repetition a man securely unites his past and future selves to the present reality and unifies them into one durational person. 'He does not run after butterflies like a boy; nor does he stand on tiptoe to peer at the glories of the world, for he knows them. Neither does he sit like an old woman at the spinning wheel of recollection...Indeed, if there were no repetition, what then would life be? Who would wish to be a tablet upon which time writes every instant a new inscription?...If God Himself had not willed repetition, the world would never have come into existence. He would either have followed the light plans of hope, or He would have recalled it all and conserved it in recollection...'(P. 34 f.)

Plainly, repetition goes infinitely beyond the simple theme of recovery of love and raises questions of tremendous philosophical concern, in particular about the nature of and identity of the person. Its ultimate import is religious consolation, but this is contemplated against a background of philosophical issues. First, S.K. had dared to hope for a 'repetition' with Regine, then, despairing of this—and of much more—he concluded that when one learns the *good* by means of suffering he has gained not only the best kind of learning and instruction, but, what is more important, the best Teacher. If one takes this occasion to learn from God, then he is strengthened 'in the inner man'. The more extended religious development of the concept of repetition undoubtedly was elaborated as a revision of the book after Kierkegaard received the crushing news that Regine had become engaged to her former sweetheart, Fritz Schlegel, thus making repetition of love a mocking illusion.

The opening and main portion of *Repetition* is a whimsical and ironical interpretation of repetition, but the closing portion deals

THE AESTHETIC LITERATURE

with it as a moral responsibility, and—when this cannot be attained—as a religious possibility. Since so strange a love letter as this had to be disguised in order that only the beloved would recognize its personal reference, S.K. continued here to treat objective persons and situations, but to do so anonymously. Thus a strange love story is told, in fact a secret mirroring of S.K.'s own love affair. A lover makes the startling and discomfiting discovery that he enjoys his memories and dreams of his beloved more than he enjoys her. With a sense of unworthiness he flees in shame, hoping to find anew the meaning of his life.

It is particularly noteworthy that the concept of repetition as one's taking himself anew in a religious manner, of being born again or having eternal life, never becomes completely evident in this book, which ends instead with a question mark and an anguished cry. The real answer to the question of the possibility of repetition (as was true through much of the authorship) was offered in the discourse which 'accompanied' the aesthetic book, viz. 'Strengthened in the Inner Man', which appears in the *Three Edifying Discourses*. Because *Repetition* is a merely 'aesthetic' work it is not permitted to offer the assurance of religious repetition but is allowed only to explore its meaning and to raise the question of its possibility.

Although the first portion of the book is, as mentioned above, less ethical or religious and is marked by humour, it raises crucial philosophical problems. It explores the problem of the unity of personhood and of identity within change. Repetition is said to reconcile the static Being of the ancient Eleatic philosophers and the Flux of Heraclitus by virtue of the fact that becoming is not simple or absolute change but is instead repetition. It is being-within-becoming, or repeated identity through change. Further, it is argued that anything sound in Hegel's concept of mediation is actually repetition. (P. 52) Often S.K.'s treatment is highly poetic. 'Hope is a charming maiden but slips through the fingers, recollection is a beautiful old woman but of no use..., repetition is a beloved wife.' (P. 34) As Plato sought intimations of the eternal within the present by means of *recollection*, so Kierkegaard seeks the eternal in future repetition. Socratic recollection is *pagan* for it will allow nothing to have being *except that which has already been,* thus excluding creation. Repetition is modern (and Christian) because that which is repeated has in it the novelty and voluntary commitment of the repetition. (P. 53)

Kierkegaard proceeds to characterize three attitudes towards repetition, progressively gaining depth. First, there is (aesthetic) repetition which comes to be feared as boredom. Second, when it is recognized that this cannot be escaped, one may at least seek novelty within monotony, by means of shrewdness but to no avail. Although a kind of repetition, essentially unsatisfying, is thus experienced even at this level, a sharp distinction is here evident between the aesthetic and those stages above it. As the constant or the abiding is the mark of the ethical and the religious, so the temporal and momentary are distinctive of the aesthetic. Gay moments fleet away, pleasures are but for the moment and pains endure too long. While time holds promise of good things to come, it carries one inexorably towards privation, old age and death. There is no hope for enduring value in duration. Only in the repetition which defies time is there a possible salvation, and a successful repetition of such magnitude as this is an introduction of the quality of the eternal. Accordingly, one should properly and finally, in an ethical and religious manner, seek repetition as the enduring continuity of personal existence and value. Then the question becomes: Is repetition as personal self-identity possible?

As a parody of anyone who seeks satisfaction by the repetition of external things or environment, S.K. humorously describes a second visit to Berlin. In this case the repeating of former delights is found to be impossible because the very recollection of them in the past robs the repetition of novelty and interest. How wonderful was the first visit to the great city—the journey, the metropolis, even the cosy dwelling, and above all the theatre where the actors had transported the audience into a kingdom of fancy and delight. With the second visit everything has become changed into a kind of mockery of what had been experienced before. The visitor again attends the theatre to see two comedians, Beckmann and Grobecker, 'lyrical geniuses who plunge into the abyss of laughter and then let its volcanic force cast them upon the stage'. Unfortunately, whereas originally he had been charmed by these 'children of caprice', now, at the attempted repetition, the only thing repeated is 'the impossibility of repetition'. (P. 65) It seems to follow from such experience that if ever there is to be a repeti-

THE AESTHETIC LITERATURE

tion it must come inwardly, and with free commitment. Repetition must be religious rather than circumstantial, a kind of God-given peace shed upon one's subjectivity. Furthermore, such achievement of inner constancy and purpose must come by an existential leap rather than a natural unfolding, not by necessary dialectic, as with Hegel. Becoming is never logically necessary, for if it were such then it would already have been.

Part One thus ends with despair of aesthetic repetition, and Part Two turns to the ethical (and subsequently religious) possibility. Whereas in aesthetic repetition one wistfully recalls a sense of wonder, anticipation, and fond dreams, and vainly wishes to return to all delightful beginnings, e.g. on waking to find one's bed as cool, neat and refreshing as at bedtime; in the ethical repetition there is a desire for recovery of the *self* rather than of external delights. Ethical repetition is a constancy of ethical purpose. However, the experience of the tragic lover in *Repetition* makes it clear that ethical repetition is no more possible than is aesthetic repetition. Only God can perform the miracle of restoring the broken self to its integrity and wholeness. (Pp. 73, 117, 136)

Repetition can never be a precisely identical recovery because the person himself always changes, as well as his situation. Repetition, as Croxall points out, is therefore not mere 'resumption' at the place where one was before, but a 'taking anew' in which 'something has been added (by God) to the shattered personality, which is now "taken again" in its pure and pristine form'.[57] Something of the inner meaning of this can be inferred from S.K.'s love affair. That repetition is not resumption, for example, a return to engagement and subsequent marriage, but is a religious substitute for this was required in Kierkegaard's case by his inability to enter upon marriage. Further, that it included a spiritual restoration of that which was lost is reflected in his hope for a spiritual reconciliation with Regine and an enduring friendship with her, although without marriage. There is thus a subtle duality in this concept. By bringing the eternal into time, Christ bestows eternal meaning on human experience and relations; the human experience is taken into and becomes a part of one's God-relationship. Yet this human love which is so blest is no longer simply subject to the changes and sorrows of ordinary experience but is secured within pathos and change.

In Part Two there is presented a series of letters from the anonymous lover who appears in Part One, written to a friend, 'Constantine' (faithful). The latter comments that fortunately the disconsolate young man did not seek 'enlightenment from any world-renowned philosopher' or professor but rather from Job, who does not 'cut a figure in a university chair' but who sits among ashes and lets fall casual hints. Just as Job was compassionately treated by the very God who rebuked him, so the lover hopes to have a repetition of love (including even marriage) as the outcome of his suffering and resignation. Yet even if his suffering should have no earthly solution, it may at least receive a heavenly benediction. With Job, the disconsolate lover cries out, 'The Lord gave, the Lord hath taken away, blessed be the name of the Lord'. Yet neither Job nor the lover (Kierkegaard) is tranquilized. One demands an explanation from God himself, with a total unwillingness to accept the 'gossip and rumour' of men. (Pp. 115, 102) Job lost, yet won, his argument with God, and gained a repetition, when all conceivable probability pronounced it impossible. Spiritual repetition is God's granting the impossible.

As Kierkegaard waited for a Job-like thunderstorm and divine voice to solve his problems he learned instead that Regine had become engaged to another. This accorded with his own half-hearted plan when he wrote *Either/Or*, but now that it was an actuality it was difficult to bear. In bitter—too bitter—irony (apparently changing the original MS), he now praised her feminine magnanimity (she 'nevertheless acted magnanimously towards me—if in no other respect, at least by forgetting me'), and tragically concluded: 'I am again myself. This self which another would not pick up from the road I possess again. The discord in my nature is resolved.' (P. 125)[58] The personal tragedy in the situation must not obscure the profound spiritual conviction which S.K. wanted to convey, viz. that he *had* indeed gained a repetition, and that spiritual repetition was therefore possible. God had given him an authentic self and a spiritual purpose, in the very moment of his terrible loss. What this meant to him is

THE AESTHETIC LITERATURE

suggested by this statement in the *Journals*: 'Two things in particular occupy me: (1) that, whatever the cost, I should remain intellectually true, in the Greek sense, to my life's idea; (2) that religiously it should be as ennobling as possible.' (No. 588) Nevertheless, in severe self-judgment, Kierkegaard regarded his re-birth as only poetic or reflective, falling far short of a complete religious recovery due to a weakness of faith. As a poetic form of repetition his experience did no more than enable him to return to his concern with ideas which as objects outside the self were 'aesthetic' and not profoundly spiritual. (P. 136) If he had gained true faith he would have returned to Regine.

One sentence near the beginning of the treatise strikes the reader as a profound and impressive, if somewhat qualified, truth when applied to S.K. himself: 'The young girl was not his love, she was the occasion of awakening the primitive poetic talent within him and making him a poet.' (P. 40) The closing lyrical ejaculation demonstrates this same fact: 'The chalice of inebriation is again held out to me, already I inhale its fragrance, already I am sensible of its foaming music—but first a libation to her who saved a lost soul which sat in the solitude of despair. Hail to feminine magnanimity! Hail to the high flight of thought...Hail to the dance in the vortex of the infinite! Hail to the breaking wave which covers me in the abyss! Hail to the breaking wave which hurls me up above the stars!' (P. 127)

Such passionate outbursts make it easy for the modern reader to interpret *Repetition* as a poetic expression of personal feeling and to discount the profundity of the idea of repetition and S.K.'s central religious concern. Yet personal experience has inspired the poetic in S.K., and schooled him in existence. Out of his experience emerged the conviction that repetition in its various forms, sought or achieved, is central to all human existence.

One basic aspect of repetition is its emphasis on the abiding nature of the self. In view of his insistence on freedom, a critic might have expected Kierkegaard to emphasize change, perhaps in the fashion of Bergson, but instead he stresses constancy. He feels that in the Heracleitian flux there is always more than enough of change. Novelty is no miracle. The great need is rather to find a way to include permanency of character. It is this very miracle of deliberate self-identification and determination which is distinctive of and definitive of man. 'He who would only hope is cowardly, he who would only recollect is a voluptuary, but he who wills repetition is a man, and the more expressly he knows how to make his purpose clear, the deeper he is a man.' (P. 34)

It is still more important that repetition reaches beyond the temporal. As Socrates sought the eternal by recollection, so Kierkegaard senses the *eternal* in the future; the future challenges not only by its requirement of decision but by its infinitude.[59] Dread arises as the imagination is staggered by this incalculable infinity and uncertainty which lies ahead, and the self sinfully falters, seeking support in tangible things. The self may escape from this dread by understanding that literally every experience is in a mysterious fashion God's good gift. Obviously, if the future is the arena of the eternal, then the present too is pregnant with limitless possibility. Even the past is not a lost treasure but can retain its meaning, secured by the eternal.[60]

The emergence of the eternal within the future is a result of God's entrance into time. It might be said that Kierkegaard would agree with Nietzsche that (at least for modern men) 'God is dead', and that western civilization is heading towards a loss of the religiously grounded values. However, whereas Nietzsche would hasten the process, and therefore proposed a transvaluation of values and the replacement of the virtues of sympathy and humility by the self-affirmation of the superman, Kierkegaard urged an inner rebirth of the old values. If God is dead in Christendom then he must be born anew in the hearts of men, giving them new birth. This is the ultimate significance of repetition. For the individual it means that integrity of personhood comes from a God-given rebirth of the proper self. To morally struggle for recovery of the self which has been violated by sin only deepens the sense of incapacity. True existence therefore cannot be moral growth or self-cultivation. It necessitates a divine act whereby the self is restored to its wholeness.[61]

It is clearly this recovery of the eternal which is the deepest and most subtle significance of repetition, although a second element is also crucial, viz. that to *be* as a person is to *become*. The emphasis on the eternal appears in the criticism of Job who is viewed as something less than a hero of faith since he sought a recovery of

THE AESTHETIC LITERATURE

mere earthly blessings and because his experience was only 'trial by probation' rather than tranquility gained by being at peace with the eternal. (P. 115) However, the thought of the eternal is not clearly set forth in *Repetition*, so much as in *Sickness Unto Death* and later works. It appears most clearly in certain of the *Christian Discourses*, particularly 'The Joy of it—that when I "gain all" I lose nothing at all'. Man is 'compounded of the temporal and the eternal'; he was created for fellowship with God. However, since man has violated this relationship, the eternal now lies out of reach as only a beckoning hope. In the deepest sense it is this element of the eternal which is repeated or recovered in the event of repetition, and it is repeated *backwards* in time. That is to say, the eternal which lies before man *in the future* ceases to be merely a hope for the future and in some mysterious way is brought back into the present. This may occur, for example, in the reality of forgiveness which is grasped in faith, or in the sovereignty of God in which one places his trust while living in a world of uncertainty and rebellion. Above all, that which connects the temporal and the eternal is holy love which defies change by its abiding. As sin consists of losing the eternal through a concern for the temporal, so repetition is a recovery of the eternal within the temporal, a return to the purposes of creation. True spirituality is repetition because of the fact that the eternal 'lays out only a small piece at a time', in instant after instant luring man onward and upward with the severity of insecurity but also with the gentleness of hope.[62]

It is with a certain disdain for the *moment* (or anything transitory) and in a yearning to escape from the temporal into eternity that Socrates (or Plato) held the doctrine of recollection. The learner does not really change in the Socratic moment of learning. He only recollects what he had momentarily forgotten. For S.K., the change in the moment is radical—from sin to grace, from despair to faith, from error to truth.[63] There is continuity of the self in repetition ('recollection forwards'), yet with free self-determination. Whereas recollection restores the changeless reality of the past, repetition extends the reality of the past into the future, in a free, creative adventure, a commitment to the values of the former self.

A point of dispute is the 'anti-historical' character of S.K.'s treatment of the 'moment' of repetition. Are successive moments discrete, lacking continuity? S.K.'s conviction is that one cannot make Tuesday's decision on Monday, so that past decisive moments are no longer decisive. A decision can be repeated; one can have the 'repetition', but it cannot be securely stored away. It does not really follow, as has been charged, that 'the science of history is unimportant' because of this.[64] Not only were the former moments important when they were on the knife-edge of the present, but they remain important in helping the self to identify that with which it wishes to identify itself. To be a self is to have repetition of authentic decisiveness, as one commits and re-commits himself in acceptance of the paradoxical intrusion of the eternal into the temporal in the person of Christ. Repetition is the acceptance of the eternal *in time*.

What is particularly important is that the eternal is not a future compensation for earthly loss, but is a new, divinely granted way of regaining eternally that which was temporally lost.[65] Obviously, the lost earthly treasure is not recovered in an earthly sense. A friend who dies is not brought back to life only to die the second time; instead he is somehow regained eternally, as 'a transfigured friend'.[66] By bringing temporal values into one's God-relationship something of the quality of the eternal is distilled upon them. The fact that S.K. comforted himself over the death of his father and the loss of Regine by bringing them into this God-relation rather than substituting the God-relation for them makes it clear that for him the eternal was not a replacement for lost earthly treasure. It was instead a religious repetition or transfiguration of the earthly treasure, in addition to the God-relation. Repetition seems to become a spiritual transfiguration of lost earthly values rather than a simple recovery of them.

Kierkegaard was fully aware of the obscurity of the 'eternal' element in man which, in his language, is possessed or gained by repetition. In heaven, for example, there is no pomp, honour, or marriage. Perhaps one does 'gain his own soul' by losing the whole world, yet there is no clear indication of the nature and status of this soul.[67] However, there is a way in which the presence of the eternal in the temporal world is indicated. If a lover is heartbroken over loss of the beloved, he may despair not only of love but also of God, and to do so is to abandon the eternal on account of the temporal. Correspondingly, if one can 'let go of the temporal' in such a manner as to indicate that it is for him only a temporal and not an absolute loss, this is then 'a precise indication of the presence of the eternal in the loser'.[68] Dying to the world is not repudiation of the world but is a learning of the relative price of earthly treasure in contrast to the absolute price of heavenly treasure. In a final sense repetition is a securing of the eternal.[69]

7. FEAR AND TREMBLING

Fear and Trembling. A Dialectical Lyric. By Johannes de silentio. October 16, 1843. Translated by Walter Lowrie. Princeton: Princeton University Press, 1941. Translation revised by Howard A. Johnson in *Fear and Trembling* and *The Sickness Unto Death*. Garden City: Doubleday, 1954, Anchor paperback A 30. (Page references are to the original edition.)

This book is a study in faith, and thus it adds the third, religious stage to the two previously defined modes of existence. In biting irony, Kierkegaard says that, following Hegel, no one is content with faith, but 'goes right on' to something higher, viz. philosophy. He draws a charming and shrewd analogy. The ancient philosopher Heracleitus proved that all is change, eternal flux, by denying that one could cross the same river twice, but a foolish disciple 'went farther' by denying that one could cross the river even once. This 'improvement' of the argument actually destroyed it, for if one cannot cross the river once then motion is impossible, which is precisely the Eleatic position against which Heracleitus was waging war. 'Poor Heracleitus, to have such a disciple!' (P. 193) So too the Hegelians, by going a little 'farther', were destroying faith even though giving it lip service. In contrast, S.K. proceeds to focus on faith, and does so with remarkable outcomes.

'Fear and Trembling!' Why this fantastic title? It is to make the point unforgettable that one's God-relation does not consist of being a bourgeois family man and citizen; it calls for strain, strangeness and the unexpected. If Christ's God-relation brought him to a cross, the disciple's path will surely bring him into a tense relation with society and social conformity. Yet the man of faith will also be a common-place citizen and a family man. Indeed, if he were pointed out, one would exclaim in astonishment, 'Good Lord, is this the man? Is it really he? Why, he looks like a tax-collector!' (P. 53)

The book was written and published in conjunction with *Repetition*, which also is concerned with the religious stage. The books are also alike in that both take their initiation in S.K.'s broken love. The astonishing hidden message for Regine in *Fear and Trembling* is that just as Abraham was called upon by God to sacrifice Isaac, yet received him back at the hand of God, so perhaps S.K., who had in anguished faith sacrificed his love, might likewise receive it back at the hand of God. *Repetition*'s religiosity had tended to remain a sublimation of thwarted earthly love. However, in *Fear and Trembling* the concept of repetition is deepened. Abraham does not renounce his earthly love, nor does he possess it only in the 'transfigured' form of *Repetition*. By faith he is enabled to actually secure it by the grace of God. He receives God and also all that he had lost. S.K. is quite aware of the fact that he himself is not a man of great faith like Abraham; if he were then he would *remain with Regine*, not abandon her. Thus in *Fear and Trembling* religion is in no sense a substitute for reality.[70]

Fear and Trembling qualifies the position of Volume II of *Either/Or*, which had so exalted marriage as to make it a universal duty. According to the latter was not S.K. himself wrong in renouncing marriage? Here he brilliantly denies this by discovering meaning in religious faith and rejecting Hegel's insistence that the individual must always submit to universal ethical rules. There is room for the exceptional case. Just as the ethical transcends the aesthetic, so too the religious experience transcends the ethical and can even set it aside. Yet S.K. as an 'exception' hopes to recover the universal.

This beautiful and profound book, scarcely understood in Kierkegaard's day, has subsequently won such esteem as to justify the author's secret comment: 'Oh, when once I am dead—then *Fear and Trembling* alone will be enough to give me the name of an immortal author.' (P. xxvii) The book begins with a panegyric on Abraham who, when required by God, hastened to the sacrifice

THE AESTHETIC LITERATURE

of his only son 'as though it were a festival'. In the ensuing section entitled 'Problemata', faith is therefore depicted as trust in the absurd in that faith trusts God even when he slays. There follow treatments of three problems: (1) religious suspension of the ethical, (2) absolute duty to God, and (3) keeping silent about duty to God. For the most part the meaning of faith is demonstrated by reference to Abraham and his 'sacrifice' of Isaac. It has been argued that the patriarch is only a symbol for S.K. and that 'Isaac' is really Regine whom he had sacrificed in love. This identification probably has some historical foundation, but it is more true to say that S.K.'s personal tragedy furnished the passionate energy and sensitive awareness which made possible an accurate and remarkable analysis of Abraham's situation, and of the others which are treated in conjunction with it. In any event, the outcome and concern of the book is with the nature of religious existence, whether applied to S.K., to Abraham, or to the reader.

Abraham was no hero. Instead, he was a man of faith, trusting and obeying God even when faith required what was rationally absurd and morally offensive. He is not merely resigned to God's requirement but believes that God will give back what he is taking away. Reason demands of God: How can the promise of Abraham becoming the father of a nation become true if his only son is destroyed? Morality would protest against the human sacrifice. Faith transcends these objections and trusts God even when he seems to violate rational and moral principles, and obscurely it hopes to receive Isaac back. Several problems emerge and are treated with meticulous care, among them the problem of silence. Does Abraham (anyone) have a right to keep silent about such a dreadful crisis as this, or should he confide to others that he must slay his son? S.K. argues for the unutterable quality of life at the spiritual level. If Abraham acted on ethical principles alone, then out of his responsible relations to others he would tell them of his dreadful duty. If he were moved by aesthetic principles alone then he would tell no one of the matter for fear of giving pain. But as a religious man he cannot speak of his own experience of God's will because its significance is uniquely individual and therefore incommunicable.

Fear and Trembling demonstrates the important point that the transcendent element or divine authority in Christianity is paradoxical, a fact which is seldom considered. Duns Scotus held that adultery, murder or polygamy would be right if God willed them. Not so, Kierkegaard! Thus Walter Kaufmann is mistaken in saying that S.K. stands for a blind authoritarianism. Kaufmann says that Kierkegaard admired Abraham 'for not looking at the content of the commandment to sacrifice his son and for not concluding that it was not divine and could not come from God'.[71] This is a beautiful half-truth. In *Fear and Trembling* Kierkegaard made it clear that Abraham *did* look with anguish at the content of the commandment and that he fully understood that God's command to sacrifice Isaac would make impossible of fulfilment God's own promise to build a nation of Abraham's seed. Accordingly, Abraham's attitude (and that of Kierkegaard who idealizes him) is not one of 'utterly blind obedience'. *Open-eyed*, Abraham sees that God is contradicting himself. Yet he trusts the God of promise against the requirement of sacrifice even while he obeys the dreadful command.

Christian faith recognizes the validity of moral principle. For example, if a pious fool, wanting to imitate the godly Abraham, proposes to sacrifice his own son, he is guilty of overlooking the essential point that God's will is for parental love and care, and that, for him as an individual, God has presumably not required the paradoxical suspension of the ethical. Thus it is evident that S.K. is just as vehemently opposed to romanticism's cult of individuality which makes each individual a law unto himself (stressing private moods and experience) as he is to the rigid Kantian legalism which sees no possibility of religious exceptions to the ethical.

This point of view is borne out in the closing portion of the book which deals with the problem of secretiveness. Several remarkable stories are told in which the heroes maintain a strange and improper silence, not, however, because of any relation to God but for aesthetic reasons. This Kierkegaard will not allow. One's moral duty, under universal principle, cannot be set aside for personal reasons. Only faith can so relate one to the absolute God as to suspend the normal moral requirement. Abraham makes the issue clear. Either he is responsible to God for his dreadful deed or else he is a monster, never to be forgiven.

THE AESTHETIC LITERATURE

Kierkegaard's view of the ethical appears Kantian in the sense that it is identified as a strictly universal principle. The moral obligation is an unqualified imperative and when an Abraham makes himself an exception to the universal rule he has abandoned the ethical and has moved into the realm of faith. Kierkegaard is eager to show that whereas Agamemnon, Jephthah, and Brutus had a moral ground for human sacrifice, Abraham had none. His act violated universal moral principle and separated him from society. He is willing to obey God, even in defiance of his own best moral sense. (P. 87) In this respect, faith is 'self-annihilation'.[72]

Recent critics have argued that the ethical is not necessarily universal and that if it was proper for Abraham to sacrifice Isaac then to do so was ethically right, i.e. whatever is right is ethically right, and in the case of Abraham there was (hypothetically) a divine justification of a *seeming* immorality.[73] The issue may not be critically important and may even be somewhat verbal. What S.K. would insist upon is that in such an instance there is a 'teleological suspension' of the ethical in the sense that faith then is not acting on the basis of rational moral principles. The man of faith still understands the universal imperative of the ethical, but he feels obliged to temporarily set aside or suspend it, without necessarily being able to give a rational justification for doing so. Faith does trust that there is a higher kind of rightness in the divine intervention, but it cannot understand it. The requirements of faith are for man so shrouded in mystery that it is not legitimate to think of them as a higher 'order' of the ethical.

The ethical may then be replaced by religious paradox (rather than by a higher ethic), but the ethical principle remains valid. Whereas the aesthetic is dethroned by the ethical (and then within the ethical is regained so that the totality of existence becomes beautiful), the ethical stage is not dethroned by the religious, but remains a proper relationship to God. Indeed, 'in all eternity', it retains its high position.[74] It is important that what occurs is a suspension of the ethical, rather than an annulment. The ethical is not set aside but strangely held in abeyance, in response to a higher divine purpose. Indeed, perhaps it would be less confusing and truer to the spirit of Kierkegaard to say that the suspension does not so much hold the ethical in abeyance, but instead peculiarly transforms it, with the result that the moral principle continues to function, but in a relative rather than an absolute manner. Thus love for God may cause love for neighbour to take the opposite expression to that which is ordinarily required by duty. (P. 105) All of this would seem to indicate that Kierkegaardian paradox is not ultimate irrationality. It is instead an acceptance of that which appears to violate human morality and even human reason, but with the trust that ultimately God's ways will be vindicated and their reasonableness made evident. This must not be interpreted to mean that the paradox is *somewhat* plausible, or is a reasonableness of a lesser degree. Rather, to the human understanding, the paradox does give offence and is absurd, but faith adds that with God the evidently impossible is actually possible.

In the light of the above, faith takes on unexpected and astonishing properties. Faith is not a believing of the probable—nor of the improbable, nor is it merely an 'assurance of things hoped for'. Faith is instead trust that with God all things are possible, that God can fulfil even the promise which He has shattered, indeed, that *with God all things are possible*. Even the 'impossible' is possible. We find this put in a remarkable formula in *Sickness Unto Death*: 'Inasmuch as for God all things are possible, it may be said that this is what God is, viz. one for whom all things are possible..., for God is that all things are possible, and that all things are possible is God; and only the man whose being has been so shaken that he became spirit by understanding that all things are possible, only he has had dealings with God.'*

Another of the very precise meanings which faith acquires is that of immediacy after reflection. It is *after* reflection in that faith is not preparation for reflection or reason, or that religion is not a preparation for philosophy as it was for Hegel. Yet faith is not *after* reflection in the sense of resulting from it, for faith comes

* *Sickness*, p. 62 f. Geoffrey Clive makes similar observations in his study of S.K.'s 'teleological suspension of the ethical'. Basic ethical requirements, he points out, must not be rejected by religion, but faith may 'suspend' them, as in the case of Abraham, where faith required not only murder but precisely the killing of the one to whom one had the greatest obligation. Two other qualities of faith are noted: (1) a suspension of reason, for Abraham believed an absurdity, viz. that God contradicts himself, and (2) the quality of miracle, i.e. the affirmation that with God all things are possible. ('The Teleological Suspension of the Ethical', *The Journal of Religion*, April 1954.)

THE AESTHETIC LITERATURE

only with a leap or act of will. It is a state of 'immediacy' in that it is a coming to grips with reality. It is an experience which is not mediated or established by reason and which is incommensurable with evidence. It is to be noted that there can also be a religious awareness (or immediacy) prior to reflection, an immediate consciousness of God.[75] This too is 'immediacy' in that the natural religious consciousness is not mediated or caused by nature's splendours, but is a free religious sense to which one moves by a kind of leap from the glories and mysteries of nature. However, prior to reflection, this religion is only a natural religious wonder or awe, very different from the faith which alone can give one purity and reconciliation with God. Indeed the natural religious awe (immediacy prior to reflection) may actually stand in the way of faith because it tends to conceal the crucial fact of sin.[76]

Furthermore, faith is given precise definition by putting it into relationship to resignation. It is not resignation, although 'infinite resignation' is the 'last stage' before faith. Faith does include infinite resignation before God but it also includes *trust* in face of the absurd, that what one sacrifices in resignation God will nevertheless restore; it is resignation with divinely inspired trust added to it. Abraham still believed in God's promise in the very moment when God required him to destroy the instrument of promise.

It may be acknowledged that Kierkegaard sees a kind of rationality in faith. Although the man of faith rises above the law he does this only out of reverence for the Lawgiver. Yet S.K. denied that man can avoid mystery or have any simple and comprehensive understanding of his relation to God. He is unimpressed by the wisdom in Hegelian synthesis. Accordingly he deliberately shocks the reader by compelling him to take Abraham seriously. He shocks those legal moralists who ignore subjectivity and look for universal principles, doing so by exalting a man whose virtue was his very willingness to perform the most terrible deed. He shocks those who thoughtlessly want to imitate great men by forcing them to consider the true nature of the strange and dreadful deeds to which great men have been led. He shocks those who want a neat and rationally unified world by showing how faith can expect the impossible. He shocks the preacher who makes a pretty fairy tale out of Abraham, without sensing the perilous and momentous issues involved. Faith, one may conclude, is bound to mystery.

It is somewhat remarkable that this relatively early treatment of faith makes the sharp distinction (in the 'Preliminary Expectoration') between general religiosity and Christian religiosity. Later these two were termed 'religiousness A' and 'religiousness B', respectively. In *Fear and Trembling* general religiosity is exemplified by a knight of 'infinite resignation', and Christianity by a knight of faith. What can resignation accomplish? It enables a man to 'become clear' to himself with respect to his 'eternal validity', gaining a sense of transcendence and of the infinite by freeing himself from the claims of finite things. This constitutes an abandonment of the world in an attempt to escape its oppressive mastery and a renunciation of temporal values in an endeavour to gain a sense of the eternal. Such religion is man's deed, a knightly defiance of all circumstance in a rather pathetic attempt to lift oneself by the bootstraps to a larger world. (Pp. 66 ff.)

Does the knight of faith succeed in grasping the eternal whereas the knight of resignation fails? Yes, but this is not the difference of immediate importance. Instead, the man of faith *regains all that the knight of resignation has sacrificed*. This is enormously important in view of the charge of otherworldliness made against S.K. He says that the man of faith is given back by God all the earthly treasures he was willing to sacrifice—although perhaps in a transformed fashion. 'By faith Abraham did not renounce his claim upon Isaac, but by faith he got Isaac.' (P. 70) The rich young man who should have given away everything would be told by the knight of faith, 'By virtue of the absurd thou shalt get every penny back again. Can'st thou believe that?' For the Christian to regain the creation in which God has placed him should be a source of joy, for if he does not really love it then his 'resignation' is of no consequence. (P. 70) Like Epictetus, the Stoic, who counselled suicide as an open door to enter if the house becomes too 'filled with smoke', the man of resignation develops an 'aloof and superior' attitude towards the world, and a note of sadness which betrays his 'heterogeneity with the finite'. In contrast the man of faith loves the world. 'With infinite resignation he has drained the cup of life's profound sadness, he knows the bliss of the infinite, he senses the pain of renouncing everything, the dearest things he

THE AESTHETIC LITERATURE

possesses in the world, and yet finiteness tastes to him just as good as to one who never knew anything higher...' (P. 55 f.) Even though faith may seem like a simple mood of trust, it is here shown to be actually complex, having resignation as a preliminary, and gaining a joyous life in the world only by virtue of 'the absurd' which is God's achieving the 'impossible'. Thus by resignation one first makes a 'movement of infinity', dying to the world, but faith is a 'double movement of infinity' in that it also regains the finite world by means of the infinite. What *Fear and Trembling* neglects to add is that there are in fact no such steadfast knights as are here portrayed but only persons who falteringly strive to fulfil these ideals.

There is an issue of theoretical difficulty and perhaps even of confusion relative to the nature of faith as here treated. Kierkegaard identified the ethical as the *universal*, and accordingly regarded the religious stage as individualistic, a *particular* exception to the universal. Abraham turns from duty to faith, not because of sin and grace but because of the strange particular requirement which God imposed upon him. Abraham is not portrayed, according to the usual categories, as a sinner who turns from divine law to divine forgiveness. Faith is specifically viewed as his unique relationship to God. 'Faith is precisely this paradox, that the individual as the particular is higher than the universal...for the fact that the individual as the particular stands in an absolute relation to the absolute [God].' (P. 82)

Although S.K. structures his concept of religion as *exceptionality* rather formally, thinking of it as a simple submission to the will of God which *might* require something in conflict to the universal moral rule, it is clear that this was not a mere hypothetical possibility for him, but an anguished awareness of such of life's concrete dilemmas as the breaking of an engagement. He might have said, indeed should have argued, that universal principles frequently do not offer complete answers for the problems of life's critical moments, as in the issue of pacifism, or in that of which person is to be saved when some must die. Clearly, the religious life takes on an aspect of precarious artistry and fearful responsibility, as one haltingly tries to be responsible to God in an incompletely charted way of life. In this regard every religious man is an individual, in some respects exceptional, indeed exceptional even in the way he observes the universal moral law. Yet there may also be exceptions to such exceptionality of universality as is illustrated by the legend of the merman who rises out of the sea to seduce Agnes.

This story presented in 'Problem III', may have had a kind of autobiographical significance for Kierkegaard, and it is important in pointing to the role which the ethical norm assumes for such an 'exception' as S.K. After seducing Agnes, the merman wishes, because of her faith in him, to abandon evil and enter into moral marriage, only to discover that ethical obedience to the universal and normal life of holy marriage must for such a sinner be replaced by a life of sorrowful repentance. For him to be earnest requires that in penitence he go beyond morality into the salvation which can be wrought only by the miracle of God's mercy. (Pp. 144 ff.)

Two critical points need to be made with reference to Abraham as an exemplar of faith. First, Abraham does reveal the supra-moral quality of religion. The essential import of religion is the righteousness of God and its ethical requirements, but religion is the ground of morality, not morality the ground of religion. Accordingly, it is the divine imperative which is crucial rather than its customary and proper expression. The fact that there can be—even in an exceptional instance—a suspension of the ethical shows the sovereignty of God to be absolute. Abraham's deed is not moral but is rather religious, in contrast to Jephthah's sacrifice of his daughter, done to fulfil a dutiful vow. (P. 86) Apparently there is no moral ground for Abraham's deed and no moral principle to be derived from it. Here is a divine imperative which violates at least the customary ethical principles and a faith which rests on no clear ground of rationality or plausibility. In this sense, faith is not only a dying to the world in order to grasp the eternal but is also a venturing out of the universality of the ethical into the singularity of the irregular and the insecurity of the exception. Faith is a personal God-relationship.

Second, Abraham does not reveal the distinctive nature of *Christian* faith, even though he is the hero of faith. Christian faith presupposes sin. In Christianity the opposite of sin is not virtue but faith. This faith is not simply awed trust on the part of a righteous Abraham. It is man's response to a divine corrective and

THE AESTHETIC LITERATURE

so is the means of recovery of an authentic relation to God. Thus it is necessary to recognize a pre-Christian quality in Abraham and his relation to God. Abraham introduces the authentic religion of faith, but faith in the mysterious God rather than the mysteriously redemptive God. In the companion volume, *Repetition*, S.K. makes it more clearly evident that Christian faith is a rebirth of purity under divine forgiveness.

Even though it was presumably not immediately evident to S.K. himself, his treatment of Christian faith as an 'exception' involved the assumption that the exception should in some sense be the normal rule. Everyone should be an exception in that God chooses to approach all men in the strange mercifulness of Christ rather than simply in the legal propriety of universal obedience to divine will. Moreover, every believer is an exception in that God calls upon him to sacrifice the normal. For example, one is enjoined by Christ to sacrifice his father, son, or wife (Luke 14:26). Every believer must be in a state of fear and trembling over what his God-relationship may require.

It is important in this connection to recognize the strange duality in religion's effect on earthly relations. The one effect is precisely the element of exceptionality and sacrifice. Nothing is to be given idolatrous equality with God. Discipleship does indeed even require one to 'hate' father and mother, and an Abraham must be ready to slay his son at God's command. Yet Abraham continues to love Isaac while doing the hateful thing, else slaying him would not be sacrifice. An analogy is offered. A husband requires his wife to leave father and mother, but does not require her to reject them. Instead, her love for them is a guarantee of her love for him. This brings us to the second effect of religion on earthly values. God's requirement of absolute love does not result in simple otherworldliness, nor in lukewarmness to relative values. Even while it forbids making them into idols, it makes them more precious and imperative. Love for neighbour is the more sacred by virtue of union with God. (P. 110 f.)

One enormously important passage regarding the exceptional individual is the treatment of Shakespeare's Richard III, a person who is portrayed by Shakespeare as physically deformed, cheated by nature, so misshapen that the dogs barked when he stopped near them. S.K. comments on the cruel habit of mind for society to think of witches as hunchbacked and to think of cripples as morally depraved. With obvious reference to his own physical deformity he insists that the one thing which a noble and proud spirit cannot endure is pity, and that this was the origin of the demoniacal character of Richard III. In this passage not only is light shed on S.K.'s personal anguish, and on the concept of the demoniacal, but also the clear fact that for him 'the universal', as in marriage, is the glorious and good state of which he is deprived, and that the universal (as marriage) is not in any sense a lower morality to be renounced by the higher religious consciousness. The suffering 'exception' may be able by God's grace to find his misfortune also a medium of blessing, but it is never to be exalted over the universal. This issue is critically important, the more so because it seems to have become clouded in S.K.'s later years. (P. 163)

Even with some possibilities of divergent interpretation, religion here takes on the aspect of radical individuality. Because faith does not rest on evidence or upon reasons but is prepared for by despair and is in fact a response to divine intervention, the 'knight of faith' cannot persuade or effectively communicate with anyone else relative to faith. He can, however, bear witness to the power of God which is available to every individual. If religion appears in this light as a dramatic intervention in existence and 'a teleological suspension of the ethical', it is so because men are needy and Christ, by his own affirmation, came to be a saviour. Usually the condition of need appears to be the outcome of sin but a Richard III, an Abraham, or a Kierkegaard reveals that need can also take other forms. Salvation is therefore an all-encompassing grace and faith is a comprehensive person-to-Person encounter.

THE AESTHETIC LITERATURE

8. THREE EDIFYING DISCOURSES

Three Edifying Discourses. By S. Kierkegaard. October 16, 1843. Published to 'accompany *Repetition* and *Fear and Trembling*. Translated by David F. and Lillian Marvin Swenson in *Edifying Discourses*, Minneapolis: Augsburg Publishing House, 1943 (volumes reduced from four to two in 1962 ed.). The first discourse also appears in *Edifying Discourses, A Selection*, ed. by Paul L. Holmer. New York: Harper & Brothers, 1958, Harper TB 32. (Page references are to Vol. I of 1943 edition.)

This little book offers more specifically Christian answers to the problems posed in *Repetition* and *Fear and Trembling*. When a frail soul can find no healing for its wounds, what then? When a shattered spirit seeks inward strength but finds brokenness repeated rather than strength recovered, what then? The answers are that love for God is one's proper resort and that, in turn, divine love can triumph over human tragedy and sin and restore a soul to spiritual strength.

The first two discourses are both entitled 'Love Shall Cover a Multitude of Sins'. It is suggested that love *uncovers* or reveals the sins of those who think they are righteous, but covers the sins of those who repent. S.K. gave great emphasis to repentance, in part a reflection of his own consciousness of sin. In his journals he gave this dramatic picture of the role of penitence: 'And this is indeed the way Christianity has always gone through the world, between two thieves (for such are we all), of which only one is penitent and said that he suffered deserved punishment.'[77] To him Jesus said, 'This day shalt thou be with me in paradise'. For such a penitent, love does not even weep over the multitude of sins; if it did this, then it would have seen the sins, but it 'covers their multitude'.

The first discourse is addressed to 'the perfect', i.e. to those who seek to express Christian spirit when confronted by evil in the world about them. Their love is to cover the neighbour's sins. (P. 66) Here the Christian ethic is strikingly portrayed. Confucius and the Pharisees would have one love the righteous but treat the unrighteous with justice, certainly not with love. The Christian is to love the sinner and thereby overcome his sin.

The second discourse develops a similar theme. However, in contrast to the first, it is addressed to 'the imperfect', who, face to face with God, discover a multitude of sins in their own lives. (P. 83) The discourse comforts the guilty person with the assurance that his sins also are covered by the love of God. This is illustrated in the story of the woman who was a sinner, and who wept at Jesus' feet. The self-righteous Pharisees easily discovered the multitude of her sins, but Christ's love covered the sins and discovered in her that which the world did not discern, viz. her depth of love, and, since love had not triumphed in her, 'the Saviour's love came to help'.

'Strengthened in the Inner Man', the third discourse, expresses the religious consolation which *Repetition* could not find; the despairing soul is restored and strengthened if he can thank God for his sufferings. The outward life is deceptive; prosperity seems to mark one as fortunate but properly it is a cause for anxious concern ('Can a rich man be saved?'). God is a Spirit and it is the inner spiritual witness which must be heeded. Good fortune *may possibly* manifest the grace of God but, on the contrary, it might even express the 'wrath of heaven'. To transform suffering into a witness for the truth and to transform disgrace into holy honour is like causing the lame to walk. It is to follow in the example of St Paul who, having nothing to boast of, boasted of his tribulations. (P. 97) Thus it is possible to be strengthened in the *inner* man even when one's striving seems in vain and when one's world seems to be falling in ruin. Spiritual victory is not to be had in securing the things for which one longs, and God can transform loss of that which is desired into gain.

This discourse is very important in correcting a common misunderstanding about Kierkegaard, viz. that he wanted to replace earthly existence by heaven, and time by eternity. Here it is plainly stated that when one becomes troubled about his earthly existence he can turn to God who restores life in the world to healthy balance by giving it a legitimate *second* place. The spiritual man can take delight in prosperity, knowing that greater glory lies ahead. If misfortune befalls him this too he can accept in peace because he is still conscious of the eternal. (Pp. 106, 112) However, the strength from the eternal can be received only spiritually. 'God is a Spirit and therefore can give only spiritual testimony, that is, in the inner man, every external testimony from God, if one could imagine such a thing, is only a deception.' (P. 103)

9. JOHANNES CLIMACUS, OR DE OMNIBUS DUBITANDUM EST.

Although never completed, and therefore appearing in the *Papers* rather than the *Works*, an English translation has been published: *Johannes Climacus, or De Omnibus Dubitandum Est*. Translated with an assessment by T. H. Croxall. Stanford: Stanford University Press, 1958. Includes a sermon.

There is an interesting story in back of the title. 'Johannes Climacus' was a name borrowed by Kierkegaard. This legendary John, a Greek monk, was called the 'climber' (Climacus) because of his book *The Ladder to Heaven*. So too, S.K. makes no pretence of having spiritually arrived but he is striving to reach the goal. S.K. is Johannes at the foot of the ladder, asking how to begin the ascent. This treatise explores doubt which is a barrier to the ladder. (P. 19) Although the book is incomplete and difficult to read, partly because of its use of Hegelian jargon, and only easily interpreted in the context of other completed writings, it is a significant work and throws some light on the development of Kierkegaard's thought.

Regarding the issues and the persons referred to in this treatise a word of caution is needed. To the student of philosophy it will be obvious that there is explicit and specific reference to the provisional doubt of Descartes. However, *Johannes Climacus* is primarily an attack on S.K.'s tutor, H. L. Martensen, who agreed with Descartes that philosophy begins with doubt. (P. 20 f.) For three years (1837-39) Martensen had lectured on the history of modern philosophy and had greatly stressed this Cartesian principle. Even prior to *Johannes Climacus*, in a projected but never completed satirical comedy entitled 'The Conflict Between the Old and the New Soap Cellar', Kierkegaard attacked this conversion of doubt into a kind of academic springboard.[78] Similarly, in *Fear and Trembling* (p. 170), he portrayed Faust as a true and passionate doubter, unlike 'these scientific doubters who doubt one hour every term-time (semester) in the professorial chair, but at other times are able to do everything else'.

For some time Kierkegaard had been profoundly concerned with the varied forms of 'negative' spirit, including the *ironical* form of doubt in Socrates, *provisional* doubt in Descartes, and genuine *personal* doubt such as he himself had experienced. However, S.K. was perhaps even more concerned with two other forms of negativity, viz. sensuality and despair. Very early he had planned an elaborate trilogy which was to explore three legends as illustrative of the three forms of negativity: Faust, Don Juan, and Ahsverus (the Wandering Jew) as symbolic of doubt, sensuality and despair.* The plan was never carried out but the essential concepts and their symbolic representatives do occupy large roles in S.K.'s writing.

In *Johannes Climacus*, which explores the doubt-form of spiritual negativity there is outlined a three-fold epistemology and ontology: (1) *Actuality* (reality), thought of as a realm of *immediacy*, i.e. the perceived world (or given), which is not reflected upon and therefore cannot be doubted, just as also it cannot be 'true', since affirmation of truth is possible only where there is a possibility of doubt. (2) *Ideality* ('speech'), regarded as a set of categorial structures which are imposed on actuality when one attempts to express or interpret the actual. Ideality is plainly other than and an addition to actuality, actuality always being presupposed by ideality. To be humanly conscious requires one to go beyond dumb immediacy into ideality. (3) *Consciousness*, which is a knowing relating of reality and ideality, and is not possible without the presence of both. There is no truth (or doubt) in either the immediacy of actuality or in the forms of ideality, but only in the relations and collisions of the two in consciousness; only in consciousness are truth and doubt possible. (Chapter I)

It is noteworthy that the role of doubt in Descartes is taken

---

* Cf. W. Lowrie, *op. cit.*, Vol. I, p. 77. The projected (1838) treatment of Faust opposed romanticism's notion of a repentant Faust by insisting that worldliness follows inevitably after doubt to despair. When Martensen published an identical interpretation of Faust—originating in a common intellectual background—S.K. abandoned his project with bitter disappointment. (*Irony*, pp. 26, 359.)

chiefly by *despair* in Kierkegaard. Doubt is viewed by him as merely an intellectual function and, as an inability to draw a conclusion, it is the consequence of limitations of evidence or of inference. Doubt is the opposite of rational conviction. Despair, however, is far more important because it is a negativity participated in by the whole person, although especially by the will. Its opposite is faith. 'Doubt is a despair of thought, despair is a doubt of the personality.'[79] The Greek sceptics make it evident that doubt is not merely intellectual but is an act of will, i.e. a refusal to give assent, for which reason doubt cannot be overcome by increase of knowledge but only by a readiness of will.[80]

Kierkegaard was unwilling to permit even doubt to be a coldly impersonal attitude, interpreting it rather as spiritual negativity. In a state of doubt a person feels restrained and bound, as if losing something of freedom by a kind of external necessity. To gain truth the spirit must be free, for which reason S.K. could never agree with Descartes in thinking of doubt (necessity) as a preliminary step on the way to spiritual truth. Moreover, whereas Hegel sought to resolve doubt by disinterested and systematic knowledge, Kierkegaard feels that wherever there is (existential) doubt there is *interest* or concern and mere objective information cannot resolve such anxious doubt. One cannot 'annul doubt by changing interest into apathy'. Knowledge is not the goal for a (faithless) doubter, nor dare faith be viewed as incomplete knowledge because faith involves a passionate concern which is lacking in objective knowledge. Since faith concerns one's eternal salvation it evokes passionate interest and, correspondingly, doubt concerning salvation involves suffering which is not present in mere uncertainty of a scientific nature. Further, whereas factual uncertainty can give way to knowledge by assimilating its object, doubt can never give way to faith by possessing its object. God retains a remoteness in faith, as also in doubt, again demonstrating a dialectic of passion.[81]

In only one of the three ontological modes (actuality, ideality, and consciousness) is true repetition—a concept of great significance for S.K.—possible, and together with it the related attitudes of faith and doubt. There is no repetition whatsoever in mere *actuality* for the reason that whatever (e.g. a granite boulder) is actual in a given moment is simply itself and is not a re-occurrence of a previous thing. That there is no repetition does not mean that all things are unlike one another. Rather, even if two things in the world were absolutely alike, yet each would have its being in itself. Each would be a facsimile of the other but not a repetition. In *ideality* likewise there is no repetition because an idea or truth is a changeless, immutable whatness or essence. However, when ideality and reality collide in *consciousness* then repetition may occur. 'When...I see something "in the moment", ideality intervenes and explains that it is a repetition.' (P. 154) Repetition or recollection occurs only in consciousness and relates to the structuring of reality by means of ideality.

Many challenging thoughts emerge in *Johannes Climacus*, including an existential view of both the doubt and the doubter. Descartes tried to get unquestionable truth out of doubt (*dubito ergo sum*), but Kierkegaard complains that the 'I' of 'I am' is already present in 'I think', so that it is presupposed rather than established by means of proof. Further, he feels that the 'cogito ergo sum' is defective in that its 'I' is an abstraction, not a concrete existing person. In the *Concluding Unscientific Postscript* S.K. develops his protest against Descartes more colourfully: 'If I *am* thinking, what wonder that I *am*?' The first proposition says more than the second and includes the second so that the 'conclusion' is actually not so much an inference as a reiteration.[82] S.K. argues that it is absurd to treat Descartes' 'thinking thing' as a being and, moreover, the first being to be doubted. The *thinking* is an act of an existing person who is related to other persons and to his world more importantly in ethical ways, if also fundamentally in cognitive ways. It is this understanding of thought, will and mood as qualities of man as he finds himself in the world (and not as subjective qualities) which has found emphatic reiteration in subsequent existential philosophy. In his *Journals* (461), Kierkegaard sums up his judgment: 'The method which begins by doubting in order to philosophize is just as suited to its purpose as making a soldier lie down in a heap in order to teach him to stand up straight.'

In *Johannes Climacus* Hegel is included in the attack, along with Descartes, for he likewise tried to start in presuppositionless fashion with bare 'being' which is subquently enriched by 'nothing'. Elsewhere S.K. had whimsically imagined a dialogue between Socrates and Hegel: '*Socrates:* What presupposition do you begin with? *Hegel:* With none at all. *Socrates*: Splendid! Then I suppose you do not begin at all? *Hegel:* I not begin, who have written twenty-one volumes?' (P. 61)

Kierkegaard insists on the necessity of some presuppositions, for himself, particularly those of the solitary individual and God. It might almost appear that S.K.'s position is an exact contradiction of that of Descartes who declared *'cogito ergo sum'*. For S.K., the case is rather *'sum ergo cogito'*, I am, therefore I think. A man's existence is a presupposition of his thinking and certainly not to be deduced from it.[83] The existing individual is exactly the truth-minded, doubting anxious consciousness. He must be ignored neither by an objective Hegelian system nor by a mere human mass or majority. Yet neither is he a self-expressionist in the style of Sartre, nor a romanticist indulging in feeling, nor, still, a self-sufficient eudaemonist. Instead, he is a Christian who attains his own being and repetition only in humility before God.

In *Johannes Climacus* Kierkegaard leaves much unsaid. He insists that doubt cannot lead to truth and that there is an immediate apprehension of one's personal existing. Yet how the full truth can be grasped is here left unanswered. Elsewhere the answer which is offered is that the only way to prove the truth of Christ is to take up one's cross and follow him,[84] and that the only way to understand God is to love him, since God is love. Thus, 'to love and to know are essentially synonymous'.[85] However, when this takes place, love does not become other than love by serving as an instrument of knowing. Neither does love come to possess the aesthetic delight and immediacy of friendship or affection. Christian love remains mysterious and insecure as it issues from the risk of faith. Existential truth, never absent in spirit, is fulfilled only in confrontation with God.

The sermon which the editor appends is a helpful supplement to *Johannes Climacus*. It clarifies Kierkegaard's understanding of religion as it relates to truth and doubt. The sermon, not elsewhere translated, was preached by S.K. during his student days, on February 24, 1844, as part of his formal preparation for the ministry. (P. 40) The theme, '"The Wisdom of God in a mystery", versus "Worldly Wisdom"', charts the trend which subsequent thought was to take. Christianity is not a natural piety, nor is it a segment of ordinary knowledge or culture. The wisdom of God is so strange a gift to man that it is inescapably a stumbling block to the Jew and foolishness to the wise Greek. The wisdom of God is a mystery which no eye hath seen nor ear heard and which has not come up from within the heart of man. Wherever the wisdom of God in Christ is present it has come down from above and dwells in the heart by faith.

10. FOUR EDIFYING DISCOURSES

> *Four Edifying Discourses.* By. S. Kierkegaard, December 6, 1843. Translated by David F. and Lillian Marvin Swenson in *Edifying Discourses*. Minneapolis: Augsburg Publishing House, 1942, 1962 (volumes reduced from four to two in 1962 ed.). The first of these discourses also appears in *Edifying Discourses, A Selection*, ed. by Paul L. Holmer. New York: Harper & Brothers, 1958, Harper TB 32. (Page references are to Vol. II of the 1944 edition.)

These discourses like the previous ones continue to develop the themes of *Repetition* and *Fear and Trembling*. When one—as Kierkegaard himself—has lost what he most dearly loved can he still believe that God bestows good gifts? The first three discourses relate to hope for the disconsolate, i.e. the problem of *Fear and Trembling*.

'The Lord Gave, and the Lord Hath Taken Away' is a study of Job. To whom better than to Job could S.K. turn for consolation? But can Job be correct, that *the Lord* would take away? Was it not rather evil men who slew Job's servants and was it not a windstorm which destroyed his house and buried his children in the rubble? No, in a strange act of faith, Job could defy the evil men and the evil winds and say, 'It is not you, you can do nothing—it is the Lord who takes'. (P. 22) Confronted by mystery and tragedy in which the loving God seems incomprehensibly to take away the treasures, Job still stands firm. He is dumb, unable to understand, but still he cries out, 'Blessed be the name of the Lord'.

The next two discourses develop the identical theme, 'Every

Good and Every Perfect Gift is from Above'. Men discover that their well-intended gifts turn out to be anything but good and perfect gifts. A son may lose his life by means of a father's loving gift, perhaps a gun. Perfect gifts do come to men, but *only from above*, and no one can bestow any good thing which he has not first received from God. God alone is ultimately good and therefore He is the perfect gift. To have need of Him is not a mark of deficiency but is precisely, as for St Augustine, man's perfection. Since God is love, love likewise is a perfect gift. Love makes the giver as well as the receiver richer. The two are not separated by the gift because love bestows equality.

Was Kierkegaard unconcerned over moral and social reform? This accusation has been made. It is true that he felt that not only does every good gift come from above, but also that whatever comes from above is a good gift, and that men should be thankful even for their tribulations. However, this was not intended to be an ethic of quietism or resignation. Indeed, it is not an ethic at all, for at this point S.K. was not asking how to bring about social justice but godliness. S.K. would have men earnestly strive for the good but would counsel faith rather than despair if the outcome is not to their satisfaction. He persuaded the believer to trust in the mysterious power of God; good and perfect gifts *do come*, and they come from above. It is notable that Kierkegaard does not postpone God's good gifts to a post-temporal heavenly compensation but instead reinterprets earth's experiences so as to find providence having its way here in joy and sorrow alike.

The last discourse is entitled 'To Acquire One's Soul in Patience', and it has an important relation to the problems of both *Repetition* and *Sickness Unto Death*. The discourse offers a clear statement of man's existential situation. The soul is a relation between 'the temporal and the eternal'. (P. 76) If the soul tries to escape the tension of its duality by turning either to mere worldly finitude or mere supra-earthly infinitude it is guilty of despair and violates its very nature.[86] How then can a man become master of his own life?

The strange but Biblical answer is that a man does not possess a unified self but must acquire it, and at that with anguished patience. The discourse points out however, that if a man *owns* his soul he should not need to acquire it, and that if he does *not* own it then he is not in a position to acquire it. The difficulty is that man is himself only in an ironical and precarious fashion. It is God who properly owns the soul—although God freely offers it to man—and it is the world which gains false title to it. Therefore, man must acquire his soul *from* the world, *of* God, and *through* himself. There is a special danger of a person confusing mere knowledge as to what the soul is, with genuinely possessing it. In knowing about the soul a man may be deceived into supposing that he has already acquired it, whereas to be truly oneself and to be master of one's destiny is accomplished only in patient action in the midst of terrifying expectations and worldly deceits.

It is an oddity of fate that because of such views as are presented in these discourses Kierkegaard should not only be accused of losing ethical concern in quietism but also should be accused, by other persons, of being a moralist rather than genuinely religious. Theodor Haecker makes the latter charge, on the ground that S.K. remained for ever concerned with *acquiring* the soul and of *becoming* a Christian.[87] However, 'acquiring' one's soul was, for Kierkegaard, not an ethical task but a matter of faith and love in which one responds to grace. Becoming a Christian is not a moral endeavour. In this becomingness one endures the tension between sin and faith in a state of forgiveness, never leaving spiritual insecurity behind.

11. TWO EDIFYING DISCOURSES

Two Edifying Discourses. By. S. Kierkegaard. March 5, 1844. Translated by David F. and Lillian Marvin Swenson in *Edifying Discourses*, Minneapolis: Augsburg Publishing House, 1945, 1962 (volumes reduced from four to two in 1962 ed.). (Page references are to Vol. III of 1945 edition.)

'Successful Personality.' 'How to be a Real Person.' If these were the titles of these meditations they might attract more of the notice which they deserve, and the titles would not be far amiss. Their pregnant message may easily escape one's attention. The thoughts explore such crises of life as can lead to despair or suicide, but which also, as indicated in the previous discourse, could help one to 'acquire his soul' and become an authentic person. Although these meditations are intensely religious, they aim to contact a man at the relatively elementary level of religiosity beyond which most people scarcely seem to progress. The themes are therefore man-centred rather than Christo-centric.

The first discourse, 'To Preserve One's Soul in Patience', is a reminder of life's perils, such perils as men tend to hide from rather than to face with courage. 'What is this existence where the only certainty is the one we never get to know with certainty, and this is death! What is hope? An importunate tormentor we cannot get rid of, a smooth deceiver which outlives even honor...' (P. 25) Yet, when a man has lost everything dear to him has he indeed lost all? No, there is something eternal which may still be preserved and which he must yet strive to possess—which (as Epictetus emphasized) no one can take from him—his own soul. For the Christian there is a special ground for confidence in the assurance that with every temptation God has also provided a way of escape. Clearly then one cannot simply *be* a self but must *preserve* his selfhood, and for doing this patience is the key. The solutions and crucial decisions of proper existence 'must be arrived at slowly, little by little... It is patience alone that prevails...' (P. 30) Patience is the correlary to divine providence.

The second discourse, 'Patient in Expectation', takes as a model the prophetess Anna, who served God night and day. Was she an aged saint? So she is described in the Biblical narrative. However, she is better understood as a young widow who had lost all that life seemed to offer and turned her loss into blessing, turning her impoverishment and sorrow into an expectation 'fruitful for the eternal'.

Anna's long years, 'all the expectation of the ages concealed in her devout form', were consummated in the welcome she gave to the infant Jesus, a saviour expected by all who looked for the redemption of Jerusalem. Men who complain about their personal misfortunes or who are bruised in their struggles with the world ought to learn from this patient woman. 'If a man... knew how to set the seal of patience on what he understood, oh, then would his life... still be spent in joyful surprise.... For there is only One who is truly the everlasting object of wonder, and that is God; and only one who is able to halt the wonder, and that is man...' (P. 63)

12. THREE EDIFYING DISCOURSES

Three Edifying Discourses. By S. Kierkegaard. June 8, 1844. Translated by David F. and Lillian Marvin Swenson in *Edifying Discourses*, Minneapolis: Augsburg Publishing House, 1943, 1962 (volumes reduced from four to two in 1962 ed.). The second discourse also appears in *Edifying Discourses, A Selection*, ed. by Paul L. Holmer. New York: Harper & Brothers, Harper TB 32. (Page references are to Vol. III of 1943 edition.)

This volume seems somewhat more detached from Kierkegaard's personal problems than is the case with the previous discourses. Yet it develops similar themes, and like them manifests on the one hand a sombre wisdom and on the other the power of hope.

The first discourse echoes a nearly universal distress and might appropriately have been entitled, 'How Maturity and Wisdom Spoil Life'. It notes that youth thinks naturally of the Creator, even though it knows very little about the creation. The title is accordingly an admonition: 'Remember Now Thy Creator in the Days of Thy Youth.' There is a spiritual simplicity which is common to youth, says S.K. 'When one grows older, then everything becomes so wretched. God in heaven must sit and wait for the fates to decide whether He exists, and finally He comes into being by means of some proofs...' (P. 82 f.) Here is a protest, to become formidable in later works, against the pretensions of such philosophers as Descartes who offered to *prove* the reality of God. S.K.'s insistence, like that in more recent times of the British historian Butterfield, is that religion must be available to the simple-hearted and untutored, and that a peasant or a child is undoubtedly less patronizing towards God and more genuinely religious than are the intellectuals.[88] Maturity's sophistication ought not destroy the unaffected religion of youth. 'Woe to him who separates manhood from its youth.' (P. 92) An interesting feature of the discourse is the existential treatment of truth which appears in it. Although it is evident that S.K. does not question objective truth, which is valid regardless of the individual's concern, he insists that there is also another kind of truth which concerns the individual as a person, and brings blessing if appropriated in action. (P. 71) Of such a nature is the awareness of God's love. True awareness of this love is impossible except through one's own loving responsiveness.

Does religious faith make an actual difference in life? This question is answered in the second discourse, 'The Expectation of an Eternal Happiness'. This seemingly commonplace theme was as troublesome to the nineteenth century as it is to the twentieth century, and Kierkegaard was well aware of the problem. Secularists want to hear nothing of eternity, positivists question its meaning, and 'religious' people often want to think of religion as an ingredient in culture. As S.K. pungently comments, the eternal is like an infirm pensioner who lives by the wretched crumbs which fall from the tables of the rich. (P. 97) This little treatise is central to Kierkegaard's religious thought. It states a theme which is at the heart of the great *Postscript*, of the provocative *Sickness Unto Death*, and indeed of the entire later authorship. To be human is to be involved in time and eternity, and to be Christian is to see all of earth's joys and sorrows against the background of an eternal happiness, which, however, remains objectively uncertain in that no *temporal* assurance can be given for it. (P. 113)

The title of this second discourse indicates that for Kierkegaard Christianity is an *expectation*, not a present possession. He militantly opposes the notion that finite man can actually exist in, or unqualifiedly enjoy the eternal. To exist as a Christian is to be *concerned* about the eternal, to come into relationship with God but only in a state of expectancy. The existential goal is an expectation of eternal blessedness. God remains transcendent, even though he breaks into time so as to make a re-directing of man's life possible. The eternal is not for Kierkegaard, as it seems to be for some existentialists, a mere function within time, yet neither is time swallowed up in eternity, as for the mystics. Instead, even at his spiritual best, man remains caught in the enormous strain or tension between time and eternity.

Significant light on the issue of the relation between existence and the eternal is found in the somewhat later *Christian Discourses*. There it is indicated that eternity is *not* an infinity of time, precisely because an infinite succession of instants could never gain wholeness, could never escape from the 'once', would for ever be marred by succession and stages.[89] Joy in eternal blessedness signifies that one is *fully present* with God, without past and future. 'Joy is the present tense with the whole emphasis upon the *present.*'[90] Thus in eternity there is no 'existence' because there is no temporal succession and no straining for repetition. Nevertheless, despite its nature, the eternal, in another form, is not absent from earthly existence; to exist is to grasp the eternal in time.

'The Expectation of an Eternal Happiness' proposes that such expectation performs the 'impossible' in that it 'works in heaven and on earth'. Faith gives mankind treasure in heaven so that a person will become reconciled to God and to himself, gaining at last a peace which surpasses human understanding. Yet the religious expectation is not only an anticipation of heaven. It helps one to understand his mysterious temporal existence, so that his present heavy burdens are seen to be only 'light afflictions, which are but for a moment'. It reconciles a man to his neighbour, friend, or enemy in regard to whatever is essential. It dissipates greed and breaks down barriers. On earth we struggle competitively against one another in pettiness of spirit, but the quest for the eternal does not bring one into conflict with anyone. Death levels all men in poverty and eternal life elevates all to the equality of purity and joy.

The last discourse moves in the direction of Christ-centred thinking, rather than reflecting chiefly on human experience. The theme is 'He Must Increase, but I Must Decrease'. These are the worlds of John the Baptist near the close of his ministry. It is natural that everyone should prefer to see the sunrise rather than the sunset. Even so John! His Biblical role must not deceive a later generation into overlooking the pathos of his life. His sun was setting. Yet his sombre words are a re-direction of focus for the human spirit. They are the herald's final cry of joy when he 'hears the bridegroom's voice'.

THE AESTHETIC LITERATURE

13. PHILOSOPHICAL FRAGMENTS

Philosophical Fragments Or A Fragment of Philosophy. By Johannes Climacus. Published by S. Kierkegaard. June 13, 1844. Translated by David E. Swenson. Published for the American Scandinavian Foundation. Princeton: Princeton University Press, 1941. Revised, with an introduction and commentary by Niels Thulstrup, translated by Howard Hong. Princeton University Press, 1962. (Page references are to the revised edition.)

This little book, the title more literally translated 'Scraps', is anything but careless fragments. It is artistically conceived and treats with relative simplicity and at times with rare beauty the most complex philosophical issues, especially those pertaining to man's relation to ultimate truth. The poetic quality of style may even pose a problem. The book is (at times) so sparkling with Kierkegaardian style ('like a classical drama in five acts') and so expressive of the author's ideas that there is a danger that the reader may overlook the depth of philosophical orientation. The book is steeped in Plato and all the ancient philosophers, and it bristles with issues which plagued Kant, Spinoza, Leibnitz and all the modern philosophers. This is a great and creative treatise, containing, almost incongruously, pages of lyrical beauty, intellectual profundity and spiritual reflection. It did not, however, immediately upon publication attract attention, but entered the world 'without fuss or fury, without shedding of ink or blood' on the part of reviewers, those 'tailors of the literary world'.[91]

The *Fragments* is strangely objective. It refuses to speak of Christ, wilfully referring to him as 'the God'. Since the book presents Christianity as a system, S.K. thinks of it as a kind of falsification, and therefore presents it here as a problem of thought rather than a doctrine. The reason is that he wanted to unravel the theoretical confusion of his age which, partly under the aegis of Hegel, saw no particular difference between the content of Christianity and of speculative idealism. On this score the *Fragments* is devastatingly effective. The later *Postscript*, which seems somewhat like it, presents a very different issue, the existential matter of how to become a Christian, whereas the *Fragments* undertakes a theoretical definition of Christianity as contrasted with idealism. Yet the contrast must not be too severely emphasized, for in the *Postscript* (pp. 18, 340) S.K. makes it clear that the *Fragments* also, though in a veiled way, was concerned with man's *personal* relation to Christianity. While Hegelianism is under attack in the *Fragments*, the issues are broader than that. S.K. wants to deal with a man-centred philosophy at its very best (an ideal humanism), and show its limitations, in contrast with Christianity.

Although this book is not avowedly Christian in point of view (appearing under the pseudonym of Climacus and listing S.K. only as 'responsible for publication'), the central theme is the astonishing news of Christianity. Socrates, 'the connoisseur in self-knowledge' whom Kierkegaard came to admire so greatly, appears here not so much in historical accuracy, but rather as a representative of the best of human insight and teaching; yet his attempts to understand man admittedly end in perplexity. The Christian message of the eternal God entering time, of the transcendent becoming a part of world history, makes a startling contrast to human systems of thought, for left to himself sinful man at best finds God a perplexing Unknown. If communication is to occur between 'the God' and man, it is God then who must take the initiative. A problem remains however. How is communication (and love) possible between the transcendent God and man? Appropriately, Kierkegaard illustrates the Christian perspective, which forms the backdrop for his reflections, with a charming parable.

A king falls in love with a humble maiden. 'Then let the harp be tuned, let the songs of the poets begin to sound, and let all be festive while love celebrates its triumph. For love is exultant when it unites equals, but it is triumphant when it makes that which was unequal equal in love.' (P. 33) However, there arises a kingly doubt in the king's heart. Would his queen be happy if she recalled that she was but a humble maiden? Even though she might be content to be as nothing, the king, wanting to honour her as an equal, would be unhappy. More likely still, the humble girl, simply because she knew nothing of kingliness, would not even understand that there existed a problem of how unequals might become equal.

THE AESTHETIC LITERATURE

Might the king shower riches upon her so that in the wonders of the palace she would never recall herself or her origin? This would be a tragic deception, for 'no one is so terribly deceived as he who does not himself suspect it'. (P. 36) Or might the king go to live in her humble cottage and prevent her grief by bringing such glory to the scene as to cause her to forget herself and think only of him? This too would be deception, and her 'happiness' would be as vain as that of a lily which might think that God loved it because of its fine raiment.

If the union cannot be brought about by elevating the humble one, it can only come by a descent of the king, who comes as a servant, in a beggar's cloak. Moreover, the cloak does not half conceal and half reveal a king's cloak beneath it, for love seeks equality *in truth* and not in pretence. Thus stands God, whose servant-form 'is no mere outer garment'. God becomes *true* man. He suffers all things and even dies for his beloved, creating equality in lowliness and redeeming the lowly. To a voice which protests that this poem 'is the most wretched piece of plagiarism', the poet replies that he did not steal the poem. It is God's own poem, but so different from human poetry as not to be a poem but rather a *Miracle*.*

There is a startling feature in the parable which sets Kierkegaard apart from most believers. Most Christians veer towards docetism, even though doing so unwittingly; they think of the God-King *assuming the form* of a servant but not really being a servant. The King lays aside his royal cloak *for a moment*. S.K. insists that the servant's garb becomes God's proper garb. It is the very nature of divine love that it freely seeks equality with the

---

* If this is Christ why does S.K. refer hypothetically to 'the God?' Is it to gain the attention of reflective minds, attention which might be reluctantly given to a forthright Christian message? This is intimated in the pseudo confession that the story is not hypothetical but is 'God's own poem'. On the contrary, Zuidema has accused S.K. of what S.K. alleges against Hegel, viz. that he mythologizes the Christian incarnation, that he is concerned only with 'a pseudo-theogony', an Absolute Paradox, and *uses* the incarnation as a symbol of it. (Zuidema, *Kierkegaard*, p. 37.) Both S.K.'s frank reference to 'God's own poem, his maieutic method, and his profound sensitivity to Jesus as a person make Zuidema's provocative theory highly implausible. Arland Ussher takes the same stand as Zuidema: 'But of course Kierkegaard is not at all primarily concerned with what Jesus taught; what matters to him is the irrational "Paradox", the atom of the eternal Faery-World inserted into the temporal This-World...' (*Journey Through Dread*, p. 33.)

133

loved one. In incarnation God does not empty Himself or lay aside his glory. It is the very glory and love of God which cause him to literally become man and seek equality with the unequal and even defiant beloved. (Pp. 39, 40) The equality which Christ gains with sinful man is so genuine that sin is both revealed and overcome by it. Christ makes the sinner conscious of the eternal, first as that from which he has alienated himself, and second as that which he is enabled to recover through forgiveness.

The underlying problem of the *Fragments* is man's relation to spiritual truth. The 'project of thought' is opened with the Socratic dilemma (Meno): What one knows he cannot seek (since he knows it), and what he does not know he cannot seek (for he would not know what to look for). The real issue raised by the peculiar dilemma is a very simple one, viz. whether one can get religious truth out of ordinary rational experience (needing no revelation), or, as S.K. phrases it, whether one can get the eternal out of the merely historical. Socrates was humble enough—or honest enough—to admit that man cannot generate the eternal, or save himself. Either he cannot help himself or else he has the help of memory in saving truth, which it is his responsibility to recover by 'recollection'. For Socrates (or the Platonic Socrates), self-knowledge must contain knowledge of the eternal, or man is lost. The familiar conclusion is that man is indeed by birth acquainted with eternal truth, but has forgotten it, and needs a maieutic teacher to remind him of it. Human teaching, by this view, is only 'accidental... a vanishing moment', which contributes no content. Insight comes from a kind of spiritual introspection, and presupposes only rationality and an occasion which jolts one into self-awareness, a chance reminder of what is already known. On this account, truth is rational, and it is in the exercise of divine reason that men recover it.

Christianity's contrast is bold, but not simple. Its disclosure of God grows in dimension as the difficulty of revelation begins to emerge. Man's problem is not mere ignorance of the eternal but, more seriously, his taking offence at its revelation. Therefore, God must prepare the human heart to receive truth; repentance is the preparation for revelation, and in order to be Teacher, God must enter man's world as Saviour. Yet the latter step is the greatest difficulty of all, a very paradox or 'absurdity', first because eternal salvation ought not depend on so uncertain a thing as an historical event (a 'once upon a time'), and second because God should seemingly not qualify his eternity by entering into time.

Clearly, this presents a doctrine of sin, a fact commonly overlooked in the *Fragments* because it chiefly alludes to the problem of revelation by means of the Socratic concept of ignorance. Yet we find here a clear anticipation of *Dread*'s formulation of original sin. The most elemental fact about man, according to the *Fragments*, but one so subtle that it cannot be grasped unless God himself point it out, is original sin. From the perspective of the hopes and alarms of common existence, it means that, far from being able to evolve out of war and evil (as the nineteenth century fondly dreamed), the human race's most splendid attainments are invariably stained with blood and guilt. Man is always guilty before God.

Stated in the peculiarly intellectual language of Socrates, the problem of sin is however formulated in terms of truth and error. If the learner is not already in the truth, how can he recognize it when it comes, a problem the more difficult since eternal truth, when it is presented, bears no hallmark of worldly wisdom, neither rational certainty nor even attractive probability? In view of the difficulty, man's teacher must be 'the God' himself, presenting man not only with the content of eternal truth, but with the condition for recognizing it as well. The truth of revelation cannot be either an element in the wisdom of rational man, or a great intuitive insight of some prophetic soul, but must be the miraculous, self-authenticating self-disclosure of the Eternal in time.*

More simply, Socrates could only remind a pupil of what the

---

* Kierkegaard uses an example from Aristotle to illustrate man's spiritual bondage to error. The man who throws a stone guides it only until it leaves his hand; and similarly the virtuous or vicious man, who was once in control of his actions, may now lack such power. S.K. adds illustrations. The child who spends his money on a trinket cannot later trade in his worthless toy on a good book. 'And so there was also a time when man could have bought either freedom or bondage at the same price, this price being the soul's free choice and commitment in the choice. He chose bondage; but if he now comes forward with a proposal for an exchange, would not the God reply: Undoubtedly there was a time when you could have bought whichever you pleased, but bondage is a very strange sort of thing; when it is bought it has absolutely no value, although the price paid for it was originally the same.' (P. 20) Such bondage pupil already knew, but Christ, the Eternal in time, imparts new life and truth. Therefore in this Moment one is born of the Spirit, faces the future with hope rather than looking back in a Socratic quest for recollection, and, in the deepest sense owing nothing to any man, cherishes a truth which is divinely imparted. Kierkegaard's essential concern is with a Christian view of truth. He states the problem of truth with precision but near mystification on the title page: 'Is an historical point of departure possible for an eternal consciousness; how can such a point of departure have any other than a merely historical interest; is it possible to base an eternal happiness upon historical knowledge?' S.K. insists that it is incomprehensible that eternal salvation can be decided in time but that Christianity nevertheless affirms it, and that seventy years or five minutes are as adequate for this purpose as 170,000 years.[92]

The issue at stake is not the eternal *nature* of God but the *temporal* existence of God, i.e. the possibility of and significance of a Christ who occurs in some point-moment of space and time. The purpose is to show that Christianity cannot be summed up in any general philosophical propositions (as in idealism), and that the idealists (or humanists or naturalists) could assimilate Christianity into their systems only by destroying it. Far from being a plausible system of philosophical truths and humanistic insight—perhaps uniquely distilled into the life and sayings of Jesus—Christianity consists essentially of the 'absurd' claim that in the Instant the eternal God entered into time. The issue is pointed up in the contrast between Socrates (wisdom) and Christ (revelation). Kierkegaard gives the highest praise to Socrates as a human teacher, with deep insights and great humility—rare in the modern world of proud professors. The explanation is that for Socrates any teacher, however great, is accidental, a mere occasion for the learner's awareness of rational truth which already lies within himself. In contrast, Christian truth comes as a shocking proclamation from an historical man, outwardly quite human, but who claims to be God.*

---

to error is the effect of a decisive choice, the free forfeiture of freedom. It casts light on both the need for a divine conditioning of heart to receive the news of the eternal, and the—humanly speaking—absurd nature of the proclamation.

* The problem of the *Fragments* rests on the familiar distinction between necessary (analytical, rational) truths and mere matters of fact (synthetic,

THE AESTHETIC LITERATURE

The mild tone of the above argument is deceptive. Actually, the *Fragments*, like *Repetition*, makes a dramatic break with idealism which (as Fichte) assumed that man possesses an inward truth or an immediate awareness of the divine. S.K. argues that man is in *untruth* and that he requires a God-given repetition or new birth. It is this rejection of idealism's basic assumption which causes the *Fragments* to wage war on Socrates. Divine truth cannot be recollected; it must be given afresh by God who becomes like man in order to bridge the chasm between God and man. Such revelation offends man because it reveals his sin and also the humiliation he imposes on God.

Kierkegaard is no mere anti-Hegelian voice crying in a nineteenth-century philosophical wilderness, for his protest is against a whole stream of thought. Not only Hegel, but Kant, Fichte, and many others tended to view factual particulars as unimportant in comparison with eternal truths, and at the most as helpful examples of the eternal. By Hegel, Fichte and Kant, Christian revelation, because it was an *historical* event, was viewed as of lesser importance even if true. In one sense S.K. is closer to Hegel than to Kant and Fichte, because Hegel—unlike Kant and Fichte—thought of even the historical truths of religion as necessary and eternal (and thereby not trivial), even though imperfect expressions of a truth which in its most perfect form is philosophical rather than religious. For Kierkegaard, revelation is imprinted by the historically particular, but it is not thereby deficient with reference to the eternal; moreover it is not necessary but free, even to the point of apparent absurdity.

For the disclosure of eternal truth what is required is not a wise man but a God. Such a teacher is here described not only as a Saviour and Redeemer, releasing the learner from his bondage to untruth; but also as the one who judges man in his responsibility to the disclosure, and, finally, as one who atones for the guilt of

empirical). The latter need not be true but happen to be correct. S.K. was profoundly impressed by G. E. Lessing's insistence that the *factual* reports about Christ lack the necessity of the analytical and therefore can never have certainty, and can be accepted only by a leap of faith. S.K. concludes that Christianity does claim to have eternal truths (not mere probabilities) but that these are far from having the self-evidency of Cartesian principles. Indeed, in a sense, they violate rationality. Christian truths, being neither factual probabilities nor self-evident rational certainties, suddenly appear in a new light which S.K. terms paradox.

the learner in his having first chosen untruth. At this point, a voice again objects, saying that this 'is the most ridiculous of all projects' because it offers as a supposedly new idea something which turns out to be nothing but familiar Christianity, so to speak charging admission 'for exhibiting a ram in the afternoon' which could have been seen gratis in the forenoon. Yet suppose no one bothered to look at the ram in the morning! Then the peculiar exhibition is necessary after all.

We may now ask about the nature of this strange God who, in order to show men what he is like, becomes like men; and who, in order to teach men about the eternal, translates the eternal into an event in time. What is the nature of this communication, and how is man to react to it?

Does Kierkegaard mean to affirm the objective reality of a transcendent God who works such wonders? M. Wyschogrod has argued that pure being (the eternal, the transcendent) 'does not exist' for Kierkegaard, on the ground that if it 'exists' it cannot be pure.[93] In any case this judgment must not be pressed to mean that the eternal is unreal in itself and is only a quality or possibility within human existence. God is real, transcendent, and eternal. Moreover, for men to genuinely exist is to accept their duty in relation to God's will. Man gains the eternal by standing before God in moral responsibility, making not this nor that choice, but choosing his self in his 'eternal validity'.[94] Man has no divine quality or element of transcendence native to himself, but he becomes himself by being related to the transcendent God. Human existence comes about by response to transcendent ultimate Being, and such existence is the object of revelation.

Thus while it is true that Kierkegaard could scarcely be more suspicious of man's attempts to chart the transcendent, he is no positivist. The transcendent is, for him, meaningful and real—but paradox. It is not simply the as-yet-unknown, in principle intelligible but to date hidden; and neither is it nothing. It is a limit to reason, an Unknown which magnetically draws reason on, but with which reason collides and with which it grapples in paradoxical passion. 'The Reason cannot advance beyond this point, and yet it cannot refrain in its paradoxicalness from arriving at this limit and occupying itself therewith. It will not serve to dismiss its relation to it simply by asserting that the Unknown does not exist, since this itself involves a relationship. But what then is the Unknown, since the designation of it as the God merely signifies for us that it is unknown? To say that it is the Unknown because it cannot be known, and even if it were capable of being known, it could not be expressed, does not satisfy the demands of passion, though it correctly interprets the Unknown as a limit; but a limit is precisely a torment for passion, though it also serves as an incitement.' (P. 55)

Kierkegaard seems to be saying that something in the nature of rational man impels him to grasp for the transcendent reality which, by his very nature, he cannot hope to know. To be human is in part precisely to be unwilling to live in the severe confines of the empirical; it is to have a passion for the transcendent. 'The supreme paradox of all thought is the attempt to discover something that thought cannot think.' (P. 46) It might be noted that the notion of an elusive Unknown, for ever tantalizing but eluding human reason, would not be popular with positivistic philosophers. Kierkegaard might well respond, however, that indeed no man avoids some encounter with the Unknown, and that the very zeal of the positivists to eliminate the metaphysical is a demonstration of their concern with the metaphysical, busily occupying themselves with the transcendent in an attempt to be rid of it. It would perhaps have been happier if S.K. had referred to this quest for the limit as an anomaly rather than a 'supreme paradox'. That which is anomalous is man's persistent attempt to outreach himself. On the other hand, the limit or transcendent has no evident self-contradiction or paradox in it. It is more plausible to claim—as S.K. does—that paradox emerges when the transcendent God humbles himself to become the God-man.

S.K.'s comments on reason's restless outreach towards the Unknown seem to evidence shrewd psychological observation and provocative philosophical reflection. Yet what he says can be properly understood only if brought into relation to his central concern, Christian experience. The significance of 'the Unknown' is not entirely evident here but does become apparent when one understands that the ultimate reference is to God-in-Christ who remains the Unknown even in self-disclosure. From this vantage point, knowledge is replaced by faith, error by sin, and reason's trying to think the unthinkable is seen as man's passion for seeking out God, yet rejecting him because the price of humility is too high. To love Christ offends because man must then abandon self-love. (P. 59) Strangely, the doctrine of the Unknown may well be the only strictly Christian point in the *Fragments*, i.e. the realization that when poetry gives way to Miracle, as man is confronted by the Unknown-God (God as unknowable, in Christ), then man resents and despises that for which he most passionately longs. The crux of the matter is not that the Unknown is God—because this is true only for faith, not for speculative reason—but that the God who is apprehended by the Christian is still the Unknown.

Not only does the transcendent take the form of an unknown in all of experience, a perplexing limit for the human mind in its general activity; in the Christian revelation of the Moment in time the transcendent meets reason as an Absolute Paradox. Revelation, when it at last comes, comes not as a straightforward answer to the questioning mind. When the Eternal freely chooses to communicate with men, its communication is not what they would like to hear; told in a manner seemingly appropriate to a god. God desires not the adulation of men, as in the role of an omnipotent wonder-worker. He comes not in the form of awesomeness, but in that of a humble servant. The royal King of the parable disguises his nature and appears as a simple man, in order to make genuine love possible. In so far as this Servant is naturally known he is human; his being also God remains unknown. To intimate his presence the Unknown God gives a sign. 'Such a sign when given is as capable of repelling the learner as of drawing him nearer.' He takes the form of a servant in order to be a common man, yet with thoughts unlike those which fill the minds of commen men. 'He is not concerned for his daily bread, like the birds of the air; he does not trouble himself about house and home, as one who neither has nor seeks a shelter or a resting-place; he does not turn his head to look at the things that usually claim the attention of men.... All this seems indeed beautiful, but is it also appropriate?' (P. 69 f.) Christ's utter devotion to his task offends many, but attracts some, mostly humble people, and becomes the gossip of the market place. But that this 'news of the day should be the swaddling-clothes of the Eternal', is possible

THE AESTHETIC LITERATURE

only in the consciousness of those to whom God gives the Moment as the occasion of faith.

We are then introduced to faith. A divine paradox cannot be judged by human wisdom. The learner cannot respond with rational belief which is based on good reasons, for without the gift of the divine condition of faith the claim that the Eternal has become a particular event is foolishness. Only for God-given faith could it be evident that God has become a man among men, in some out of the way corner of history. Kierkegaard does not here elaborate on the charm or winsomeness of such a paradoxical revelation, although he sees such values in its ambiguous nature. What he is intent upon making clear is that before such divine 'news' man remains free and responsible; assent is not forced upon him with either logic or evidence. Divine truth does not overwhelm men *en masse*. The individual has his choice to set reason aside and live happily in faith with the Paradox or else to repudiate the Paradox in an attitude of offence.* Faith is not knowledge since the Paradox cannot be known, nor is faith either required or precluded by lack of knowledge. While denying that faith is an act of will—since only God gives its possibility, Kierkegaard expressly suggests that for the person confronted by the Paradox both belief and faith (or rejection of them) require an act of will. Error roots in the assent one gives or denies to the given, not in what is given. (Pp. 102 f.)

The element of paradox in both faith and revelation cannot be overstated. About the only suggestion of divinity in the historic Jesus is the odd fact that he had no job and spent his time in care of others. Apart from this, his message is sheer news/information/ gospel, of a non-celestial and unlikely character. He sets aside his

---

* What is it for reason to be 'set aside'? Certainly not simply to be renounced as it comes to be replaced by the certitude of faith. Faith cannot convert probabilities (or rather, improbabilities—as of incarnation) into certainty. In faith man still rationally recognizes the uncalled for character of the divine deed and the mystery of it (paradox). But in trust he no longer demands the ability to comprehend. Neither does he any longer use the inability to comprehend as a justification for refusing to repent and to love. J. Heywood Thomas makes it quite clear that, on the one hand, paradox does not cease to be paradox by virtue of its being necessary for faith; thus, S.K. is not a rationalist in disguise. On the other hand, according to Thomas, S.K. is not an irrationalist since true subjectivity or faith is a grasp of truth which is really objective. Cf. J. H. Thomas, *Subjectivity and Paradox*, Oxford: Basil Blackwell (1957), pp. 72–6.

glory to approach man, in response to which man must set aside reason to possess faith. This grace-faith relation precludes the possibility of either an empirical or a rational foundation for religion. We now see in a mirror, darkly; only in heaven will men see face to face. S.K. was particularly irritated by Martensen, his tutor, who thought man could rise above doubt since, as he believed, all knowing is 'knowing-with' God. S.K. thought this an impatient 'attempt to have the perfect before its time', an unwillingness to accept man's earthly lot.[95]

One is tempted to ask, could not the Unknown, the God, ever become *empirically* evident? No, S.K. replies; 'divinity is not an immediate characteristic'. Empirically there is evident only a strange and humble man (in the course of time disguised with man-made halos and the paraphernalia of myth added by imaginative and reverent men). Only to the learner who accepts the God's own freely granted condition for faith do the empirical contents disclose the God himself, paradoxically lodged within. All that transcends the merely human in the Moment, i.e. the God incognito, is fact for faith alone. That a strange man lived and walked and died in history is empirical; the awareness that God was in this event is itself a miraculous gift of faith.

In seeking the Unknown, reason cannot actually imagine a possible character of the transcendent. Man cannot even imagine how God can be *unlike* him, any more than like him. The most one can do is to project the familiar and relative empirical qualities in the direction of absoluteness—never reaching it. (P. 55) Since the Unknown cannot be conceived it follows that, should the Unknown turn out to be God, there is an infinite difference in quality between man and God.* This inability of reason is not a

---

* Herbert Wolf maintains that at the outset the *Fragments* expresses a Socratic-Platonic idealistic principle which sets the infinite against the finite, that in the 'Interlude' it seems semi-Aristotelian, but that eventually S.K. abandoned these positions and shifted to existential thinking. (H. Wolf, *Kierkegaard and Bultmann*, Minneapolis: Augsburg Publishing House (1965), pp. 54 ff.) It may be more fair to say that this supposed 'Platonism' was a vehicle for Christian concern for the eternal and that in the later existential emphasis this concern was never lost. Further, while Wolf's complaint may well be taken that the term 'eternal happiness' is defective in that it heavily underscores happiness, it is the phrasing which is deficient rather than the concern for the lure of the eternal.

THE AESTHETIC LITERATURE

fault, however, because both likeness and unlikeness of God and man are to be grasped primarily at the level of value experience. Unlikeness is evident in man's sin, and a redemptive likeness is to be found in love.

God is no more rationally demonstrable than empirically evident. To argue from his works in nature is to no avail. 'The works from which I would deduce his existence are not directly and immediately given. The wisdom in nature, the goodness, the wisdom in the governance of the world—are all these manifest, perhaps, upon the very face of things? Are we not here confronted with the most terrible temptations to doubt, and is it not impossible to dispose of all these doubts?' (P. 52) The point is that the one who believes it possible to demonstrate God's existence already assumes it, and the poor soul who requires a proof has no evidence with which to start. God has chosen to confront man as a person but if reason seeks to supplant grace and faith then God no longer deals with man as a person but acts 'objectively' towards him, so that 'the world' actually does not present a personal God.[96]

Kierkegaard arrives at the conclusion that proving the Eternal is not fit business for reason and he has at best compassion and at worst biting sarcasm for those philosophers who try. 'When the Reason takes pity on the Paradox, and wishes to help it to an explanation, the Paradox does not indeed acquiesce, but nevertheless finds it quite natural that the Reason should do this; for why do we have our philosophers, if not to make supernatural things trivial and commonplace.' (P. 66) Even if God's being could be established by proof, nothing would thereby be accomplished, for it is not God's 'being' which is of importance. Instead, it is God's 'existence', if it may be called such, i.e. his available presence or relatedness-to-man, which is of religious concern and this is grasped only in love and faith.[97] God must be presented to man for existential choice rather than for philosophical reflection. Jesus presents a sign at which one may either scoff or pray, and it is only for faith that he is the Christ. It may be recalled that Jesus never attempted to prove his truth, but declared, 'If any man will do the will of my father, he shall know of the doctrine whether it be of God'.[98] S.K. comments: 'Act according to the precepts and commandments of Christ, do the will of the Father—and you shall have faith. Christianity does not lie in the least in the sphere of the intellect.'*

It remains to attempt to ascertain what S.K. means when he asserts that God is the absolute Paradox, and what is entailed by the claim that for human reason God must remain an enigma. Already for Socrates, any Socrates, God seems paradoxical in the sense of being an inapprehensible limit to thought, but in Christianity there is an *absolute* paradox in that the separation of man from God is now seen to be not a mere accident of fate or a character of the creature but instead a fixed and absolute necessity resulting from sin. Sin has spoiled the relation of man and God. (P. 58 f.) In itself this separation of aliens is rationally comprehensible. However, the absolute paradox becomes 'the Absurd' when God, in redemptive sacrifice, loves the unlovable in the 'appalling' disclosure of the offensive Christ.[99] Certainly, the 'absolute paradox' does not represent ultimate irrationality within God. Rather, God upholds the rational order by setting the order aside. Nor does God cease to be himself when he becomes a suffering servant, a King incognito; but rather he does these 'impossibilities' in order that transcendence as unmerited, re-creative love may be effectually introduced at a level of experience where man is free to witness and believe or be offended and crucify. The maximum of rational understanding in regard to the distinctive Christian matters of faith, such as sin, incarnation, and forgiveness, is to comprehend that these matters defy understanding.[100]

Although in this work Kierkegaard deliberately framed the concept of transcendence (central in paradox) in philosophic language, it is clear that he does not want the problem of transcendence to remain reflective. It is essentially a religious issue and can be dealt with properly only existentially. True, God remains theoretically transcendent and manifests this in omnipotence—with him *all* things are possible. Yet the meaning of

* *Papirer*, XI¹ A 339. The evil of 'proofs' of God is that they put intellectual conceit in place of the *suffering* which Christian existence calls for. 'To prove the existence of one who is present is the most shameless affront.' The only way to 'prove' God is by worship, or by loving one's neighbour—thereby grasping an intimation of God as love. Were it otherwise, the man with the highest I.Q. would have the surest hold on God. (*Postscript*, pp. 485, 501 f.; *Works of love*, p. 74.)

omnipotence for an existential thinker is to be found in the experience of faith—which could only come from God—and the mystery of divine love which 'takes itself back' or restrains itself in order to make men free and independent in their response to the giver.[101]

Man's task is not to intellectually comprehend transcendence either in general or in the form of strangeness in incarnation; the task is to existentially confront sacrificial love. Here the transcendent is grasped as divine love which risks being despised and endures the 'unfathomable grief' of the defeat of love as God seeks to gain understanding with man without violating man's equality in freedom. Transcendence is misunderstood love and kingly grief. (P. 35) Even the ancient Jews had a faint intimation of God's problem when they said no man could see God and live. 'Not to reveal oneself is the death of love, to reveal oneself is the death of the beloved.' (P. 37) Yet transcendent love will not 'alter the beloved' in order to overcome his resistance, but alters *itself* in humiliation. (P. 41) Incarnation is a strange bridge between the two alternative threats (death to love or to the beloved). It is not an escape between the horns of the dreadful dilemma for it leads to crucifixion. God *hiddenly* reveals himself so as not to destroy the integrity of the beloved, yet the death which befalls his love is transformed in omnipotence into the only power which is able to save. Dying love is still a bridge between man and God. Its dying still reveals the power of God and wins the penitent.

In one sense Kierkegaard's notion of the paradox does involve (non-paradoxical) irrationality in man's quest for God, much as in neo-Platonic thought where God is grasped in mystical awareness because he transcends reason. So too, S.K. thinks of reason reaching a limit where its problem-solving function is cut short. The intellect is, after a fashion, for ever attempting a glorious suicide in that it is always trying to solve *all* problems, after which it would have no further task. The intellect is for ever beating on the doors of the Unknown but can never open them. However, this element of irrationality is not true paradox in that rational contradiction is not present, but emerges only when God becomes incarnate and when the eternal becomes temporal. (Pp. 47, 50) Further comment on the concept of paradox appears in the appendix at the end of this unit.

Other aspects of the *Fragments* which merit special attention are its treatment of Biblical criticism, contemporaneity with Christ, the nature of history and change, and of 'natural' religion. So-called 'higher criticism' of the Bible was coming into prominence in Kierkegaard's age. His response to it is largely incorporated in his concept of contemporaneity. The essential problems posed by higher criticism are how eternal salvation can properly depend on historical (thereby limited and even uncertain) documents, how to overcome the apparent disadvantages facing later generations of believers as contrasted with fortunate 'eyewitnesses', and how historical events or even the historical Christ can give non-historical knowledge of God. The answers, it should be remembered, are given by Johannes Climacus (John the Climber), who is climbing towards Christian truth; therefore the answers are relatively speculative and immanent rather than openly Christian.

In Kierkegaard's day scripture was under attack on the ground that it seemed to furnish a poorly documented account of Jesus' life and work. S.K.'s reply is pleasing to neither fundamentalists or liberals, but it is close to the position of Luther. The Bible does not, in his judgment, and in the very nature of empirical data could not, offer sufficient empirical evidence for religious *belief*, but Spirit-inspired faith does find the eternal Christ in the historical Jesus. That to which the Bible writers essentially certify is not the historical facts but that in faith they have found the historical Jesus to be the son of God. Accordingly, Biblical criticism is in a strict sense irrelevant.* It is S.K.'s theory of the decisiveness of the moment which gives him a foundation for his attack on higher criticism. Christianity is not a corpus of tradition or a mass of reputed history which requires validation by scholarship. The believer does not need to survey the evidence in order to arrive at a conviction of the accuracy of Christianity. Instead, he finds himself confronted by a very simple but paradoxical disclosure of Christ and either responds with faith or offence. The 'after history' of Christendom is interesting, but irrelevant for faith, and can even delude by its pretentious 'successes'. However,

---

* *Postscript*, p. 27. Herbert Wolf notes the astonishing Kierkegaardian ring in Albert Schweitzer's insistence that the spiritual force of Christ cannot be detected by 'historical knowledge of the personality and life of Jesus', which quest for the historical Jesus may be 'even an offence to religion'. (*Wolf, op. cit.*, p. 10 f.)

it is not true that there is no issue of historical objectivity. That Jesus appeared in time in the kind of role indicated in the gospels is a necessary historical presupposition. Yet he did not 'prove' his Messianic character, for if he had done so there would be no room for offence—or faith. The only possible 'proof' of Messiahship is to be found through discipleship.

The issue receiving the most extensive treatment in the latter part of the *Fragments* is that of 'the contemporary disciple' and 'the disciple at second hand'. The question is by no means peripheral, but is essential to the basic theme of ultimate truth and how man is to relate himself to it. It is a natural corollary of the questions previously raised concerning the evidence (or lack thereof) for religious truth, reason and paradox, and divine as opposed to Socratic teaching. If the Eternal comes as an event in history, how is it to be equally available to all generations? If revelation consists not of profound insights available to all rational men, but of an actual affront to reason, then how can men of all generations equally relate themselves in faith to the 'news of the (now long past) day'? The events of the past are irretrievable and in danger of becoming ever less meaningful.

Kierkegaard argues that the possibility of faith must not depend on happenstance, as for example being in the neighbourhood when Jesus passes by. In such case, one might be contemporaneous only with Jesus' eating and walking, and could well respond with unfaith. 'I ate and drank in his presence, and he taught in our streets. I saw him often, and knew him for a common man of humble origin. Only a very few thought to find something extraordinary in him; as far as I am concerned, I could see nothing remarkable about him, and I was certainly as much a contemporary as anybody.' (P. 84)

The solution of the problem is implicit in the notion of faith as something not founded on objective historical evidence—despite its focus on an historical event—but on a God-given possibility. If the God in time is a paradox, then no superficial contemporaneity will produce faith. However much one may romantically long to directly encounter the God-man, belief would be no easier were this possible. Such a meeting might have the advantage of making the alternative possibilities of faith and offence more vivid, and the need for decision more evident, but the absolute Paradox would not thereby be less a folly or hurdle for reason. On the other hand, were one to console himself with the thought that the remoteness of the event gave better perspective, with a test of time for faith, he would again have overlooked the character of revelation. The passing centuries only tend to 'surround faith with a noisy chatter' not so likely to have been originally present. The fact is that what is once a paradox is always so, and subsequent events (the growth of the church, for example), will never serve to make the paradox to be any less paradoxical. Perhaps one must most beware of covering over the absolute Paradox with such a blanket of myth as to make a quasi-objectivity of it, thus helping one to become a 'well-drilled chatterer, in whose mind there is no suspicion of the possibility of offense, nor any room for faith'. (P. 117)*

A radical consequence is that if Christianity is paradoxical it cannot become a settled heritage or an accepted tradition. One can only be returned to the challenge of God's humiliation, so that he does not find himself in a later point in the 'tradition' but is on identical footing in matters of faith with people of all generations. For faith, time itself is really immaterial; one is at no disadvantage for not having been an eyewitness. Inasmuch as faith, whenever it occurs, is based only on the condition granted by the Eternal, there can be no such thing as discipleship at second hand. Every disciple is a contemporary of God in the only significant sense of contemporaneity. Events in the flow of time are at the best occasions for spiritual awakening, and at worst distractions. It is imperative to overlook the burden of spiritually irrelevant fact, whether or not one happens to be an immediate contemporary of the Moment. The true Moment is fixated by having the eternal penetrate it, so that it gains an identity of its own. It is no longer simply *in* time, because 'time', being durational, cannot be broken into true successive discrete units. The latter day witness is reminded that it is his duty never to relay the news of the Eternal

---

* That the confrontation or paradox is the essential fact of incarnation rather than an elaborate biography of Jesus is summed up—though undoubtedly oversimplified—in this amazing and much disputed statement: 'If the contemporary generation had left nothing behind them but these words: "We have believed that in such and such a year the God appeared among us in the humble form of a servant, that he lived and taught in our community, and finally died", it would be more than enough.' (P. 130)

in time except in its naked purity—as the paradox which it is, an offence to reason, and the occasion for the moment of truth.

Further, it would be a grievous mistake to think of contemporaneity with Christ as a like-mindedness which spans the centuries, as might be the case with modern admirers of Socrates. Only the guilty person who is contrary to the mind of Christ but who receives the condition of faith from God himself can become a contemporary in that he—as one present—feels judged by the love of God and redeemed by that love. (Pp. 85, 131) To be a contemporary of a pretty baby Jesus is not being contemporary with Christ. To admire such a one is not even to be religious; it is only to have an aesthetic feeling.

Does S.K. really mean that the history of the church is of no significance whatsoever, as has been charged, or that if it has any significance it is only as an obstacle in the way of individual discipleship?[102] In a single sense, yes. The true Christian history is confined to God's entrance into history in the person of Christ. The history of the church is not a part of this divine deed. On the other hand, even though S.K. points sharply to falterings within historic Christendom, he also recognizes proper Christian life and teaching within it. The history of the church is significant just as a sermon may be significant, for edification, proclamation and witnessing. In his comments on the church, the principle of 'the corrective' must be recognized. S.K. sees no need to defend historic Christendom with reference to its worthy endeavours, but he is profoundly impressed with the perils of self-deification and complacency within it.

In a section of the *Fragments* entitled 'Interlude' there is presented a rather difficult discussion of the essential nature of history and change. The casual reader might be quite misled as to its real intent. It does plainly incorporate an interesting theory of the nature of change but it is much more—or less—than a philosophic doctrine such as that of a Heracleitus or Bergson. Kierkegaard felt that in order to make room for faith he had to free human experience from the shackles of necessity. Man constantly experiences the pressures of causal forces, but by virtue of man's freedom his history is not an unfolding of necessity (as with Hegel's 'Spirit') but is properly a response to challenge and confrontation. For S.K., facts of history, particularly of human history, do not belong in a 'system'; through freedom they escape the net of scientific explanation.

This entire argument involves a theory of reality which regards actuality as involving an interplay of immutable *essences* (like Plato's Ideas) and *being* (the changing world order). In S.K.'s view, concrete existence, such as is the concern of the historian, and ideal whatness or essence, which is the concern of the mathematician or philosopher, cannot ordinarily be divorced, even though also they must never be confused. The two synthesize in all processes. 'Necessity is the [point of] union of possibility and actuality.'[103] This means that 'necessity' is that unchanging plan, pattern, meaning or whatness which is present as the essential meaning of an actual thing but was already present in identical form when this thing was not yet real except as a possibility. As that which alone is present in a given thing both when it is merely possible and when it has become actual, this unchanging 'necessity' (whatness) is indeed that which unites possibility and actuality.

Whereas Spinoza held that the more perfect an essence is, the more real it is, S.K. maintains that if a fly exists it is just as real as God is. 'Factual existence is subject to the dialectic of Hamlet: to be or not to be.' (P. 51) Further, while reflection can ponder how to interpret an existent by naming it (e.g. as star or fly), thus identifying it with an essence or whatness, reflection can not in any way prove that there is such a being. Indeed, it cannot even, in the strict sense, define it because to do so is to convert existence into whatness or essence. (Pp. 50 ff.) It is existence rather than essence to which S.K. gives primary attention, and the dramatic quality in Kierkegaard's thought concerning existence is that, among other existents, he accepts with full seriousness the reality of the subjective self. Such personal existence is demonstrated by faith which freely and subjectively acts, without compulsion from reason, whereas the purely objective thinker has no authentic selfhood and merely reflects the beliefs which reason acquires.[104] The leap of faith, because it is an act of the self, in freedom, points to the reason for identifying existence with subjectivity or passion. It is self-activity. Its more obvious manifestation is emotion, such as concern, but probably volition is more fundamental.

THE AESTHETIC LITERATURE

Because Kierkegaard's concern was primarily with responsibility in existence rather than with philosophic structures as such, he did not elaborate on the concept of necessity, although his thought brings to mind many philosophers of essence or whatness, such as Russell, Whitehead, Santayana, and Plotinus. On the other hand, S.K. did spell out his theories of the *actual* (existence, being) and of the *possible* (as occurring in repetition).[105]

What then is the nature of 'coming into existence'? The subject which comes into existence must remain unchanged while coming into existence. Otherwise it is not the same subject as the original subject, but something else. Yet this subject which is a 'being' after it has come into existence is only a 'possibility' prior to that event, so that the change 'is a transition from possibility to actuality'. Such transition occurs with freedom and never by necessity. 'Everything which comes into existence proves precisely by coming into existence that it is not necessary, for the only thing which cannot come into existence is the necessary, because the necessary *is*.' (P. 91) If anything is necessary it is not possible, but instead is inescapably actual.

Everything which comes into existence is historical, and that history is the realm of freedom is demonstrated by the fact that the very immutabilities of the past nevertheless did not simply exist from eternity, but came into existence. Only man has a true history. 'It is the perfection of the Eternal to have no history...' On the other hand, it is the perfection of nature that it has no history other than in the sense that it once came into existence, i.e. is marked by events. Although man can probe into what nature once was, the natural really *has no past*; it *exists* only in the present. For man, however, there is a unique possibility for 'reduplication, i.e. the possibility of a second coming into existence within the first coming into existence'. (P. 94) It is a possibility for transcending the moment of time by an identification of the person with his past self and future self, in responsible personhood, so that there is a repetition of the self. Even though man can no more exist in his past or his future than can a geological process or an animal, yet he can identify himself with past and future so as to formulate goals, judgments, and values, and thus live in more than the passing moment. He remains responsible for his past and assumes responsibility for his future.

Michael Wyschogrod suggests that for S.K. man can never *fully* exist because to do so would mean that he is pure subjectivity, with no necessity or choice devolving upon him from the eternal.[106] That is to say, man cannot be all existence because this would exclude essence. In any case, S.K. does view man as in a striving condition whereby he seeks to continually reacquire the selfhood which is a realization of the eternal within the temporal. From this it is also clear that the kind of being which man possesses is not pure being but only 'becoming', which is a blend of ephemeral time with eternity. Only the eternal, as for Parmenides, has enduring being. Becoming grasps the eternal in a kind of temporal analogue, viz. enduring by means of repetition. Becoming is creative in that it represents self-determination in an act of freedom, transforming possibility into actuality. The becoming is also repetition, in that it is not a replacement of the past by the new but a free movement whereby the past self is recovered. This recovery is ultimately a repetition of the self in its God-relation. Becoming represents the fact that a selfhood cannot be quiescently possessed but must be for ever dynamically repossessing itself, strenuously and passionately. It is the objective uncertainty or elusive quality of the transcendent which keeps man in this straining situation.[107]

An important contribution of the *Fragments* which is largely overlooked because of its stress on the transcendent element in Christianity is the illuminating clarification of the character of natural religiosity. S.K.'s treatment is precise. General religiosity is natural and good but is *not* Christian. It lacks the transcendent disclosure. Hegel and his followers had, as it was frequently phrased and as S.K. repeatedly mentions, 'gone farther' than Christianity into supposedly universal and humanistic religiousness. S.K. accepts the value of religion and sees it as an essential preliminary to Christianity (cf. the *Postscript*), but views it as pathetic, requiring Christianity for its fulfilment.

How does religion arise, apart from revelation? It comes as the numinous, if one may borrow Rudolf Otto's term. This appears in *Thoughts on Crucial Situations* and also in the *Fragments*. In the latter, the little chapter on The Absolute Paradox, which is termed 'A Metaphysical Crotchet', explains that religiosity

THE AESTHETIC LITERATURE

arises by collision of the human reason with the Unknown, which is not any known thing but is 'the limit to which Reason repeatedly comes'. However, the limit occurs at the point of interruption of every quest and so the Unknown comes into 'a condition of dispersion (*diaspora*)'. The result is only too well demonstrated by the religions of mankind. Man, the godmaker, in his imagination may deify any form of limit which overawes him, e.g. the monstrous (as Civa the destroyer or even Krishna in his earth-devouring form), or the ludicrous (illustrated by some of the Greek sprites or the monkey god of India). 'But it is impossible to hold fast to a difference [deity] of this nature. Every time this is done it is essentially an arbitrary act, and deepest down in the heart of piety lurks the mad caprice which knows that it has itself produced the God.' (P. 56) The outcome for natural religion is that the religious mood veers from fantasy to fantasy, thence to polytheism which is the collective dream of all fantasies, or to pantheism which is an incongruous and unreconciled merger of them. 'The Reason has brought the God as near as possible, and yet he is as far away as ever.' (P. 57) This is the tragic denouement of 'religion'.

In conclusion we may ask for the final message of the *Fragments*. It culminates as it begins with a focus on Christianity's difference, the strange breaking in of God upon time, history and conscience. This constitutes one version of S.K.'s doctrine of the Moment, the instant where the eternal fixates the temporal or reveals itself in it. Here is the daring, fantastic gospel of Christianity. Buddhism seeks the eternal *outside* of time. Socrates sought it by *recollection* from a pre-temporal state. Christ places it where no one would have looked for it, in history (of all things Jewish history!). To find this Eternal, a gift of the Holy Spirit would be required, precisely as scripture asserts. (P. 137 f.) The insistence on 'the moment' can be understood only from the standpoint of revelation which, if it occurs at all, must have a point of beginning. For Socrates, since eternal truth is recollected, there is no real beginning; man recovers the spiritual life which had for a time subsided. In Christianity however the moment is that point at which God breaks into history.

APPENDIX: PARADOX

If Kierkegaard were writing for the twentieth century he would doubtless say far less about paradox and 'the absurd', and would take up cudgels against empiricism rather than idealism. In his age the chief threat to Christianity was the Hegelian attempt to incorporate Christianity into a rational structure, and it was against this that S.K. pronounced the essence of Christianity to be mystery, irrational and non-assimilable. That God became man or that the absolute became a fact of history defies comprehension.[108]

While paradox relates primarily to transcendent Christianity, in S.K.'s treatment, there is a sense in which irrationality relates to existential subjectivity. The doctrine that a self is always in a process of becoming involves a kind of irrationality, not in the sense of contradicting reason, but in that it removes the self from the static categories which are employed with reference to being. A free act of will or of faith cannot be explained by causal reference. Reason can classify instances under categories or relate them in types of necessity, but, confronted by freedom, it can do no more than recognize that it is unable to explain this kind of experience. It may sense the purposes towards which choice freely and perhaps reasonably moves, but it cannot explain or predict in a scientific sense. Apart from this consideration, however, S.K.'s doctrine of irrationality is objective rather than existential and is chiefly related to paradox.

In fairness to Kierkegaard it is to be noted that when he refers to the absurd he is thinking primarily of the human situation in which man must act but can find no adequate reasons for doing so. He does not mean that existence itself is ridiculous or that God is absurd. Neither does he mean that one should abandon rationality. What is 'absurd' is that one must act decisively *as if* all the evidence were in and reason could demonstrate the justifiability of the decision. Yet neither Christian, nor Marxist, nor humanist has any such warrant. To act without support from reason is, like Pascal's gamble, 'to act upon faith', doing so, 'by virtue of the absurd'. In doing this, the Christian says to God: 'This is what I do, bless my actions, I cannot do otherwise because I am brought to a standstill by my powers of reflection.'[109] In effect, S.K. is agreeing with the empirical thinker who cannot find a warrant for faith in God or even for love for neighbour. Yet his conclusion is different. If to love or to believe is 'absurd', i.e. cannot be supported by reason, it does not follow that one should wait with loving or believing but instead one may conclude that reason has limitations and that in being true to his decisional nature one must not wait for reason's bidding. Neither God nor man is absurd, but man's situation is at least a seeming absurdity when he must make the most fateful decisions as if they were reasonable, whereas in fact there is at the most only frail hope to support them. Absurd or no, the life of value-existence is as natural as breathing. To be human is to engage in it and while the fateful decisions eventually come face to face with ultimate mystery, the structure of value decisions is clear-cut and imperative. Choice of the good—a choice made with risk—is urged on man by his very existence, and, at a higher level, is required by Christ.

In addition to the absolute paradox (incarnation), Kierkegaard recognized lesser (and even pseudo) paradoxes, in particular the concept of the 'limit' or the unknown. Some of the paradoxes are certainly only seeming contradictions, e.g. the fact that genius depends on an accidental occasion to spark it.[110] Paradox as a common quality of thought is picturesquely identified by S.K. as 'grandiose thoughts in embryo', but he totally differentiates this from Christianity which is the 'Absolute Paradox'.[111] With reference to the Unknown, it may also be noted that such a transcendent limit imposed upon reason is not as such paradox. Paradox properly involves an element of self-contradiction whereas the Unknown (except in Christianity) is merely that which is beyond apprehension. S.K. makes this plain when he equates the Paradox with the absurd and with the possibility of offence, insisting that the absurd is essential in Christianity, so that offence is Christianity's defence against speculation.[112] Christ is the *absolute* paradox, first, in that as God he is absolutely unlike man (and therefore even unknowable), and, second, because to bridge the chasm he truly becomes like man. (P. 59)

Strangely, Kierkegaard's concept of paradox was derived in part from David Hume. As a sceptical university student, S.K. concluded that the romance between Christianity and philosophy was an illusion, to the discrediting of religion. Then, in 1836, he was struck by the treatment of Hume's scepticism by the German philosopher Johan Hamann. Unlike the Hegelians who were trying to make religion 'reasonable', Hume had written that Christianity not only began with miracles 'but even to this day cannot be believed by any reasonable person without one', since it cannot be rationally demonstrated. Hamann commented that while Hume may have written this in a spirit of scepticism that actually all of Hume's doubts about a faith unsupported by miracles demonstrate his proposition that Christianity must continuously involve the miraculous in order to be genuine.[113] Accordingly, Christianity became literally for Kierkegaard what Hume said it must be, 'a continued miracle' in any person who is moved by faith. This is, of course, the view of faith already presented by St Paul.

It must be acknowledged that Kierkegaard's treatment of paradox varies in nature from time to time, and that it is difficult to precisely define. As a result there has been sharp controversy over it. An obvious reason for the difficulty is that S.K. wrote in the fever of battle. His language at times is extreme and must be put in the frame of historic reference. Hegelian idealism insisted on absorbing religion, on the assumption that all opposites are ultimately reconciled. Therefore, to defend the very reality of religious faith, S.K. felt impelled to deny any identity of human and divine, as in a Hegelian process of 'mediation'. In consequence, at the point of faith, reason had to be sacrificed, placing outside its scope the ultimate individuality of the believer, acknowledging a non-rational foundation for faith, and, most specifically, recognizing Christ as the paradoxical God-man who represented no Hegelian natural unity of human and divine, but instead manifested an utterly incomprehensible and unnecessary incarnation of love.

At one time Kierkegaard pondered whether there might be some more radical or absolute paradox than that presented in Christianity, as, for example, for a Christ to live so utterly natural a human existence as to totally conceal his divinity. This notion he rejected, viewing such a possibility not as a more radical paradox, but rather as a simple failure to communicate within a purported communication.[114]

THE AESTHETIC LITERATURE

What does Kierkegaard most fundamentally intend by the idea of paradox? Some interpreters have taken it to be simply an intellectual difficulty over a doctrine, such as the doctrine of the incarnation, atonement, or of the two natures of Christ. However, even though S.K.'s language does at times suggest this, he emphatically denies that this is his meaning. Instead, paradox seems always to have a valuational rather than a theoretical core. It is not mere intellectual bewilderment, but is the bewildering duality and contradiction of the challenge of veiled Love which evokes alternatively love-faith or offence. The clash of the paradox is in the strange value character of God and in the conflicting tendencies of man's value response. The very attempt at treating Jesus' love as presenting an intellectual problem is itself sinful, an attempt to translate a life of value into one of cognition, avoiding responsibility by means of speculation. Kierkegaard insists that the central paradox (or Absurd) is the scandal or offence in Christ as personal Lord, and in the relation of the disciple to him. Already here in the *Fragments*, S.K. indicates that the paradox is not merely 'a folly to the understanding' but 'an offence to the human heart', in that it humbles man, who in his pride does not understand that sin prevents not only his knowledge of God but even knowledge of self.[115]

This view, that for Kierkegaard paradox represents more an affront to the concrete logic of human wisdom than an inconsistency in the formal logic of reason, is plausibly advocated by some scholars. N. H. Søe believes that in formulating the paradox as a conflict between the eternal and the historical, S.K. was in some measure betrayed by the 'orthodoxy' of his time, believing that— as in Greek thought—God can in a measure be known apart from revelation, i.e. known under the category of the eternal or the absolute. Søe draws the conclusion that if S.K. had clearly understood that, for the Christian, God is known *only* in Christ then he would not have been plagued by the paradox of eternity-historicity but would have understood in simplicity that which he did stress, viz. that the real paradox is the offence of the Christ of history to man as sinner.[116] In line with Lundensian thought, Søe intimates that the real conflict (paradox) is not of a logical character, nor within a doctrine, but is an opposition between ordinary thought and the unique Christian categories, such as the amazing, unselfish, and unmerited love—*agape*.

In any case, Søe seems altogether correct, in opposition to others, in insisting that paradox is not essentially an intellectual difficulty. This is evident in S.K.'s statement that 'it is not difficult for men to understand, but it is difficult for them to understand how much self-discipline and self-denial Christianity demands'.[117] The difficulty is not in understanding Christianity but in facing it as reality.[118]

Finally it is to be noted that the objective paradox in Christ must be answered by man's paradoxical response, e.g. in faith and love, both of which bear the plain stamp of paradox. Instead of the believer enjoying happiness, as might have been anticipated, he is called on to suffer and 'die to the world'. The sign of the divine is that 'every concept is turned around'.[119]

14. THE CONCEPT OF DREAD

> *The Concept of Dread.* A Simple Deliberation on Psychological Lines in the Direction of the Dogmatic Problem of Original Sin. By Vigilius Haufniensis. June 17, 1844. Translated by Walter Lowrie. Princeton: Princeton University Press, 1944. 2nd ed., translation revised by Howard A. Johnson, 1957. (Page references are to the first edition.)

Dread was an early, profound and subtle psychological study, laying a foundation for the investigation of anxiety as a key factor in the dynamics of neuroticism. It identifies anxiety as the ambivalent dizziness of being lured and repulsed by a possibility which is really unknown because one has not yet willed it into being. However, *Dread* is more than psychological; it is also a profound and controversial theological study of the concept of sin.

Although this book was published at the same time as *Philosophical Fragments* it has a decidedly different style, and in fact is quite different from all other writings by Kierkegaard.* *Dread* is

---

* Unlike S.K.'s other works, *Dread* was put in the textbookish style of the scholars whom S.K. was attacking. It has been suggested, dubiously, that this was done in a kind of ironic mockery. The book is exceedingly difficult, due partly to our unfamiliarity with Kierkegaard's literary sources, but more particularly to its mode of expression, abstractness and profundity.

literally a supplement to *Fragments*. Both aim to show what is distinctive in Christianity, the latter from a theological standpoint and *Dread* from the standpoint of a psychological view of the human resources with which Christianity has to deal. *Dread* treats that trait of human nature (anxiety) which makes sin possible, but which cannot be said to produce it since sin is a responsible act rather than an unavoidable part of one's nature.

Because of its abstract and difficult character, *Dread* is one of the less widely read books by Kierkegaard, and among those who do read it there are differences of interpretation. Even Lowrie, its translator, complained that there is 'too much about Adam' and about 'original sin' in it. However, many of the complaints, including this one, are basically misleading or in error. Although S.K. speaks a great deal about the matter, what he actually does is to forcefully *reduce* the 'Adam element' in the concept of sin. He argues that sin comes into every man's life exactly as it did in the case of Adam, i.e. by a 'leap' or free act, so that *every* sin is an *original* (true, uncaused) sin. If there is 'too much about Adam' in the book it is put there to emphasize that one must take his own guilt seriously and not make Adam a scapegoat. Adam is *within* the race, sinning in the same fashion as his children do, not outside or before the race so as to impose guilt upon it. The simple man is apt to know this full well, penitently, how sin comes into his life, and how he is responsible for it. He does not avoid the earnestness of penitence by blaming Adam, or by making original sin an academic question. S.K. therefore views the story of Adam's fall as 'myth' in something of the Platonic sense, i.e. a pictorial representation of a truth not otherwise comprehensible. (P. 42)

The title of this book, as also that of *Sickness Unto Death*, may conjure up strange and gloomy images. Yet just as the Cross does not make Christianity gloomy but is a symbol of hope, so dread does not make existence morbid. In fact, says Kierkegaard, it is dread more than noble reason which marks the glory of mankind. Not consciousness or even self-awareness defines personality, and certainly not such choices as animals can make. Rather, it is moral concern 'which constitutes a personality', even though the conscientious attitude may be in some cases scarcely self-conscious.[120]

Accordingly, the fact that a child is 'born in sin' (a form of dread) does not belittle the child or mean that it is cruelly burdened with an undesirable human affliction, for such dread is the 'deepest expression for its highest dignity'.[121] To experience dread is to be anxious over the possibilities of the future, to experience misgivings over one's uneasy relation to the eternal. Only a free spirit has such possibilities of existence. No animal can be thus anxious about the course of its life. Therefore dread is a mark of humanness. 'If a man were a beast or an angel, he would not be able to be in dread. Since he is a synthesis [of body, soul, and spirit] he can be in dread, and the greater the dread, the greater the man.' (P. 139) It is spirit which synthesizes body and mind and brings a sense of ultimate values into experience, 'where time is constantly intersecting eternity and eternity constantly permeating time'. (Pp. 79-80) Yet this linkage of temporal and eternal is no pantheistic blending of human and divine; rather, it involves the conviction that man, creature of time and nature though he is, finds himself prodded by an objectively uncertain but eternal God into becoming a true individual.[122] Living thus in time but with an eye to the eternal, spiritual life is marked by possibility, hope, and —more particularly—dread. Since dread is a general uneasiness before the undefined possibilities of life, and has no specific feared object, it follows that it is identical neither with fear (which always has a specific object) nor sin (which is a deed and an act of the will).

It was Kierkegaard's melancholy which prompted him to explore the concept of dread. The mystery of his relation to his father is a background for understanding his view of dread and a commentary upon it. The discovery of unexpected sin in his godly father caused S.K. to sympathetically share a feeling of guilt even though in this instance he was not himself the sinner. He felt himself impelled to evil by his despair over his father's sin, thus feeling that guilt *is* inherited and that a person is not only himself but is also in some sense identical with others and the race. If it is true, as some believe, that S.K. for a time fell into a somewhat dissolute life through the shock of discovering his father's guilt, then the thought of guilt being inherited must have impressed him the more deeply. Accordingly, he came to think of sin as emerging from prior or original guilt, as distinguished from personal guilt which follows one's own responsible sinful act, and to think of guilt as a dread of evil as yet unrealized. He found a dramatic illustration for this in his myth of King David who orders Bathsheba's husband killed so that he can marry her, then sends another messenger to prevent the murder, and waits in *dread of the sin not yet committed*.[123] It seems that S.K. was troubled also by anxieties over personal sins, e.g. sexual, which had not yet occurred or perhaps never occurred, and by anxiety over such bitterly difficult decisions as the breaking of his engagement. Further, he reports that he felt a 'dread of Christianity' even though strongly drawn to it.[124] All of this gave a deep personal awareness of anxiety as the background of sin and of responsible choice.

However, lest the fact of melancholy draw attention away from the basic issues, it should be added, first, that the structure of this concept is developed in independence of Kierkegaard's personal life, and, second, that all of his experiences show intensification —joy as well as sorrow. Thus he insisted that even in sufferings he was indescribably joyful,[125] and once he wrote: 'Properly understood, every man who truthfully desires a relationship to God . . . has only one task: always to be joyful.'[126] The important point is that S.K.'s varied moods tended to enrich all his concepts.

The term which Kierkegaard employs to designate the objectless anxiety over responsible choice is '*Angst*'. Translators generally agree that 'Angst' is only inadequately rendered by the English 'dread'. In the original term there is involved not mere anguish but forbidding anticipation, yet an anticipation which awaits 'nothing'. Moreover, dread not only views this 'nothing' with avoidance or antipathy but also experiences attraction to it. One can be lured by horror and can also long for that which he fears. Accordingly, dread is 'sympathetic antipathy'. One can dread the evil even though being bound to it and can also (demoniacally) dread the good even though conceivably not being able to cast it off. Man's temptation to sin is of this character, for man is not tempted simply by the world, by God, or by a 'serpent'. Every man is tempted by himself, through the fascination of his own dreams of the future and the possible. Thus, although in a sense dread is an 'alien power' which overwhelms one, 'yet he is guilty, he who after all loved it while he feared it'. (P. 39)

As pointed out above, since dread has no specific object, Kierkegaard regards it as a response to 'nothing'. This 'nothing' is specifically *that which spirit creates* as it begins a kind of fantasy life. While it is nothing in that it is not as yet any actual thing or event, it is still 'something' in the sense of *that which is possible* for man to spiritually do or become. Commitment to the eternal is thus one of the possibilities of this nothing. Despoiling the eternal in an attempt at animality (for man can *not* succeed in being an animal) is another possibility. That S.K. should designate this object of anxiety as 'nothing' is thus not intended to indicate that it has no being or significance, but rather that it is what man has not yet produced but may produce in his life adventure.[127] Moreover, the character of the 'unknown' object varies, not only with circumstance but also in relation to one's life stance. For example, for a Buddhist or Hindu the dreadful state is to be an individual through failure to enter Nirvana or the unity of Brahman. For the Christian, for whom alone genuine sin is possible, sin is the basic object of dread and true individuality is the spiritual goal.

There is a philosophy of human nature which is incorporated in *The Concept of Dread*. Before the fall into sin, as S.K. interprets it, man was human but had no knowledge of good and evil, and therefore was without significant goals. However, by losing innocence, he gained a knowledge of good and evil and therefore must now look to the future and its possibilities with uncertainty, anxiety, and hope. Becoming involved with choice involves man in successive events and so makes him historical rather than simply eternal. Nevertheless, choice also tends to carry man beyond time and into the eternal. The explanation is that true choice is an act of freedom, and 'finite' freedom (finite implying imposed limitations) is a self-contradiction. This does not mean that finite man is free in all regards but that what freedom he does possess is *true* freedom, in its own way absolute or infinite. True freedom is of necessity infinite and 'does not arise out of anything'. (P. 100) For Kierkegaard, man is destined for freedom, for the infinite, and for the eternal to which the infinite is akin. S.K.'s concern for a free and absolute commitment to the eternal changes with the passing years, so that the way to the eternal is increasingly a way of renunciation of the finite and temporal. Whereas at first he thought of man as properly a synthesis (although *absolutely* committed to the eternal and only *relatively* to the temporal), he eventually seemed to be moving towards the position of Socrates, that the wise man wants to die in order to gain the eternal. This plainly constitutes a major dilemma in his thought and in his personal life.

With reference to anxiety, divine discontent, and unrest being distinctive of the human spirit, as opposed to mere animality, Kierkegaard quotes Hamann. 'This dread which we experience in the world is the only proof of our heterogeneity. For if we lacked nothing, we should do no better than the pagans and the transcendental philosophers who know nothing of God and like fools fall in love with this precious world; no homesickness would attack us. This impertinent uneasiness, this holy hypochondria, is perhaps the fire whereby we sacrificial animals must be salted and preserved from the decay of the passing age.' (P. 145)

How then does 'spirit' emerge in man? Before falling into a state of sin man has no profound sense of dread. The innocence of Adam is a state of ignorance, not knowing good from evil. He is indeed constituted of soul and body but is not yet spirit, for spirit in man is on the one hand an aspiration for the divine and on the other a love for the world. As spirit, man becomes stretched between finite and infinite, stretched almost to the breaking point. Thus *fallen* man is spiritual, filled with dread, yet dreaming of God. Moral consciousness, spiritual yearning, dread, sexuality, and the humanness of the race all emerge together. In a strange sense, one might almost propose that prior to sin Adam was somehow pre-human, lacking his essential (spirit) self.

Implicit in this view, as for Hegel, is an emphasis on freedom as a mark of spirit. S.K. might have entitled this treatise 'The Birthplace of Freedom', for what he wants to show is how freedom, the greatest human gift, originates. It comes into being, he believes, as one begins to have a troubled awareness of something unreal, which might be real, indeed which may become real if one should will it so. This possibility is not, not yet and perhaps not ever, a reality; and therefore it is not a feared *object*. Yet because of the necessity of decision which this possibility imposes on man the situation is one of anxiety, pregnant with possibility and responsibility. How unlike Greek eudaemonism this is! For Aristotle the ethical life is a *fulfilled* life, the confident self-realization of the Greek aristocrat. For Kierkegaard it is the *unfulfilled* life, the life of challenge and decision. It is in view of such facts that Paul Holmer insists that the importance of the Kierkegaard literature lies not in its description of fact but in a 'presentation of possibles' and of 'a theory about these possibles'. These possibles are not theoretical hypotheses but are instead practical alternatives.[128]

There remains a mystery in the notion of freedom. In language like that of many idealists but actually reflecting Christian perspectives, S.K. held that paradoxically man is authentically free only to choose the *good*. If one 'chooses' evil, which is for ever alien to his proper nature, one is in effect failing to exercise his freedom and makes himself a slave. Thus, in contrast to the genuine freedom with which one chooses the good, there is as its alternative a yielding (albeit a commitment) to evil which, subjectively, is guilt, and objectively is necessity or external compulsion. (P. 100) Thus man may enter into slavery by means of a responsible act which is, nevertheless, self-destructive in that by it he is surrendering his freedom.

Because man's freedom is the opportunity for changing bare possibles into actual facts, it involves man in the concreteness of time. This is serious in that time threatens man with change, limitations and even death. S.K. is insistent that time, as experienced in human existence, is durational and cannot be broken into a succession of discrete moments. 'Precisely because every moment, like the sum of the moments, is a process, no moment is a present, and in the same sense, there is neither past, present, nor future.' (P. 77) The spilling over of past into present and the impingement of the present upon the future makes each one of these moments meaningful only within a totality of duration. Nevertheless durational time lacks meaning because of endless flux and indeterminate succession. The fluidity of temporal duration can be put in a fixed and clear perspective only by being related to the eternal. The eternal makes contact with time and illuminates it in the 'instant' (moment of revelation-and-faith). The instant is a true (unfleeting) present in that its fixity of meaning liberates the person from the endless flux. The eternal comes into time in such way that man may gain an absolute relationship to himself, and thus become spirit. (Pp. 76-80) In this doctrine

THE AESTHETIC LITERATURE

there is an interesting parallel to Reinhold Niebuhr's insistence that no final judgment of history can be made within history since the judgment itself would then come under judgment, and that therefore history can be truly judged only from a fixed Messianic point outside it. The difference for Kierkegaard is that the eternal does not wait for the instant at the end of history, but may transform any moment.

The place of dread in life, and Kierkegaard's philosophy of man, can better be understood by contrasting his views with those of some later existentialists, whom he considerably influenced. We find in his thought the roots of Jaspers and Heidegger, as in the notion that dread is distinctly human, marking a free response to possibility. Yet S.K.'s precise meanings for 'nothing', the nature of man's peril, and the possibilities of hope are abandoned by such men as Jaspers and Heidegger. S.K. thinks of the object of dread as being nothing in that it is not yet existent. The choice which permits possibility to become reality is fearsome because of its responsibility, finality, and uncertainty. There is an anxious indecisiveness in the face of uncharted possibility, a premonition of an unknown peril, particularly a premonition of an evil into which one may move by one's own wilfulness. The secular existentialists also emphasize the requirements of responsible freedom, yet tend to replace anxiety before the possibilities of the eternal with a dread of death. This likewise is 'nothing' (i.e. not yet come to pass), but it threatens the self as an external annihilation rather than as a subjective indeterminateness or self-betrayal. Clearly, for Kierkegaard, dread is essentially a spiritual attitude, having to do with spirit's relation to itself and to God, whereas for the secular existentialists it is more akin to fear (of an external threat) except that it has no actualized object in either case. For the secular existentialists, dread is a facing of the pathos, uncertainty, and finitude of life, and thus may challenge one to reflective self-determination—a kind of naturalistic spirituality. For S.K. it is rather a religious awareness of one's tenuous relation to the eternal.

It is to be further noted that in spite of the prominence Kierkegaard gives to dread, he assigns a lesser role to it than do the secular existentialists. They accept his point that dread or anxiety stirs anticipation, freedom, and spirit, and that without it human existence is a mere body-mind process, a sort of animal-vegetable life, with no spiritual element. However, for S.K., this is only a starting point, because dread is followed by sin, which in turn—for the Christian—issues in repentance and faith. This makes dread fundamentally preparatory, and the sin which may emerge from it is the very beginning of religious experience. Sin is recognized as such only in a distinctively Christian kind of awareness. It is not a mere sense of guilt (as failure), but a sense of wilful disruption of the relation to God and thereby a radical sickness of the self and a violation of its proper nature. It is in turn only the believing that one's sins are forgiven which gives spiritual maturity, in that this experience gives a fuller self-awareness. Therefore, sin is not simply a misdemeanour which is forgiven and then has no further significance; instead, in forgiveness there occurs a revelation of man's state of radical alienation from his proper self and from God, together with a divine healing of this disease.[129] It is precisely because of the radical character of dread and sin that they throw open the door to the holy, and it is the subsequent sin, forgiveness and spiritual clarity which Kierkegaard stresses over mere anxiety.

If for Kierkegaard dread is a starting-point for spiritual realization (dread, sin, repentance, faith), yet dread does not cause sin, nor does sin cause repentance. Each comes in a free movement. Further, there is a proper order but no simple succession among these experiences. From penitence one can again revert to sin (and to dread), perhaps more easily for having faltered in this way before; the path is now well trodden and easily followed. It should be noted that to return to dread is not necessarily to return to sin, nor is the return to dread necessarily a retrogression. Since dread helps man to be *spirit*, i.e. a creature facing the possibilities of his own being and freedom, *great dread* is a quality of a spiritually great person. That Christ in Gethsemane suffered in agony as he contemplated the possibilities of the future emphasizes the fact that dread is not evil but is instead an aspect of spiritual responsibility. Dread helps one understand where he stands, where he ought to go, and thus prepares the way for the life of holiness.

In attempting to account for sin, mankind's common speculative error is to explain its coming about by a series of, in themselves, pretty, little, innocent changes. Such thinking 'paints a fantastic picture of *how* man was before the Fall, and gradually, as the understanding chatters about it, the assumed innocence becomes little by little, in the course of the twaddle, sinfulness—and so there it is'. (P. 29) In contrast, the Genesis account is frank and consistent, holding that 'sin came into the world by a sin', i.e. 'sin presupposes itself'. (P. 29) This makes it clear that evil is not caused by good, or a mere lack of goodness; nor is it brought about by a kind of unfortunate oversight or accident. Nothing but evil can cause evil. There is no gradation by easy, if careless, little steps from good to evil. When evil occurs there is a radical change. Sinfulness came to Adam precisely by his first sin, so that the unprecipitated 'leap' or deed is a new and evil quality. However, to deny that there are quantitative gradations from innocence to evil does not mean that there are no gradations of evil in any sense. Thus there is a merely ethical guilt which emerges, for example, when one comes to hate the good which he also loves. Such guilt is not yet sin because it is not an act *before God*. True sin is no mere misdeed or accumulation of misdeeds but is a rejection of eternal responsibility. Only defiance of the transcendent brings one to sin, and here the 'very least guilt' constitutes a total alienation from God. The 'smallest' guilt, if it is before God, has an absolute quality, just as the widow's penny represents a complete or absolute gift to God.[130]

If sin is an act of alienation of oneself from God, it seems to follow that all men have the same experience of sin which Adam had. They too lose innocence only by personal guilt, and for men who have leaped into sin to then idly speculate as to what might have occurred if Adam had not fallen is to sinfully attempt to be 'spectators' of Adam rather than being penitents. Adam does not cause his children to sin. Neither is any tempter responsible for one's sin because in the temptation the tempter 'really said nothing'; he only presented the nothingness which makes one giddy.[131] Prior to the plunge into sin a person is in a state of ignorance or dreaming. So long as one remains in this state of innocence one only dreams of the possible, and is ignorant in that there is as yet no actual object to be apprehended. What then is one specifically anxious about? 'Nothing. But what effect does nothing [i.e. the existential alternatives] produce? It begets dread. This is the profound secret of innocence, that at the same time it is dread. Dreamingly the spirit projects its own reality, but this reality is nothing, but this nothing constantly sees innocence outside of it.' (P. 30) Animals have no dread because they lack spirit, and children manifest dread as a 'thirst for the prodigious, the mysterious'.

Even though Adam did not cause every man's sin, yet there is a kind of inherited sin. On the one hand, Kierkegaard claims that it is not guilt which is inherited, because each man can be responsible only for his own deeds. What is received from Adam is dread, spirit, sexuality, knowledge of good and evil, and oneness with the human race. In order to acknowledge that sinfulness is somehow transmitted and yet is always a free act, S.K. identified the effect of *original* sin as dread. It is the kind of mental state out of which sin can emerge, while the actual sin remains a free deed. Yet inherited sin remains a paradox for S.K., defying reason in that it combines the ethical (guilt arising from free choice) with the biological (hereditary determination).[132] Inheritance of sin stands essentially for the continuity of the race; every man is an Adam, and is both an individual and a part of the race. (Pp. 26, 30 f.) No one lives unto himself alone. The race is so unified that even Eve is described as derived from Adam, and the individual discovers the race within himself even though he is responsible for what he is and becomes as an individual. Man is free, yet finds in himself a despoiled creation, a corruption which is the legacy of the race.

In the concept of original sin, Kierkegaard makes manifest and seeks to overcome an apparently contradictory duality, which presumably is paradox although not being precisely so designated. He is insistent that sin cannot be explained by a cause other than itself or by anything outside the person, for then sin would not be sin and would not involve guilt. Yet he cannot simply dispose of original sin. He regarded it as paradoxically true that there is a guilt in original sin, so that guilt is inherited.[133] At this point of difficulty, an understanding of S.K.'s motive is important. As explained above, he had not wanted to deny the inheritance of a common corruption, but he did want to make it clear that every man sins by a free act and is personally responsible. The problem is that if subsequent sinfulness is an effect caused by Adam's sin, then such 'sinfulness' is determined whereas the original sin was free, in which case the two must be thought of as essentially different. All genuine sinfulness must retain the same freedom which the original sin had. What S.K. is protesting against is the thought that by consequence of Adam's sin his children are so lost in a state devoid of freedom that they cannot responsibly act. S.K. concludes by insisting that Adam is *inside* the race, not prior to it, and that every man is at the same time both himself and the race.

Kierkegaard certainly throws himself open to the accusation that by equating original sin with dread he has in fact abandoned the doctrine or original sin, and that his 'adherence to this doctrine is purely verbal'.[134] Yet his struggling assertion that man nevertheless *inherits* guilt makes it clear that the charge must not be carelessly made. The historic doctrine of original sin may well be paradoxical, and S.K.'s interpretation may thus understandably contain an element of inconsistency. Further, a counter charge might well be made against his critics. As S.K. himself puts it, if Adam's children are sinners simply because of what Adam did, then they are not really sinful at all because they are not personally responsible. Whatever judgment be made regarding the success of S.K.'s involved arguments and the problem of paradox in them, his points are impressive, viz. that sin must always be sin and involve personal responsibility, whether in Adam or his descendants, that Adam must somehow be viewed as within the race rather than prior to it, and yet that guilt is somehow inherited.

Particularly in view of Kierkegaard's inclination towards asceticism in his later years, the special connotations of sin presented in this work are important. Even in this early writing a negative attitude towards the sensual is prominent. Sin is identified as a disruption of spirit with a concomitant falling into sensuousness and sexuality. This does not mean that sensuousness or sex are in themselves evil. What is intended is that sensuousness is a basis for dread in that it epitomizes enslavement to the bodily, the temporal and the finite, and that sexuality represents the most extreme form of this enslavement. (Pp. 44, 65) Sexuality, as treated here, is not biological sex, which man shares with the non-moral animals and which he must have had prior to sin. Human sexuality involves a deformation by sin, and reveals an evil halo over man's potentialities. All sensuous capacities—including sex as the most intense sensuous experience—are fraught with evil if also ideal possibilities. The monk may try vainly to live as if sex were unreal, on the ground that in heaven it will be non-existent. (P. 63 f.) However, this is futile in that it disregards the actual and good order of creation. The proper task of spirit is not to denounce sex or the life of the senses but to bring them 'into conformity with the destiny of spirit' in such manner, in the former instance, that triumphant love becomes, in a manner, forgetful of the sexuality which supports but also threatens it.

Inescapably involved in the states of true sensuousness and sexuality are an improper yielding to the finite and a forgetting of the eternal. The bodily life is in itself good, but the proper goal of spirit involves mastering of bodily impulses because they are momentary, involving temporary rather than eternal goals. The basic principles which S.K. enunciates are those of proper balance, with absolute commitment to the eternal and relative commitment to the temporal. However, already in *Dread*, S.K. seems to falter in his earlier (cf. treatment of *Fear and Trembling*) glorification of the normal and universal duties of an earthly and temporal nature, moving in the direction of the later asceticism.

A final consideration regarding sin is the unique temporal sequence it may exist in as related to dread. Although S.K. initially treats dread as anxiety *before* guilt, he also points out that dread remains after sin. When sin occurs its actuality is still a kind of 'nothingness' in that it is an illegitimate reality before which the spirit quails. Dread can then appear in a variety of forms. On the one hand it can serve as a support for repentance and faith, the latter being possible—in the strict sense—only for the sinner. As the sinner places his trust in God's forgiveness and seeks to follow Christ in suffering obedience, dread of the evil to which he is still bound offers support for a Christian life. On the other hand, faith can be threatened by continuing dread, as one dreads the good which is laying hold upon him. In such dread of the good, S.K. sees the aesthetic life coming to its ultimate finality. At this point, when one so unrelentingly clings to the worldly as to reject the eternal, he is not merely in despair; his state is precisely demonic. (P. 137)

This dread which occurs as a result of sin is referred to as subjective dread. It contrasts with objective dread which is

THE AESTHETIC LITERATURE

possessed simply through one's membership in the human race and which is the condition out of which actual sin emerges. Strangely, in view of S.K.'s usual opposition to Platonic perspectives, his view of subjective dread is reminiscent of Neoplatonic notions of spirit gazing down into the mirror of dead matter, becoming enamoured of its own image and thereby falling. Dread, either prior to sin or after sin, is a dizziness of freedom, when freedom 'gazes down into its own possibility, grasping at finiteness to sustain itself'. (P. 55) In this dizziness freedom may succumb.

15. PREFACES

> *Prefaces.* Light Reading for the Different Classes at their Time and Leisure. By Nicolaus Notabene. June 17, 1844. Not translated; portions quoted are translated by Paul David Johnson. Appears in Vol. 5 of *Vaerker*.

This whimsical work was made to 'accompany' *Concept of Dread* (published the same day), perhaps partly to counterbalance the gravely serious character of that work. As a rule, an aesthetic work was accompanied by a discourse or sermon, but how unlike a sermon *Prefaces* is! The explanation is that *Dread*, even though regarded by S.K. as aesthetic—perhaps because of its psychological nature—was still too religious, too serious and direct, to have a sermonic accompaniment. Therefore it was given this ultra-aesthetic accompaniment, by which S.K. had the opportunity to manifest a lighter and more whimsical side of his personality.

The author professes to confine himself to the writing of a series of prefaces, on the ground that he had promised his wife not to write a book. Why would a budding author make so strange a promise? Because his pleading wife could not endure the book as a rival for her husband's affections. An author, she says, is even worse as a husband than a man who spends his evenings at his club because the author is absent even when he is at home, staring into space like 'Nebuchadnezzar reading the invisible writing'. To be an author when one is a husband is open infidelity.

Happily, the author finds a certain gain in being able to write only prefaces. For the reader what unexpected gain if he could limit himself to prefaces and not bother with the books introduced by them! Certainly it would be a delight unintended by the authors. Prefaces have a quality all their own, are much more subject to literary fashions than are the books themselves. 'Now they were long, now short, now daring, now shy, now still, now careless, now worried almost repentant, now overly confident...'

What is a preface? It is a lyric. 'A preface is a mood. To write a preface is like sharpening a scythe, like tuning a guitar, like chatting with a child, like spitting out the window. One doesn't know how it happens, the desire just comes, the desire to write a preface, the desire for these silent whispers when the night falls. To write a preface is like ringing someone's doorbell to fool him; like walking by the window of a young girl and looking at the cobblestones, it is like swinging a cane in the air against the wind, like tipping your hat without greeting anybody. To write a preface is like having done something which deserves a certain amount of attention; like having something on your conscience which tempts intimacy...; it's like standing on Valby Bakke looking for the wild geese.'

'Like this it is to write prefaces; and what about the one who writes them? He appears and disappears between people like a crocus after winter and a fool during summer. He is hello and goodbye in one person, always happy and carefree, pleased with himself, really a light-hearted do-nothing...'

Although this strange work (who other than S.K. would write a book consisting only of a series of prefaces?) is full of fun and irony, it actually represented much more than that. There are shrewd and sarcastic observations about Hegelian philosophy which could begin with nothing and conclude with the Absolute, about authors, and most particularly about literary reviewers and critics. The reading public receives its share of sarcasm in the suggestion that it finds a book useful, at least as a New Year's present and as a supposed proof of culture, if not for reading.

The immediate source of the book's inspiration was the error of S.K.'s friend, Professor Heiberg, who reviewed S.K.'s *Repetition* but missed the whole point of the book. Heiberg felt that the author had rather lost himself at just the point where Kierkegaard had in fact turned from jest to earnestness, i.e. from the aesthetic to the religious view of repetition.[135] On first reading Heiberg's review S.K. thought of replying to it in a book which was to be entitled 'New Year's Gift', with Nicolaus Notabene listed as the author and with an indication that it was published 'for the benefit of the asylums'.[136] This plan eventually gave way to the volume of *Prefaces*, in which Heiberg as well as others became an object of painful satire. Earlier, says author Notabene, he had rested in a festive mood of admiration for the professor, i.e. after he had succeeded in comprehending him. More recently, however, he has felt inadequate even to make a firm conclusion and so suspends judgment as to whether the melancholy of the times will be overcome by the professor's later 'astronomical, astrological, chiromantic, necromantic, horoschopic, metascopical, chronological studies'. However that may be, it is nevertheless a stroke of luck, thinks Notabene, if not for astronomy, then for theology, that Professor Heiberg has taken up astronomy.

16. FOUR EDIFYING DISCOURSES

> *Four Edifying Discourses*. By S. Kierkegaard. August 31, 1844. Translated by David F. and Lillian Marvin Swenson in *Edifying Discourses*, Minneapolis: Augsburg Publishing House, 1945; 1962 (volumes reduced from four to two in 1962 ed.). The first discourse also appears in *Edifying Discourses, A Selection*, ed. by Paul L. Holmer. New York: Harper & Brothers, 1958, Harper TB 32. These four together with the previous fourteen discourses were soon collected by S.K. in one volume of eighteen *Edifying Discourses*. (Page references are to Vol. IV of the 1945 edition.)

This volume develops in simple religious phrasing that which Kierkegaard later put in brilliant but abstract Hegelian form in *Sickness Unto Death*. Its thought is that to be human is to be stretched taut between heaven and earth. The tension is acute. The struggle is bitter. However, the godly man succeeds in attaining the heavenly goal *in that* God succeeds in conquering him.

KIERKEGAARD'S AUTHORSHIP

The first meditation, entitled 'Man's Need of God Constitutes His Highest Perfection', is the most profound of these discourses. Its accent is on heaven, on man's yearning for it, and on God's strange way of drawing man to himself. By himself (as mind and body) man cannot master himself. To attain his true nature he must be born of the spirit, so that the new 'spirit' self conquers through response to God. The outward self must come to nought while the spirit becomes sanctified by God's love through a 'strenuous re-acquirement of one's self'.

Yet what is to turn man to the eternal when, although destined for it, he remains infatuated with earthly glory and outward things? 'Does not the eye aim its arrows outward every time... desire stretches the bowstring?' (P. 23) The answer is that man has a need for the eternal, which constitutes his greatest perfection but which is most deeply stirred only on the occasion of earthly loss.

Man is but a babe—in spite of middle age or advanced years—being weaned from earth, a child lying 'at the breast of time in the cradle of the finite'. For the child of earth, life for a time may be enchantingly beautiful, but as pains of disappointment arise he is taught to die to the world so that eternal life can take possession of the soul. (P. 34) In a famous passage in *Fear and Trembling*, obviously related to this, it is told how a mother may blacken her breast so that the infant will no longer desire it.[137] By analogy, man, at the breast of the temporal, craves earthly bliss, but God seeks to wean him for the larger life. To attain the realization of need-for-the-holy is to be perfected, and become suited for fellowship with God. Thus a lack, a state of need, is the beginning of fulfilment; it is man's greatest perfection in that it turns him from transitory values to the eternal.

The message of this notable but edifying rather than specifically Christian discourse is, for Kierkegaard, an unqualified truth, yet it is incompletely stated. The need for God, expressed in a new aspiration for the Eternal, is indeed the highest perfection of man as he enters the portals of religion for the first time (religiousness A or general religiosity). However, when he discovers in bitterness that he cannot attain God by his striving then his highest perfection takes on a new form, that of need for God as a Christ or saviour (Christianity—religion B). This unstated fact becomes evident only in the later writings.

THE AESTHETIC LITERATURE

The next discourse, 'The Thorn in the Flesh', extends the previous theme but with an earthly application. If man's head is above the stars, his feet drag in the muck. St Paul's irremovable 'thorn' is a reminder that even an apostle may not remain in the 'third heaven', and that the union of earthly life with eternal happiness is always an unstable marriage. Man looks for tranquility, but lo things change! Yet the thorn in the flesh is not without meaning; it is given so that one will not be exalted above measure. No one should wish for the most deeply spiritual life—like that of Paul—unless he is willing to have the heaviest suffering. 'God deals with a man as the hunter and the hunted: He pursues it to exhaustion, then he gives it a little breathing time to gather new strength, and then the chase begins again.' Whatever the thorn which wounds the flesh may be, the man of faith shall find that the wound may work for good, so that God's grace is sufficient.

Because of the familiarity of the Biblical 'thorn', Kierkegaard's position will almost certainly be misunderstood by the reader. Is it not an accident if one has a painful thorn in his flesh? St Paul's reference suggests a unique affliction. However, this is exactly contrary to Kierkegaard's meaning. The thorn of which he speaks comes to all by birth, for through birth man becomes 'exposed to the danger in which he now is'. (P. 77 f.) Such universal suffering results from dread and the perilous tension between time and eternity. 'To have been made unutterably rich in God, and now to be crushed to flesh and blood, to dust and corruption!' (P. 61) This outcry has the ring of Schopenhauer's protest against existence, but the fact is otherwise. Earthly existence is a mysterious blend of anguish and lovely dreams, of creation and despair. It is 'beautiful enough as a halting place for one who expects an eternity, but not beautiful enough to make a man forget that he is still only on the way'.[138]

More important still, suffering must be seen in relation to sin from which it results and to salvation to which it points. Until one recognizes that suffering is related to guilt he wrongly thinks of it as a mere externally caused misfortune.[139] Yet the thorn in the flesh is not mere punishment. It may even be a blessing, if it helps the believer to sense his guilt and keeps him in fear and trembling before the holy God. (Pp. 53 ff.) Since Christ came to save sinners, the suffering which restores man to awareness of sin is also a means to reconciliation, only, however, if one dutifully accepts the suffering and turns it to good purpose.

The third discourse is entitled 'Against Cowardice'. It intends to answer the question of how man can be faithful in the difficult marriage of earth and heaven. Cowardice is the great danger against which the striver must be on guard in the midst of tensions between guilt and faith. Cowardice keeps a man from knowing what is good. It prevents him from doing good, and even from acknowledging the good which he does. In courage one should dare to champion the good in the face of the world's misunderstanding or contempt, recognizing that the suffering is 'an ordeal from the hand of God'. The righteous man may cringe before the noisy tumult. It is difficult to endure the scoffing of sinners. Yet courage can be born anew by one's retiring to inwardness and silence. 'Everything which is good in man begins in silence, and it is fit that God essentially dwells in secret, so also the good in a man dwells in secret.' (P. 104) How distressing it is if one lets the tumult of life break his courage, so that he loses the God who dwells in secret!

The final discourse deals with spiritual culmination. Its vivid theme is 'The Righteous Man Strives in Prayer with God and Conquers—in that God Conquers'. The earnestness of prayer, its striving character, and its paradoxical submissiveness are set forth. In prayer man strives and conquers, but only by being conquered by God. 'Or was it not a victory, that instead of receiving an explanation from God, he was himself transfigured in God, which transfiguration consists in this: that he reflects God's image?' (P. 142) Far from involving paradox or trickery, the discourse sets forth a simple principle, the theme already developed in the first discourse, of man's being weaned from time to eternity. The earnest man strives, pleading for the granting of whatever he may passionately desire or bitterly need. Yet in the dialogue of silent denial and qualified approval, the man of prayer begins to learn that the longing in which he strove has begun to slip away. Not knowing how he should rightly pray, the man of prayer nevertheless receives the correct answer from God, and eventually learns to ask for the good gift which he may already have received. That which is granted him is an inwardness which has

THE AESTHETIC LITERATURE

the constancy of the eternal and which thereby reflects the image of the divine. (P. 142) Dag Hammarskjöld has given a vivid negative expression of this same thought: 'Your cravings as a human animal do not become a prayer just because it is God whom you ask to attend them.'[140] God himself is the only adequate object of man's concern. Therefore, at its best, prayer goes beyond petitions and becomes silent adoration for the reason that there is no longer anything for which one can pray.[141]

17. THOUGHTS ON CRUCIAL SITUATIONS IN HUMAN LIFE

Three Discourses on Imagined Occasions. By S. Kierkegaard. April 29, 1845. In English: *Thoughts on Crucial Situations in Human Life.* Translated by David F. and Lillian Marvin Swenson. Minneapolis: Augsburg Publishing House, 1941. The second discourse also appears in *Edifying Discourses, A Selection*, ed. by Paul L. Holmer: Harper & Brothers, 1958, Harper TB 32.

It is strange irony that this wonderful little book in which Kierkegaard offered answers to some of the profound questions raised in the *Stages* was rather ignored, the more strange in view of its great beauty. Reflecting in turn on a confession of sin, a wedding, and a funeral, it explains: (1) what it means to seek God, (2) that love conquers all, and (3) the decisiveness of death. In fact, the three discourses somewhat exemplify S.K.'s three stages of existence. Wonder (seeking God) represents the aesthetic awareness of reality, manifesting desire. Married love represents *ethical* duty, although reaching beyond it. Death stands for the eternal and its impingement upon man in judgment and redemption, and thus represents *religious* fulfilment. Nevertheless, it is to be noted that these discourses, like the *Edifying Discourses*, are not 'fully' Christian in that they do not develop the more specifically Christian categories such as atonement.

The first discourse, 'On the occasion of a confessional service', portrays *natural* religiosity as wonder. This discourse is not an ecclesiastical commentary on the practice of confession, but is instead an existential exploration of what happens to man when his wistful wonder succeeds in coming into the fear and bliss of God's presence. (P. 13) At its most elementary level the experience is a sense of the awesome in nature, reflecting S.K.'s poetic sensitivity to nature, which expressed itself in love of woodlands, lakes, and quiet flower gardens.[142] 'When the forest darkens in the evening hour and the moon loses itself among the trees, when the natural magic of the forest seizes its prey, and the pagan suddenly sees a wonder...then he sees the unknown, and expresses his wonder in worship.' (P. 13 f.) Wonder is the sense which in unreflective immediacy one has of the divine, and it is a kind of awe before the Unknown.[143] This thought is similar to that of R. Otto's *Das Heilige*, yet is more sensitively developed and shows more appreciation of the bliss element which S.K. relates ambiguously to fear.

In this primitive and imaginative pagan consciousness God comes to be 'the inexplicable whole of existence'. Whatever overpowers the soul whispers of God. 'When the sea lies deep and still, inexplicable, when the wondering mind gazes dizzily down into its depths until the unknown seems rising up to meet it, when the breakers roll monotonously over the beach, overwhelming the soul..., when the rushes whisper in the wind and again whisper, and therefore must wish to confide something to the listener—then he worships.' (P. 14) However, when the wondering soul turns seeker and intently strives after the unknown, trying to turn the faint intimations of God into open vision, then the unknown vanishes. Enchantment is lost and the straining and striving become filled with distress. As wonder ends in seeking, so seeking ends in despair, a despair which seems to say that there is no wonder. At this point the relation of natural religion to Christianity begins to take form in S.K.'s perspective. While his contemporary Albrecht Ritschl was arriving at the astonishing conclusion that Christianity's revelation discloses what all men should already have understood, viz. the completely unmiraculous fact that God is loving, Kierkegaard focused on the quite unlike natures of natural religion and Christianity. The latter is not merely a deeper form of natural religion, or a reminder of its truth. Christianity is instead the miraculous attainment of that existence, of which natural religion wistfully dreams or towards which it vainly strives.

THE AESTHETIC LITERATURE

The sense of wonder in nature is a crucial point. The above passage pertaining to the sea, like that about the lovely forest nook in the *Stages*, reveals a rare poetic sensitivity. Yet S.K. vehemently repudiated romanticism's notion that God discloses himself in nature or can be proved by its evidence. Instead of sharing romanticism's feeling of kinship between man and nature, S.K. agreed with Pascal—or Bertrand Russell—on man's lonely unlikeness to nature. Man is a 'wanderer' who is overawed by the majesty of the stars but has a melancholy awareness that the universe does not understand him and can come to no agreement with him.[144] She does not hear man's dying scream or whimper in the vast unfeeling silences. Do the trees, in their whisperings, have something to confide? 'I do not hear the trees in the woods relating to me old legends.' All they can whisper is 'the twaddle they have so long been witnesses of'.[145] Elsewhere S.K. indicates that God alone and not nature is the ultimate object of wonder, which wonder is so natural to man as to be characteristic of youth and never absent in the grown man unless wilfully violated.[146]

In its preliminary stage, wonder is profoundly aesthetic, the mood of childhood and of the poet. Its culmination is a passionate grasping towards God as 'the inexplicable whole of existence, as sensed by the imagination in the least and the greatest everywhere', comparable to the mysterious Tao which the Chinese philosopher Chuangtzu sensed making its presence felt in the commonest things of experience. (P. 14) The very sense of wonder obliges the soul to seek after that which is already present, for that which is wonderful is elusive. Yet to engage in seeking spoils the wonder, interrupts it, by placing the wonderful beyond reach. It is for this reason that all primitive religion begins in wonder, continues in seeking, and ends in guilt, idolatry, superstition and despair. (Pp. 12–15) What happened in pagan religion occurs also in the late adolescence of the youth who likewise comes to despair on finding that wonder vanishes when he deliberately sets out to find it. The youth becomes a tragic positivist as he becomes a man, seeing the glorious Unknown turn into an incomprehensible and meaningless nothing. Then the springtime of youth is lost and the young person becomes an 'eternity old'. (P. 16)

If wonder in nature is lost to the seeker it is still available to him in an unexpected place, viz. within himself, where God turns seeker. As wonder in nature leads to superstition, so that natural religion becomes a kind of idolatry (and polytheism or pantheism), the wonder of God in nearness to the self remains both blessed and fearful. Inward wonder is not an awed stillness before the majesty of the mountains; it is a stillness where the soul is naked before God, surrounded by the silences of the eternities, and where God's judgment breathes through the solitude. (P. 4) It is fearful to gain this solitude because in it one discovers that man *was* the place where God was to be found, but now man has changed. Inward wonder is therefore replaced by guilt. As this change occurs, seeking God becomes confession, for man discovers in his guilt that God is seeking him out. 'No man can see God without purity, and . . . no man can know God without becoming a sinner.' (P. 9)

For the sinner to receive the seeking God requires penitential sorrow and sincerity which are found only in the solitude where one is alone with God. A dying man whose bed is surrounded by his family still dies alone. Similarly, a person making confession is as solitary as the dying man because each guilty man must give his own accounting. (P. 2) Yet in a wonderful way, by entering the stillness of solitude, each man becomes identical with his neighbours, sharing with them the joy and peace of the eternal. Not in social activism, but only in prayerful solitude is a beautiful concord with men to be found.

Even if it must be by solitary confession, is it not more wonderful that after nature's radiance has turned to ashes man can still find wonder in himself? Perhaps the crux of the new wonder is that one actually possesses what he aspires towards and what he violates, viz. the presence of God. (P. 19) Instead of tracking down the deity, man trembles over being himself the locus of the divine. (P. 20) Such a one asks for no proofs of God. In fact, to try to 'prove' God would be to ignore him. It would demonstrate that the reasoner is unwilling to confront him. 'Proofs of God are wrongly based for they seek intellectual conviction, the possession of an overwhelming idea. Instead, God must be dealt with in terms of his sovereign moral will and grace.' (P. 21) As primitive or natural wonder was destroyed by reason, so, in this second stage, wonder over the inward life can be nullified by reason. As the aesthetic experience of wonder culminates in despair, so too

THE AESTHETIC LITERATURE

ethical wonder can issue in its own form of despair and, hopefully, in repentance which is the characteristic feature of 'religion A'. In this writing Kierkegaard does not press his analysis to the point of indicating the wonder which is inherent in the distinctive Christian categories (e.g. atonement, love and paradox), although obviously he could have done so. In fact, whereas for Hegel wonder gives way to comprehension as faith is replaced by knowledge, for S.K. wonder grows more profound as religion becomes more authentic.[147]

The second 'crucial situation' which is explored in this volume pertains to a wedding, and its concern is not sentiment but ethical duty. The theme is 'Love conquers all'. S.K. agrees with his 'Judge William' of *Either/Or* that in marriage love becomes duty, but here he goes farther in stressing religious earnestness (rather than humanistic happiness), and also (characteristic of the life of faith) he makes the duty not a once-for-all resolution but a daily commitment. 'The marriage pledge is indeed like a garland of everlastings, but love weaves it, and duty says it must be woven—each day from the blossoms of the moment.' (P. 44) Mere lovers are unconcerned about the future, unconcerned about a promise or a curse; yet marriage introduces these serious terms.

Kierkegaard's treatment of marriage is impressively unlike that of the general world of literature. In popular fiction courtship is generally the greatest of all themes, but for both the aesthetic and moral sense of Kierkegaard it is marriage which is the more challenging. Romantic novelists have pictured the course of *true love* as a struggle to overcome every obstacle (in earlier India even the obstacle of the first wife), thereupon living 'happily ever afterward'. In sensual fiction the interest is in *false love*, treated with neither the delicacy nor the understanding which appear in S.K.'s gifted treatment of seduction. S.K.'s view of marriage looks to an existential growth in love, not an automatic happiness but a dedication before God. Marriage is transfigured by the eternal and from the eternal it gains the enablement for growth in beauty. Marriage is not mere love, nor even is it love plus a wedding vow. Marriage imposes the duty to daily renew before God the garland of everlastings with the blossoms of the moment. Even successful marriage has no complacent status but involves a daily earnest endeavour. Thus to consult God about one's love does not merely serve to arrest attention and to quicken the conscience. Instead, it makes the marriage relationship (as should be the case in any other relationship) a part of one's God-relation, so that the marriage not only fulfils the will of God but is a means for expression of one's God-relationship.

If Kierkegaard finds unexpected solemnity in a wedding, so 'At the Side of a Grave', the last essay, portrays less of sorrow than most people would expect to find in it. At the grave, S.K. finds hope, and vastly more of earnestness than is the case with most mourners. Jaspers and Heidegger have learned from him the decisiveness of death, with the ensuing realization that to exist in earnest is to live in view of one's own dying, in such fashion that one's life can be seen in its totality of meaning. When death comes it will not permit one to add a letter to the story of a life.

It is particularly important that for Kierkegaard the decisiveness of death does not stand for oblivion. Unlike Jaspers and Heidegger, S.K. does not regard death as 'nothing'. Death does reduce vanity to lowly equality, yet earnest faith sees in this fact a beautiful symbol of equality before God. Consciousness of death becomes an earnest call to responsibility. Whereas Johannes the Seducer had advocated uninhibited fun, S.K. says that since in the grave there is no remembrance, 'not even of God', that one should be faithful in remembering God while he yet lives. Finally, the meanings to be found in inexplicable death, whether terrifying, peaceful, or hopeful, cannot be learned by rote, nor by reading, but only 'by him who worked himself weary in the service of the good'. Dag Hammarskjöld has given a close parallel to S.K.'s thought: 'There is only one path out of the steamy jungle where the battle is fought over glory and power and advantage—one escape from the snares and obstacles you yourself have set up. And that is—to accept death.'[148]

Even Marjorie Grene—no disciple of Kierkegaard!—notes that he comes to close grips with reality in taking seriously man's deep consciousness of death, his being afloat over the perilous '70,000 fathoms', in contrast to the shallow comfortableness of pragmatism which passes by on the other side when death or sin puts in its appearance.[149]

18. STAGES ON LIFE'S WAY

Stages on Life's Way. Studies by Sundry Persons, Collected, forwarded to the press and published by Hilarius Bookbinder. April 30, 1845. Translated by Walter Lowrie. Princeton: Princeton University Press, 1940.

Almost any judgment can be made of this fantastic book. It is brilliant but at times tedious. It is almost shockingly candid and yet full of mystification and concealment. It is a kind of repetition of the aesthetic works but has new and astonishing contents. It lays bare Kierkegaard's sufferings in a way which will offend some readers, yet it is not an autobiography but instead a religious persuasion which aims to lead the reader out of the aesthetic life and even beyond merely moral existence. This book, somewhat repetitious of earlier writings, served to bring the problem of S.K.'s love to the religious solution which had, for the most part, been concealed in the earlier treatments.

'In Vino Veritas' (The Banquet), the first of three sections, represents the aesthetic life. It is a work of great artistry, modelled slightly after Plato's Symposium, although in no sense being dependent upon it. The Symposium praises love; the Banquet derides woman. The second (ethical) portion of the book is a defence of marriage by 'Judge William', and thus is a rebuttal of the Banquet which champions eroticism without a sense of responsibility. For S.K., as for Catholic mysticism, there were two understandings of woman, the temptress who leads man into sin and the mother who leads her child to God. This duality appears not only here and in *Either/Or* but is perhaps even more pronounced in S.K.'s final writings, particularly the *Instant* and the edifying discourse entitled 'The Woman that was a Sinner'.

Possibly less astonishing than the Banquet but more perplexing, and to some readers offensively personal, is the long final section of the *Stages* entitled 'Guilty?/Not Guilty?' which consists largely of Quidam's Diary. This is the record of S.K.'s own love affair, skilfully transformed into an artistic work, recording so intimately his relationship to Regine that perhaps it ought never have been published. In his defence it may be said that the furore of its critics seems grossly inappropriate on two counts. The first is that in his own day probably only one person other than Kierkegaard was able to clearly recognize the autobiographical nature of the diary. The other is that this 'diary' is not only a work of literary art but also a critically important treatment of the religious stage of experience. It presents religion not as a doctrine but instead as life experience.

In its entirety the *Stages* has a remarkable perfection of form. Its subtle and effective employment of varied literary devices and styles is perhaps as great or greater than in any of S.K.'s other writings. The large pieces of prose persuasion, diary, banquet speeches, epistle, and narrative are obvious. Less conspicuous are some of the smaller units, in particular certain short stories which are tucked into the diary, each one possessing a different form. Regarding these, F. J. Billeskov Jansen comments: 'With unrivalled skill he imitates in turn the Old Testament ('Solomon's Dream' and 'Nebuchadnezzar'), Herodotus ('Periander'), Shakespeare's King Lear on the heath ('A Leper's Soliloquy'), and the contemporary Danish novel ('A Possibility'). So great is the concern for style in these perfect *pastiches* that a gulf seems to separate the writer of the Diary from the six tableaux which he presents as his own work; the stylistic virtuosity here has to some extent had an effect contrary to that intended by the novelist.'[150]

In fairy-tale manner a group of strange friends attend a fantastic banquet, remarkable in every detail. The banquet is held at a lovely nook in a forest. 'Here it always is quiet, always beautiful, but most beautiful . . . now when the harvest sun holds a vesper service, and the sky turns a languishing blue; when the creatures take breath after the heat, when the coolness is released, and the leaves of the meadow shiver voluptuously, while the forest rustles; when the sun thinks of the evening when it will cool itself in the ocean, when the earth prepares for repose and thinks of thanksgiving...' (P. 34) The five banqueters arrive at a beautiful hall where intoxicating music, flowing wine, enchanting perfumes, and the choicest of foods help to set the stage for the heady speeches which follow. Their extreme and terrible exposes of woman and love are neither evil nor simply false. They are instead remarkable irony. They tell painful but needed half-truths which only a psychologist can ferret out, but they do so in a

THE AESTHETIC LITERATURE

derisive manner which by its very mockery calls for loving reassessment.

All of the speakers are 'aesthetes', i.e. they take a worldly view of woman, thereby excluding any sense of the spiritual. There is a progression in the speeches from the merely inexperienced to an attitude of utter contempt, a movement away from the spiritual. In Plato's Symposium, by contrast, the speeches on love move towards the spiritual. Each speaker is a sharply defined personality.[151] The 'young man' symbolizes the melancholy which rests in indecision regarding life's possibilities. Constantine, on the other hand, is illustrative of experience-hardened understanding. Victor represents sympathetic irony. The tailor stands for demonic despair, and Johannes represents cold-blooded evil.

It is evident that pleasure is only an 'either' (one of two alternatives) for all of the aesthetes. Clearly they are not animals following impulse, since they very well understand that there also exists an ethical 'or', which, however, they do not accept. S.K. sees their attitude as an avoidance of choice rather than an emphatic renunciation; it is dallying in pleasure. The aesthetic experience is that by which a man is immediately what he is.[152] Thus the aesthete is fully human, quite informed about values—perhaps even Christian values—but his being informed is no guarantee of his moving into a comprehended but more demanding realm of existence. Accordingly, the aesthetes exist only in the moment, enjoying that which presents itself rather than setting deliberate goals for themselves.[153] The closest that the aesthete can come to an either/or is, 'If you marry you will regret it; if you do not marry, you will also regret it'.[154]

The first speaker at the strange banquet is the 'young man' who has lived in abstract thought and knows little of the world or about love. He fears love and finds it ridiculous. He occupies himself with *reflection* and therefore avoids personal commitment (is non-ethical). He will not risk involving himself in the mysteries of love, marriage and paternity since he cannot 'understand' them, yet he senses the tragedy of his being surrounded by so great a force as love which he feels obliged to let pass him by. (P. 52) The young man observes that it is comical that the two 'halves' when united don't make a whole but 'one and a half'. People 'fall' into love, indeed with anyone, and end in momentous parenthood.

There is no reasonable explanation for love taking the specific direction that it does. Adam fell in love with Eve simply because there was no other lady available. If a man falls in love with a girl because of her femininity then he is not in love with a particular sweetheart but only with an instance of femininity, which is certainly no compliment to the sweetheart as a person.

The young man offers what may be taken as a shrewd and bitter commentary on the sex addicts of the twentieth—or any other—century, noting the fact that the race wins a victory over the individual (in reproduction) just when the individual had supposed that he had gained freedom and mastery. (P. 56) He also poses the impressive question for a confused and debauched age as to whether paternity should be viewed as the most terrible of eventualities, or, second, as an accident which befalls one, or indeed as the loftiest of all tasks. (P. 59)

The second speaker is Constantine (steadfast), who is also the host at the banquet. He also appears in the S.K. literature in the role of author of *Repetition*. Constantine is an abstract intellectualist, yet he experiments with life and subjects it to cold analysis. As opposed to man's steadfastness he sees in woman nothing but changeable twaddle. 'Far be it from her candid soul to want to deceive anyone, she meant all she said, now she says the contrary, but with the same lovable frankness, for she is ready to die for the contrary.' (P. 62) Woman may become transformed in a day, may go off like a rocket on New Year's Eve, and if she fizzles out in nonsense or unfaithfulness can anyone seriously challenge her to a duel? If woman be taken simply as a jest of the gods then she can be delightful, but if taken seriously she is dangerous. In view of her fickleness, to view woman ethically makes the entire matter a joke. Constantine clearly is in a kind of despair, for it cannot be really amusing that woman must be considered as a joke. The lover must make false aesthetic amusement out of what is actually an ethical tragedy, viz. that woman's 'seriousness' is never dependably serious. (P. 61) Perhaps as with Schopenhauer, seriousness is a pretence in an insecure endeavour to please. To make a game of provoking these deceits in woman is the greatest sport. (P. 64)

Victor Eremita is the next banquet speaker. He is a religious recluse, standing aloof from men and even more aloof from women. He is also the pseudonymous editor of *Either/Or*. Regarding marriage he notes that it involves the most incongruous features, including Christian duty and pagan sexuality, sentimentality and scheming convenience. Victor thanks God that he was not born so strange, mixed, complex a being as woman. She is never the same, moving from the ridiculous to the sublime, and thence to the trivial. First, a girl is an inferior boy, then she becomes exalted as an 'Empress in love's far-reaching realm of exorbitant speech, and titular Queen of all the exaggerations of tomfoolery', and finally turns out as plain Mrs Peterson on Bathhouse Street. (P. 69) Ideality comes into a man's life through a woman's influence, but not by means of the woman he marries. No poet ever became a poet because of the girl he got, 'for through her he only became a father'. Nor did any saint become holy by means of the girl he got, for surely a saint never married. (P. 70)

Woman's honour, says Victor, is her capacity (by simply appearing at the right moment, and at that by a stroke of luck—just any woman will do) to inspire ideality in man, to awaken his latent idealism, and even to arouse his consciousness of immortality. She is the inspiration of all poetry and song. However, if she marries the poor fellow who worships her, then life becomes humdrum for both of them. The only way to escape from the commonplace is for the beloved girl to die, thus remaining an ideal inspiration for her lover; or else to be unfaithful to him (the sooner the better) in order to give him ideality through pain. This thought is undoubtedly a strange projection of S.K.'s own suffering. Profoundly in love, yet unable to marry because of his feelings about his father's guilt and about the evil which infects human sexuality (and perhaps other reasons also), S.K. was doomed to an anxious poetic contemplation of love. Coming thus to a poetic awareness of existence which he could not otherwise have attained, he glorified the poetic approach to life even though he suffered under it.

The Ladies' Tailor, himself something of a dandy, veers towards bitterness. He says that woman is a silly creature of fashion, logically consistent only in becoming more and more crazy. Yet there is purpose in her madness. 'As in heathen Prussia a marriageable girl wore a bell which served as a signal to the men, so likewise is the existence of a woman of fashion a perpetual bell-ringing...' (P. 76) The sinister tailor delights in assisting woman in her madness. This feminine weakness is a moral degeneracy as woman uses even churchly attire as a status symbol and a means of rank over against her lowlier sisters, thus reducing even the holy to the contemptible and depraved.

The last speaker is Johannes the Seducer who professes to take woman just as she is. He does not belittle woman as do the other speakers but instead appreciates her, prostituting her to his own desire. Love, says he, is the highest enjoyment. A man who does not partake of it is a 'Wesleyan Methodist'. Love is not something to *think* about but something to zestfully experience, as suggested by an old song which says of a kiss: 'Es ist kaum zu sehen, es ist nur für Lippen, die genau sich verstehen.' The gods made woman 'delicate and ethereal as the mists of a summer's night and yet plump like a ripened fruit, light as a bird', yet they hid her perfection from her in the ignorance of innocence and modesty. (P. 85) She is a deception, irresistible by virtue of being resistant. Johannes makes it clear that he does not let himself become deeply involved emotionally, for then he could not contemplatively enjoy the situation. Thus he is a seducer, although he claims no great proficiency as such, indeed acknowledging his inferior skills in seduction. In *Either/Or* he explains: 'To love only one is too little; to love all of them is a surfeit; to know one's self and love as many as possible . . . so that each girl gets her own proper nourishment while the consciousness embraces the whole—that is enjoyment...'[155]

The strange addresses come to an end and the speakers fling their wine glasses from them in a kind of libation to the questionable gods of the underworld, then close the door to the nether regions. As they walk quietly homeward, they happen upon a scene of marital happiness and devotion, involving Judge William and his wife. Victor succeeds in stealing a manuscript which the judge had written. Finding that the manuscript contains a defence of marriage, Victor sees to it that it is added as a second and antithetical portion of the *Stages*.

Quite understandably, this contrasting treatise, 'Various Observations About Marriage in Reply to Objections', is an urgent moral protest and reply to the aesthetic banquet speeches. The judge defends love, but, far more emphatically, he portrays marriage as the highest goal of existence. Marriage requires 'resolution' in addition to the immediacy of love. The boasted 'ideality' of the aesthetes is a hollow mockery because ideality without resolution is insignificant. Through love's resolution the heavenly is disclosed. Love apart from marriage is commonly given too much praise. A seducer has such impudence as to think that he knows what true love is and also to presume to share in its delights. Although love is immediate and aesthetic and is essential to marriage, marriage represents an act of free commitment, an act of will, so that it does not simply issue from the love experience but is instead a religious dedication of life. Such an act of dedication is an attempt to bring the eternal and the absolute into temporal existence. In marriage the lovers *promise* to love, thereby giving a quality of finality to affection which is otherwise subject to change.

As opposed to a pessimistic Schopenhauer, the treatise argues that marriage enriches feminine loveliness. 'Woman as a bride is more beautiful than as a young girl, as a mother she is more beautiful than as a bride, as wife and mother she is a good word spoken in due season, and with the years she becomes more beautiful.' (P. 141) Love is a gift of God but it cannot be fully possessed apart from marriage, with the consequence that marriage becomes a sacred duty, although there are—as in Kierkegaard's own case—exceptions to this rule.

Judge William's enthusiasm for marriage has certainly not declined here, as compared with his views in *Either/Or*. However, he seems less confident of easy success in fulfilling the ethical responsibilities of marriage. He still insists that one can be a good husband in spite of his imperfections if he will humbly recognize his inadequacies. (P. 122) As if to counteract the dreadfully pointed attacks on woman in 'The Banquet' he presents a lyrical tribute to woman as godly mother. 'Mother-love is soft as pure gold, and malleable in every sense, and yet whole.' (P. 137)

Near the end of the 'Observations' there appears a mysterious and important digression which suggests that there may conceivably be a godly exception to the universal order of marriage. If there be such a man (S.K. himself), with a deeper understanding he will be able to speak of the glories of marriage, manifesting a fervour of which any married man is incapable. He must not fail to love the universal (i.e. to honour marriage), even though under some peculiar responsibility to God he makes himself an exception to it. It has been suggested that this departure from the ethical universal into *individual* religious responsibility represents a transition from the ethical to the specifically Christian. This is perhaps the case, and it is true that for S.K. the specifically Christian life involves severe individuality, suffering, and radical commitment, all of which are in contrast to the quiet peace of the ethical life. On the other hand, the specific insistence that the 'exception' must love the universal and wish to remain within it seems to make it incontrovertible that S.K. at least at this time, viewed the Christian life as normally incorporating the ethical universals, including marriage, while bestowing upon them a deeper religious sensitivity. (Pp. 173-75) Apart from this issue, it is notably true that the treatment of the ethical at this point brings one to reflect upon the religious stage which lies beyond it.

The final section of the *Stages* is 'Quidam's Diary'. The publisher, Frater Taciturnus (Brother Silent) gives a lyrical if fantastic account of how he found the diary in a lake. Accompanying a naturalist who was studying marine life, he had worked through a treacherous bog—a 'border conflict' between lake and land—coming at last to the emerald water where, in the awesome stillness 'the ear grasped in vain for a support in the infinite'. A heavy rosewood box, sealed in oilskin, became caught in the naturalist's equipment, and could scarcely be drawn from the bottom; it was as if the lake would yield its deep secret only with a sigh. When the beautiful box was broken open its key was found within! 'Thus it is that morbid reserve always is introverted.' (P. 182 f.) Among highly symbolic objects (a page of scripture, a withered rose, a jewelled cross—all telling of love, duty, and suffering) was a beautifully written diary which centred on the question whether a soldier who is likely to be killed in battle or a person warring with unconquerable melancholy (Quidam's case) has a right to marry and impose suffering on another soul. The issue arises only because *Christian* marriage imposes the duty of openness and candour.

Lest one take this unit to be simply S.K.'s exact diary, it is to be noted that it consists of three unlike but precisely blended portions. The elements of the first portion, all written of a morning, do read like exact recollections of S.K.'s romance, although as if

THE AESTHETIC LITERATURE

they were being recalled later, a year to the day. The second portion of the 'diary' consists of successive reflections written at the midnight hour, but now looking back to the broken engagement and seeking some healing for the broken heart. The third portion is a group of six stories (Solomon's Dream *et al.*) which symbolize the problems which emerged in S.K.'s childhood home.

In the entire authorship 'Quidam's Diary' is perhaps the truest expression of Kierkegaard's life and feeling. Almost offensively it tells the very words with which he tortured Regine and himself. Yet because the diary is so autobiographical it lacks some of the dramatic character of earlier writings. 'Quidam' is so truly S.K. that he lacks the vividness of type which marks the other pseudonyms; he is too complex and too genuinely human for that. If religion as an absolute individual responsibility to God shines forth in the diary, there is still concealed what this exceptionality involves for S.K. himself. Or rather, the sacrifice and sorrow which religion imposed on Kierkegaard are revealed in the mysterious stories which are so wonderfully formulated as to give revealment in concealment, all of them relating to S.K.'s sense of involvement in his father's guilt.

The diary is perhaps unduly extended. It endlessly turns upon itself in painfully sensitive analysis of moods, doubts, self-accusation and suffering. Yet it may be that the candour of the writing as well as its artistry helped prevent S.K.'s contemporaries from suspecting that it was literally the story of his own life. However one judges this baring of the heart, one should still realize that the writer's primary aim was a noble one, to carry the reader from aesthetic contemplation, through ethical commitment and its failure, towards the religious suffering through which God can save.

In the diary Kierkegaard describes, with understandable anonymity, the devious ways by which he thought of trying to solve his problems. For one, he thought that perhaps in marriage he could hide from Regine the deep melancholy relating to his father, shielding her from his secret sorrows. Then, in revulsion at the thought of such deception, he felt he could gain spiritual integrity only by sharing everything in love. In the end, he chose to do neither, but to humiliate himself before Regine in order to help her liberate herself from him and escape the burdens which love would impose upon her. His suffering finally succeeded in giving his beloved both freedom and eventual happiness. Yet this did not end S.K.'s difficulties, as Quidam makes clear. A more profound issue arose, as to the sense and degree of S.K.'s (Quidam's) own guilt in the matter. Each year he felt it necessary to retrace the sorrowful steps, repentant, yet unable to be certain of any guilt calling for repentance. (Pp. 240–45)

At this point the *Stages* becomes a forthright study of the religious stage of existence. Christianity is a special God-relation which does not actually solve earthly problems but gives the spiritual composure by which suffering can be endured. God is not 'a dear old grandpapa' who indulges people, but one who educates the soul for communion with the divine by means of the discipline of faith in the midst of suffering. The sense of the religious is here more personal and existential than in *Fear and Trembling*. In that work God speaks to Job in the distant voice of thunder. Here his voice, indeed grounded in scripture, comes to express itself through inwardness and conscience. God speaks not from the transcendent heights but from the inner transcendence of an inviolable voice. God uses man against himself, speaking through the mysteries and inwardness of his life, requiring him to stand in lonely individuality before the infinite. (P. 342 f.)

Perhaps the most distinctive—and disturbing—feature in this outlook is that whereas God was initially thought of as offering a solution for suffering, now a second kind of suffering, divinely imposed, is thought of. The Christian life comes to be viewed as distinctively marked by suffering. The deeper the suffering the greater is the religious awareness, even though this suffering is transfigured in holy joy.[156] Lest a psychoanalytic bent cause the interpreter to read sheer morbidity into this deviation from the psychology of 'adjustment' (Was any noble man ever well 'adjusted'?), we may be reminded, first, that suffering is thought of by S.K. as resulting from sinful deviation from moral law; second, that his account treats *Christian* suffering as a distinct category, sharply distinguished from all other kinds of suffering; and third, that for him suffering is not an end in itself but a means of weaning one from ego-centric desire to the love of God. Finally, he would add, not only are earthly joys ennobled and earthly sorrows made spiritually meaningful but also all of existence is given the security of eternal blessedness through one's God-relation.[157]

THE AESTHETIC LITERATURE

Reflection on suffering is particularly prominent in the difficult but important epistle by Frater Taciturnus, attached to the diary. The ordinary (aesthetic) view of suffering is that it is a misfortune which accidentally befalls one. The aesthete wants to know nothing of suffering, although he might find the persecution of a hero interesting. On the other hand, the religious man does not grieve over misfortune for he understands that before God all men alike are 'exposed to the blows of fate'. What he does grieve over is his inward guilt, a guilt which becomes transparent as he stands before God. At the same time the Christian is joyful, although his torment is that he stops halfway, guiltily failing to press through to the joy made available to him by God. The religious experience is thus a conflicting duality; the joy of God's presence is counterbalanced by the falterings of one's own faith. If this religious transformation of Kierkegaard's own suffering is disturbing, at least it must be acknowledged that he is remarkably accurate in characterizing the kind of experience which the New Testament depicts in its account of Jesus' prayerful agony in Gethsemane or in his turning to the Father in forsakenness on the cross.

It must be noted that Kierkegaard does not intend to spin out a dogma concerning suffering, but rather to comprehend actual suffering. As the Old Testament's anguished question as to why the righteous suffer is transformed into the New Testament *revelation* that the righteous (and God most specifically) *do suffer* (the mystery being not in the least reduced by the revealment), so S.K.'s understanding of suffering is grounded in mystery. He does not propose to eliminate mystery by rational explanations. His journals show the burning enigma which underlies his 'doctrine'. Thus he protests: 'A man denies himself in order to please God, and everything goes wrong...' Before such efforts a human father would, he says, dance for joy, but God seems to be angry with the godly. Suffering must surely be God's way of winning a soul, yet God seems to be 'out of his senses'. A modern Job must complain, 'Only when I have to do with him, and really do his will, does he seem to be angry.'[158] Clearly Kierkegaard does not begin with a harsh dogma of God's weaning a man from the world by means of suffering; instead he reflects on his own abiding suffering and trusts that the transcendent and inscrutable God must somehow be mysteriously using it. That the Christian's becoming a sacrifice is spiritually purposive is indicated in the injunction to be 'salted with fire', for to be salt is 'to be for others'. Salt by itself is not food, but it lends savour to food.[159] The consequence is that whereas Marxists and many religionists alike think of belief in a personal God as a source of comfort and consolation, S.K. insists that faith in a God who 'tempts' one and requires 'the most terrible decision' is in a real sense torture, if also it is eternal blessedness.[160]

In conclusion it may be asked what the essential purpose of the *Stages* is and how it relates to Kierkegaard's personal life? In this work he appears to have had two fundamental aims, the first being the intent to show the utmost of charming beauty. He sought to reveal the aesthetic consciousness and capacity in its finest expression. The second aim, more fundamental, was to show that there is a pervasive pathos in the aesthetic. This is not merely the haunting sense of incompleteness which remains when the artistic dream is found to be impossible of attainment. Instead, the pathos is in the inability of anything external to man to satisfy him as spirit. Most obviously, this is demonstrated in boredom, a familiar theme with S.K., boredom being a wearying of old treasures.

In addition to the despair readily recognizable in boredom, there is a more subtle and ironic form of aesthetic pathos, particularly in man's futile attempt to absolutize the relative. An example of this is the strange alternation between *fleeting* kisses which are of the moment only and *eternal* vows of love. What could be less eternal than a kiss? 'Two loving souls vow that they will love each other in all eternity; thereupon they embrace, and with a kiss they seal this eternal pact. Now I ask any thinking person whether he would have hit upon that!... The most spiritual is expressed by the very opposite, and the sensual is to signify the most spiritual.'[161]

The pregnancy of the aesthetic, its pointing beyond itself, and its inability to capture that which it loves had previously been dramatized by Kierkegaard's definition of a poet (cf. treatment of *Either/Or*). The same irony appears in the *Stages* in the suggestion that if a woman 'is really to awaken ideality in her husband she must die', since only then can she cause 'all the great things poetry attributes to her', but that if she fails to die 'her significance in this regard becomes the more doubtful the longer she lives'.[162] These comments, not those of the authentic Kierkegaard but only of one of his whimsical pseudonyms, are intended to suggest both the vivid delight in the sensuous life and its incapacity for fulfilment.

The very use of the term 'aesthetic' tends to lead to an over-simplification. It is quite as important that the aesthetic is pathetic because it leads to an *uncommitted* life as because it is pleasure-seeking. As uncommitted, it is marked by inconstancy, and may even be demoniacal if it rejects any meaning for life itself. It lacks even the 'fixed measures' which are evident in the Heracleitian flux. The rationality in the aesthetic life has no profound sense of selfhood and tends to prostitute life to trifling or unworthy goals. The aesthetic life is nevertheless human existence. It not only includes a measure of rational reflection and selective enjoyment, but even seems to involve a kind of faith—in the self, in the world, and perhaps an orientation towards order and purpose. It tends to move towards natural religiosity. Yet there is no natural development of this life into a higher (moral or religious) existence. Movement to the higher stages can come only by a dethroning cf the aesthetic in a decisive act.

To what extent can the meaning of the *Stages* be reduced to the autobiographical? This final question forces itself on any reader who is familiar with S.K.'s strange life. Analysis has shown that the book is autobiographical to a rather astonishing and even embarrassing degree, not only with reference to Regine, but also to S.K.'s childhood, youth, and religious experience. However, these facts were apparently undetected by the people of his own age. It seems clear that 'The Quiet Despair' in the diary describes S.K.'s melancholy relationship to his father, and 'Solomon's Dream' seems to revolve about his suffering over his father's shame. In a myth it is related that Solomon discovered the terrible guilt of his father and that the royal majesty is actually a mark of sin which shall lead to the ruin of the entire family. This is the 'great earthquake' of S.K.'s own life in which he discovered how his father had once in childhood cursed God because of the hunger and cold he had to endure, supposedly thereby bringing doom on himself and his children.* Kierkegaard's relation to his

---

* *Journals*, 556, 243. Cf. *Stages*, pp. 236, 220, 191, 298, and Lowrie, *op. cit.*, Vol. I, pp. 45, 70, 75, and 125 pertaining to these stories. It is common to view

father is also symbolized by the story of the Leper, and that of King Periander who secretly murdered his queen out of jealousy. The deed was then discovered by his son who, because of it, turned against his father and went into exile. It is clear that writing the symbolic stories served as a catharsis for Kierkegaard; he relieved himself of suffering, even though he permitted no one to truly understand. In his *Journals* (447) he wrote: 'I will try to rid myself of all the black thoughts and dark passions within me by writing "The leper's meditation".'

There is also another and perhaps deeper sense in which the *Stages* has self-reference. At the end of the work it is pointed out that in religious utterance even though none of the 'listeners' were to take heed there would still be one hearer who would be seriously moved, viz. the speaker himself. (P. 420) It is not, however, the speaker *qua* speaker who is affected but rather the speaker as one individual whose heart is open to the message.

Some scholars have even supposed that the exquisite if somewhat demoniacal Banquet was not a mere literary creation spun by the poet out of his rejected impulses, but that it is a poetized report of a banquet which actually took place, with S.K. (Constantine) paying the enormous bill. If this should be correct, then the gay deviltry which there makes mockery of love might be interpreted as an exhibition of the youthful sophistry and moral indecisiveness of Kierkegaard's earlier years. The more likely interpretation appears to be that the young man ('A', Quidam) represents S.K. as he was before he fell in love. Some of the other speakers reflect in limited degree other sides of his personality, except for the Seducer (who reflects an acquaintance for whom S.K. felt contempt). In any event, it is important that the Banquet is described as 'recollected', seeming to imply that it is past and transcended so far as S.K. himself was concerned. Judge William expresses the true Kierkegaard better than any of the strange aesthetes. However, he too has been transcended, for he is scarcely aware of the ethical dilemmas and the sense of guilt which in the diary lead one beyond mere morality to religion.

this sense of family doom as irrational and even morbid, out of keeping with S.K.'s faith in God. Without rejecting this criticism, it is also to be noted that this thought took on a sensitive Biblical understanding of providence, so S.K.'s —or any man's—seeming doom is actually a blessed call to a unique way of obedience under God's strange sovereignty.

THE AESTHETIC LITERATURE

However intriguing these issues may be to 'psychological morticians', they are of relatively little consequence. In the case of either a Shakespeare or a Kierkegaard it is a riddle to what extent the hideous nightmares or fair visions employed are their own rejected (or enacted) possibilities. Even in the case of a more common man, one may ponder the extent to which strange dreams born in the night are revelations of a hidden and somewhat schizoid character. Nevertheless, as in a Greek tragedy, S.K. offers to all men—including himself (one of his most important readers)—the benefit of catharsis and existential challenge. As added benefits in the one-sided emphases of the pseudonyms, one may find brilliant half-truths and psychological insights, displayed in a literary production of great artistry.

19. CONCLUDING UNSCIENTIFIC POSTSCRIPT

Concluding Unscientific Postscript to the Philosophical Fragments. A mimic-pathetic-dialectical composition, an existential contribution. By Johannes Climacus. Published by S. Kierkegaard. February 27, 1846. Translated by David F. Swenson and Walter Lowrie under the title *Concluding Unscientific Postscript.* Published for the American Scandinavian Foundation. Princeton: Princeton University Press, 1941.

Imagine a church member who wonders whether he is, after all, a Christian and becomes perturbed over the matter. His wife, not liking 'such a fuss' about little issues and anxious to maintain the social equilibrium, might mildly scold him:

'Dear husband of mine, how can you get such notions into your head? How can you doubt that you are a Christian? Are you not a Dane, and does not the geography say that the Lutheran form of the Christian religion is the ruling religion in Denmark? For you are surely not a Jew, nor are you a Mohammedan; what then can you be if not a Christian? It is a thousand years since paganism was driven out of Denmark, so I know you are not a pagan. Do you not perform your duties at the office like a conscientious civil servant; are you not a good citizen of a Christian nation, a Lutheran Christian state? So then of course you must be a Christian.' (P. 50)

The twentieth-century reader may be inclined to agree with the perplexed wife. How odd that Johannes Climacus, the author, should ask how to become a Christian when he already believes that Christianity can make eternal blessedness available! If he believes that it has this boon to bestow is he not already a Christian? To Kierkegaard, however, this reaction is irreligious evasion, since any worshipper of lust might believe in God but steadfastly avoid him. What saddens S.K. is that the multitudes of churchmen seem to have so little concern about eternal life and values. What they want is a pastor's benediction pronounced on their worldliness or their failings. In protest S.K. heaps grim irony upon them. If all are Christians then no one is a heretic, no matter what he stands for. For intellectuals, Christ is a remarkable professor and the apostles, a kind of 'little scientific society'. (P. 193) For the masses, on the other hand, Christianity is a sentimentality or even a very refined means of pleasure-seeking.

As opposed to all such hypocrisy, Climacus asserts his existentialism; Christianity has to do more with the way men exist than the ideas they profess to accept. Most apologists ask, 'What must I believe?' Kierkegaard asks, 'How do I stand in the presence of God?' In so far as reflection is involved in personal existence its primary purpose should be to bring one's life to clarity rather than to develop an objective system of doctrine. A farmer and a housewife will likely have no difficulty in understanding the claim which faith makes upon them, but a college sophomore—or professor—may have grave difficulty in escaping the notion that Christianity is a set of dogmas to be reflected upon and argued about. If one is truly existing then Christ's paradoxical meaning or significance for life is not difficult to discern; but, defining Christianity as a *world-view*, one may not in the slightest be moved to accept it. The very notion of a 'world-view', or world historical perspective, popularized by Hegel, is dangerous. It tends to obliterate the lowly individual in the vastness of world movements and also deludes him as to what is important, for unfortunately it is seldom virtue which gives one a great name in history. Thus a Hitler occupies a large niche. What ought to concern man is not taking a role in history or having a world view but to 'will the good'. (P. 120)

This very large book, S.K.'s great philosophical treatise, was written with unusual art and unexpected humour.* The title seems strange. Its intent might be rephrased: A Final Unpedantic Treatise, in the Nature of a Supplement to the 'Philosophical Fragments'. It was meant to be so final as to bring the entire authorship to an end, after which the author would become a country pastor. Instead, an apparent lack of public understanding and appreciation of his cause led him to transform this work into a preface to another large, and more explicitly religious, literature. As a postscript to the *Fragments*, this was no small footnote, but an exhaustive elaboration—chiefly an examination of the rational or speculative attempt to come to terms with Christianity. It was 'unscientific' or unpedantic as opposed to the pretentious works of the professors who, in S.K.'s judgment, obliterated personal reality in the process of explaining it and destroyed the life of the human spirit by analysis or dissection.

The 'author', John the Climber, stands at the foot of the 'ladder of heaven', asking how to climb. This makes it emphatic that the *Postscript* is not an objective description of Christianity but is instead a treatment of the subjective problem of how to become a Christian. 'How may I, Johannes Climacus, participate in the happiness promised by Christianity?' (P. 20) In contrast to all the 'scholars' who seem to assume that what is important is one's comprehension, and that if a man is able learnedly to define Christianity that then he *is* a Christian, S.K. insists that only by a kind of 'leap' can one make 'the qualitative transition from no belief to belief'. (P. 15) The contrast between the *Fragments* and the *Postscript* is important. Whereas the *Fragments* asked a formal question about the nature of Christianity, the *Postscript* personal-

---

* It may be noted that, in spite of Kierkegaard's melancholy, there appear here, as in many of his other writings, not only unexpected thrusts of humour but even major engagements of the same, as in the narrative by Johannes Climacus of how he entered into authorship (The Task of Becoming Subjective), and even a formal treatment of the role of humour in religion. S.K. bemoans the lack of a place for humour in Hegel's Absolute, in interesting parallel to F. C. S. Schiller's diatribe on Hegel in the famous comic issue of *Mind*, Christmas, 1901.

ized the question, asking how one can—and cannot—relate himself to the objective revelation. The *Fragments* asked how the Eternal (absolute, unqualified, necessary) is related to the temporal (fortuitous, accidental, free) in the objective Christ. The *Postscript* asked how the eternal can be related to the temporal in the believer, and how his eternal happiness can be grounded in an historical point.

In a few trenchant opening pages (Book I), the *Postscript* sweeps aside an 'objective' approach to Christianity, such as might be attempted by either philosophy or orthodoxy. S.K. had the highest regard for philosophy ('All honour to philosophy.' P. 54), but he would not allow it to be, for complacent men, a substitute for religious passion. Christianity cannot be proved or disproved by reference to scripture either, for faith is not belief resting on evidence. Neither can certainty be sought within the church, which, in so far as it is anything beyond a human and historical institution, is itself an object of faith—something to be believed in rather than having demonstrable certainty. The weight of Christian history adds no element of plausibility for faith, and the eighteen centuries tend only to bathe one in comfortable delusion. (Pp. 30, 41, 45 ff.) In corresponding fashion, it is argued that Christianity cannot be given the objective support of philosophy. Speculation may be able to reflect on doctrine, and at that perhaps quite unfavourably, but it cannot evaluate faith because the only way to appraise this is by experiencing its passion. (P. 51)

Because the *Postscript* is so deeply religious it was not given any accompanying discourse. Yet S.K. did not view it as distinctively Christian; rather it aimed to lead one away from philosophical speculation *towards* authentic Christianity, just as the aesthetic works were aimed to lead one away from aesthetic concern to Christianity. The religion expressed is in part the 'immanent' religion of the *Edifying Discourses*, a kind of natural religion, certainly informed about the true nature of Christianity and readily projecting itself in that direction, but unable to become decisive Christianity except by a leap of faith. This transformation must come by an effort of the will and is not facilitated by intellectual comprehension of the history or doctrine of Christianity. Nevertheless, if not distinctively Christian, the book does focus

THE AESTHETIC LITERATURE

on Christian themes; and in effect (although this is not expressly stated), it adds a fourth stage or sphere of existence to the aesthetic, ethical, and religious stages. This fourth sphere is religion B or Christianity which can be reached from general religiosity (religion A) only by the same kind of decisive leap as is involved in the other movements. For the comparative study of religion, S.K.'s treatment of 'natural religion', as it compares with Christianity, is exciting and definitive (treated already in the *Fragments*). He now designates natural religion, which has only human nature as its origin, 'religiousness A' as opposed to Christianity which is 'religiousness B'. He notes that the general religiosity must be present before one can move to authentic Christian categories (Cf. pp. 493-98). It is the paradoxical character of 'B' which precludes the possibility of an objective or scientific approach to it, necessitates subjectivity, and hence provides the main theme of this book.

Although the *Postscript* is perhaps S.K.'s greatest work, it may be somewhat briefly reviewed here, relatively speaking, because its major themes are also treated in relation to other writings. Some of the major topics are faith, paradox, authority, dying to the world, and truth as subjectivity. Some earlier concepts are refined here, e.g. the stages and their mutual involvement. Here it is made clear that the basic alternative (either/or) of life is between the aesthetic and the ethical, in that the ethical life inescapably issues in religious concerns, and further that these natural or immanent religious concerns find their fulfilment (if also negation) in Christianity. Thus Christianity fulfils the ethical life as well as the primitive religiosity, even if it also sets both of these aside or dethrones them. For that matter, it is evident that even the aesthetic sphere is not repudiated by the ethical-religious life, but is redeemed and incorporated within it.

The *Postscript* is intended to point the way to religion, away from the scepticism of objective reason. But religion is not all of a kind, and the *Postscript* carefully distinguishes and defines. At the lowest level, the aesthetic stage of existence, the religious impulse is only a sense of wonder or awe. In turn, the religious aspect of the ethical life is chiefly a sense of the divine imperative of the moral law. Religion as a distinct category begins with the realization that only through God's power are the problems of existence resolvable. Yet in the form of 'religion A' even this genuine religious awareness lacks such basic Christian qualities as atonement and grace. If Christ is present he is thought of as a pattern rather than a saviour.

There is a dilemma in viewing natural religion as being immanent. If religion is a grasping of the transcendent, how can religiousness A be only immanent? The explanation is that the infinitude which man grasps is in this case merely a quality within his own person, and the transcendence is only a transcending of finite values. An example would be Socrates who as an idealist ambiguously wished to die to the world in order that his immortal soul might be liberated. (P. 496) On the other hand, religion B is the religion of objective transcendence in that it offers a Christ or saviour.

Kierkegaard regards natural religiosity as based upon a double myth, first, that if one searches in his own soul he will find God (immanence) and, second, that if he strives diligently he will attain the holy (optimism). The two myths add up to religion as a *human* quest for the divine. Religion A may be thought of as pagan or pre-Christian, yet it is the common form of religiosity even among 'Christians'. It lacks the severity of Christianity's demands, blunts the sense of sin, and has no profound understanding of forgiveness and salvation. Further, it panders to man's desires, offering comfort, release from trouble, and the security of a carelessly indulgent God. In sharp contrast, Christianity reveals both the gravity of sin and the hiddenness of God, and calls on the forgiven disciple to take up his cross and follow. Thus Christianity rests on two principles contrary to those named: first, that if one searches his heart he will find there a sinner (sin), and second, that the transcendent God has acted to introduce his sovereign love into man's existence (incarnation). These principles add up to religion as a *divine* quest. (Pp. 184 ff., 494 f., 509)

The optimism of religion A may in fact take the form of a most dire 'pessimism', as in the religions of India where it is supposed that only after the most severe torments, most extended reincarnations, and most sacrificial endeavours is it possible to attain the spiritual goal. Yet even the 'pessimistic' version demonstrates the inherent optimism of all natural religion, viz. that the divine power which is in man will eventually win through. (P. 515 f.) Christianity denies the optimistic premise of such religion. It denies that the individual is in immediate possession of, or can personally achieve, knowledge of God; and still more it denies the existence of a natural, or naturally attainable, right relation to God. Thus the human spirit finds itself alien to God, or, in the language of Kierkegaard, natural 'subjectivity' is 'untruth'. It is only in relation to the paradox of the incarnation that *in faith* subjectivity gains truth. (Pp. 185–87) In part, this truth is a new consciousness of sin, showing that the shallow sense of guilt which was present in religion A is but a hint of an actual radical alienation between God and man. In part, Christian truth is an awareness of the reconciliation of forgiveness, whereby the eternal enters into man's temporal experience. Whereas in the shallowness of religion A, man's central problem is nothing more than his falling short of the goal, the problem in Christianity is the possible offence man may take to God's strange way of healing the breach between man and himself. (P. 494) Nevertheless, even though natural religion is strikingly different from Christianity and does not lead to it, it is not possible for one to enter into Christianity except by passing through 'religion'. (Pp. 494, 346, 516)

It is the emphasis on the strange intrusion of the transcendent in religion B which provides the basis for the main theme of the *Postscript*—the subjectivity of truth and the failure of objective reason to find existential truth. If man is so alienated from God that the divine message may be a stumbling block and an offence; and if the transcendent and eternal appears to man as a paradox in a 'moment' of history, then, manifestly, human reason is not the appropriate means for man's approach to God. This leads S.K. to reflect on the role of 'proofs', and to set them in sharp contrast to faith and humble suffering, which he regards as the two essentials for a successful grasping of eternal blessedness. Attempting to prove (or disprove) anything which is objective and historical can end only in approximation, with the consequence that neither the church nor Bible can be decisively established (or overthrown) in this fashion. More than that, it is nonsensical to seek to prove religion by rational argument. With biting sarcasm S.K. depicts the confused parson who confesses that he isn't much of a philosopher and 'must be content with faith'. (P. 32) To try to prove the existence of God is a shameless insult for it shows that the reasoner is really ignoring God. If he took God seriously he would worship. (P. 485) For the scientist to put God to the test empirically is equally offensive. 'The physicist uses the microscope as a dandy uses opera-glasses; only, the microscope is focused on God.'[163] The rational approach to religion focuses not on responsible commitment to an active God, but on intellectual comprehension and verification of objective doctrine. There is even a sense in which an established probability for Christianity would threaten faith, making it a treasure one could carelessly or disinterestedly possess, like money in the bank. (P. 30) Therefore, everyone is placed equally distant from faith, no matter how learned, and can move to it only by an act of commitment.

In the *Postscript*, as in the *Fragments*, the fact that transcendent Christianity is paradoxical is central. Not surprisingly—since this fact has to do with man's inability both to understand and trust—it also is one of the most difficult and controversial of Kierkegaardian topics. It is paradox above all which undercuts the efforts of objective rationality. Paradox is not however a quality of truth itself. Truth 'becomes paradoxical by virtue of its relationship to an existing individual'. (P. 183) Paradox, at the most elementary level, is the availability of no alternative but a leap of faith, taking a risk on the most crucial issues, without a rational support. But in Christianity there emerges *the* paradox, far more radical. The object of Christian faith is not only an 'objective uncertainty', but when it is seen for what it truly is, is so unlikely as to be offensive. God-in-Christ is absurd in that in him the eternal becomes that which it cannot rationally be, viz. the historical; the eternal becomes a moment. Approached humanly the difficulty is that an historical datum (Christ) is presented not as simply historical but as the eternal itself which has violated its own nature in becoming temporal. (Pp. 508, 512) Christianity is also 'absurd' in that man can never really comprehend how the eternal could become a mere moment in Roman times. There is a contradiction in that 'the historical fact here in question is not a simple historical fact, but is constituted by that which only against its nature can become historical, hence by virtue of the absurd'. (P. 512) Thus faith can never be objectively certain, nor highly probable, nor even a little bit probable.

THE AESTHETIC LITERATURE

In noting that Christianity is 'absurd', S.K. did not mean that its paradox constitutes nonsense but only that it is humanly incomprehensible and implausible. In fact, reason even has important roles within Christianity, ascertaining the genuine claims of faith, and distinguishing paradox from nonsense. The latter could never be accepted by faith, whereas the incomprehensible paradox is accepted by faith even though it is 'against the understanding'. (P. 504) It may be debated whether in fact human reason can make the distinction indicated, but at least S.K.'s contention makes it clear that he regards paradox as that which is incomprehensible to man, yet is comprehensible to God, a situation which would not be the case in true self-contradiction.

In regard to the meaningfulness of metaphysical terms Kierkegaard shows an interesting parallelism to positivism, which denies that the absolute (or eternal or God) can have cognitive meaning because all such meaning is empirical in origin. S.K. held that Socrates failed to realize the eternal by means of 'recollection' and that Plato nullified the infinite Idea by trying to make it an object of contemplation. In this connection, two basic thoughts emerge: (1) That the disclosure of the Eternal-in-time by Christ is a veiled paradox, acceptable (if not thereby less mysterious) only to faith, and (2) That the concrete meaning which the eternal has for man is gained *existentially*. The latter means that when one has infinite concern or a passion of inwardness that then he attains a limited human awareness of the absolute, the unqualified, the infinite, even though the latter cannot be apprehended as an object or quality of an object because God's presence and omnipotence are not of that character. (Pp. 184 n., 189, 219) The quality of the infinite is intimated by unqualified or infinite human commitment. In his journal S.K. states that the apprehension of the objective *absolute* is possible only through man's *absoluteness of submission* to God.[164] Still other existential intimations of transcendence are in the widow's 'mite' which in God's sight is equal to the greatest gift, and that the most righteous man is a mere sinner before God. In man's relationship to God it is thus evident that absolutes are involved whereas even in moral society, existence is based on comparatives and relativities. Even the very meaning of God is transmitted through the empirical. Since God is transcendent, so that a great gulf or absolute difference exists between him and man, faith cannot describe him as he is in himself. Thus S.K. existentially defines 'God' to mean 'that all things are possible' which to man are otherwise impossible.

Not only God but also every other religious concept is given a personalized or subjective meaning in the *Postscript*. For example, quite impressively, and in anticipation of Heidegger, S.K. stresses the personal significance of death, not death as any kind of theoretical or general fact, but the disturbing fact of one's own impending but temporally uncertain death. So too eternal life is not a beautiful doctrine to be believed, or understood, but a reality which must somehow express itself in a person's existence. It is not a subjectivistic desire but a proclamation which owes its power to its paradoxical character. On the one hand, *happiness* is a quality of existence and a goal of striving. On the other hand, the *eternal* is the non-temporal ideality, quite separated from the life of desires and striving, frustration and achievement. An eternal or non-temporal happiness thus is as puzzling as is the God who became man, but it is also the 'impossibility' which God promises, a real existence which has the bliss of the eternal. Because it is transcendent, however, eternal blessedness cannot really be defined in its own nature but only 'in terms of the manner of acquisition'. (P. 382) This acquisition comes by joyful quest in suffering, as by faith one accepts the improbable Word that God became man for our salvation. (P. 397) It is fundamental that the joy, striving and suffering are characteristic of both man's quest for God and God's quest for man, because love always suffers in the presence of sin and love is both God's attitude, and an attitude which he evokes in man.

Because of the enormous emphasis which he placed on eternal blessedness S.K. expected protests and questions about it. 'Could you not inform me what an eternal happiness is, briefly, clearly, and definitely? Could you not describe it "while I shave", as one describes a woman's beauty?' (P. 351) His answer is: (1) Value experience cannot be made an objective of empirical investigation; love, for example, is not composed of objective sense qualities. (2) Absolute or eternal values can be grasped only *existentially*, i.e. by their serving as the magnetic pole around which all earthly values are re-oriented. Thus, while the eternal does transfigure human existence, it still lies beyond the earthly existence and is apprehended only as *expectation*. (P. 360)

The underlying factor of transcendence upon which paradox rests appears in a variety of ways, so that the concept of paradox has a number of applications. Among these is the 'instant' (the moment of contact with the eternal), in which absolute decisiveness is a mark of the eternal. Others are the objectively unjustified and undetermined leap of free choice, the 'individual' (person of faith) who accepts God's self-disclosure, 'spirit' which is a synthesis-in-tension of body and soul, and 'authority' which is the sign in Christ or in his representatives pointing to the presence of the transcendent.

Precisely because Christianity claims absoluteness or transcendence a special problem of authority emerges, the more critical because of God's unwillingness to make revelation manifest in an objective scientific manner. First, transcendence appears in Christ, the problem here being how the eternal can enter into time, and the divine into the human. Second, it appears in the church, the problem now being how the transcendent Christ-meaning can be communicated by one man to another. Specifically, it may be asked whether and how a man can witness for Christ. Certainly not directly. There have been men who could speak with a divine authority, but they were apostles. Others, like S.K. himself, who may be conscious of a divine 'governance' in their lives are still not able to lay claim to being 'witnesses to the truth'. Thus while an apostle, not by virtue of wisdom but simply by virtue of being called, can seek to set souls at rest, the most that others can do is to prod men from their spiritual lethargy, to inspire them 'with concern and unrest'. (P. 346) Unless it be by an apostle sent by command, even the introduction of Christianity into a heathen land may not be a religious act but a merely aesthetic one or even an all too human act of conquest by military power. (P. 388)

With the paradox of a mere moment of history claiming eternal significance, and the failure of all speculative attempts to justify the claim of authority, the rational quest of the transcendent is supplanted by faith. It is faith and not knowledge which bestows eternal blessedness. Furthermore, faith is not an acceptance of what is only probable but not certain; it is rather an acceptance of the uncertain and improbable. To have faith is to accept the paradox, 'the Absurd', and yet certainly not on the ground that it is absurd, but in spite of its improbability. Improbability in itself is no merit, but it happens that God in his wisdom chose or did the unlikely in order to overwhelm and redeem the unhappy, the glory of which is evident to the redeemed.[165] From this it should be evident how grave is Marjorie Grene's misunderstanding when she accuses S.K. of a 'sheer intellectual delight in the absurd for its own sake'.[166]

That faith, which constitutes man's truest relation to God, is never a secure possession, but an attitude of awe and trust blended with fear and trembling.[167] In contrast, a simple confidence in the (true) facts of religion does not constitute faith because such an attitude might still leave one in a wrong relation to God, devoid of the tension required by the presence of the holy. (P. 67) This interpretation might be taken to exclude 'simple childhood faith' but S.K. seems to imply that such spontaneous trust is appropriate in given instances, above all in childhood, but that this is not mature faith. Above all, mature faith is trust in Jesus' assurance of forgiveness. By it the believer becomes a 'new creation', even though the full release is a heavenly promise to be trusted rather than an immediate experience in the world.*

One of Kierkegaard's expressions which has provoked a great deal of criticism, and which is very closely involved in the doctrine of subjectivity expounded in the *Postscript*, is the reference to faith as a 'leap'. S.K. sensed a dilemma in this notion in that a leap would seem to deny faith any vital relation to the content of truth. In his journals he sought to clarify his position. Faith requires a leap in that it does not rest on the standards of objective rationality, or on empirical evidence. One must thus leap into the realm of revelation where God has come as paradox. However the word 'leap' fails to accurately express the full thought because the believer certainly does not, in S.K.'s view, hurl himself senselessly into the realm of the holy. He acts in obedience to God and

---

* *Journals*, 581. The Catholic philosopher, Regis Jolivet, agrees that faith is a gift of God but objects that S.K. wrongly rejects reasons for believing 'in something which transcends reason'. (*Introduction to Kierkegaard*, p. 56.) S.K. would agree that there are objective points of reference (as incarnation and scripture) which are essential for faith, but would deny that they are *reasons* for faith. Not only are such claimed reasons in fact quite unconvincing, if they were so, then faith would be caused by them and could not be a gift of God.

THE AESTHETIC LITERATURE

certainly in a kind of meaningful response to his felt need, his existential plight; yet he must act boldly for in obedience he finds himself in a state of suspension, without earthly support. Faith is thus person-to-Person obedience to the divine will, an obedience which rests on the humanly unverified authority of Christ. The radical nature of Christian faith, as distinguished from a mere trusting extension of belief beyond the limits of available evidence, is indicated by a contrast with the faith of Socrates. Whereas the latter had a religious faith in a God who remained objectively *uncertain*, the Christian accepts a divine disclosure which appears to the natural man as improbable and even absurd.[168]

Kierkegaard maintains that the leap of faith is a 'how', i.e. a manner of gaining truth, but that when this occurs there is also a 'what' or content which is given. 'Here,' he says, 'quite certainly, we have inwardness at its maximum proving to be objectivity once again.'[169] The 'what' or object which thus determines faith is the paradox. If this language discourages or outrages the reader, it should at least be clear what is intended, that Christianity is not meaningless nonsense, but specific and meaningful paradox—in relation to which man must choose. The justification of the obedient leap of faith is, furthermore, real to the faithful, even though it never becomes public or objective in the scientific sense on pain of ceasing to be faith. As S.K. likes to phrase it, the eternal appears in time, the universal becomes particular, Christ becomes the God-man, involving in any case the unbelievable thought that God has changed. Any attempt to reduce the gravity of the problem by blurring the distinction between opposites appears to S.K. as a pantheistic falsification. From the standpoint of man, the paradox means that actual sin, which can never become unreal as fact, is nevertheless covered or obliterated. It is precisely because God does the 'impossible' that there is an object capable of evoking faith, so that man comes to 'believe by reason of the absurd'.[170] It is this notion of an objective truth grasped in the objective uncertainty by the subjectivity of faith that defines the central issue of the book.

The most perplexing doctrine of the *Postscript*, and the one around which most of the others revolve, is the notion of religious truth being grasped by faith, or as S.K. phrases it, that *truth is subjectivity*. This subtle thesis must be carefully defined, particularly because it is usually seriously misunderstood. How critical the issue of subjectivity is can be demonstrated by noting that so careful a student as Marjorie Grene could say that S.K. eliminated altogether any conception of an 'objective truth of Christianity'.[171] This is totally false. Kierkegaard rather means to show that whether one is a Christian does not depend on historical or scientific evidence, on logical inference, nor on the accidents of birth, geography or culture, but instead on his divinely-enabled leap into the realm of faith. He did not mean to deny the objective basis of truth, nor the objective Christ-in-history to whom faith responds; nor did he mean to say that it is immaterial whether or not Christianity is objectively true. What he did mean is that the only way a person can apprehend the truth of Christianity, and the only justification by which he dare call himself a believer, is by being existentially or personally related to the truth. If Christianity were a doctrine then one could come to have a certain external knowledge, but not faith, for only an intellectual response is involved in knowledge. Christianity is not a doctrine although doctrines may grow out of it; it is a divine deed to which man must respond by an act of will. 'Faith is precisely the contradiction between the infinite passion of the individual's inwardness and the objective uncertainty.' (P. 182) Just as 'objective' means any datum so colourless as to be 'extraneous to the movement of existence', so 'subjective truth' is a passionate grasping of what apart from faith is uncertain. (P. 278)

At this point the twentieth-century reader is hampered by outmoded terminology. 'Subjectivity' was not misunderstood in S.K.'s Hegelian era, and indeed it was a more or less unavoidable term. Hegelians identified reality with truth. Therefore they would expect S.K. to say that subjectivity is truth, *if* he held that the existing *subject* constitutes one's reality. This is exactly what he did maintain. One can gain the truth about himself only by first becoming an ethical self, and one can have truth about faith only by experiencing faith.

That subjectivity is truth is essentially a Socratic or Platonic principle; it seeks absolute and eternal truth but seeks it within the self. The kind of subjectivity referred to is utterly remote from personal whims. It seeks exactly that absolute and divine truth which Socrates hoped to find by means of 'recollection'.

Earnest subjectivity is thus the point of disclosure of genuine objectivity. Nevertheless, that 'subjectivity is truth' means something very different for Kierkegaard than for Socrates, in two regards. First, man is not so immediately in possession of eternal truth as to be able to regain or recall it by earnest self-discovery. Instead he must depend on God's presentation of the Eternal-in-time, Christ. Second, recognition of such truth in no wise assures a life lived in accord with it. Left to himself, man wickedly takes offence at the truth and wishes to live in untruth.

Kierkegaard is famous for having said that one's interest in his existence (his valuational becoming) constitutes his very reality, and that to become thus subjective is his greatest responsibility. (Pp. 279, 119, 142) Man must first reject the objectivity (outward orientation) of the aesthetic life wherein he is a slave to things. Next he must develop the responsible inwardness of duty and self-fulfilment, but a still greater subjectivity is found in the life in which exists a passionate tension of concern for eternal blessedness (religion A). (P. 51 f.) Nevertheless, far from asserting that even such subjectivity is truth, S.K. insists that it is untruth. By this he means that even natural religiosity is only a yearning after the divine and not a possession of that eternal truth which Socrates thought was hidden in the soul. (P. 185) Accordingly, the question is raised whether, beyond this passion, there may be something more concrete in the form of truth, which might satisfy the Platonic desire and quest.

The thesis which emerges is that Christianity is this highest subjectivity and that in Christianity it becomes true, *paradoxically*, that subjectivity *is* truth. Implied in the notion of subjectivity is the thought that such truth dare not be thought of as a plausible doctrine or fact which a soul can comfortably possess. Indeed, the element of the 'absurd' in Christianity, whereby God became a Jewish boy, needing to grow in wisdom as in stature, and leading to glory by way of humiliation, is so great that instead of Christianity releasing the believer from the dynamics of existence, it deepens the strain. It makes suffering essential to life and the way to joy, and requires a total re-orientation of the worldly self. Christian life is thus the most profound and most passionate subjectivity. Truth becomes subjectivity in that the disturbing 'truth' of the God-man is apprehended and appropriated not as a rational dogma but in a passionate inwardness. This is the most profound form of personal existence and is a grasping of the eternal not directly but through the *expectancy* of it.[172]

There are various and even positivistic strains in this position. One of these has to do with the completeness and certainty of knowledge. Empirical knowledge is available to man, but scientific objectivity never attains finality. Yet in the realm of the metaphysical and in particular in one's value judgments, there is a critical need for finality; in regard to duty or to God the kind of tentative generalization or approximation which is appropriate in science will not do. Scientific scepticism, the habit of cautiously suspending judgment, when applied to matters critical to existence, results only in frustrated passionate need. However, the semi-agnosticism of Kierkegaard differs profoundly from the view of a Goethe, Comte, or a Sartre, all of whom either avoid metaphysical issues or indulge in self-expressionism as a substitute for knowledge. S.K. holds that man's unquenchable thirst for the infinite manifests itself in Christianity in a process of personal appropriation. (P. 102) S.K. dares to call this state 'truth', subjective truth for an existing self. Strictly speaking, it is faith which functions in lieu of final truth.

That subjectivity is truth is not an epistemological theory in the usual sense. It does not affirm that subjective experience has a mysterious correspondence with objective fact, still less that it replaces it. S.K. does mean that the only way in which ethical or religious reality can be grasped is by existing ethically or religiously. There is not intended the slightest depreciation of either scientific fact or logical entailment; these are quite appropriate in science and logic. However, it is insisted that there can be no ethical or religious knowledge apart from living with values. Values are not to be treated primarily as *objects* of knowledge although obviously one may reflect profitably upon them; they are subjective modes of existence. They are not subjective, however, as in the emotivism of much recent value theory, where they represent essentially arbitrary and personal feeling and choices. They are rather, for Kierkegaard, personally and passionately needed and chosen aspects of life which have a perfectly objective or real, but hidden, humanly speaking, relation to and grounding in the transcendent absolute. (Pp. 176 ff.)

THE AESTHETIC LITERATURE

Kierkegaard makes his existential notion of truth clear when he insists that a man who prays truly and earnestly to an idol is *in the truth* because he is unwittingly in relationship to the true God, whereas one who prays hypocritically to the true God whom he nevertheless properly conceives is *not in the truth* and actually worships an idol of his own desire. (P. 179 f.) There is no intention here of denying objectivity in the realm of values any more than in cognitive science. The point intended is that the immediate concern of the individual should be whether or not he is in the truth-relationship, i.e. whether his existence has the proper orientation. In the case of Christianity, which is S.K.'s chief concern, there is the additional consideration that to be in the truth the believer must not only be immediately concerned about his truth-relationship but also, as explained before, must by the subjective leap of faith hold fast to an objective datum (Christ) which is presented as an *objective uncertainty*. 'An objective uncertainty held fast in an appropriation-process of the most passionate inwardness is the truth, the highest truth attainable for an existing individual.' (P. 182)

By this Kierkegaard intends that it is impossible for man to grasp spiritual reality by empirical concepts.[173] If man were to apprehend himself intellectually (by concepts) he would grasp only his possibility or whatness, his ideal nature. It is only as man consciously wills to be this self that he achieves an actuality which can be apprehended. Only through the moment of volition or faith is there the actuality of subjectivity (selfhood) which truth can represent. Here reality is not a static entity to be recorded as upon an unliving photographic plate, but something to be actualized and grasped by participation. To speak of God as an 'objective uncertainty' which is grasped in passionate inwardness is utterly unlike the paradoxical double-talk which some have tried to make it. Very simply, it means that if one were to treat God as an objective certainty, like any 'thing' in the world, then one would be essentially unrelated to God's person, to his godness. To merely reflect or ponder on God is to degrade divinity. Only in the passion of inwardness is God's reality as will, love, judgment and redemption properly confronted. For man it is not God's theoretical locus which matters; it is his stance which must be faced. For a man without faith, God does not 'exist' even though this faithless and loveless human correctly believes in the eternal being of God, because to 'exist' is to stand in a person-to-Person relation.[174]

The *Postscript* is not only what its name implies, a culminative treatment of earlier works and thoughts. It is also a remarkable preface to all that is to follow, charting the issues of the violent authorship which culminated in the open 'attack' on Christendom. Protesting that Christianity had been made so easy that the 'Christians' were really pagans, S.K. tried to show how difficult it is to be a Christian. He objected to lukewarmness, pointing to the severe demands of the Christian life. He called attention to the elements of absurdity and offensiveness in Christ, and noted the imperative fact that 'truth is subjectivity', i.e. not an idea to be toyed with but a conviction to be held with passion. Whimsically, he indicated that just as the most difficult leap is for a man to jump in the air in a standing position and land in the same spot, so 'it is easier to become a Christian when I am not a Christian than to become a Christian when I am one', i.e. landing in the same spot. (P. 327) A pagan feels a challenge to make the leap, but a person baptized in infancy is tempted to think that he has already arrived at his spiritual goal and thus senses no occasion for decisiveness.

The Christianity of little children properly but gullibly appropriates a baby Jesus, three wise men, and a star, to say nothing of the gingernuts; but such religion represents a kind of universal natural piety, a fantasy-inwardness, and it lacks the decisive Christian categories which require commitment—the absurd, suffering, and discipleship. To force a child to face Christianity's severity as if he were a man is a sin against childhood, but it is nevertheless stupid to think of childhood as being the distinctive Christian age. (Pp. 521-32) It is nonsense to think of such credulous and undiscriminating 'simple childhood faith' as a point to which the adult should return. Faith is not the point of man's origin but is his ultimate goal. It might be objected that S.K.'s view of faith harmonizes much better with his attack on bourgeois complacency than with the accurate reading of a child's heart. In any event it is clear that while he would not force the sin-grace consciousness of the adult upon the child mind, he does protest against the prolongation of childhood's religiosity. The unadulterated prettiness and cheeriness of the latter prevents the consciousness of sin which is crucial for the fully developed self. The intent is not to force every little child or great grandmother into existential passion but to make every mature sinner aware of the realities of his existence, an awareness which must lead to such passion.

Imagine an organist who plays the hymns properly Sunday by Sunday but on Christmas or Easter celebrates with a gay waltz! This is the kind of folly of which the church in general and preachers in particular are said to be guilty, doing reasonably well for Christianity on common days but on festival occasions, moved by enthusiasm, ascending from the higher to the *lower*, moving from the mature to the childish. (P. 531) Seeking or proclaiming childish assurance, one actually makes faith impossible. Both the orthodox preacher who can *prove* God and the pietist who claims some warm and tender presence of the divine are betraying Christianity by making it a certainty, i.e. an object of knowledge rather than of faith. To the contrary, Christ is always a paradox and challenge.

Kierkegaard's attack, both in this and later works, was not simply on the state church but on a prevailing misconception of religious life, a confusion of Christianity with worldly virtue. The Middle Ages felt that there was something in the world which could not be harmonized with the thought of God, and therefore men tried to 'break with the finite' by entering the cloister. For S.K. the issue is different. It is not a retreat from a corrupted world which he advocates but a more clear-cut dedication to the infinite as contrasted with the finite.

The reason for this proposed break with the finite is an insistence upon the need for the personal existential choice of a fundamental *telos* in life. S.K. felt that so long as one habitually repeats the daily rounds of unthinking or impulsive acts—eating, drinking, working, marrying, procreating—he is not a real self but only an instance within which 'the race' is repeating itself. Only by resolute decision, an absolute choice before God, can one possess his personal selfhood. On the other hand, an absolute commitment to a relative end is not possible. The true goal of existence must be a devotion to the absolute. This fact raises a certain doubt about the ethical mode of existence. Judge William went so far in glorifying the ethical as represented by marriage that he might seem to be more concerned about a godly home than about God.

Does Kierkegaard here mean to renounce man's relative and earthly goals, e.g. replacing marriage by celibacy? He seems to have wavered over the issue and yet not dared to do so, for this would have led him in the direction of a Gnostic view of incarnation and creation, viz. that God could not have created so dubious a world and that he did not really come to earth in Christ, but only pretended to do so in order to lure souls away from the evil world. S.K.'s basic intent is to say that the Absolute must have the absolute place in life and the relative a relative place, and that the relative can be transfigured by the absolute. Simply to ascetically avoid earthly relations in order to seek God would be to violate God's will. God has placed man in the worldly order.[175] To take a pleasant walk in the deer park can be a religious act in which one happily accepts the kind of existence which God has allotted to man. (P. 440 f.) All normal human relations are to be transfigured by being made the Christian graces and duties.

Nevertheless, there remained an ascetic strain in Kierkegaard which in later years was to have violent expression. In part, this tendency manifested a protest against the moral laxity and indulgence of the age. S.K. pointed out that if he had lived in the medieval period he could not have been a monk because at that time the monk was wrongly regarded as a saint (with special merit deriving from his way of life), and further noted that the monk's supposed 'inwardness' became only a 'special outwardness'. (P. 363) A monk can be guilty of pride, selfishness, and of his own special kind of worldliness, demonstrating thereby the fact that man cannot exist and really escape from the finitude of the world. Nevertheless, argued S.K., in the modern world—and particularly in a Protestant land—there is no need to fear the perils of monasticism. The opposite perils cry for attention. Accordingly, he was severely critical of Protestant ethics and specifically of Luther, for taking the monk out of the cloister and for reducing the Christian ideal to little more than civic righteousness. Protestantism intends to make all of life holy, but risks making the holy just another, if moralistic, part of secular life. Catholicism seemingly proposes a double code, first a superior way of life, as removed from the world as possible; and, second, an inferior and barely (hopefully) adequate way of life, more mixed with the world, so as to include marriage, children, property, a business career, etc.

Lowrie is correct in insisting that this issue is grave and is misunderstood. S.K.'s immediate complaint was that Protestantism was permitting almost any morality or aesthetic sentimentality to masquerade as religion. He points out that while man must live 'in the world' he must not be misled into living 'of the world'. While a man must take account of civic responsibilities, recreation, health, the economic life, and social obligations, all of this must never be confused with man's relation to God. Concern for 'eternal happiness' is an *absolute* concern for the absolute end, whereas concern about marriage or one's job is a *relative* concern about a relative end. In eternity it will make no difference whether one married or how he was employed. The two kinds of concern are both legitimate but must never be confused: 'Nor is it true that the absolute end becomes concrete in the relative ends, for the absolute distinction that was fixed between them in the moment of resignation will secure the absolute *telos* [end or goal] against fraternization every moment. The individual is in truth in the relative ends with his direction towards the absolute *telos*; but he is not so in them as to exhaust himself in them. It is true that before God and the absolute *telos* we human beings are all equal, but it is not true . . . that God or the absolute *telos* may be placed on a level with everything else.' (P. 359)

It is because Kierkegaard denies the possibility of 'fraternizing' between the absolute end and the relative life goals that he is a Christian rather than a mystic; he emphasizes faith rather than communion or immediacy in relationship to God. Even though the eternal gives validity to the temporal, serving as the magnetic power which attracts all value aspiration, yet, in contrast to mysticism, it never becomes an earthly possession, but remains for ever the *expectation* of faith. Unlike some kinds of otherworldliness, the other-worldliness of Kierkegaard does not warrant the criticism of being a compensation for life's hardships. Instead, the 'eternal' is for him the source of the driving passion which brings earthly existence to honesty and to heroic dedication. Its significance for the existing person has been aptly described by David Swenson: 'There is the rest and the peace, the final consummation, the consciousness of a victory not again to be jeopardized, the happiness of looking back upon sufferings endured in a good cause... Sailors battling in an angry sea and straining every nerve to reach haven before the boat is engulfed and their lives lost, will scarcely understand the [worldly] principle that the value is in the struggle, not in the attainment.'[176]

From this it should be evident that, while religion is the ultimacy of existence, the super-earthly fulfilment of religion would no longer constitute 'existence'. Bluntly, in heaven there would be no 'existence', although S.K. deliberately refrains from any such comment. Existence is the straining process of becoming, in a passionate expectancy of the eternal. There will be fulfilment but fulfilment will spell the end of becoming. S.K. insists that the Christian must focus on the expectancy of the eternal and on his earthly existence, not upon the *realization* of the eternal or the trans-existent.[177] This is not so much a philosophical avoidance of the speculative as a faithful religious adherence to the New Testament which focuses on Christ as the *Way* (rather than describing, e.g. by analogy, what it is to which the way leads). Obviously the goal is to go beyond the existential experience. Nevertheless, expectancy is the only form in which the goal is now available and consequently existence must be one's central concern. This existence requires and is formed by faith which is a revolutionary acceptance of the improbable, resting on divine inspiration, but still requiring a decisive leap of bold venture.

To avoid the error of seeing asceticism as implicit in S.K.'s premise—an error into which perhaps both he and Lowrie fell in some measure—it is essential to grasp his central thesis which is that man's existence is 'a synthesis of the infinite and the finite', and that therefore man's duty is to live absolutely with reference to absolute goals and relatively with reference to relative goals.[178] Neither the earthly life nor the quest for God dare be slighted. S.K. would agree with Kant that doing one's absolute duty may have unhappy consequences; concern for the absolute *telos* will not free one from the normal perplexities of life in the world of relativities. In fact, a would-be Abraham who thinks he has such an 'absolute' duty to God as to sacrifice his son, may instead be a fool or insane. The absolute does not replace the relative, nor does it even resolve the perplexities of the world. What it does accomplish is to show that the relative *is* relative.

THE AESTHETIC LITERATURE

In this light, Kierkegaard's growing inclination to asceticism is as much a violation of his own fundamental principles as is the bourgeois cult of earthly goals. If the worldly man fails to behave absolutely towards God, the ascetic fails to deal relatively with the relative (but essential) goals. S.K. well understood that in a sense monasticism attempts the impossible, trying to deal only with the absolute while renouncing the relative. Yet he hoped that a portrayal of the severe Christian ideal would challenge the complacent worldling to honesty and humble confession. In fact, says S.K., Luther was right in rejecting monasticism, because monasticism is an artificial attempt at solving the problem of the Christian's relation to the world; it attempts to solve ultimate problems by means which are mechanical and institutional rather than spiritual. Yet, rejecting the false method may well obscure the fact that there remains a necessity for man to free himself from worldliness. A fresh focus on the ideal of monasticism might therefore be employed to reveal at least the nature and gravity of man's spiritual enslavement, even though the true means of escape will be 'infinitely more exhausting' and will require religious suffering.[179] The suffering results precisely from the fact that man wants to commit himself *absolutely* to merely relative ends. He is unwilling to place God before father, wife, or child. (P. 412) Before accepting the lordship of Jesus man wants to marry a wife, bury his father, or inspect his property.

What more can be said on the relation of the absolute to the relative goals of life? Clearly the Christian will continue to live with worldly treasures, but they will be relative. The relation to God may make use of them, but it cannot pour itself exhaustively into the relative ends, because the absolute relationship may possibly require the renunciation of them all. (P. 363) To make certain that his worldly treasures are only relative and have not become idols, the religious man may propose to resign them, not as if they were evil but with the understanding that only when one is willing to sacrifice his dearest treasures is he really serious about the ultimate treasure. Asceticism seems to emerge here but it is really aside from the point; God may instead will that one live in common comforts. The point is only that if anything remains which one is unwilling to sacrifice for God then this is certain proof that one's God-relation is not triumphant. (P. 353) The spiritual life is never secure; one must for ever live in the world, cherishing it, clinging to loved ones, but willing to love God more. Instead of living like a monk, the Christain will probably be indistinguishable from others in society but neither earthly treasure nor earthly loss can destroy him because he has treasure laid up in heaven. (P. 367 f.)

Kierkegaard uses an expression for humility towards God which is subject to grave misunderstanding; 'self-annihilation', he says, 'is the essential form for the God-relationship'. By this he means what Luther intended in the principle that man can do nothing spiritually for himself, that he is 'as nothing before God'. (P. 412) But to be as nothing *before* God does not involve a mystic merging with God. Certainly the 'annihilated' self does not vanish, nor is it destroyed. It remains intensely real in its concrete striving. The Christian understands that 'the greatest exertion is nothing' but that at the same time this is precisely what God requires. (P. 414) To be annihilated is to rise to the most intense spiritual exertion, but to trust fully in the grace of God. If self-annihilation is the very contradictory of mysticism, it is equally alien to monasticism which attempts to renounce the world and the self by a peculiar 'external expression', indeed by a queer kind of worldliness as a meritorious substitute for authentic spiritual inwardness. (P. 412) The distinctive feature of true self-annihilation is the corrective suffering which remains as one persistently seeks to love God with all his heart and soul, making this his absolute *telos*, with the result that he suffers over having to treat all other values as merely relative ends. (P. 363)

Because of his stress on suffering and on seeking the eternal, Kierkegaard is often charged with other-worldliness, not without some justification. Yet primarily he is existential rather than other-worldly. To be Christian is not to dutifully wait for heaven; it is to enter into blessedness and joy at once by allowing one's entire selfish existence to be sacrificed to and transfigured by an eternal good. Only if one's existence in the world is transformed is religion actual. When the selfish man asks what he can get out of eternal life, S.K.'s ironic answer is that instead of getting something he has everything to lose—his pleasures, possessions, pride, even his 'righteousness'. What is worse, all he 'gains' is suffering. Nevertheless, this subtle answer is incomplete. He who loses the whole world gains his own soul, and suffering is—for selfish man—the bridge to joy, a joy which is not postponed for heaven but which distils peace in the restless soul. Then the relative values of an earthly existence become valid and beautiful by being restricted to their proper relative position. Their dethronement by the absolute *telos* at the same time gives them justification. (P. 364) This transfiguration and validation of the relative by the absolute never involves merger of them; the absolute is not a mere capstone. It never 'fraternizes' but instead remains transcendent. (P. 359)

Why is Christianity essentially suffering? There are many kinds of suffering, including painful accident and ethical martyrdom, but Christianity as suffering is unique. The stereotyped explanation is, of course, sin, but this in turn is to be understood as man's idolatrous deification of earthly values, treating an earthly love or delight as if it were divine. Christian suffering is precisely the dying to the world, a being weaned away from all that one normally cherishes. (Pp. 412 ff., 432, 446) The reason for the weaning from the world is not that the world is evil, but that man evilly makes an idol of it. The sinner gives absolute place to relative values and only relative place to absolute values. S.K. is here only saying in abstract language what Jesus expressed more simply in Matthew 10:37, 'He that loveth father or mother more than me is not worthy of me'. Thus on the one hand Christian suffering is a dethroning of temporal treasures in order to acknowledge the eternal. On the other hand suffering is the hungering of the yearning soul waiting for the fulfilment of eternal blessedness which cannot yet be possessed. For S.K., perhaps the most pathetic distortion of existence is for a man to cling to the ephemeral beauty of nature or the qualified constancy of human love as if it were absolute and eternal. That one suffers in yearning after God is the surest proof of one's relation to God.[180]

The complexity of the interrelationship of relative and absolute goals has led to various misunderstandings Thus Marjorie Grene failed to comprehend the relationships of the stages, believing, for example, that S.K. would renounce ethical existence in despair and commit himself to the subjectivity of religious (non-moral) solitude and nothingness when standing in the presence of the transcendent God. Rather, ethical universals (and also aesthetic satisfactions) are never left behind even though the ethical law is dethroned by grace; the religious man is to love the universal even though by grace he may happen to be an exception from it. In fact, religion is the category of fulfilment, whereby the ethical and life in its entirety shall be redeemed from despair and where righteousness shall be given a heavenly security. Grene's supposition that nothingness and sufferings are as such the goals of existence is astonishing in view of the abundance of evidence to the contrary.[181]

Another confusion which should be dispelled by the evidence noted is that the underlying issues lie in a conflict between Protestant and Catholic forms of piety. The issue is rather how the relative *teloi* and the absolute *telos* ought to be related. S.K. seems to make an important point in insisting that these cannot fraternize, that they must never be confused, and that the religious duty might even in a given instance require a teleological suspension of the ethical (cf. *Fear and Trembling*). Yet the questions are not thereby answered as to how the two functionally relate to one another. The basic issue is defined but the *Postscript* does not offer a complete answer. That there must be a relationship between absolute and relative goals is obvious. Man is straddled precariously with one foot on earth and one in heaven. In view of S.K.'s own insistence on the incarnation of the transcendent in the immanent, we might expect him to propose that the relative *teloi* offer empirical meaning and content for the absolute *telos* which otherwise would remain hidden because transcendent, and further that the absolute overcomes the multiplicity, the confused rivalry and the inadequacy of the relative. Yet such concrete proposals are wanting.

APPENDIX: SUBJECTIVITY IS TRUTH

This strange proposition needs some further comment. It is ironic that Kierkegaard should have offended so many by saying that subjectivity is truth, when in fact he sought to demolish the idealistic assumptions of such thinkers as Fichte, Schelling and Hegel that subjectivity is truth. They, like Plato, thought that if one searches his truest heart he will find reality, truth, and perhaps God. S.K.'s view is that if one searches his truest heart he will find a sinner and will come to guilt and suffering. Only by a miracle can man's subjective awareness possess God or eternal truth, and it is on this miracle that he focuses.

For men today this entire issue is obscured by the Hegelian climate with which S.K. had to deal. He would be far better understood if he had simply identified his labyrinthine study as an exploration of faith's relation to reason. However, in Hegel's system faith had been absorbed by reason, so that faith was a mere preliminary step on the way to philosophic truth. Therefore S.K. felt obliged to abstract faith from reason, and to insist that they are different in kind. Whereas reason gives a cold and passive assent to what is factually so, faith is a value commitment or an ethical act whereby one not only discovers what it is like to exist by actually existing but also discovers the nature of the value world which is sovereign over him. It is in such existential matters that subjectivity plays its role.

There is a sense in which religious truth lacks the rigidity of objective truth relations. While the believer is dealing with an objective God and with the lordship of Christ, yet the kingdom of value is *what ought to be* rather than what is; God's meaning is that which is possible rather than actual; and Christ's sovereignty is a pleading rather than an inescapability. Existence is what one makes of his possibilities, and the only way to grasp its truth is by existing, i.e. experiencing the subjectivity of passion and choice. Furthermore, inasmuch as to be spiritual is to be free it follows that what occurs in the realm of spirit cannot be causally 'explained', and is therefore 'irrational' at least to the extent that to be rational is to find causal explanations.

The tangle of unwieldly words in which S.K. phrases his thought are, interestingly, not wholly of his own devising. Not only was his problem created largely by Hegel, but the terms and ideas he used in attacking it were largely borrowed. He followed Lessing in holding that truth is not merely intellectual possession but must involve passionate value concern and a commitment of will.[182] Accordingly, he makes truth a quest, a 'venture which chooses an objective uncertainty with the passion of the infinite'. (P. 182) Further, the commitment or act by which one transforms an idea into his personal truth is, again in a word borrowed from Lessing, a 'leap'. The term 'leap' does not imply that one's act of acceptance occurs in a split second but that it is only by an *act* that one can transform a concept into truth. (P. 151 f.) As a lover does not justify his love by reasons, so too faith says simply, 'I believe', and then perhaps finds reasons. Or, perhaps one had noted some reasons and then chosen to believe, not being really impelled by the reasons but only by 'the witness of God'.[183]

The simple objectivity of existential truth is excluded not merely by the fact that the truth-appropriation process is one of value-existence, but also because that which is ultimately responded to is never a thing-like object but likewise a Subject. By transforming the eternal into an intellectually cognized thing, man makes it impossible for himself to communicate with it. God is actually separated from the knower, his personhood being lost sight of. (P. 178) Ultimate truth for man is to be found in a subject-Subject relation, in which value-consciousness is deepened to the point of greatest intensity. It should be obvious from this that the 'truth' to which S.K. is referring is not ordinary earthly truth but only Christian truth. In grasping the truth of earthly things it is certainly *not* the case that subjectivity is truth, because things are not subjects but only objects and do not enter into an 'I-Thou' encounter. The truth of a scientific doctrine is certainly not settled by faith. Truth is normally not subjective, even though it presupposes the subjectivity of consciousness.

Clearly then it is not enough to say that Kierkegaard equates subjectivity and truth. Not only is some truth not subjective; some kinds of subjectivity have little to do with truth. The diverse kinds of subjectivity need to be differentiated. For example, a dog's consciousness is subjectively private, but S.K. is not referring to the psychological when he refers to the subjectivity of truth. Closer to the point at issue, a pietist may believe whatever his emotions require, but Kierkegaard's subjectivity is not intended to allow such a privilege.

The kind of subjectivity intended is that kind of passion which is aroused when a man encounters the passion of God and finds himself responsible to it. If one truly encounters God, one cannot view him from the standpoint of a spectator. (P. 339) Christian responsiveness is thus not speculative or contemplative but impassioned and dutiful. Christ is not encountered at all unless he is sensed as the Way, and therefore he can be appropriated as truth only by walking in the Way. Christ does not say, 'Understand me', but 'Follow me', and in the life of discipleship grace and truth take possession of the disciple.[184]

There is a certain paradox involved in this view. On the one hand, the subjectivity of faith is a gift of the Holy Spirit. Yet it is not *caused* by the Spirit, but rather receives its enablement from God, and thus empowers one to make the leap which is not causally determined but is a free act. Furthermore, subjectivity is an act of will which is devoid of rational support. Its freedom is even a kind of 'absurd' commitment since the believer accepts a Christ who scandalizes the intellect by making the eternal an event in fluid history. To fully exist is to assume the risk of accepting or rejecting that which can appear true *only to faith*. Relative to such existence, only 'indirect communication' is appropriate, not persuasion, since there is no evidence but instead only challenge.[185]

It must be immediately added that the subjectivity which is faith is objectively grounded. It is not mere emotionality or a non-objective mysticism, but fellowship with the historic and eternal Christ. S.K. finds objectivity so necessary that he insists that man can attain true subjectivity only by manifesting infinite concern with eternal truth so as to evidence it in his living. Subjectivity does not spin out its own cocoon but responds to and grows in depth in relationship to the transcedency of God, appropriating the content of revelation and grounding itself in it. Yet the objective character and substance of the eternal never requires assent, and man remains free to reject the paradoxical revelation as an offence to reason.*

In this light, Kierkegaard's use of the term 'subjectivity' is unfortunate because it cannot be separated from objectivity. There is no such thing as faith but only faith-in-God, no such thing as

* Pp. 540, 183. Whereas Torsten Bohlin wanted to think of paradox as a theoretical and artificial means of opposing Hegelianism and of subjectivity as S.K.'s own personal awareness of God, Valter Lindstrom and J. Heywood Thomas have more plausibly argued that subjectivity is only the inward correlary of external paradox. Subjectivity is the acceptance in the passion of faith of that which cannot claim rational grounds. Cf. Thomas. *Subjectivity and Paradox*, pp. 45 ff., pp. 115 ff.

subjectivity but only subjectivity-appropriating-objectivity. Further, this element of faith is not an odd appendage to existence. Life in all of its relations is transformed by the subjectivity-objectivity; when man chooses himself absolutely he brings the sovereignty of God into all his living.[186]

By his rejection of the traditional separation of subjectivity and objectivity Kierkegaard parted company from the tradition of Schleiermacher as emphatically as from Hegel. He protested primarily against Hegelian speculative cognition of the Absolute, because of Hegel's enormous influence. Yet he would find Schleiermacher's religion of emotion (as a feeling of dependence) equally unchristian. Faith is not universally and spontaneously generated but is an individual response to the eternal God who has entered into time.[187]

Finally, it may be asked whether S.K. was not wrong in saying that subjectivity *is* truth. Harry S. Broudy has argued plausibly that S.K. should at the most have said that subjectivity is a 'necessary condition' to truth. The difficulty, he says, is that S.K. confused 'communication' with 'a special non-cognitive outcome of communication', i.e. the experience, mood, or even self-awareness which cannot be communicated but can perhaps be evoked. If one acknowledges this distinction, says Broudy, the subjectivity of existence and the importance of indirect communication in such an area as art would be acknowledged, but the philosopher would still possess objective communication.[188]

Broudy's insistence on careful use of terms is appropriate, and his distinction between awareness, the object-of-awareness, and the relation between them. If truth is thought of as an accurate grasp of reality, and if reality (in this case God) can be grasped only in the passion of love and faith, then passion may be the means of awareness but hardly the truth-relation itself.

In any case, the import of the matter can be summed up by contrasting S.K.'s position with that of Nietzsche. Gregor Malantschuk puts it this way: 'Kierkegaard's subjectivity is a blend of truth and what is individual, whereas Nietzsche's subjectivity is a blend of what is arbitrary and what is individual. For Kierkegaard it is truth which determines and transforms the individual; for Nietzsche it is the individual who determines what truth shall be.'[189]

CHAPTER III

THE CHRISTIAN WRITINGS

Is it super-irony that the *Concluding Unscientific Postscript* stands not at the end of Kierkegaard's vast writing but at the midpoint, that it seemingly has no special reference to science, and finally that it is six times as bulky as the *Philosophical Fragments* for which it was intended to be a 'postscript'? No, it is not really strange. There are, as previously indicated, rational and straightforward explanations. For one, Kierkegaard did plan to *conclude* his authorship with the '*concluding* postscript', and become a pastor, probably of some little rural congregation, or (as he conceived it at a somewhat later time) a theological professor.[1] As to the *Postscript* being 'unscientific', what S.K. chiefly intended to indicate was that he was avoiding the professorial style in an attempt at staying close to human experience. Further, there are suggestions here of his unhappiness with his contemporaries' growing preoccupation with and trust in the objective methods of science. Finally, the concluding writing would appropriately speak with greater comprehensiveness and finality than the *Fragments* or any of the other earlier works which in volatile, kaleidoscopic and fragmentary mood and fashion raised issues but did not finish nor even adequately explore them.

In time however all this was changed because the commitment to Christian faith and life which had been the imperative need for Kierkegaard—and, in his judgment, for everyone else—suddenly became for him a completely real personal experience. In a relatively short period of time which centred in the Easter season of 1848, he came to be assured of the forgiveness of his sins and was convinced that God deliberately and really 'forgets' sin. He even believed that with Christ's help his melancholy and sense of isolation from others might be broken. S.K.'s conversion—if it may be called that, for he had never really ceased to be a Christian—was not a mystical experience but an overwhelming joy at the full realization that God is loving and that even one's suffering is made under providence to serve the purposes of love.

The immediate consequence of all this was that whereas formerly in all his writings he had sought to 'wound from behind' (to make room for God but 'not authoritatively'), now he was free to speak openly, even with the authority of a 'witness'.[2] As a Christian, S.K. had always understood that, although the maieutic method is essential for self-awareness, true Christian communication must ultimately be witness-bearing, since eternal truth is not 'in the subject (as Socrates understood it) but in a revelation which must be proclaimed'.[3] Yet as a person Kierkegaard had been able to write only wistfully, longingly of Christianity as a well-understood possibility, whereas now it was for him a glorious presence. He was 'in faith'. The radical consequence was that, often in response to particular occasions, a great new authorship came into existence. It was direct rather than indirect, bluntly, outspokenly and uncompromisingly Christian rather than somewhat aesthetic or 'immanently' religious, and candid rather than maieutic and evocative.[4]

The new sense of responsibility to speak directly as a Christian carried with it a new life stance. S.K. had always felt that one's expression must be in conformity with his manner of life; writing is a deed of the person. Accordingly, he now felt a responsibility to openly *act* as a Christian if he were to write as one. Two notable events came in consequence of this. The one was his prompt attack (cf. unit 53) on the *Corsair*, an offensive and destructive popular journal, in which attack he willingly incurred suffering in the cause of righteousness. The second was his equally daring and even more important attack on the church for its hypocrisy. In a very important sense, the entire literature after the *Postscript* is not so much a literature—great and central though it be—but rather a series of formidable Christian deeds.

Being 'in faith' does not give complete certainty or simple security. Therefore, even though Kierkegaard—or any believer—speaks boldly he speaks at the same time with utter humility. He must never doubt that God is love, but must always doubt whether he loves God. Because of this emphasis on *Christian* doubt, the wound in the heart which drives one ever back to penitence, some have questioned whether Kierkegaard really was Christian. Arland Ussher argues that it remains uncertain whether S.K. 'really sought sainthood through despair, or whether he was fascinated by despair when he thought he was in love with sainthood'.[5] Similarly, Zuidema asserts that S.K. did not attain a consciousness of possessing faith, and that he had only an 'unhappy love of religion'.[6] Such interpretations are plainly contradicted by many of S.K.'s own statements, and are completely in conflict with his life of prayer. In large part they rest on a misunderstanding regarding the 'becoming' of a Christian. For S.K. to intimate that he was only in a state of becoming does not mean that he felt himself to be only on the way to faith. Rather, in the state of faith one is still only a 'becoming' Christian, living in a state of forgiveness even though unable to leave sin and insecurity behind. Indeed, faith itself, like God and the church, is an object of faith. Since faith can have no rational security, S.K. even dares to define it as a kind of anxiety, uneasiness, or doubt, 'a perturbing thing', nevertheless constituting more a state of offence with the strange Christ who also evokes love than an intellectual scepticism.[8]

The question may be raised whether the Christian literature properly begins with or after the formal and comprehensive statement of the *Postscript*. Actually, in a sense, both are the case. Kierkegaard allies it with the aesthetic writings by making it pseudonymous (Johannes Climacus), yet makes it authentically his own by listing his own name as the one responsible for publication. Likewise, although clearly directed to religious ends, the *Postscript* remains profoundly reflective, whereas in the later religious writings the reflective element of a philosophical nature largely vanishes.

Finally, the task of Kierkegaard in authoring the Christian writings is very simply stated. It is not to extol Christianity but to define it in such bold outlines that there can be no confusion as to its nature and no escaping its confrontation. Hegel made Christianity a pretty symbol for the 'truth', i.e. for his system. Culture addicts have identified it with civilization. Sentimentalists have made poetry of it. Legalists have transformed it into a new Judaism. S.K. comments: 'What was more honest in former days about even the most embittered attacks on Christianity was that there was approximate acceptance of what Christianity is.'[9]

20. ON AUTHORITY AND REVELATION: THE BOOK ON ADLER

On Authority and Revelation: The Book on Adler; or a cycle of ethico-religious essays. Not published by Kierkegaard. Translated with an introduction and notes by Walter Lowrie. Princeton: Princeton University Press, 1955. Kierkegaard did publish one of the essays from it, 'On the Difference Between a Genius and an Apostle', in *Two Minor Ethico-Religious Treatises*. The excerpt is from pp. 103 ff. The book was written and twice revised in 1846–47.

This largely unnoticed book, not published by Kierkegaard himself, is actually the beginning point of a great new authorship. It laid the foundations for most of the great concepts which followed and marked a sharp change in S.K.'s understanding of himself and his life work. The somewhat unreadable book relates to an eccentric pastor (Adolf Adler) who claimed to be writing new revelations under the guidance of Christ. Adler was a very learned man, a disciple of Hegel, and a successful pastor. Apparently becoming deranged, a 'vision' turned him against Hegel and led him to publish certain 'revelations' in a large volume of sermons. Professing to be a kind of Messiah, he approached Kierkegaard and in effect offered him the role of a John the Baptist. These events became the occasion for a prodigious amount of reflection on the part of Kierkegaard, not so much about Adler himself as about the underlying issues, such as the nature of revelation, the nature of religious authority in general, and more specifically the difference between an apostle and a genius. He felt it necessary to identify the basis for distinguishing between what is objectively Christian, what is personal interpretation, and what may even be subjective delusion. (Pp. viii ff.)

A bitter personal experience under which Kierkegaard was

suffering at the time undoubtedly had much to do with the strange fascination which Adler had for him. It was at just this time (1845) that Kierkegaard had felt obliged in Christian responsibility to attack a clever but unworthy journal, the *Corsair*. In particular, S.K. was incensed because P. L. Møller, one of its editors and a debauched person, had attacked S.K.'s diary of his love affair ('Guilty'/'Not Guilty' in the *Stages*) on moral grounds, even though praising the aesthetic element of *Either/Or*. Cleverly and satirically, Møller parodied its contents: 'She must be made free, because only then will she belong to me, and she can then get engaged again and marry whom she will; but nevertheless she is married to me.'[10] In his reply S.K. complained that his pseudonyms Hilarius the Bookbinder and Victor Eremita had been praised in the *Corsair*, in spite of their deficiencies in character, and hinted at Møller's true character. In response, with cruel humour, the paper played repeatedly on S.K.'s frail and misshapen body, in particular hammering on the fact that his one trouser leg hung lower. 'We all know from experience that *either* the two legs of trousers are equally long, *or* that the one is longer than the other.'[11] 'Either/Or' came to a strange and bitter usage, and children shouted this after Kierkegaard on the street. Far from regretting the situation, S.K. rejoiced over the privilege of suffering for the good, even though his anguish was very deep.[12]

Adler's being laughed at and scorned as a freak was painfully reminiscent of the derision being heaped upon Kierkegaard, when even the better element of society was afraid to come to the latter's defence, but the similarity took on a very unusual importance in that each man was professedly suffering for a godly cause. For Kierkegaard it became imperative to identify the sense in which the Christian is called to suffer for righteousness. Thus there ensued an exploration, with microscopic analysis, of the perilous role of the prophet and social critic. There was needed a meticulous discrimination between a St Paul, an Adolf Adler, and a Kierkegaard. This was particularly true because, on the one hand, S.K. never dared to think of a divine revelation or apostolic authority being bestowed upon him, and, on the other, he nevertheless was conscious of a wonderful 'governance' by which God made use of his life.

If Adler's errors called for definition, the opposing errors of mobs and masses of unthinking and even evil men also called for comment. Not only in *On Authority* but in other works soon to follow, S.K. found it necessary to call attention to the loss of responsible individuality in the social mass, and to the consequence of the necessity of righteous men suffering under public abuse.

A third factor in Adler's case led to still another major trend in Kierkegaard's judgment and life. In a sense, it was the fact that like S.K. himself, Adler had made a qualitative leap 'from the fantastic medium of the Hegelian philosophy . . . into the sphere of religious inwardness'. (P. 150) S.K. noted that this queer man had been brought up as a 'Christian' and become a pastor, during which time he was really a heathen, and that when he came nearer to actually being a Christian he was dismissed from the church (indeed, on good grounds of dubious sanity). Yet these events made it clear that there was a great illusion in supposing that one is a Christian simply by virtue of belonging to the 'church'. In spite of his derangement and false pretensions, Adler was one of the few who clearly understood that Christianity must be a living force and not simply a holy event of a bygone time or a wistful hope for a remote future. (P. 155) The church was as guilty of delusion in regard to its being authentically Christian as Adler was about his 'revelations'. These reflections led S.K. to conclude that he himself was only a poet (without authority), that he was a true individual (as all ought to be), that he was a strange exception to the normal pattern of life, but one who should help to clarify the truth, and finally that the church—however noble it may be—dare not assume that it is literally Christian. All of these themes and convictions become the real burden of the works which subsequently came flowing in swift succession from Kierkegaard's pen.

In spite of the importance of the *Book on Adler*, the author could never bring himself to publish it, for fear of further humiliating a man who had been deposed by the church. Instead, at a later time, he published a small but important section of it which made no reference to Adler and only oblique reference to himself. He felt compelled to seek a distinction between his own emphasis on subjectivity ('truth is subjectivity') and the irresponsible mysticism of Adler. True Christian subjectivity, he insisted, must of necessity have an objective foundation, in that it must be related to the historical and external revelation (the 'God-man').

Who can offer revelations? Kierkegaard replies that only an apostle can declare God, and he does this by virtue of his unique authority which comes from a special relationship to Christ. Thus a mere fisherman who is authorized by Christ to do so can speak with authority, but a genius who is not so authorized cannot communicate God. He can perhaps edify, but only 'indirectly', and as one without 'authority'. S.K. makes it plain that he is only a lowly genius, pouring out his books under the governance of God, hoping that they might serve as mirrors for readers to discover themselves in their existence.

Although largely unnoticed, *On Authority and Revelation* is important both because of the significance of the topics with which it deals, and because it discloses a firm place for an objective datum of revelation within S.K.'s 'subjectivity'. He argued that there is a necessary objective 'historical element in Christianity', viz. the paradoxical fact that God came into existence in human form under the Emperor Augustus. Objective scripture and history are essential for modern Christianity, just as seeing and hearing Jesus were essential in the first century. The disciple believes '*by means of*' such experiences but, since these are not self-authenticating, he comes to faith only '*by virtue* of the condition he himself receives from the God'.[13] However, the historical element must never be confused with 'the history of Christianity'. (P. 58) 'The Christian fact has no history, for it is the paradox that God came into existence in time . . . and though Christianity were to last another ten thousand years, one would get no further from this paradox than the contemporaries were.' (P. 60 f.)

The long centuries of the church may even stand in the way and confuse, seeming to imply that Christianity is becoming more plausible with its centuries of 'success'. One cannot become a Christian by relating himself to this 'after-history', and the gospel itself neither has been nor becomes 'assimilated' in history. One can become a Christian only by being lifted out of his own century so as to become a 'contemporary' of Christ. This in no sense implies that one becomes like a first-century Christian or that there would be any particular advantage in living in the first century, but only that one must somehow come face to face with

Christ if one is to be moved to faith like the apostle John or to offence like Judas.

Nevertheless, the Christian is not contemporary with Christ in the same way that an apostle was, for an apostle was specially called to make proclamation of the gospel. The ordinary Christian can indeed speak as a Christian but he is without authority. His message stands on its gospel strength and is not supported by his personal witness. Even an apostle does not inject his personality into his communication. Yet he is for ever and uniquely an apostle, and may well become a martyr because he is a 'witness for the truth'. Kierkegaard viewed the authority of the apostle not as simply an historically grounded pre-eminence but as deriving from the transcendent authority of Christ himself. Therefore the apostle was thought of as sharing in Christ's paradoxical transcendence. (P. 112) God appoints a man 'to have divine authority' which comes 'from another place and has nothing to do with cleverness or wisdom'. Accordingly, apostleship is not historically demonstrable, although obviously an historical reference is involved. The authentication of the apostleship, like that of Christ himself, is given only in (non-rational) faith, and is dependent on faith in Christ. An apostle has no proofs; he simply asserts his apostleship and proclaims his gospel, and the believer is then related to the message—not to the apostle.

In this simple assertion or witness of the apostle there is a distinctive quality which intimates the element of transcendent authority. An apostle is willing to die for his truth, and his martyrdom is a profoundly impressive witness. In contrast, a truth for which the sponsor is not willing to be sacrificed is unpersuasive.[14] However, even true witnessing is not proof but only a sign because faith is not convinced by reason but by one's being obedient to the Spirit's prompting.

Kierkegaard's emphasis on authority, as of apostles or even of ordained ministers, may seem strange, particularly in view of his subsequent attack on the clergy and his insistence that he was himself without authority. Nevertheless, there is no contradiction in this. By his criticism and self-abasement he wished to exalt *true* authority in contrast to the hollow and assumed authority of mere officialdom. It is precisely the nature of Christian authority that it speaks with earnestness, positiveness, and finality rather than with (aesthetic) meditation or (rational) argument. Christian authority commands, enjoins, proclaims. It does not ponder or dally but requires a choice and insists on the possibility of the hearer being offended by a lowly Christ. Unless *being offended* with Christ is a definite possibility, faith can be no more than a casual acceptance of the traditions in which one happens to have been reared. In this light it is important that the Christian message must be spoken with no other persuasion—no rational proof or enticing charm—than bare, undemonstrable authority.[15]

Kierkegaard's stress on being contemporary with Christ led him to contrast the individuality of the Christian with the individuality offered man by modern society. The French revolution caused him to make it emphatic that political reform cannot solve mankind's fundamental problems. In its attention to human welfare, social revolution may pretend to be concerned with the individual, but it leaves out the one thing essential, the 'God-relationship in the individual'. Liberty apart from God ends in an equality of mediocrity, and fraternity becomes egoistic collectivism, 'a monster of fairyland with many heads, or, more correctly and truly, with a thousand legs'. (P. 193) This is a dehumanization which parades under the banner of humanity. It is this which S.K. calls a 'dissolute pantheistic contempt for the individual',[16] replacing God with a virtually deified state-crowd-mass (as in Nazi or communist or even democratic power systems). This mass reduces the individual to the self-less and irresponsible position of a mere number in society. The appalling catastrophe of the totalitarianisms of the twentieth century make very clear how important is S.K.'s approach to the solving of social ills. The individual must be re-born.[17]

Further treatment of this work appears under the heading *Two Ethico-Religious Treatises* where the crucial excerpt from it is reviewed—'On the Difference Between a Genius and an Apostle'.

21. ON THE DIFFERENCE BETWEEN A GENIUS AND AN APOSTLE

'On the Difference Between a Genius and an Apostle.' This essay is the more important part of *On Authority and Revelation: The Book on Adler*. Although the entire work was subsequently published, Kierkegaard himself refrained from doing so and instead published only this selection from it. He included this essay in *Two Ethico-Religious Treatises* (section 33), where it is chiefly treated in the present study, but also in *On Authority* (section 20).

22. A LITERARY REVIEW

A Literary Review. By S. Kierkegaard. March 30, 1846. This work (*En literair Anmeldelse*, Vol. 14 of *Vaerker*) has not been translated in full. It concerns an anonymous novel, 'Two Ages', but more importantly it is an impressive expression of Kierkegaard's view of society and of the individual. The more important part appears in English under the title *The Present Age*, under which heading it is here treated (section 23).

23. THE PRESENT AGE

This work is the more important part of *A Literary Review*, which is not translated in its entirety. This selection appears in *The Present Age* and *Two Ethico-Religious Treatises*. Translated by Alexander Dru and Walter Lowrie. London: Oxford University Press, 1940. Reprinted in *The Present Age and Of the Difference Between a Genius and an Apostle*, with an Introduction by Walter Kaufmann. New York: Harper & Row, 1962, Harper TB 94. The *Review* and the *Treatises* (one of which is *Of the Difference*) are here treated separately. (Page references are to the Torchbook edition.)

THE CHRISTIAN WRITINGS

In his Introduction, Walter Kaufmann notes that there is a real danger that readers will *not* take offence at this book, even though in it S.K. 'strained to be offensive', especially to parsons and professors. The reason is that even though his 'is now a name to conjure with', yet Kierkegaard's 'central aspirations are almost invariably ignored'.

Kaufmann is quite right in arguing that S.K.'s interpretation of his own age was faulty, e.g. in holding that in such an age it was unthinkable that there could be revolution and decisiveness. The revolutions which swept over Europe in the nineteenth century demonstrated his radical error in this regard. Kaufmann may even have a point in his objection to Kierkegaard's contention that the age required not mere reflection but more passion, although one might wonder if they are not talking about essentially different passions, especially considering S.K.'s concern for intelligent government and good social order. In any case, however, the book has the merit of speaking to conscience in any age about the shabby way in which men tend to lose their individuality in the sodden mass of society. How applicable to the humour of today's mass media is the possibility which S.K. here imagined, and which supposedly would never (sic) come to pass, that wit might sometime be 'transformed into its shabbiest contrary, a trivial necessity, so that it became a profitable branch of trade to manufacture... and buy up old and new witticisms'. (P. 40)

Already in his doctoral dissertation, at the outset of his career, S.K. was distressed by the follies of his 'age', with its easy convictions which took the role of truth, and its incessant talk about pathos of which it was scarcely capable. Its symbol, he suggested, is a wide-open mouth, 'for how else is one to visualize a true... patriot except he be making speeches, how else should one visualize the dogmatic face of a profound thinker except with a mouth able to swallow the whole world?' Taking comfort in numbers which seemed to relieve one of the necessity of being a significant individual, the age despised isolation and could not even conceive of a person 'going through life alone'. People meddled in one another's lives to such an extent that the whole city was inclined 'to take upon itself the honourable task of proposing' for a lover.[18]

In *The Present Age* the charge is made that society is in many ways guilty of dehumanizing people under the very pretence of taking care of them. 'For a time, committee after committee is formed . . . but in the end the whole age becomes a committee. A father no longer curses his son in anger . . ., a conflict which might end in the inwardness of forgiveness; on the contrary, their relationship is irreproachable, for it is really in process of ceasing to exist . . .' (P. 44) By a horrible levelling process individuals become afraid to be themselves and feel secure only in mass humanity. No matter how great the nonsense nor how evil the deed, if a few people can 'add themselves together' then they dare to do it. 'Twenty-five signatures make the most frightful stupidity into an opinion, and the considered opinion of a first-class mind is only a paradox.' (P. 79) Culture itself tends to make men insignificant copies, abolishing individuality, and world history is a noise-maker in which men take refuge to avoid their personal responsibilities.[19]

Loss of individuality has its charateristic effects, according to Kierkegaard, such as 'reasoning', superficiality, talkativeness (which loses the vital distinction between the time for speech and the time for silence), and flirtation (in which one 'dares to touch evil' and 'fails to realize the good' even though he desires the good).

Kierkegaard's journals greatly expand upon these observations. For example, he insists there on man's gaining liberation from the mass by seeking the riches of solitude. 'Even if I were able to say in a loud voice something which everyone would highly esteem, I would not say it if it had to do with religion, because it is a kind of religious indecency to suppose that everything depends on shouting loudly whereas true religion depends solely upon quiet talking with oneself. Alas, everything now is reversed: instead of its being important for religion that every individual walk alone and enter into his closet, there to converse softly with himself, one believes that everything depends on shouting.'[20] Unlike animals, which benefit from the impulse to be in a herd, man must learn to be solitary because God deals with persons and a person is always single.[21]

Kierkegaard claims that whereas an 'animal-definition' of man may conceive him largely in terms of social responses, a true understanding of selfhood will relate it to the eternal. Accordingly, the measuring stick of the human spirit is the question of how long one can bear to be alone.[22] However, the individuality which is deepened in solitude does not involve a withdrawal from society. Indeed, for people who have become or chosen themselves, before God, and only for them, does authentic sociality become a possibility. Although Kierkegaard himself is not a social actionist, the concept of the individual is a presupposition to social action. Where men are not individually responsible their society collapses into some kind of living mechanism or totalitarian mass. There is, however, the religious possibility that one who has suffered in the levelling process may learn by it to discipline himself in lowliness.

If true individuality is not isolationist in character, neither is this protest against the social mass in any sense anarchistic or revolutionary. Actually, Kierkegaard was a conservative, on the side of social order and suspicious of the rabble and of disruptive influences. His respect for authority was evident in his loyalty to the government and also in his loyalty to the head of the church. Equality gained by mob action, by revolution or violence would be at the lowest common denominator and would not constitute an equality of responsible and unique individuals. In reflections reminiscent of Plato, S.K. argues that even democracy is much the same as tyranny except that in a democracy not one man but 'the crowd' is tyrant.[23] This by no means signifies that S.K. was simply a traditional conservative. His conservatism rested on a recognition of the fine line which separates the demos from the mob when once its members no longer feel individual responsibility to God and listen to the preachments of an incendiary. Equality of rascals or of vain sophisticates will not do. For humans who invariably differ sharply among themselves, communism's attempt at making people common is both comical and frightening. S.K. underscores this by pointing to the glory of uniqueness which is available to every man.[24]

Until this book, Kierkegaard wrote, for the most part, pseudonymously and evocatively. Here he begins to speak more directly and in his own voice, protesting vehemently against the insincerity, hypocrisy, and lack of integrity of his generation. In connection with his conflict with the *Corsair* (cf. unit 20) he had come to the conclusion that in order to be a religious author he could not simply write sermons; he had to be polemical, challenge evil and endure persecution. Christianity must be a force in the world. 'A victorious religious author [suffering under no opposition] who is *in the world* is *eo ipso* not a religious author.'[25] His own age, Kierkegaard felt, was particularly guilty, an age which levelled men *down*, so that no man was allowed to be greater or nobler than another. S.K. thought of himself as an exception, perhaps an unhappy one, but nevertheless a deliberate individual, willing to suffer for being different. As such, he persistently addressed himself in his writings not to a public, a crowd, but to the 'individual', a kind of timeless person, unbound by the age in which he lived, who would will to be himself.

The ideas of this work and others helped to popularize and deepen the understanding which has developed in the twentieth century of the levelling effect of the mass. Kierkegaard's concept of the public as a threat to personhood has been eagerly taken up, not only by existentialists such as Jaspers (*Man and the Modern Age*); Marcel (*Man Against Mass Humanity*), Jose Ortega y Gasset (*The Revolt of the Masses*), and Nicholas Berdyaev (*The Fate of Man in the Modern World*), but also by social thinkers unrelated to existentialism.

24. EDIFYING DISCOURSES IN VARIOUS SPIRITS

> *Edifying Discourses in Various Spirits.* By S. Kierkegaard. March 13, 1847. The three large portions of this work have been published separately in English, and here are so treated, under the titles: *Purity of Heart, The Lilies of the Field* (or, *Consider the Lilies*), and *The Gospel of Suffering.*

This large volume of discourses, still called 'edifying' by the author, nevertheless is formidably Christian. The style and message varies considerably as one moves from one to another of the three very distinct parts of the work, i.e. from the treatment of purity of heart to the message of the lilies of the field, and finally to the significance of suffering. It is quite appropriate that the dissimilar units have been published separately in English.

However, there is a sense in which the three parts of the total work manifest a unity, giving illustration to the familiar three stages. The second unit, a charming treatment of the lilies and birds, is highly aesthetic. The first unit, dealing with purity, is ethical, and the last unit is profoundly religious. Nevertheless, even the poetic utterance leads to the presence of God, and the ethic (purity) is a *religious* ethic which is concerned with obedience to God—an obedience which is conceived of essentially as a single-minded openness to God.

25. PURITY OF HEART

> *Purity of Heart is to Will One Thing.* This work, published independently in English, is Part I of *Edifying Discourses in Various Spirits,* published on March 13, 1847. In English: *Purity of Heart.* Translated by Douglas V. Steere. New York: Harper & Brothers, 1938; revised ed., 1948; Torchbook paperback TB 4, 1956. *Purify Your Hearts!* Translated by A. S. Alderworth and W. S. Ferrie. London: C. W. Daniel Co., 1937. (Page references are to the 1956 edition.)

The title 'Diary of the Seducer' (*Either/Or*) will attract more attention than will 'Purity of Heart'. However, the purpose of *Purity of Heart* is not to attract and entertain those inclined towards seduction but to edify those who are seeking wholeness of character. As a definition of purity and as a plea for integrity this book is a classic of devotional literature. Of it the Danish scholar Eduard Geismar has written that it is the best book with which to begin an acquaintance with Kierkegaard. 'It seems to me that nothing that he has written has sprung so directly out of his relationship with God as this address.'[26]

As with *Works of Love,* the purpose of *Purity* is not to make men pure but to so dramatize the life of holiness as to furnish a mirror in which all of one's dreadful blemishes can be plainly seen. *Purity* is really a pathway to repentance. As he realizes what it is that singleness of purpose requires, the penitent cries out: 'Alas, but this has not come to pass . . . Each day, and day after day, something is being placed in between: delay, blockage, interruption, delusion, corruption. So in this time of repentance may Thou give the courage once again to will one thing.' (P. 218) Man is unlike all of nature. For the animal there is a time to leap with joy and a time to die. So too, 'when the flower is dead, the story is over'. For man there is not only change and passing time but an unalterable constancy which derives from his contact with the eternal. The clearest demonstration of it is repentance which, even though it is always tied to a particular hour, viz. the eleventh hour (hour of judgment), is nevertheless always the same because every hour is the eleventh hour. (Pp. 35 f., 42)

Despite its bland title and its seemingly mild utterance, *Purity* has been likened to shock therapy because of its ability to bring the reader to a fearful honesty with himself. S.K. meant these discourses to be read aloud in private meditation as one prepared himself for public confession. Therefore they offer no consolation but instead demand honesty. Confession calls for a collected mind, collected, that is, 'from every distraction'. It is painstaking research in personal responsibility. A physician—even a pastor—asks about one's health and life circumstances, but eternity is not interested in these; it compels a man to be responsible for the condition of his own soul.

Section 12, a good point of beginning, treats 'the listener's role in a devotional address'. Kierkegaard uses an impressive analogy. Whereas one who listens to the discourse wishes to be a passive hearer, he must instead be like an actor on a stage. The edifying discourse is then only a humble prompter, behind stage, suggesting the actor's lines which then the actor must speak for himself. The actor must in earnest repeat the lines on the stage of eternity, with God as the solitary audience. The prompter does assume that the actor has the best of intentions but it asks him the painful question as to whether by his manner of life he is succeeding in willing only one thing—the Good.

Unhappily, men are like Adam, furtively hiding. Adam thought he could conceal himself from God and from the truth by slipping among the trees. Men today are still more clever; they hide among one another in a crowd of nonentities where even God cannot distinguish one from another. Among these other nonentities a man vainly indulges in comparisons, excuses and evasions. However, in eternity there will be no crowd, no mass, but only individuals, and therefore no place of concealment. Eternity will not ask how many others had the same opinion—the same wrong opinion. Moreover, 'the larger the crowd the more probable that that which it praises is folly', so even in the temporal world one should beware of the crowd. (P. 191) If for the sake of conscience one is ridiculed by the crowd, this ridicule can be like a warrior's wound, a badge of honour on the breast. 'Eternity asks solely about faithfulness, and with equal earnestness it asks this of the king and of the most wretched of all sufferers.' (P. 210)

What then is purity of heart? The answer offered is strange, yet it is Biblical and impressive. It is to will *one* thing, i.e. the all-encompassing good which is the will of God. S.K. treats with relentless concentration the perils of double-mindedness, and also the barriers to willing one thing (such as willing the good only out of fear of punishment or for the sake of reward). In such cases a person is not really loving the good but only himself, and thus is compromising the good. At the very best, he is guilty of loving the good only up to a certain degree but not in wholeness and faithfulness. Inasmuch as only the good is a unity, to will anything other than the good is double-mindedness. Moreover, to have two wills—thereby being in inner conflict—is despair; whoever rebels against God is in despair.

In the rush of daily life there is a temptation to compromise the good, or to be 'reasonable', but if one truly wills the good then he puts his cleverness to use in preventing such evasions. Thus he does all for the good and is willing to suffer everything for it. The absolute necessity for having good conscience is for a man to *be an individual*, rendering his account to God. 'For he who is not himself a unity is never really anything wholly and decisively; he only exists in an external sense—as long as he lives as a numeral within the crowd...' (P. 184) Whereas an angry man believes that he is expressing himself in his act of vengeance, later, in recollection, the deed may become loathesome to him. Thus for a true individual there is an inversion of customary and relative value judgments. In eternity there will be no place to which one can flee from truth and conscience, for in the infinite 'there is no place, the individual himself is the place'. (P. 186)

If the disclosures of shameful truth about oneself make the light of eternity frightening, how much more fearful is the ignorance of the sinner who stumbles through life, crushing, bruising, and yet of whom it must be said 'he knew not what he did'. (P. 51) Imagine it, that one might come to the point of death without ever coming to understand who he was and what he had done!

It is only the prayer of confession which brings one to truth and to the possibility of reconciliation. Only by speaking aloud in the stillness does one's enormity begin to be evident—to himself, although it was long known to God. Yet even this repentant man can be guilty of concealing the truth from himself. S.K. imagines a criminal who, after punishment and penitence, cuts away from the past, and begins a new and distinguished life in a strange community. He is deceptively at peace, managing to exclude his painful memories from awareness. Then one who knew him in his shame recognizes him and the reformed criminal is brought back to reality and to despair. His trouble was that he had repented *once upon a time* and then forgot his true self and his repentance. Against this stands the unbreakable truth that one's past is for ever his own. 'It is eternally false, that guilt is changed by the passage of a century.' True repentance is 'a silent daily anxiety', and such honesty before God will preserve one against inward collapse in the face of truth's disclosure. (P. 45)

In conclusion, it must be acknowledged that, for the casual reader, there is almost a monotone of reiteration in this book's insistence that purity of heart is to will one thing, the good. However, it is just this recurrent theme which makes it evident that this work is distinctively Christian in that it exalts purity on one ground only, viz. that this singlemindedness is the acceptance of God's claim upon man. To do good or will the good for any other reason—as reward or fear of punishment—is not truly to will the good.

THE CHRISTIAN WRITINGS

26. THE LILIES OF THE FIELD

This work, published independently in English, is Part II of *Edifying Discourses in Various Spirits*, where it bore the title 'What We Learn From the Lilies of the Field and the Birds of the Air'. Translated by David F. and Lillian Marvin Swenson in *The Gospel of Suffering* and *The Lilies of the Field*. Minneapolis: Augsburg Publishing House, 1948. Also translated by A. S. Alderworth and W. S. Ferrie in *Consider the Lilies*. London: C. W. Daniel Co., 1940. The second discourse of Part II is in *Edifying Discourses, A Selection*, ed. by Paul L. Holmer. New York: Harper & Brothers, Harper TB 32. (Page references are to Swenson's translation.)

What is it to be human and how can one reconcile himself to being human? Here is Kierkegaard's answer to such existential questions. True, the central admonition is the Biblical 'Consider the lilies', but the outcome is 'Consider man!' Some of S.K.'s most beautiful writing appears in this work.

Considering the crescendo of human wailing, the title of the first discourse is interesting. It is 'On Being Content With What it Means to be a Man'. The reader is asked to consider the lilies *of the field*, but the name lily is deceptive to people who think of lilies in terms of such potted flowers as Easter lilies. The flowers we are called to consider are not rare plants. They have been tended by no gardener. Instead, uncared for, they grow in profusion, 'standing in a host, of so many colours, yet each of them as good as the rest'. See how they still grow, Kierkegaard urges, even though nobody cares for them. The lily succeeds without striving. It is beautiful without assistance. If it could speak to an anxious man, the lily would say, 'Should it not be just as splendid to be a man?'

A charming parable is told, one of Kierkegaard's great contributions to the literature of the ages. A lily was standing by a running stream, well known to some nettles and a few tiny flowers of the neighbourhood. The peace of the lovely lily was disrupted by a wicked little bird which, to put on airs, told of lovelier lilies elsewhere and of their greater abundance in more favoured spots. The troubled lily began to wonder why it had to be so secluded, with nothing but stinging nettles for company. Yet it sought not to be unreasonable. 'I do not demand the impossible, to become what I am not, as, for instance, a bird, but my wish is only to be a magnificent lily, or maybe the most magnificent.' (P. 180) And so, by agreement, the little bird cut away the soil from the little flower's roots and flew with it 'to the place where the splendid lilies bloomed', there to plant it among them. But, alas, the lily withered and died. Man is such a lily, and the little bird is the poetic and seductive anxiety in him which makes him unwilling to accept himself.

Consider also the birds of the air. Pertaining to them Kierkegaard tells what has become an equally famous parable. Once there was a wood-pigeon which lived happily 'in the lowering wood, where wonder is found along with shuddering'. The wood-pigeon came to know two tame pigeons and talked with them about the conditions of life. Previously it had let each day carry its own troubles, but on learning how the farmer stored up loads of corn for the tame pigeons to eat it began to worry about its future security. The wood-pigeon began, like the farmer, to gather in store, yet it never seemed to have more than what was sufficient for the day. Troubled, not by want but by anxiety, the wild bird finally dared to join the tame pigeons, and at night went with them into the pigeon loft. When the farmer closed the loft and found the axious bird he killed it, releasing it from its anxiety, and made a meal of it. The wood-pigeon is a symbol of man, whose need is to be content with being a man. Man is 'as little capable of sustaining himself as of creating himself'. Men are cared for, indiscriminately, by the heavenly Father. Accordingly, anxiety is man's sin.

The second discourse turns attention from man's degradation to his glory. Its humanistic title is 'How Splendid it is to be a Man'. Yet how contrary is man's mood: 'If then God so clothed the grass of the field!' Yet no lily is clothed in greater loveliness than another, for the loveliness of each is its being true to its nature. From this one may be reminded that if one lady is dressed in more beautiful raiment than another it is not God who has given the finer raiment. Such differences are external and trivial. The 'being clothed' of the lily is precisely the same as its being a lily.

So too, for man to be beautifully clothed by God means for man to be adorned by the glory of humanness.

How splendid is man! Animals may have eyes, but the faculty of looking belongs only to man. Man alone stands erect, and is thus an uplifted being. So too, man is the only creature blessed with delicate, imperious, creative hands. The lily is not like God because the lily is *visible*, but man is *spirit* and so he is in the image of the invisible God.

Man must be like the birds, free of anxiety for the morrow, yet it is no virtue in the bird that it knows no anxiety. It cannot be anxious because it lives only in the present moment. But in man the temporal and the eternal come into immediate contact. Therefore, whereas the bird sows not, nor reaps, but procures its food as a 'vagabond' out in the fields, man works, and thus resembles God who also works, even unto the present time. Man's proper glory is to have the tempting gift of knowledge, yet to retain his creaturely integrity and authencity in godly trust.

The last discourse, 'The Blessedness that is Promised in Being a Man', extends the analogy of man and nature. In nature, there is endless change and variety, thronging life but also sudden death, gay songs of birds but also unfathomable suffering. The lily that flourishes today in indescribable splendour is tomorrow cast into the oven. Two sparrows are sold for only a farthing. Indeed, one of them has no value at all.

In contrast there is blessedness in being a man, such blessedness as frees him from the mysterious pathos of nature. He is not a puppet in the hands of the eternal, but is given the privilege of choice between God and mammon. The lily has no privilege of choice; it serves the glory of God but cannot do otherwise. The bird does not serve two masters, although only unwittingly does it sing God's praises. Man likewise cannot serve two masters, but he can and must *choose* which master he will serve. It is impossible to choose God *and* mammon, for to choose both is to avoid choosing. Only when man is like the lilies, dependent on God, and yet unlike the lilies is freed of anxiety and reconciled to God by choice, only then is he properly himself. For one who seeks first the Kingdom of God, divine righteousness shall be added—for the Kingdom is righteousness.

Finally, it is to be noted that, however Biblical this book may be, it is also a clear exposition of Kierkegaard's own existential thought, i.e. of existence as the unique kind of being which man possesses, marked by choice before God, marred by anxiety, and gaining fulfilment only by so decided a leap as is made possible by the grace of God.

27. THE GOSPEL OF SUFFERING

> This work, published independently in English, is actually Part III of *Edifying Discourses in Various Spirits*. Published in English as: *Gospel of Sufferings*. Translated by A. S. Alderworth and W. S. Ferrie. London: J. Clarke, 1955. Also translated by David F. and Lillian Marvin Swenson in *The Gospel of Suffering* and *The Lilies of the Field*. Minneapolis: Augsburg Publishing House, 1948. The fifth discourse is reprinted in *Edifying Discourses, A Selection*, edited by Paul L. Holmer. New York: Harper & Brothers, 1958, Harper TB 32. (Page references are to the Swenson translation.)

This work begins with a sharp attack on the common churchly understanding of 'following Christ'. Is it permissible for the comfortable and complacent Christian to thank God for letting Jesus suffer so that the disciple may be comfortable? A vivid pictorial answer is given. Imagine a brave ancient warrior who leaps out in self-sacrifice to draw the enemy arrows on himself. Is one of those whom he shields by his suffering a 'follower'? Not unless he follows *into danger*. To follow Christ means to take up one's own cross, walking the way Christ walked. The solitary anguish of a follower seems tragic, but if a child is learning—with bumps and bruises—to walk and cries out complainingly, 'I am walking alone', its mother will say, 'That is very wonderful'. For the Christian it is still more wonderful so to walk in loneliness because he is alone only for the reason that Christ has gone on before him to prepare a place for him.

These eminently 'Christian' discourses are not clever or entertaining. Unlike the aesthetic writings, they were not written to charm the sophisticated or to arouse curiosity. The author's hope was to give comfort and strength to any anguished Job who in spite of suffering dedicates himself to righteousness. Casual readers may find these pages somewhat laboured and lacking in S.K.'s customary wit. Philosophers will find them deficient in his familiar dialectic. However, sufferers will find here profound thoughts for reflection, and, in the end, every man (above all every Christian) is a sufferer. In this work Kierkegaard's interpretation of Christian existence becomes more precise, indicating the absolute requirements which Christianity imposes and the suffering —nevertheless transformed by joy—which it entails.

The title of the book is misleading, for suffering is certainly not the content or the goal of the gospel. It is nevertheless one essential part of the inevitable outcome of dedication to the gospel. The believer must take up his cross and go in the way Christ went, and he must go alone. Like Christ he may find himself needy, forsaken and mocked, for the sake of the good. Yet his burden becomes light in the thought that one is suffering for his guilt because this focuses on the compassion of God and on the fact that the source of misery is not in God but in man. Even more joyous is the fact that the familiar Biblical assertion that 'narrow is the way' does not so much signify that the way itself is narrow but that *narrowness is the way* to the good. If an earnest person finds himself in tribulation he may well be assured that he is on the right way. The light affliction of the moment worketh eternal glory, not as an earned reward but as a happiness which is inherent in the good. In spite of the book's sombre title, there is nothing morbid in its stress on joy in suffering. It reiterates the Biblical assurance, which is also demonstrated by the lives of the apostles, that courage in suffering transforms defeat and derision into victory. The man of faith should never envy those who are not suffering because his affliction is a ground for trust that he is on God's way.

How dreadful then must the burden be which one bears in following Christ? The answer is, 'The burden can be light'. Nevertheless, that Christ's yoke is easy is a matter of faith; its lightness cannot be seen but only believed. The Christian is spared from no suffering but if he understands that his experience is spiritually profitable then it becomes the easy 'yoke of Christ'.

The meekness which God requires enables man to bear the heavy burden lightly. Imagine a cruelly treated slave. 'To bite at the chain is to bear it heavily, to ridicule the chain is also to bear it heavily..., to bear the bond of slavery as a free man may carry a chain: that is bearing it lightly.' (P. 37) Meekness in suffering hides guilt and overcomes sin. Thus Jesus looked meekly at Peter who had with curses denied him thrice. His meekness concealed Peter's guilt and offered the reconciliation of forgiveness to relieve the consciousness of sin.

Christian patience is not to be confused with Stoic apathy or disdain. The image of an Indian warrior bravely enduring torture is not to be identified with the Christian acceptance of suffering. The Christian does not admire indifference to pain, but, acknowledging the suffering, gives it new meaning, that 'suffering trains for eternity'. Jesus learned the Father's way through suffering, but men are eager to learn more quickly and much more easily. The instruction which suffering offers is the lesson of patient obedience, as expressed in the prayer, 'nevertheless, not my will, but Thine'. Far from being indifferent to suffering, the Christian recognizes in it both a dreadful schooling and a peril, the greatest danger being that one may learn nothing at all from it. Happily, the 'longest schooling [suffering] trains for the highest; the school which lasts as long as time, can train for eternity'. (P. 61)

A humanist might well complain that neither suffering nor Kierkegaard's view of it makes sense. As John Stuart Mill argued in his essay on nature, nature strikes down the noble and the vile indiscriminately, in what would be criminal fashion if judged by moral standards. Even Scripture echoes the protest: Why must the righteous suffer? Kierkegaard is profoundly aware of this problem. Already in the *Postscript* (pp. 256, 259) he had indicated that apart from religion suffering is only circumstantial whereas the Christian suffers also from the burden which paradox imposes on reason. In this new work he develops a provocative thesis, '*Man always suffers as being guilty*', i.e. all suffering ought to be given a religious connotation. It does not follow and is not stated that evil is part of a divine plan or that all suffering—of animals as well as of men—is a consequence of sin, although S.K. does neglect the Biblical theme that evil and suffering are an enigma and alien to God. The important point is that he is not here involving himself in the issues which plagued St Augustine and Leibnitz; he is not attempting a comprehensive explanation of evil. He is not thinking of collective guilt, or of the measure of suffering being proportionate to the amount of guilt. Instead, his concern is with spiritual therapy, a Biblical response to evil rather than explanation of it. He only wants to say that, regardless of the origin of one's sufferings, the only proper way to accept them is by standing before God as one who is in guilt. Suffering can then become a source of joy in that it is apprehended as a purifying expression of God's love.

Whose judgment can one trust regarding a proper response to suffering? Surely, thinks S.K., the statement of a dying man ought to be taken very seriously. Then how impressive is the testimony of the thief who was cricified with Jesus! 'We receive the due reward of our deeds,' he said, 'but this man has done nothing amiss.' As compared with his neighbour, a man may be relatively guilty in one regard and innocent in another, but, says S.K., the dying thief understood that before God man is always guilty because religious guilt does not consist of occasional misdeeds but of an unwillingness to be the kind of creature God ordains. While the innocent Christ cries out, 'My God, why hast thou forsaken me', the penitent thief should have exclaimed, 'My God, forgive me because I have forsaken Thee'. The sufferer Job was humanly righteous and he was therefore understandably indignant when his neighbours suggested that he confess his sins so that God would cease punishing him. Nevertheless, Job was guilty *before God*. In their consciousness of guilt such sinners should find an unexpected cause for joy, viz. to know that God is not cunning, that it is not God who has deserted the sinner, and that the real cause of the alienation lies in man. If man were indeed forsaken by God this would leave him with no task to perform, but even the dying thief had the task of contrition to perform. For every guilty man there is much to do. He has a future with goodness and hope.

Underscoring Kierkegaard's religious optimism—his melancholy notwithstanding—we find his remarkable reformulation of *'narrowness is the way'*. The Biblical way from Jerusalem to Jericho offers an illustration. It is narrow, difficult and dangerous. Yet how differently the narrow way was followed by the Samaritan than by others! One travelled it as a just man, another as a robber. The priest and Levite walked it in thoughtlessness and meanness of heart. Only for the despised Samaritan was it an opportunity for showing mercy. By external circumstance the way was evil, but by moral resolution the Samaritan made the narrowness, the evil and the suffering, to be a way of glory.

From this a sufferer should learn what his task is. Others may not have to walk in such afflictions as he experiences, but he should waste no energy contemplating other and more delightful roads. Instead he should use his strength, which under God is always adequate strength, in journeying on his godly path. 'But when an affliction is the way, then the affliction cannot be taken away without taking away the way, and there cannot be *other ways* [than God's way], but only a wrong way.' (P. 11) Further, if affliction is a way then it must lead somewhere, viz. to eternal life, betokening not human dignity but a religious hope. Godly sufferers 'are more than conquerors' because they succeed in transforming the dread enemy into a friend. Yet what if despite his faith and hope the torment seems to become unendurable to the afflicted one? This is an illusion, for though one lose even his life he still gains victory in faith. The sufferer ought to take consolation in the thought that 'the way *on* which a man goes certainly does not go over his head', but is a *path* under foot to be trodden. There must be a determined plan of action. The sufferer must *walk*, thus guaranteeing to himself that there is a *way*, knowing further that for every temptation God has also made a way of escape. (P. 116)

Kierkegaard is greatly concerned lest the sufferer lose perspective, failing to see the anguished moment in the light of the 'happiness of eternity'. A light affliction worketh an eternal glory. Only when a sufferer has the eternal as the other quantity with which to counterbalance the scales can he know that his affliction is really light. The grave danger is that in the busy way of life and under the pressure of affliction, like the driver who travels by his own bright lights and therefore cannot see the eternal but distant stars, one may neglect to guide himself by the eternal. He may be preoccupied with the blinding light of the moment. A man is most oppressed by suffering when it seems to accomplish nothing, but the tribulation becomes light if the goal is eternal life. The Roman soldier was brave because he knew that dishonour was more to be feared than death, but the Christian is still more brave because he knows a greater hope, i.e. that no sacrifice need be unprofitable in the victorious kingdom of the good.

Not unexpectedly, the *Gospel of Suffering* leaves many questions unanswered and some unasked. However, in the last discourse, 'Courage in Suffering', the author turns to one of the more subtle of the perplexing problems related to suffering. The issue is whether there may not be a grave peril of spiritual pride in suffering. May not the supreme guilt be for one to claim that he is suffering for the right, self-righteously imposing guilt on his opponents? While it is contemptible to fail to confess one's faith, it may be presumptuous to do so when confession is not called for. When early Christians refused to deny their faith in spite of Roman torture, their confession of faith was at the same time a witness or proclamation to those who tortured them. However, if a modern Christian confesses his faith to other Christians this may be not so much a proclamation of Christianity (for the hearers already know it) but instead may be a boastful judgment upon them. Its effect may be to say that they are *not* Christians or at least not as good Christians as the one who is witnessing. The confession which in a pagan community is 'identical with proclaiming Christianity' may become in a reputedly Christian community a sectarian conceit or a proud judgment on the supposed hypocrisy of others. (P. 143 f.)

It appears then that there is a kind of spiritual hiddenness about the life of suffering, as of faith in general. Humility rather than spiritual pretension must prevail. The apostles rejoiced that they could suffer for the name of Christ. For them, and for any believer, courage in tribulation can 'take the power away from the world and...transform derision into honour'. (P. 147) In the life of any believer confession of faith in suffering may be called for, yet no man dare boastfully point to his suffering as a badge of virtue. Indeed, some men thus impudently 'set their glory in their shame'. (P. 148) In any event, however, when men do persecute the faithful, perhaps even believing that they are honouring God in doing so, then it is shameful to fail to be a witness against evil for fear of suffering.

The lives of the apostles are a beacon on the way. They accepted as honour what the world called disgrace. They were not bitter, did not upbraid; instead, they attended to God. If one is wrongly put to death and dies 'with a witticism on his lips', that is 'the triumph of paganism'; but a saint dies not with a witticism but a prayer on his lips. It is a prayer of thanksgiving for the grace which makes all things work together for good to them that love God. In a world which crucified Christ, the disciple comes to understand that although he may be offered subtle and false honour, he will inescapably suffer for the good, and will be treated as a criminal or as a fool.

In conclusion it may be noted that in this work we find much to support the very common charge that Kierkegaard thought of Christianity as an imitation of Christ which seeks to share in Christ's sufferings. In his defence it must be kept in mind that whatever problems this emphasis on suffering may suggest, Christ did bid his followers to take up their crosses and follow him.

APPENDIX: SUFFERING IN THE LAST WRITINGS

The theme of suffering grew in prominence in Kierkegaard's last writings, and it is a recurrent topic in the last journals. His numerous statements do not constitute a unified doctrine, yet there is a clear and very important pattern within them. Although the doctrine of suffering is neither validated nor invalidated by S.K.'s own experience, it is clear that there is something autobiographical in this development, as in the insistence that the more one concerns himself with the eternal the more embittered he becomes with the temporal.* S.K. imagines Christianity saying to him that it was God's love which made it impossible to enjoy life, but that this sad truth had to be hidden until he could endure Christianity's dreadful judgment upon mankind. (XI^1 A 210)

Suffering is not of a single category. There are varied kinds and significances of suffering. Quite apart from the problem of evil or the consequence of sin, there is a natural foundation for much

* *Papirer*, XI^1 A 472. Note that the many following references to the *Papirer* will simply cite the location.

suffering. The more significant existence is the more difficult it is. Thus an animal's life is more difficult than that of a plant and a wise man's life is more difficult than a simple man's. Christianity makes man supremely significant and therefore makes his existence 'as difficult and painful as possible'. (XI¹ A 194)

That suffering is proportionate to the significance of life is the background for the doctrine that suffering results from man's being *spirit*. In earlier works, like Volume II of *Either/Or* and *Sickness Unto Death*, S.K. had insisted that man must not attempt to be pure spirit, but that by God's will be is properly blended of the finite and the infinite. In his last writings, S.K. came to emphasize not a balanced synthesis but a synthesis in which 'the absolute is fatal for relative being'. (XI² A 205) He argues that suffering is unavoidable if one serves the 'absolute absolutely' in a 'conditioned world', (XI² A 56) or where spirit is joined to the animal creation. (XI² A 246) Negatively, spirit means to will that which the body shrinks from, and thus is a dying to the world. (XI¹ A 558) Clinging to that which is animalistic, mediocre humanity says of Christ that he has a devil and that religion spoils life. In contrast, Christ addresses Peter as Satan when Peter wants to shield Jesus in an earthly fashion. The Absolute imposes unrest whereas humanity seeks material satisfaction. (XI¹ A 516) This tendency to identify suffering with the accent on spirit does not necessarily involve a doctrine of sin, and, in fact, frequently makes no reference to sin. From this standpoint, man's torment is simply a divine lure; God attracts men by means of unrest, disturbing existence for the sake of intensity. (XI² A 29) 'The Spirit is fire, and Christianity is incendiarism. And by nature man shrinks from this fire more than from any other.' (XI² A 41)

Quite as often Kierkegaard explains suffering as a consequence of sin, and it is possible that 'spirit' in the previous category is not to be understood as spirit *qua* spirit but as fallen spirit. At any rate, S.K. insists that it is not possible to love God and to be happy in the world because God is in opposition to the world. (XI¹ A 279) Sin as cause of suffering is not evident to the natural man; indeed, mankind is so accustomed to its wretchedness that it is quite pleased with its condition. (XI² A 201) God's punishment for sin is his separation from the sinner, a separation so radical that it is even hidden from the sinner that he is suffering any punishment. (XI² A 96) Sin is thus a fact of Christian revelation; Christ expressed a shocking absolute pessimism when he refused to have anything to do with the wretched world except in love to be slain by it. (XI¹ A 482) The distinctive feature of sin as the explanation of suffering is that it is not the sinner as separated from God who suffers, but that suffering comes about in the endeavour to save the sinner. Grace turns earthly existence which is pleasing to the natural man into intense suffering, so that the worldly situation will cease to be important to him. (XI² A 182)

The repetitious formula under which S.K. sums up this phase of his doctrine in these last writings is that since man is 'conceived in sin' and 'born in transgression', his very existence is a crime, the world is a vale of tears, death is his punishment, and procreation should come to an end. (XI² A 157) However violently a critic may wish to disagree on such issues, mankind is in debt to Kierkegaard for his reminder that there is no place for easy optimism. The cuddly babe all too soon demonstrates the universality and depth of evil. The inner collapse of civilizations or societies, and the subtlety of evil in high places and within the form of 'righteousness', suggest a profound malignancy.

At the same time the question may be raised whether Kierkegaard did not veer in the direction of Gnosticism's doctrine that the world is evil by creation, and that salvation is an undoing of creation. He insists that it is not a Christian view that God wants to make something splendid out of this world, but rather 'that this world has come about through a fall away from God'. Everyone born into it 'merely augments the mass of perdition'. God wants to reclaim the world which has fallen but cannot do so by simply destroying it because it must return to him in freedom. (XI² A 434)

So far it has been noted that there is a kind of natural suffering, the more intense as life becomes significant; that some suffering is tacitly acknowledged as a kind of enigma; that there is suffering which results from spirit's renunciation of the earthly and its quest for the eternal; that suffering may result directly from sin but results from it most intensely as spirit seeks the holy and renounces the worldly. The most important concept of suffering remains to be cited, i.e. specifically Christian suffering. The offence of a lowly Christ which brought suffering upon him finds a certain

THE CHRISTIAN WRITINGS

parallel in that the believer must likewise suffer in relation to God's love. (XI² A 422) The Christian is called upon to suffer precisely because he is *willing to suffer*; no one is so hated by the world 'as he who freely gives up that in which men naturally live their life'. (XI¹ A 327)

Christian suffering is often misunderstood, even by Christians. For example, the 'whole suffering of the middle ages', such as fasting and self-denial, was not Christian at all because there was in it no conflict with men and no suffering for the truth. (XI² A 396) True Christian suffering may or may not involve persecution. It tends to do so because it renounces the values to which the world clings. Thus it offends by opposing conventional sociality and the mediocrity of the crowd; it intends to shut up the single individual in relationship to God. (XI² A 65) Often Christian suffering is quite inward, and not at all bodily. The Christian suffers not only *for* the truth but *from* the painful truth, e.g. in the realization that the 'progress' of civilization which causes a general sense of well-being in society is spiritually worthless or even retrogression, or from the discovery that 'everybody being Christian' is an optical illusion, or that this 'splendid world' is a tissue of lies and evasions. (XI² A 438) The goal of Christian existence is therefore to come, at the cost of suffering, to 'the supreme degree of disgust' with this tawdry life. (XI² A 439)

Not contradicting these views but certainly expressing a different theme is another perspective on Christian suffering, to the effect that suffering is God's means of testing and training a soul. Far from being punishment, or even a weaning away from the world, such suffering expresses God's love and his intent to train the Spirit. The more tormented the earthly life, the more blessing there may well be in eternity. (XI¹ A 299) Specifically, God tests the soul with suffering to see if it can then still believe in divine love. If it failed to do so God himself would suffer infinite pain. (XI¹ A 405)

28. WORKS OF LOVE

The Works of Love. By S. Kierkegaard. September 29, 1847. Translated by David F. and Lillian Marvin Swenson. Princeton: Princeton University Press, 1946. Translated with an introduction and notes by Howard and Edna Hong. New York: Harper & Brothers, 1962, Harper TB 122. (Page references are to the Hong translation.)

Whatever its virtues, worldly love unhappily includes or issues in a multitude of sins. It covers sex murders, selfish vanity, and greedy possessiveness. In this great book Kierkegaard offers his corrective. For him too, love must cover the multitude of sins—but to hide them in godly grace. Christian love is the redemptive power which overcomes the vulgar forms and expressions of love, ennobles the splendid but still pathetic forms of natural friendship and romantic love, and issues in its own good works. The book makes many unexpected observations which leave the reader wondering why no one had thought to focus on them before.

Far from being a treatise on 'works' or 'work righteousness' (as involved in theological debate), this is a treatise on love. Nevertheless it does not treat love as a sentiment but instead love *as it works*, for, according to S.K., if love does not work it is not genuine. This sizeable treatise is Kierkegaard's greatest writing on Christian ethics. It is an ethic only in a special sense, however, for it does not discuss the wistful and frustrated morality, the reasonable good behaviour, of the natural man, but specifically the life to which the Christian is called and which becomes possible only by the power of God.

As a tranquil lake is fed by a hidden spring, so man's love wells up from the hidden spring of divine love. Consequently, the loving spirit is hidden, and S.K. does not propose to portray love itself so much as the fruits by which it is known. These fruits (good works) have no claim to merit but are the ways in which the hidden love expresses its power. Furthermore, there is a hiddenness even about the 'fruits'. While a good tree cannot live without bearing fruit, yet an evil tree may also bear fruit. 'Good deeds' may be performed for outrageous motives by evil men. Therefore one 'tree' cannot judge another; a man cannot securely judge his neighbour. The hidden life of love does have recognizable fruits, but their spiritual origin is so concealed that no one can say with finality in a given instance that love is or is not present. Thus, if a person be asked whether he is speaking out of love he might humbly reply that it may be only out of vanity but that hopefully his speech is a manifestation of love. (P. 343) Love is the invisible life of the spirit and the source of Christian social concern. To assert that S.K. leaves the individual 'hermetically' sealed off from others is true *only* in the sense that the individual is compelled to face God alone over the issue of whether he is or is not loving towards his fellow-man.[27] There is a mystery about the human heart which makes it impossible for anyone to say boldly, 'I love you with Christian love'. He can only hope that it is true.

Even though remaining mysteriously elusive, the works of love are a joyous expression of freedom and spontaneity. They are the spontaneous expression of one's very being after he has been transformed by faith. Christian service is then for Kierkegaard as for Luther a life of freedom, even though to be truly free is paradoxically to accept the role of a bond-servant of Christ.[28] Thus the apostle does not write 'Thou *shalt* love', but 'Beloved, *let us love* one another'. Kierkegaard comments: 'You do not hear in these words the rigorousness of duty... but neither do you hear the intensity of inclination, of poet-passion... It is as if the apostle said, "Dear me, what is all this which would hinder you from loving... ?" It is as if you should not need to be commanded, because to love human beings is still the only thing worth living for... Truly a profession of faith is not enough.' (P. 344)

Because Christian love has a divine origin it expresses itself very differently than does natural affection. Indeed, rooted in the eternal, Christian love possesses no romantic charm. It does not perish like earthly love, but neither does it blossom like romance, and so no poet will depict its unexpected occurrence or charm. (Pp. 26 f.) Furthermore, Christian love differs from sentiment and sympathy in being *imperative*, in seeming contradiction to its spontaneity, its free and joyous expression in the lives of the faithful. 'You *shall* love—this, then, is the word of the royal law.' (P. 40) Romantic love may be far more exciting than love which is transformed into duty, yet only dutiful love is secure against change, jealousy, and hate.

Is this Christian duty a Kantian imperative? Indeed it is categorical, but on non-Kantian grounds. It does not seek to universalize the need of man or his value. A Christian loves his neighbour because it is the will of God that he do so, not because the neighbour needs or merits it. There is a second difference from Kant in that Kant thinks in terms of universal law whereas S.K. thinks of an absolutely personalized love for the neighbour. The neighbour is always a distinct individual, not another instance of the human race. Neighbour-love is free of the abstractness and aloofness from real persons which often characterizes 'concern for humanity'. It is not detachment which causes the Christian to love equally his friend and foe but instead his generous compassion. There is a final difference from Kantian legalism in that in a double sense the Christian ethic is one of grace. On the one hand, Christian love is made possible through divine grace, a power without which one could not fulfil the good, and on the other hand the believer's love is itself gracious in that it reflects and manifests something of divine compassion.

In summing up Kierkegaard's general concept we may borrow the definitions of a later scholar, the distinguished Swedish theologian Anders Nygren, for S.K.'s interpretation is a precise but less formally structured anticipation of Nygren's views of *agape*. Such love is a kind of creative fictionalism which always views the neighbour with compassion and as one's equal, regardless of what he is in fact. Whereas ordinary love causes the lover to be 'changed into the likeness with the beloved', Christian love seeks to transform the beloved into likeness to God.[29] It is the divine love and divine will which transform all things and which alone constitute the foundation for Christian morality. At this point S.K. is also exactly in the position of Luther, and is subject —if one disagrees—to the same criticism. Nygren's familiar terms may be taken as summarizing the thought: (1) Christian love is *uncaused* by the object because the neighbour is not charming but is a sinner. Why love such a neighbour? Because it is the will of God. The Christian therefore does not *fall* in love; love is an imperative. (2) Love is *unmotivated* in that by loving his neighbour one is not seeking to obtain something. (3) Love is *creative* in that instead of merely responding to some good in the neighbour, it bestows good on him and establishes a fellowship of reconciliation.

(4) Love is *spontaneous* in that it springs directly from the life of faith.[30]

In interesting and important ways this doctrine of love exhibits existential concerns. Kierkegaard's personal way of life illustrates the point and throws some light on his ethic. Far from being a haughty aristocrat, he showed profound concern for his fellow man, anxious lest he might fail to show some simple courtesy to the commonest of men.[31] Nevertheless, the Christian love which he manifested did not confine itself to 'doing good' for the neighbour in an activistic way. He felt responsible for the neighbour's very relationship to God, understanding that thereby he might even occasion resentment by compelling the neighbour to face his spiritual situation. Christian love is concerned with inwardness rather than with external circumstances, although by no means will it ignore the latter. Here it may be noted that Marjorie Grene is guilty of an astonishing misunderstanding in claiming that for S.K. the Christian's whole concern is for eternal blessedness for 'my own little I'.[32] It is true that he invited such misunderstanding by the way in which he phrased his problem. Yet both in his understanding of the nature of the self and in his personal manner of life, he demonstrated that it is this concern about eternal blessedness for the (not little!) self which frees the self from rapaciousness, and for gracious love.

In existential fashion, Kierkegaard makes the issues of love intensely personal. The injunction is fearfully personalized: '*Thou shalt love.*' An evasive Pharisee who wishes to avoid the duty to love may try to confuse the issue by asking who the neighbour is to whom he owes this obligation, but when it is clear that everyone is a neighbour then evasion becomes impossible. Nor dare one etherealize love by talking abstractly about loving *all* men. It is the man next to one—an actual individual—whom one is to love. Christian love is as severely individual as it is universal; it is never a concern for the mass of society but is the concern of one solitary individual for another solitary individual, and then after him for every individual.

Love, as a divine quality, is that transcendent factor which more than any other brings the eternal into human consciousness. Its abiding when most other treasures are lost intimates the eternal

(p. 24), and it demonstrates the fact that to have *being* is to reach beyond self in an act of *bestowing*. Since love is this fullness of being, all true love is a reflection of divine love. (P. 20) It treats men as if they were not finite, variable creatures but as if they possessed the absoluteness and equality of the eternal. But is this deceit? In its championing of indiscriminate love for all, is Christianity guilty of levelling all men, ignoring the sins of the wicked, the virtues of the saints, and the dignity of the noble? Does Christianity reduce all men to an impersonal and lowest common denominator? The very opposite is the case. No one is more horrified by the 'mass man' who is identical with all others than is Kierkegaard. For him, the Christian is the only true individual. He is not devoid of distinctions but instead has his differences both redeemed and undergirded by having them grounded in the eternal. It is as when a husband loves his own wife and exists uniquely in this unique relationship, yet brings the element of the eternal into the relationship by making it a matter of conscience before God.

In keeping with existential inwardness Kierkegaard's ethic is severely individualistic. It has been criticized as having little concern for the needs of society. It is true that he does not offer a programme of social reform. Nevertheless, the criticism is very poorly founded because S.K. insists on social consciousness in the Christian, for the personal ethic has inescapable social involvements. True, as S.K. sees it, love for neighbour does not specifically intend to establish democracy, unthrone kings, or promote social legislation. Differences in persons will for ever remain. The poor will be with us always, so too the wise and the criminals, although such facts neither excuse anyone from nor obviate the need for earnest social effort. Love does not try to make all alike but it does care for all *as if* they were all alike the children of the holy God. Christian morality is thus eminently *possible*, more so than any humanistic scheme of reform, because every believer *can love* his neighbour—even the most unlikely neighbour, even though he may not be able to solve his neighbour's economic or social problems, and in spite of the fact that he himself may even contribute to those problems.

Perhaps even more than Martin Luther, Kierkegaard refused to identify religious love with social reform. 'Christianity has not wanted to storm forth to abolish distinctions... but it wills that differences shall hang loosely... as the cloak the king casts off in order to show who he is... Then there steadily shines in every individual that essential other person, that which is common to all men, the eternal likeness, the equality.' (P. 96) S.K. does not disregard human need and social problems but he realistically recognizes that there will always be human differences, that these can properly be dealt with only on the basis of men's equality before God, and most important that the character of a people is not determined by the extent of their social reforms. If social work is important, the quality of personal mercy is immeasurably more so, and it is this to which S.K. wants to give primary attention. He does see possibilities of improving society. In fact, Christian responsibility calls precisely for blessing and helping others by works of love. Yet what S.K. would say to the would-be reformer is that even when men are externally helped by economic or other means, but without love, they have not been truly benefited.

The key concept in Kierkegaard's entire ethic is the distinctive category of neighbour-love. A maiden, says S.K., dreams of the future, and gazes at passing men, wondering which of them might be her hoped-for lover. For the Christian the problem is much simpler; he is to love the first person he sees. It is this duty to love the next person which converts anyone—everyone—into a neighbour, thus giving release from passionate partiality. Only in company with God does one discover his neighbour. (Pp. 64, 87) Nor does one wait for a person to improve before calling him neighbour, since love is not a man-to-man relation but a 'man-God-man' relation, with God as the 'middle term'. (Pp. 112 f.) Christ did not wait until Peter improved; he said, 'Peter is Peter, and I love him...'. (Pp. 168)

How shall one love the neighbour? As *himself*. Shall he not love the neighbour *more* than self, placing the neighbour first, whereas by nature his own self claimed this position? Perhaps surprisingly, S.K.'s answer is negative, on the ground that both the neighbour and oneself can be 'first', in that love seeks the full and unqualified good of fellowship with God for both neighbour and self. The Christian does not soar like a poet who exalts a beloved more than himself and perhaps even more than God. No poet ever sang about the very unpoetical and very unavoidable person whom the Christian wilfully calls 'neighbour'. Instead, the poet is too often guilty of gross and selfish partiality in his ecstatic praise for the one (only one) beloved. However, there is to be noted a hidden restriction of a different sort in Christian love. Neighbour-love has in it no blind adoration, no submissiveness to the neighbour's perhaps foolish wishes. Instead, one shall love the neighbour *as oneself*, i.e., as one *ought* to love oneself, cherishing only the true good for him, and presupposing intelligent and measured response.

Neighbour-love is not adoration. There is such a higher devotion, man's complete adoration of God, a devotion which is obedient to every divine wish. Such adoration must never be tolerated in love for man, where instead critical concern is to be the rule. One must not read into neighbour-love a kind of calculating balance between egoism and altruism as seems to be implicit; for example, in the outlook of the English utilitarian John Stuart Mill. Instead, one seeks the complete and true good for both neighbour and self. This is equality of perfection, not of compromise, realizable without threat of conflict because such a good is available to all at the same time. One does not deprive himself by serving others. The goal is to help the beloved to love God. Therefore, Christian love is always good, even as self-love (which is the antithesis of what is normally designated 'selfishness'), for to love oneself is to make the love of God one's goal, and this in turn cannot but lead to the love of others. (Pp. 36, 87 f., 92, 98)

As pointed out above, neighbour-love has universality in it, yet it is not a natural universality. For example, it is radically unlike the universal love fostered by the Mohist philosophers of ancient China who sought to make man's natural self-love universal on the ground that if everyone were loving towards all people then everyone would benefit. In contrast, Christian love is a universal *unnatural* love. 'You shall love yourself in the same way as you love your neighbour when you love him as yourself.' (P. 39) Such self-love is redeemed from even the most 'enlightened' selfishness. The Christian way to love oneself is clarified by neighbour-love, for by being compelled to love the neighbour one learns an 'unnatural', reforming, and holy love for himself. True neighbour-love makes evident the follies of the frivolous man, the pleasure seeker, the melancholy man, and even the ascetic. It shows how the natural man betrays himself in egoism. Christian love requires self-renunciation in that the good which is sought (for neighbour and self) is in no sense self-aggrandizement but humility and faith for the sinner. This love does not flatter its object.

How does strange Christian love relate itself to natural sentiment? The Christian imperative 'Thou *shalt* love' is really shocking to the natural man. Even positivistic thinkers like Hans Reichenbach acknowledge that humans are and will continue to be loving, without theoretical justification, but simply because humans are peculiar in this way. 'Volition', says Reichenbach, 'is not derivable from cognition. Human will is its own progenitor and its own judge.'[33] However, the humanist takes exception to the view which changes love from a natural sentiment or expression of the will into inexorable duty, a duty in which one dare not sentimentally engage. How offensive that one must *love* Hitler, Marx, and the people next door! Yet just here the Christian revelation 'breaks forth with divine creativeness'. (P. 41) What a difference there is between the mere play of emotions and this earnest command! Only when love is such a duty is it secure against change and against chance and circumstance. True, even natural love (S.K. calls it 'immediate love') has a poetic delusion of eternity about it, so that people swear to love each other for ever and ever. However, because romantic love will not acknowledge duty but lives by passion, the illusion of eternity is quickly evident —as in the divorce court. Parenthetically, it may be noted that in a sense God's own love might be thought of as a natural sentiment, although not subject to the whims and change of ordinary sentiment. God does not love because it is his duty but because love is his nature. Consequently, while man in one sense resembles God by becoming loving, his love is not a true semblance in that it is dutiful. (P. 74)

Christian love, severely unlike natural sentiment, is not even a transformed or higher form of natural love. Instead, it is alien in that it pushes earthly love and friendship from their throne. (P. 70) This does not mean that the Christian rejects earthly love. He should still love his friend with common appreciation, but the friendship will be safeguarded by the fact that the friend is also a

Christian neighbour. So too, of a wife! 'The wife shall first and foremost be your neighbour; the fact that she is your wife is then a narrower definition of your special relationship to each other. But what is eternally basic must also be the basis of every expression of what is special.' (P. 141) There is a kind of love which is profoundly and naturally present in human nature, and Christianity does not replace this natural affection. Yet it adds to it and transforms it by making it a matter of conscience before God. (P. 143)

An interesting issue which has been disputed is whether Kierkegaard's emphasis on the *works* of love represents a tendency towards a Roman Catholic rather than a Lutheran view. Some Catholics have suggested that S.K. would have become a member of their church if he had not died so young. One reason for this contention is S.K.'s criticism of Protestant failings. Another is his sympathy for (if also criticism of) monastic earnestness, and a third is the insistence in this book on good deeds, or 'works' of love.

The penetrating interpretation by Johannes Sløk is helpful in evaluating this issue. He reminds us that a man must be viewed within the framework of his age and as related to its problems. Thus, says Sløk, Martin Luther felt no need to show how righteousness produces social morality. Luther's only need was to find a source for righteousness which transcends deeds, viz. the righteousness of faith or openness to a gracious God. However, by the time of Kierkegaard, Christian morality began to appear as 'bourgeois complacency'. Therefore Kierkegaard had to find a way for faith to issue in or manifest itself in effective love. Moreover, he had to ground morality in freedom which Rousseau and Kant had made an essential concept. Therefore S.K. viewed the decision by which a person commits himself to himself, both in decisiveness before God *and* as an outreach to one's neighbour as an act of essential freedom.[34]

Thinking of the way of salvation, Luther insisted on 'faith alone', repudiating any notion of merit. But thinking of the shocking worldliness of professing Christians, Kierkegaard insisted that there could be no 'love *alone*'. Love without works is dead. Lowrie rightly insisted that S.K. was not objecting to the *doctrine* of the Reformation, but was only demanding that the church seek to practice its spirituality. Love must demonstrate its reality by bearing fruit, or else be exposed as hypocrisy.[35]

In endless reiteration, S.K. reveals that he clung to salvation by the grace and deed of God quite as much as did Luther. However, whereas Luther sensed the necessity for clarifying the way of salvation, Kierkegaard had to fight against the modern secularization of religion whereby it became little more than a pleasant inward mood with no radical effect on life. He protested that Christian love is not preferential liking (of nice people) but is rather a universal (absurd) loving of one's neighbour (anyone at hand and in need), and with no concern for the neighbour's merit or demerit, charm or repulsiveness. The pagan loves his neighbour *if the neighbour is attractive*, but it is shocking to a pagan—and ought to be startling to a Christian—that God commands a person to love everyone, regardless of what qualities he may possess. It is dramatic and inexplicable that Christianity makes love a duty. It is from this original paradox that Kierkegaard came to stress the point that love 'believeth all' (far too many) things, hopeth all things (which seems futile), and wilfully covers up the multitude of sins. Plainly, S.K.'s love is *agape* (transcendent), not Augustinian *caritas* (human love which has received a divine enablement), nor Platonic *eros* (a cherishing of the good because it is good). Finally, with the pattern of Christ's victory before him, S.K. was assured that love unfailingly makes a difference and is victorious in its unyielding power. He explained that faith cannot but issue in love because God is not only the goal of life but also the way; love is the religious aim, and also the means of attainment of it. God is '*how* one relates himself to him', so that in religion the '*how* is what', being both the holy way and the holy object.[36]

In the light of the above, we may conclude that in Kierkegaard, as in Luther, there is a Pauline theology in the treatment of the severe demands which Christianity imposes. The thought is that without a divine law as a schoolmaster, man may very well not sense the need of grace. To be prepared for the love of Christ one should measure his life by much more than civic righteousness which an ethical man (and perhaps even an aesthetic man) may fairly well fulfil. If he is faced by the demand for an absolute love, man recognizes his pathos and need for forgiveness. Thus, as

S.K. puts it, when confronted by God man is *always* guilty. It is such consciousness which prepares the heart for the love of Christ. Precisely because it is transcendent love which is required of the believer, resting on no humanistic base, the outcome is exactly the opposite of what a superficial analysis might suggest. The *Works of Love* brings a man to the need for grace, showing clearly the remoteness of S.K.'s position from that of Catholic theology.

This leads to a final complication in the relation between faith and 'works'. Not only must works follow from faith if faith is really living, but also, in a strange sense, S.K. thinks that works in the form of moral earnestness must precede faith. That is to say, there must first be genuine human existence, a value situation, with earnest striving. Then, within this, one may come to faith— or to despair. The striving certainly does not cause the faith, nor is it meritorious in the sight of God, but it does furnish the framework within which faith and its life (a 'second existence') can occur.[37]

We may finally ask what the nature of the 'works' is in which love issues? The answer to this question, occupying the last half of the book, is highly revealing and critically important. The works do not consist of passing laws, championing causes, nor even helping the needy. These latter may very well be dead works, if also it is possible that love may express itself through them. The 'works' of which Kierkegaard speaks are, in fact, hardly *deeds* in any sense, but are rather the qualities of the loving life. They are, for the most part, lifted directly out of the New Testament.

(1) Love edifies, i.e. 'builds up'. The sight of a sleeping person does not usually edify, but to see a little child asleep in the arms of a loving mother does edify. Whenever there is true edification love is present. Moreover, no one can actually create love in another. Instead, to be loving is to presuppose love as existing in the loved one, and by one's own love to fan the other's flickering candle of devotion into living flame.

(2) Love 'believeth all things'. A stupid man may believe all things and thereby be deceived, but in what is essential love is never deceived. The lover can never be deceived into surrendering love, which is the power which overcomes the world. Mistrust is the wisdom of the world. 'To believe nothing in order never to

be deceived—this seems to make sense.' (P. 221) Yet in such 'wisdom' there is only hopelessness, which deceives one by robbing him of the blessedness of love. Christ's love would not accept defeat even on the cross. So unyielding as this must the disciple's love be.

(3) Love hopeth all things—and is never put to shame, for in eternity there will be no mockers to deride anyone because he 'was foolish enough to make himself ridiculous by hoping for all things'. (P. 246) Youth throbs with expectancy but life quickly becomes a dull repetition where hope 'becomes something which nowhere has a home, and possibility a rarity like greenness in winter'. (P. 235) However, the Scriptures do not use the word 'hope' for the whole lot of worldly expectations. Only one expectation has the honour of this name and that is the hope of the good. This cannot really fail even though in the world it repeatedly fails, for in eternity it will be evident 'that it is not the result which determines honour and shame, but the expectation itself'. (P. 246) Hope for the good succeeds as goodness even if its particular expectations fail.

Christian hope grasps the eternal as a *possibility*, even though unable to assimilate it into the restless flux of time. In a sense then hope reaches beyond itself; it becomes an 'eternal' hope, already possessing the quality of that for which it longs. It 'lays hold on the possibility of the good', which is eternal. Although eternity, since it is not in temporal duration, is no more future than present or past, it yet identifies itself with the believer's future in order to lure him to itself. In its allurement eternal life is as near as it is far away, actually laid hold upon even if not possessed. This grasping is not intellectual comprehension because a despairing man *knows* the possibility but rejects it or 'ventures impudently to assume the impossibility of the good'. In contrast, hope is more sceptical about attaining good in earthly time, even by obedience to the will of God, but it is *religiously* optimistic in that it trusts that God will make the good possible in eternity. (Pp. 233-38)

(4) Love seeketh not its own, but wastes itself in helping others to become their *own*. It seeks the neighbour's own *for him*. Love does not even bestow a gift so as to put the recipient in a debt of gratitude. Rather, it gives in such a way that the gift appears to be the receiver's natural possession. (P. 255) Love's labour is thus

seemingly lost, with no reward, but in fact it is the most God-like creative work in that it helps the beloved to be a free creature rather than the lover's debtor or slave.

(5) Love covereth a multitude of sins. The sinful eye does not overlook the sins of others, with the result that their multiplicity looms larger and larger. Not so one who truly loves! He is a very dull fellow, who, as in a child's game, can hardly see the sins which are in plain view before him. Love forgets its own advantage in order to look lovingly for another's advantage. The neighbour's sins remain and since love cannot really avoid seeing them it hides them by forgiveness or by lenient explanation. (P. 268) If one refuses to forgive he adds his own sin of hardness of heart to all the previous burden, but love takes sin out of its element and destroys it at birth.

(6) Love abideth. It never fails, for if ever one ceases to be loving then it is at once evident that he never was really loving; there is no possibility of breach in holy love. (P. 282) People cannot simply 'fall out' of this love for one another. The matter is much more serious than that. They must betray and fall away from love itself, and this is a betrayal of the eternal. If a forsaken lover patiently says, 'I abide in love', then his love remains unshaken by any lack of loving response.

(7) Mercy is a work of love, even if it can give nothing—for indeed mercy has nothing to give. It is not the alms which is the work of love but the mercy which becomes the inspiration of the gift. The moral man insists that the needy must be helped and that such activism is a work of love. 'On the other hand, the eternal says: there is only one danger, this, that mercifulness is not practised; even if aid were given in every need, there is still no certainty that it was done in mercifulness...' (P. 301 f.) How comforting it is for the disconsolate soul who grieves because he cannot bring help and has no gift to offer; he still can do the one thing which is essential, i.e. he can be merciful.

(8) Love wins a victory of reconciliation, not waiting until the enemy asks for forgiveness but giving reconciliation long before it is ever sought. With infinite gentleness, love wins the *vanquished person*, not winning a victory *over* him. The strange truth never occurs to the lover that he has conquered his enemy (by means of the good), and such a vanquished person also does not know

that he has been conquered and therefore knows no humiliation. Reconciliation is a matter of the spirit, not of external relations. As St Paul did not condemn slavery but did require love between slave and master, so S.K. thinks that what Christianity is chiefly concerned with is not the social inequalities—although they must be struggled with—but the equality of men before God, an 'eternal equality in loving'. (P. 70) A lesser truth, presupposed by reconciliation is that love is in collision with evil, and wins its victory by suffering in that collision. That true love must suffer is clarified by Christ's experience with Peter when he was obliged to call Peter 'Satan' at the very moment that Peter, 'burning with love', sought to shield him. (P. 115) True love collides with earthly love which rebels against divine love, and true love is victorious.

(9) Remembering the dead is 'a work of the most unselfish love', unrequited, whereas in even the deepest devotion for the living there may be some self-seeking and hope for repayment. A dead man has the strength of changelessness over the one who loves him. He does not cause sleepless nights by being difficult, like a wayward child, but perhaps he may cause sleepless nights by his changeless integrity. By faithful remembrance of the dead a person can learn that it is no less a duty to faithfully love the living.

(10) It is a work of love to recommend love to others, both by inward self-denial and by outward disinterestedness. Everyone can praise love because praising love is not an art which is bestowed on only a few but is given to all who wish for it. Yet, if praising love does not require poetic talent, it does require self-renunciation because only by this can one hold fast the God of love and only in self-denial can one command love even for the ugly.

29. DIALECTIC OF ETHICAL AND ETHICO-RELIGIOUS COMMUNICATION

The Dialectic of Ethical and Ethico-Religious Communication. Incomplete notes for a book, comprising a first and second draft, together with marginal notations. Not published by Kierkegaard, written in 1847. Appears in *Papirer*, VIII B 141-90. The authors are indebted to Nils John Anderson for translation.

These rough, unsystematic and incomplete notes have a certain value in that here Kierkegaard speaks with some plainness about 'indirect' communication, a matter of enormous consequence both in his thinking and in his plan of writing. He viewed his task as essentially a Socratic one, not only in the sense of assisting as a midwife at the birth of truth in the learner, but, more importantly, in that the truth with which both were concerned is eternal truth. He agreed with Socrates that the 'midwife' must deal with the learner where the learner is, within whatever state of distress or falsehood he may be, and seek to progress from that point towards the eternal.

In sharp contrast to the great numbers who wish to instruct others, particularly their children, in matters of morality and religion, S.K. insists that in the main no such direct communication or instruction is possible. This misunderstanding results in part from the vast development of science, which seems to imply that all kinds of awareness or knowledge should be teachable. Instead, the moral life and the religious attitude are learned more by practicing the *art* of such living, together with observation of this art as demonstrated by noble examples. After the pattern of Socrates, S.K. holds that morality and religion are not to be forced *into* the learner but evocatively awakened in him.

By analogy, the drill sergeant or corporal does not inform a recruit about the contents of a book on military tactics but by action draws out of him the soldierly qualities which in a fashion he already possesses. The art of drill is the means of accomplishing this. Picturesquely, S.K. says that communication of the ethical means, 'to *coax* the ethical out of the individual, because it already exists inside him'.

The aim of indirect communication is not to bring the learner into a relationship to the teacher but rather into relationship to the truth. Thus it might be that the unattractiveness of the teacher, the ugliness if a Socrates, could even help by keeping the learner at arm's length from the teacher and encouraging him to grow in inwardness. Spiritual communication must be so indirect that the human teacher fades into the background, leaving the hearer standing solitary in the presence of God.[38] Further, inasmuch as the goal is to bring the learner to a personal acceptance of spiritual principles rather than to an intellectual comprehension of them (indeed, presumably already understanding them), one needs to be prodded into self-awareness in relationship to these principles, by means of irony, pathos, and dialectic.[39] This prodding challenges response, does not seek to inform.

The reason for the difficulty in communicating is that truly important teaching relates to the subjective person and his own volitions. The peril is that if one proclaims a *doctrine* about existence people may believe the doctrine but be unchanged by it. Imagine the bishop who lives in luxury and preaches about self-sacrifice! What he ought rather do is to demonstrate his truth by his way of life. Personal *existing* is thus the initiation of communication and also its goal, and in each instance it calls for a transforming of the earth-bound life under the discipline of the eternal.

What is the nature of the 'ethical' which is to be awakened by 'indirect communication'? S.K.'s provocative if incomplete reply is that this very question is unethical, since every person at least knows what it is to be morally responsible. One might interject that to explain the nature of the good to a dog is impossible since the dog cannot comprehend, and to explain it to a man is impossible because he already knows it. Presumably, what S.K. intends to say is that to make an issue of the relativity of moral judgments, by asking what is ethical, may well be an immoral evasion of one's responsibility.

In indirect communication, the communicator is obliged to make it clear that he is not the teacher since only God bestows eternal truth. He must also make it clear that the learner somehow already possesses the truth. Finally, he must acknowledge that everyone stands absolutely alone in his relationship to God. Elsewhere, S.K. strengthens the latter point by insisting on a person being an 'individual', and by his recognition of the fact that there can be no disciple of a disciple. In the present work he makes the interesting point that in ethical or religious communication there is a 'double reflection', in that the teacher is himself a learner who benefits from the response of his pupil.

One shrewd judgment is offered which reflects much of S.K.'s own manner of writing. All indirect communication, he says, is different from the direct in that the indirect is primarily deceptive. In part, the deception results from trying to communicate the ethical (i.e. to make another person ethical) when, in fact, no one can be ethical in behalf of another or will the good for him. Direct 'communication' can at the very most pertain only to insights and not to actual existence. Further, there is deception in that if one seriously wishes to give ethical or religious communication he will of necessity be ironical, i.e. he will conceal his true motives. This is precisely what S.K. had done in the entire aesthetic authorship, leading people to the ethical by causing them to first take delight in and then later (hopefully) to despair of the aesthetic. In this way the basic motive was radically different than the obvious or apparent motives of entertaining and illuminating.[40]

Finally, although S.K. did not stress the connection, there is an obvious relation between the Christian's indirect communication and Christ's own indirect communication or revelation. For Christ to say that he and the Father are one seems to be a direct communication, but that an individual and lowly man, Jesus of Nazareth, says it makes the communication indirect. Instead of plainly revealing his glory, Jesus called on people to accept him as Lord in the very moment when he was a rejected and crucified prisoner. Faith is thus the response to a communication which is indirect, ane everything Christian 'exists only for faith'.[41] It is Kierkegaard's understanding that in all spiritual matters what is revealed is also hidden and remains so. Therefore, in seeking to exert spiritual influence, the believer, like his Lord, must employ a kind of hiddenness. Moreover, just as the indirect instruction of a maieutic Socrates and the mere 'sign' or hint of God which Jesus offered were offensive, so too the indirect communication of the Christian will offend.[42]

THE CHRISTIAN WRITINGS

30. CHRISTIAN DISCOURSES

Christian Discourses. By S. Kierkegaard. April 26, 1848. Translated by Walter Lowrie. New York: Oxford University Press, 1939; Galaxy paperback 49. Included in the volume are two small books which were originally published separately and are here treated under their own titles, first, *The Lilies of the Field and the Birds of the Air*, and second, '*The High Priest*'—'*The Publican*'—'*The Woman that was a Sinner*'.

Although these discourses are called 'Christian', by which Kierkegaard indicates that they are severely earnest rather than poetically edifying, yet the book has both remarkable beauty and gentleness of spirit. This applies particularly to the first two parts, entitled 'Anxieties of the Heathen' and 'Joyful Notes in the Strife of Suffering'. In the third part, 'Thoughts which Wound from Behind', there is actually initiated S.K.'s great attack on self-satisfied Christendom. Perhaps the most impressive feature of all is the optimistic hopefulness with which the book closes, in the section called 'Discourses at the Communion on Fridays', S.K. seems to feel that after smug churchianity has been 'wounded from behind' by the presentation of Christianity's severe demands, it will be so corrected by the criticism that a spiritual consummation will follow. In the journal he wrote about this: 'The contrast between the third part and the fourth is as sharp as possible and as searching: the one is like a commemoration of the Cleansing of the Temple—and then the quiet and most heartfelt of all acts of worship: a communion on Fridays.'[43]

A simple progression is evident in the volume. It begins with a focus on 'paganism' (anxiety), next treats the joys available to the disciple in spite of his sufferings, thirdly calls attention to the actual paganism which parades as 'Christendom', and lastly moves to the culmination of faith and love at the Lord's table. In the last instance the movement from paganism to Christianity is complete. S.K.'s view of paganism rests on the conviction that the natural man typically seeks limited, temporal goods, and idolatrously makes false gods out of passing values. As a Christian, man must set his values right by seeking an eternal good or happiness.

The opening portion of *Christian Discourses* gives a remarkable definition of a Christian, by analogy to the familiar birds and lilies. It was in the sermon on the mount that Jesus spoke of the birds and lilies. 'It is at the foot of the mountain; yea, what is more, the birds and the lilies are in the company—it sounds almost as if it were turning the thing into a jest that they come along... playfully...The birds and the lilies come along as assistant teachers of a sort.' (P. 13) What is the instruction which is offered by the lilies and the birds? It is that if a man lives as do the little wild flowers and songbirds, receiving God's gifts and having no anxiety for the morrow, then he is a Christian, which, of course, these lesser creatures could never be.

Whereas the heathen are anxious over poverty, the Christian should be no more anxious than the birds. Unlike the bird, the Christian should lay up food in store, yet this store is not the reason for his freedom from anxiety. However great or small the store which a man acquires, he is to be free from anxiety simply because he trusts God. Even though the bird 'still lives' it is always in poverty, but the Christian discovers that even though he is still in poverty he can really live, in a spiritual sense. The heathen are anxious over riches (seeking more, or fearful lest they lose that which they do possess), but the birds are not anxious over riches for they have none. The Christian should be like a bird, not anxious, yet cherishing the riches God bestows upon him, using them not selfishly but as a stewardship. Again, the heathen are anxious over lowliness, wishing honour. In contrast, the birds and lilies are not ashamed of their lowliness, because they do not know that they are lowly. The Christian also should not be anxious over his lowly station but should be aware of the spiritual honour of lowliness. In this he will be aided by remembering Christ who made himself of no reputation.

The heathen are anxious over highness, lest they fall. Like the soaring bird, the Christian should not be fearful of falling, yet unlike the bird he should be aware of his responsible position and be aware of God who levels all men. All of God's lesser creatures have troubles but they do not worry about the morrow's troubles, as the heathen do. The Christian likewise ought not to worry about the morrow, but he should keep in mind that today is the gateway to eternity. Finally, the heathen have the anxiety of irresolution, wavering between two masters, Birds and lilies unwittingly serve only one master, never disobeying God. The Christian too should be obedient, yet with a freedom which the birds and lilies do not possess.

Part II of *Christian Discourses* is aptly named 'Joyful Notes in the Strife of Suffering'. Its joy is rooted in consolation and its wisdom consists of 'dark sayings'. The faithful sufferer is urged to rejoice because his anguish is only of the moment whereas his triumph is eternal. Affliction, no matter how terrible, is a source of hope, and not for oneself alone because the poorer one becomes (like St Paul or Christ himself) the richer are the blessings which he can shower on others.

> 'When the heart of man is saddest
> The harp's tense strings are gladdest.' (P. 161)

The Christian's strange ability to find joy in suffering has no simple or single explanation, but in any event such thoughts do not represent mere compensation or consolation.[44] They relate to the central principle in Kierkegaard's philosophy of man, viz. that to be human is to experience a blend of the eternal and the temporal, so that the temporal is given its proper honour only by first transferring one's dedication from earthly values to God. Earthly joy and suffering can thereby be put in meaningful perspective. The related concept of repetition likewise emerges in the thought that the goal of life is to recover the element of the eternal within the soul.

There is something quite unexpected which emerges here, viz. that the 'eternal' is not simply *future*, or beyond time; it repeats itself backwards into time in the instant of revelation, making itself available already in the temporal world, although it is grasped by faith only as paradox. Whatever is lost in time can be restored to one by the eternal (as Job received again earthly possessions), but in a new form. Man's great peril is that by wrongly clinging to the temporal he may lose the eternal. Only by being willing to lose the temporal for the sake of the eternal may either temporal or eternal be secured. When the temporal is restored by the eternal it is recovered in the present worldly order but in an 'eternal' rather than a commonplace sense. This may be illustrated by

S.K.'s personal experience. The eternal in this case is a quality of earthly life, as when—even in permanent loss of Regine—S.K. was able to keep her with him in his God-relationship. Above all, the presence of the eternal is recognized in the realization that what was lost is only a temporal loss. (P. 146) It may be noted that this theme is a religious exposition of what S.K. elsewhere phrased more philosophically, in the idea that one must relate himself only relatively to the relative and absolutely to the absolute.

The third part of the book, 'Thoughts Which Wound from Behind', hints at S.K.'s subsequent fierce attack on the complacency of the church. It encourages the disciple to consider his spiritual progress, not however in order to press on as a straining athlete, but in order that he may fall upon his knees in confession of sin and in profession of faith. Here there is the most emphatic insistence that there is no human merit in the disciple's good deeds or even in his godly suffering. Such righteousness as he does possess points to the power of God's grace in human life.

Two of the 'wounding thoughts' may be specially mentioned. The one is a new appraisal of 'The Resurrection of the Dead'.* Kierkegaard, in spite of being a pupil of Socrates, is aghast over the fact that Christendom had abandoned the Christian doctrine of the resurrection and the ensuing divine judgment, replacing it with the complacent Platonic doctrine of immortality. He protests that the idea of immortality is like a sedative which keeps one from being truly concerned about the eternal and his own uncertain relationship to it. Immortality would guarantee that, like God himself, man—indeed, any man, whether good or evil—has a blessed indestructibility. If there is any significant concern in the notion of immortality, it goes no further than theoretical questions about its probability and nature, e.g. whether in eternity one will find himself 'in the tapestry of remembrance' of his happiest earthly moments, or will be obliged to sorrowfully recall despond-

* This impressive treatment of the resurrection, as well as related treatments of resurrection, ascension and Pentecost elsewhere—as in 'The Woman that was a Sinner', and *For Self-Examination*—is very important in correcting the judgment that these matters were neglected by S.K. because of his exaggerated emphasis on imitation of Christ-in-humiliation. (Cf. S. U. Zuidema, *Kierkegaard*, p. 39; Herbert Wolff, *Kierkegaard and Bultmann*, Minneapolis: Augsburg Publishing House (1965), p. 56.)

ent hours. However, to thus speculate about immortality is blasphemy, treating God as if he were dead. In sharp contrast, the doctrine of the resurrection is existential, directed to the will rather than the intellect. Instead of offering a comfortable humanistic assurance, it causes one to tremble. For the unrighteous, the resurrection to judgment is fearful and inescapable. For the believer, it is the miracle of God's blessing. Dramatizing the issue, S.K. comments ironically in his journal: 'One of our poets is said, sentimentally, to hold the opinion that even every insect is immortal. The man is right, one is tempted to say, for if human beings as they are born today, *en masse*, are immortal, it would not seem unreasonable that insects also are.'[45]

Gregor Malantschuk develops the provocative thesis that Kierkegaard nevertheless does not exclude immortality but only corrects the emphasis, while still holding something of both views in a not altogether reconciled tension. According to this interpretation, S.K. tended to view immortality as a general potentiality for the quality of the eternal, a potentiality which is in man by virtue of creation. The resurrection then becomes a fulfilment, a divine conquest of sin and death, and the Christian awaits the resurrection as Christ's promised blessing.[46]

Whatever the role of immortality may be within S.K.'s doctrine of man, eternal life is not a simple extension or prolongation of life, as it tended to be for the Greeks. Instead, the Christian must look for a dramatic 'eternal separation between the just and the unjust'. Moreover, says S.K., earnestly addressing the reader, this applies to *me*, to *thee*. The believer's concern ought to be with the fact that the resurrection is at hand, a realization which calls for an attitude of seriousness before the Judge. Platonic immortality is, for the most part, a theoretical issue, but the resurrection of the dead is existential and decisive.

Equally challenging is the thought of the discourse entitled 'All things must work together for our good—*if* we love God'. Is the 'most fortunate' man really fortunate? Yes, *if* he loves God, for then his 'blessings' will work to his good. Is the most miserable man really miserable? No, not *if* he loves God, for then his misfortunes can be turned to his good, and he receives comfort. 'At the moment of terrible despondency... there is still one clause left, a courageous clause of comfort.' (P. 204) But the 'if' of the doubt ('Do I thus love God?') must for both the fortunate and the unfortunate alike remain to the end as 'an arrow in the heart', wounding or comforting according to one's own need. 'Beware of this "if"—in another sense, take care to love this "if".'

In this connection S.K. tells a charming story. A great theologian writes a brilliant book about the Christian concept of love and pours all his wisdom into it, carefully drawing out the implications of the love of God. Then a tragedy befalls him and he ends in misery. In this extremity he goes to a pastor, quite unknown to him, for comfort and guidance. The pastor soon discovers that the problem is quite beyond his resources but is struck by a happy thought. 'I have only one counsel left to give you; there is a book about the love of God by so and so, read it, study it, if that does not help you, no man can help you.' What pathetic irony there is in the wise man's reply, 'I myself am the author of this book'! So great is the difference between comprehending a doctrine and having personal faith. (P. 206)

This section ends, in preparation for the closing unit of the book, with a discourse marking the transition from religion A to religion B, the change consisting essentially of a radical leap of unqualified faith. Here at last Kierkegaard, always so reluctant to lay claim to being a genuine Christian, makes his confession, 'I have believed in him'. For him, such an acceptance involves the willingness to accept martyrdom if need be, or any sacrifice, for one's faith. (Pp. 244-47)

Section IV continues at the authentic Christian level. The worshiper's prayerful acceptance of atonement is portrayed as the distinctive characteristic of Christian life. Of the seven 'Discourses at the Communion' which constitute this unit, two were actually preached by Kierkegaard in the cathedral. One of them ('Come Unto Me') obviously related itself to the famous Torwaldsen statue of Christ which stood close beside Kierkegaard as he was preaching. In the beautiful statue Christ is made to appear spreading his arms in consolation and invitation. Kierkegaard puts this invitation into words. 'God grant that he who seeks may also find...; that he who comes hither seeking in the right place may also find rest for his soul. For, true enough, it is a restful position at the foot of the altar, but God grant that this in fact may be but a weak intimation that the soul finds rest in God through consciousness of the forgiveness of sins.' (P. 273)

It is not simple fulfilment which the altar represents. One goes to the communion with a hearty longing and leaves with an even more hearty longing. He does not go to the altar on rare and occasional instances for reconciliation; instead, the altar is a kind of abiding presence in the worshipper's life, for on leaving the altar he still remains at the altar of the Lord's presence. God's sacrifice and suffering in reconciliation is for ever central. Faith recalls that it was in the night when he was betrayed that Christ instituted the supper of love, taking the sorrowful rejection as an opportunity for reconciliation. (Pp. 268, 280, 288) Further, it is not the Christ who is ascended into glory who says 'Come hither', for no man has yet seen Christ in his glory. It is instead the lowly man who suffered and was crucified and who is 'the sign of offence and the object of faith' who gives the invitation.[47]

The profoundly devotional character of *Christian Discourses* is particularly evident in this closing section. S.K. makes the discourses intensely personal. The reader is directly addressed. It could be *anyone* who is addressed, but in any case it is *one*, a solitary individual. 'He who came to earth to die, died also for thee. He did not die for men in a general sort of way; oh, exactly the contrary, He died for someone in particular, not for the ninety and nine—and, thou art too wretched to be reckoned vaguely in the round number, upon thee falls the emphasis of wretchedness and guilt so dreadfully that thou art counted apart.' (P. 301)

31. THE CRISIS AND A CRISIS IN THE LIFE OF AN ACTRESS

The Crisis and a Crisis in the Life of an Actress. By *Inter et inter*. Printed in four parts in the newspaper, *The Fatherland* (July 24–27, 1848), and in 1855, after Kierkegaard's death, published as a whole work by J. L. Heiberg whose wife was the actress referred to. Translated by Stephen Crites in *Crisis in the Life of an Actress and Other Essays on Drama*. New York: Harper & Row, 1967. The first attachment, 'A Passing Comment on a Detail in Don Juan', appeared in *The Fatherland*, May 19–20, 1845 (see section 53, below, item 9). The final essay is 'Herr Phister as Captain Scipio'. S.K. never published it and it is translated from the *Papirer*. It was written in 1848.

The Crisis, interesting in itself, has a somewhat important role within the total authorship. First, it is a reminder of Kierkegaard's delightful companionship with the famous actress to whom it refers and with her brilliant husband. S.K. was in a fellowship which included Hans Christian Andersen and other gifted young men who clustered about the Heibergs. Second, the work is notable for its clear indication that the aesthetic type of experience is not something to be renounced by the Christian but is to be positively retained within the spiritual life even though not being given sovereign place. Biographically, it may be added that in spite of the happy companionship with the Heibergs, S.K. evidenced a severely critical attitude towards the lordly pretensions of Heiberg, who sat 'by the window of literature' waving to the passers-by and who might even have found Christianity a worthy subject for a musical play.[48]

The literary significance of *The Crisis* corresponds to that of the totally dissimilar *Edifying Discourses*. The latter demonstrated S.K.'s primary religious concern at a time when only his aesthetic writings received much attention. They were intended to be actual accompaniments of the aesthetic works, often issued on identical dates, but published in S.K.'s own name in order to indicate that they represented his true views. *The Crisis*, written much later, when S.K. had turned to specifically Christian writing, makes it apparent that he had not changed. Above all, it demonstrates that the author had not fallen into sombre piety because of adverse circumstance. He continues to demonstrate the deep concern for aesthetic matters and the psychological penetration for which he first became famous. Religious controversy has not robbed him of his universality of concern. The discourses proved that he was a religious writer from the start. *The Crisis* proved that he did not later lose the aesthetic interest through religious dedication. Because *The Crisis* might seem to contradict the intense seriousness of his religious writings, S.K. published it only after inner struggle and considerable delay, and then with the hope that it would show that, far from being a kind of prophet, he was a man of ordinary interests.

This work is an interpretation of the work of a great actress. It argues that her splendid performance and self-possession indicate that 'she is in the right rapport with the tension of the stage'. (P. 77) The illusion of the stage and the intently gazing eyes are a great burden to bear, as is quite evident when there is lack of rapport with the audience. Where rapport does exist, the burden is still present but it becomes light. Tension may make the actress anxious prior to the performance of the play, but under the pressure of the stage she is 'light as a bird just set free'. (P. 78)[49]

There is expressed here a basic conviction, that human greatness, including great art, is not hindered by tribulation. This was first evident in S.K.'s attack on Hans Christian Andersen, and was also expressed in *Either/Or* in his definition of a poet. Now he adds that the highest flights are made by the aid of 'hardship and the pressure of adversity'. (P. 77) Given the necessary sympathetic understanding of the audience, the very tenseness of the stage is transformed by a great artist into power. The artist is not devoid of anxiety but becomes carefree under the pressure of the creative situation.

The Crisis extends itself beyond the consideration of the given actress, and even beyond dramatic art, into a general reflection on art and art criticism. The actress, it is pointed out, must pay a high price for her art. While the 'wardrobe of the Royal Theatre' may be costly, the artist's private life is invaded by the public with the folly of its shifting whims. Indeed, art criticism seems most often to pertain to such trivialities as the artist's age or physical profile.

When time has taken the liberty of making the public's idol ten years older, then the public is provoked—with the idol. (P. 72)

An existential aesthetic theory develops. In harmony with Hegel,[50] S.K. thought of art as an observing of *timeless* principles in a medium, and of an actress as being possessed by an enduring 'idea'. She does not possess one element of genius in youth and another in maturity; instead the genius which is potential in youth undergoes metamorphosis in a reflective self-realization. (P. 89) Her genius is not that of a 'damn lively girl' but a feminine youthfulness over which time has no power. It is vivacious originality, exuberance and assurance, inexhaustible playfulness. (Pp. 87, 91, 74) Since in art as in philosophy one is attuned to the idea and since both are thus cognitive, the artistic development is actually an instance of 'the aesthetic-metaphysical dialectic'. (P. 90) By contrast, in religious existence one seeks within the insecurity of time to shape his very being by his deeds. The aesthetic is statically timeless and has 'repetition' of only an 'idea', whereas religious existence is decisively temporal and seeks repetition of the person.

Finally, what are '*the* crisis' and 'a crisis', of the title? *The* crisis for any artist is the issue whether he will succeed as an artist. *A* crisis, in the life of this given actress, was the uncertainty whether she could again successfully take the role of Juliet as she had once done, nineteen years before. The actress herself paid high tribute to S.K.'s comprehension, as contrasted with the shallowness of ordinary theatre critics. More specifically, she expressed astonishment that this 'inspired theorist' could sense and express things which artists feel strongly but cannot articulate.

A Passing Comment on a Detail in Don Juan, a newspaper article translated with the above essay, was occasioned by the return of Mozart's opera to the stage. In it S.K. does not elaborate on the opera as in *Either/Or*, but comments only on the duet with Zerlina and on Zerlina as a person. Her lines must not be sung with strong emphasis because she is befuddled, unlike Elvira incapable of understanding what it means either to be seduced or saved. She romances with Don Juan—a little, then comforts Masetto—a little. As in *Either/Or*, Don Juan is again interpreted not as a crafty seducer, appropriate to drama, but as a nonreflective immediate mood of sexuality, a force of nature which can be portrayed only by the immediacy of music.

Herr Phister as Captain Scipio, a second little essay translated with *The Crisis*, is a delightful comment on the role of S.K.'s friend as a comic captain of police. Phister's *forte* is reflection and this calls for no 'bravo' but for reflective understanding in the audience. The tippling and corpulent Scipio is a discordant person who awkwardly pulls himself and his body together, a gallant and resplendent captain and a wobbly, puffing fellow who blows a complaisant kiss only to hide a gentle belch. Apart from Scipio, what chiefly interests S.K. is that comic subtlety betrays the captain's secrets surreptitiously, and that such reflective comedy demands sensitive interpretation by the viewers instead of the vulgar 'curdling into *Gemütlichkeit*' which most people desire.

32. THE LILIES OF THE FIELD AND THE BIRDS OF THE AIR

The Lilies of the Field and the Birds of the Air. Three Godly Discourses. By S. Kierkegaard. May 14, 1849 (to 'accompany' the 2nd edition of *Either/Or*, published on the same day). Translated by Walter Lowrie and published as an appendage to *Christian Discourses*.

Kierkegaard's early writings were intended for intellectual and sophisticated readers but in his final works he turns to the common people—the plain man. F. J. Billeskov Jansen notes such a shift in this book and also calls attention to its lyrical power. 'Each sentence is given a primitive cadence and certain words are repeated at regular intervals so that our brain finally reproduces unaided the leitmotivs of the discourse; when this occurs the missionary writer has achieved his purpose.'[51] S.K.'s romanticism, with its ambivalent joy and sorrow, reappears in even this profoundly Christian work. Nature, with lilies and birds, is so beautiful, so pregnant with meaning, and so quickly subject to suffering and death. (P. 351 f.) Yet nature's beauty and melancholy alike prompt man to spiritual concern.

It seems strange that in this work of poetic beauty the author should repudiate poetry on the ground that it 'cannot come to an understanding with the gospel'. This rejection of a poetic approach to religion is a clear mark of the 'godly' earnestness of the discourses. Kierkegaard complains that sentimental people love to hear the poet exclaim, 'Oh, would I were a bird . . . like the little song-bird that sings so humbly, notwithstanding no one listens . . .' (P. 319) It is no such indulgence in sentiment, but a commandment of the New Testament, that man should learn from the birds and lilies. However, upon hearing this, the poet and his followers laugh and make a jest of the gospel.

Silence, obedience and joy are three lessons taught by the lilies and birds. Silence is the theme of the first discourse which bears the title 'Behold the birds of the air; consider the lilies of the field'. How silent are the lilies! Even the animals with their grunts and cries are silent so far as meaningful speech is concerned. 'But because it is an advantage to be able to speak, it does not follow that to be able to keep silent is no art.' (P. 322)

For man to be silent is literally to 'seek first' the Kingdom of God, yielding to divine sovereignty. What ought a man to do? Should he give his fortune to the poor? To this and a thousand activistic questions the invariable answer is that he should seek first the Kingdom of God. This makes it appear that to seek the Kingdom is to do nothing at all. In a sense this is true, for to seek God is to keep silent. 'It is man's superiority over the beast to be able to speak; but in relation to God it can easily become the ruin of man who is able to speak that he is too willing to speak.' (P. 323)

Silence is the mood of prayer. Has one striven earnestly in prayer? The more earnestly he has striven surely the less he has found to say, until, as he came close to God, he fell silent. In fact, when in prayer the believer at last becomes silent he becomes the precise opposite of a speaker, i.e. he becomes a hearer. 'He had supposed that to pray is to speak; he learnt that to pray is not merely to be silent but to hear.' (P. 323)

Obedience, as a second instruction of the lilies and birds, is set forth in 'No man can serve two masters'. Certainly the lilies serve only one master and the birds are unconditionally obedient. They are never guilty of half-measures or of 'a little disobedience'. In nature God's will is invariably done. However, because man is wilful, God manifests himself to mankind as the God of patience. The gospel commands with unexpected severity, 'Thou shalt', but then with loving compassion it takes the disobedient one by the hand, out among the lilies, pointing out that it is service of masters other than God which disturbs the beauty of the world.

Finally, from the little creatures of nature man can learn joy. 'Behold the birds of the air: they sow not . . . nor gather into barns.' These schoolmasters are full of joy because, not being anxious for the morrow, they live today. With a chorus they eagerly greet the dawn. 'What joy when the bird—who does not merely sing at his work..., but whose essential work it is to sing—joyfully begins its song...' (P. 347) This must not be misunderstood. It is not freedom from trouble which calls forth the songs of birds. The dumb creation may also gasp in pain. Almost in a miracle the birds joyously sing while the whole creation groans. Birds are joyous because they cast all their cares on the Lord and do not ponder over the gathering gloom. Or, rather, it does not occur to them not to leave all things in the hands of God and so give way to dejection.

What the birds do unconsciously man must freely choose to do. In conscious faith he can sing out in a prayer of joy, 'Thine is the kingdom and the power and the glory, for ever and ever. Amen.'

33. TWO ETHICO-RELIGIOUS TREATISES

Two Minor Ethico-Religious Treatises. By H. H., May 19, 1848. In English in: *The Present Age* and *Two Ethico-Religious Treatises.* Translated by Alexander Dru and Walter Lowrie. London: Oxford University Press, 1940. The second treatise was originally part of a (then) unpublished work, *On Authority and Revelation: The Book on Adler.* The Harper edition of *The Present Age* (1962) includes the second treatise but unfortunately omits the first. (Page references below to the second treatise are to the 1962 edition but page references to the first treatise are to the less readily available 1940 edition.)

Regarding this work as not 'in his authorship but as pertaining to it as a whole, Kierkegaard chose to make it strictly anonymous rather than fictionally pseudonymous. Accordingly it was printed by a different publisher and simply with the initials H.H. to indicate authorship.

This 'minor' book is major. If Kierkegaard had written nothing else this work would have been a startling challenge to the modern world's confused judgment on religion, which tends to retrain it in a secularized form but with no clear recognition of its transcendent character. He phrases it pungently: If an apostle is no more than (and *as much as*) a genius, then 'good night, Christianity'.

The first essay, more perplexing and probably less important than the second, treats a topic nevertheless arresting for every admirer of Socrates, 'Has a Man the Right to Let Himself be Put to Death for the Truth?' Far from being an abstractly theoretical question, this problem is in part autobiographical. In the severity of his childhood home only the image of Christ as the Crucified One was impressed upon Kierkegaard. Unlike other children he did not hear of the little child Jesus. So to speak, S.K. had no Christmas, but only Good Friday. 'Although only a child, he was already as old as an old man.' (P. 81)[52] Some poet has felt, in gazing at the Crucified, that Jesus is pleading with man, 'Take me down from the cross'. Kierkegaard's understanding of sacrificial love in atonement would exclude this, but he too came to feel the claim which the image of Jesus on the cross laid on him personally. He must do something about the cross. Although he was but a sinner, he felt that he might still without presumption, 'desire to suffer for the same cause, even unto death'. Finally, however, there came an illuminating doubt, as to 'whether a *man* has a right to let himself be put to death for the truth'. (Pp. 82, 85) Is this right rather reserved for God?

The issue seems strange. Yet we may ask whether it is not more astonishing that among all who have professed to walk in Jesus' steps—from the time of St Peter who denied Christ to avoid suffering with him, down to the present age—so few have frankly noted that these steps lead to a cross. The issue eventually became circumstantially personal for S.K. He had chosen to suffer for the truth, and did suffer. In his growing conflict with the state church he felt that it was not inconceivable that he, like Socrates, might be punished for impiety. Although it may seem preposterous, he wondered if he might be put to death for the truth and even whether he ought not choose such martyrdom. However, in humility, he is obliged to ask: Does a man have a right to let himself be put to death for the truth? This question can best be understood as a variant of the question whether Kierkegaard had the right to assume the role of a godly and suffering critic of Christendom, as he later did. The answer at which he arrived at this time was negative. He is no more than a poet, not a martyr, and is permitted only to lure men into the arena of Christianity by his poetic talents. At the end of his life he came to the opposite conclusion and dared to attack faithlessness in Christendom and even to hope for martyrdom.*

Has a man the right to die for the truth? Who but Kierkegaard would ask the question? A martyr will hardly ask if he has a *right* to martyrdom because he attends to his cause rather than to himself. Neither will worldly 'Christians' ask if they have a right to let themselves be put to death for the truth. Indeed, they will sacrifice all virtue to avoid this 'privilege'. Yet perhaps this strange question is inescapable. Consider a preacher speaking eloquently about the

* Even in the last journals, S.K. was still plagued by the doubt as to whether one has a right to be a voluntary sacrifice, whether this is not harshness to others in making them guilty of sacrificing him. (*Papirer*, XI² A 263.) Yet he came to think of his life itself as 'a kind of martyrdom', being 'trampled to death by geese'. (*Ibid.*, XI¹ A 484.)

glorious martyrs. What would be his embarrassment if a plain man, much moved by the sermon but hardly understanding the circumstances of martyrdom, came to report that he was now ready to join the noble army of martyrs! 'Then the parson would reply to him good-humouredly as follows: "Why! Merciful Father in Heaven! How did such an idea ever occur to you? Travel, divert yourself, take a laxative."' (P. 100) If the plain man misunderstood the imitation of Christ, perhaps by reason of his plainness, the preacher made a mockery of it. Clearly, S.K.'s discourse revolves about the heart of the gospel, viz. what it is like to seriously follow a crucified Lord.

In some ages the question of this essay is queer for the added reason that there are no martyrs, and none who are plagued with the question. This apparently happy solution deserves further reflection, however, for if an age has no martyrs it is not because the people of the age are incapable of murdering the prophets. It is rather because no man is sufficiently righteous to exasperate evil men to the point of killing him.

As suggested before, this treatise ought to be of interest to any who have reflected on the death of Socrates, the more so if they have compared it with the death of Christ. Has a man a right to let himself be put to death for the truth? No, replies Kierkegaard, not even Socrates who believed that he did have such a duty to truth. Love for his enemies should have prevented Socrates from making his enemies guilty of killing him. 'It is monstrously cruel to let simple men become guilty of putting one to death because they were unable to understand', or, even as may have been the case of the enemies of Socrates, because they refused to understand. (P. 118) Christ, on the other hand, could allow this because instead of imposing guilt on his enemies he was actually manifesting a loving and redemptive concern for them. Christ's death was thus not martyrdom but atonement. It was a divine and saving deed.

One might question whether the guilt which ignorant men bring on themselves by being provoked into killing a disciple or a prophet is so unique or unpardonable (presumably incurred largely through ignorance—and to be judged in Christian perspective) as to warrant S.K.'s anxiety. However, there is another consideration to be weighed. Even if a martyred Socrates thereby manifests a loving concern for mankind and not simply a stubborn adherence to truth, still S.K. feels that his act is presumptuous. He cannot claim that he is—simply and absolutely—dying for the truth. No man has such certainty of or monopoly on truth, or on virtue. The willingness to sacrifice oneself does not bestow either infallibility or the privilege of, through one's possibly foolish action, placing others in such jeopardy.

If Christ is not a martyr like Socrates, why did he allow himself to be crucified, and in what sense did he die for the truth? S.K. answers that Jesus did not die *for* the truth because he himself is the truth, and revealed this through his death as in his life. Whereas Socrates died for the truth, Christ died for the enemies who killed him. Christ refused to falsify his mission so as to be what the people wanted. 'The mighty hated Him because the people wished to make Him king, and the people hated Him because He would not be king.' (P. 89) Therefore, men had no alternatives but to adore or crucify, and Christ willed to die when men would not adore. The death of Socrates could not take away the guilt of his murderers but the death of Jesus has a power of atonement whereby truth and love are not in a state of alienation, mutually exclusive alternatives, but are reconciled to one another. In his journals S.K. throws a bit more light on this matter. Christ had the right to let men put him to death because he was Love, and love healed the guilt of those who crucified; but much more importantly he could do this because he was *Truth*. He let men become guilty of crucifying in order to 'reveal Truth to the uttermost degree'. Love cannot take precedence over truth, cannot change the actual fact of sin, but faces absolute truth unswervingly and wins a paradoxical victory over the bitter truth.[53]

There is one odd qualification which Kierkegaard adds to his conclusion. Although man must not be guilty of loving truth more than neighbour, yet an apostle has a unique relationship to Christ. The apostle is sent to bear a message and it may be that the outcome of his doing so will be martyrdom. While he cannot die for his enemies as Christ did, he is so close to Christ—not by wisdom but by commandment—that he is freed from the responsibility of making his enemies guilty if he permits them to kill him. Finally it should be noted that while any faithful Christian may be subject to persecution and might even be killed without his choosing it, that his death is then scarcely martyrdom because he does not challenge evil to yield or else destroy him. The role of the apostle is dramatically in contrast to this. This focus on the peculiar role of the apostle becomes central in the ensuing treatise.

'On the Difference Between a Genius and an Apostle', the second essay, makes a violent protest against the confusion of 'poetic inspiration' and 'divine revelation', and insists that the very existence of Christianity is being threatened by the common confusion of apostles with men of spiritual genius. They are, however, unlike in that apostles are called, while poets can be born. Kierkegaard herein points to divine authority as constituting the essential difference between genius and apostleship. A genius is still qualitatively one with the crowd, can still be brought down to a common, and even vulgar, level. On the contrary, the apostle speaks with borrowed authority. Like a mailman delivering a letter, he 'has nothing to do with its contents' but has as his sole glory the responsibility for delivering a message which is not his own. (P. 106) S.K., of course, did not claim to be an apostle, but only to know of the apostles and what an apostle is.

Walter Kaufmann is undoubtedly correct in insisting that in this work 'we find the heart of Kierkegaard', and that the message is 'not genteel, not comfortable'. If men are disturbed by the apostles' tone of authority and claim to a message of eternal significance, this is for S.K. precisely as it should be. Noting how the present age carelessly lumps Jesus with Buddha, Confucius, and other wise men, Kaufmann comments: 'The appalling possibility that Kierkegaard insisted we consider was that God's teaching might not agree completely with the predilections and the conscience of the present age.' (Pp. 27 f.) Kierkegaard was horrified by the nonsensical but nearly universal identification of Christianity with culture and wisdom. Therefore he shouted aloud that St Paul was not a genius, and that the gospel does *not* reveal what men (cultured men, at least) should all the time have understood. The reason why one should listen to St Paul is not that he was brilliant, or that he employed beautiful similes—although foolish people do persist in praising him 'as a tent-maker whose masterly work surpassed that of all upholsterers'. All that is important about Paul is that he was called to speak for God, which fact is furthermore only a faith-fact since it is not demonstrable by reason or evidence but is true only for those who are quickened by faith.

Which of the two men, genius or apostle, has something *new* to bring forth. In a sense, it is the genius, but his new offering is transitory. S.K. draws an incisive contrast between paradox and pseudo-paradox. The genius 'may be a century ahead of his time, and therefore appear to be a paradox, but ultimately the race will assimilate what was once a paradox in such a way that it is no longer paradoxical'. (P. 92) Christ, on the other hand, the God-incognito, can never be so assimilated. He remains for ever an absolute Paradox, and since *he* is the message of the apostle it follows that the apostolic message can never become a part of human culture and wisdom but is always a voice from the transcendent. Thus it is that the apostle, even though he has not a single unique idea, presents that which is everlastingly new, i.e. eternal; he speaks with timeless authority.

How can an apostle prove that he has such authority? Indeed, he cannot. Even miracles are objects of *faith*, not of demonstration, and faith is a response to the power of revelation, not 'reasonable belief'. It is also evident that the claim of Christianity is not that its message is profound. Jesus' message is to be accepted not because it is wiser than that of Plato or Confucius but because it comes as a divine assurance, the truth of which is grasped only in faith. In bitter protest against humanistic pleasantry and flattery, S.K. insists that Jesus is not the Great Teacher. Indeed, he is not even the Master Carpenter. What distinguishes him is the voice of authority, a transcendent element.

Man himself has no such transcendence, for he never really transcends other men (contrast Heidegger who views deviation from common practice as transcendence). The individual can only realize and demonstrate those possibilities which are latent in all individuals, and he is understandable precisely because he does not involve categories beyond humanness. In contrast, Jesus demonstrates a qualitative, not quantitative, difference from men; he speaks with divine authority. This unique element need not be subtle. It may even be quite simple and lucid. What Christ enjoins when he says, 'But I say unto you...' may have simple earthly meaning, and be a simple earthly deed. The transcendence lies in his right to speak with authority. At this point his enemies probably understood him much better than did his patronizing friends. His friends depict him as a good and kindly man. Christ's enemies, on the contrary, understood him perfectly. He is a blasphemer, they protested; he makes himself equal to God. Yet that, of course, is the whole point to Christianity. The mark or sign (not proof) of authority in Christ, and derivatively in his apostles, is the unconditional obedience with which they accept martyrdom in order to give a witness. (P. 159; also *Journals*, 990)

A very important fact for the understanding of Kierkegaard himself may be noted in conclusion, i.e. that this essay has profound autobiographical reference, a fact which is not directly evident and which has no necessary bearing on its objective significance. Called forth by the strange case of Adler (cf. unit 20), who claimed to be giving revelations, S.K. was challenged to think through his own role. He insisted that the righteous life for the ordinary individual, even an authentic and responsible individual, even an authentic and responsible individual, is to exemplify the God-given universal order, e.g. as father, husband, church member, or pastor. Yet the fantastic pretensions of Adler and his own peculiar life led Kierkegaard to believe that there is also a place for exceptional persons who may seek by their strangeness to bring the normal mode of existence under critical scrutiny.

Nevertheless, argued Kierkegaard (in the book from which this essay is taken), an extraordinary person cannot at the same time criticize the normal life and yet claim to be an example of it. If he makes himself an exception then he must be willing to pay the price of *being* a luminous but atypical instance, in which category S.K. chose to place himself.[54] Adler, in contrast, claimed to give new revelations but sought to establish them by means of Biblical revelation. He tried to prophesy *to* the church and yet also to speak *by* its authority. Unlike him, when S.K. later pronounced judgement on the church he did not seek its support, did not propose a real plan of reform (as one working within it), but only wanted as an extraordinary person to wound the conscience.

In this light it is crystal clear and enormously important for an understanding of Kierkegaard himself that while it is incumbent on everyone to be a true individual (normally living the commonplace life), there is also a special role for a rare exception who will not be an individual *within the universal* but an interpreter outside of it. Adler confusedly claimed to be both apostle and genius and in fact was neither. S.K. denied being an apostle (i.e. one who speaks with authority) but certainly was a genius (a 'poet'), one who sought to remind people of what apostles had actually said, and what had subsequently come to be ignored.

34. THE SICKNESS UNTO DEATH

> *The Sickness Unto Death.* A Christian psychological exposition for edification and awakening. By Anti-Climacus. Edited by S. Kierkegaard. July 30, 1849. Translated by Walter Lowrie. Princeton: Princeton University Press, 1941. Translation revised by Howard A. Johnson in *Fear and Trembling* and *The Sickness Unto Death.* Garden City: Doubleday, 1954; Anchor paperback A 30. References are to the original edition.

The title of this book comes from the saying of Jesus regarding Lazarus, 'This sickness is not unto death'. Since, nevertheless, Lazarus died and was buried, it is plain that Jesus was referring to a kind of spiritual death. It is of this death of the spirit that this book offers a morphology, revealing what happens to men's souls in night clubs, on battle fields, and in loneliness—however, not in terms of such places and circumstances but in terms of the varieties of inner despair which men there experience. Billeskov Jansen comments on *Sickness*, that it 'begins in the Hegelian manner with the vaguest of all abstractions, a metaphysical definition of man, and continues with a series of character studies which together form a brilliant portrait gallery of every type of sinner'.[55] It is significant however that S.K. does not simply give an anatomy of the dreary regions of human despair. He is able to view it hopefully as the doorway to spiritual recovery and faith, because he holds that man is not prepared to trust God until he at last concedes that he can no longer trust himself.

Whereas this exhaustive recital of forms of despair might be taken to reflect the depth of S.K.'s melancholy, it rather represents a kind of dogmatic position. He is determined to brand as despair not only the conscious form known to man but also any life attitude other than Christian faith. If the unbeliever is unconscious of despair nevertheless he has not escaped it. This dogmatism expresses the conviction of the necessity of faith for gaining wholeness of spirit.

Along with *Training in Christianity*, this work is commonly regarded as one of the author's two great religious writings. Despite its severity, rare humour punctuates the brilliant psychological-philosophical and theological analysis. S.K. himself wrote of the book: 'It is certainly the truest and most perfect thing I have written; but my relation to it must not be such as to make it seem as if it is I that come down upon all the others with an almost damning judgment—no, I must myself first of all be educated by it; there is perhaps no one that has a right to be so deeply humbled by it as I before I have a right to publish it.'[56] For fear that this very severity of judgment would give offence, in particular to Bishop Mynster, S.K. hesitated about publishing the work, despite its importance.

In an unusual sense *Sickness* is one of the pseudonymous writings. Earlier pseudonyms were used to indicate that the views did not necessarily correspond to S.K.'s own attitude. Here he enters his own name as editor to indicate his complete agreement, yet he refers to Anti-Climacus as author. The early pseudonym 'Johannes Climacus' had accurately described Christianity, yet as one not necessarily committed to it; correspondingly Anti-Climacus is the *confirmed* Christian. In contrast to both, S.K. thinks humbly of himself as one who is only a 'becoming' Christian.

The degree of involvement with Hegelian idealism and, on the other hand, the degree of genuine Christianity reflected in *Sickness* is disputed. Zuidema has argued that 'Kierkegaard secularized Christianity and Christian categories long before the development of Heidegger's and Jasper's existentialism'.[57] His interpretation views S.K.'s doctrine as essentially the story of a struggle of the self to become its absolute or infinite self (salvation) by transcending its finite (worldly) self. Zuidema concludes that this view 'is in principle atheistic, in spite of the good intentions of its author', on the ground that God is not central to the thought, but is instead only the instrument whereby the self succeeds in its process of spiritual evolution.[58] This provocative view, based on S.K.'s intense struggle for and concern with personal integrity, overlooks or sets aside his religious love and faith and his remarkable sensitivity to the personal meaning of Christ. If Zuidema's view is a possible interpretation of *Sickness*, viewed by itself, it is almost impossible to reconcile it to the more important culminative works, such as *Training* and *Works of Love*.

It is true however that S.K. gives faith an existential twist. Faith means not only trust in God but the self's willing to be itself before God. This can be given either of two interpretations, either that S.K. *uses* God as a means of existential self-realization; or, that he thinks of his relation to the creator as a natural fulfilment of existence. The first interpretation makes religion an instrumentality of existential concern, while the other would simply unfold Christianity's meaning with reference to existence. The authors agree with Zuidema that existentialism did modify S.K.'s theology at times, as in *Dread*, but hold that primarily it is Christian faith which dominates his existential outlook.

Ground covered in *Dread* (as well as in *Fear and Trembling* and other works) is re-explored here, but from a positive Christian standpoint, and with a concern for healing the 'sickness' of humanity instead of merely describing its symptoms. *Sickness* is thus in no sense a revised version of *Dread*. Anxiety as treated in *Dread* is the very mark of humanness, under the responsibility of freedom. Despair, as treated in *Sickness*, is the dreadful sickness which befalls spirit through its wrong use of freedom. Dread is possibility, but despair is actuality—sorry actuality.

In order to know how the self can be sick and in order to assist it, there must first be determined what a self is. Accordingly, an anthropology is proposed in *Sickness* which is foundational in S.K.'s analysis of the human problem. Although it is perilous to single out of so vast a complex of principles as that presented by Kierkegaard any one doctrine as being more important than others, this anthropology does seem absolutely central.

It is here argued that man is an insecure and straining synthesis of the temporal and the eternal. This synthesis, as created by God, constitutes man's uniqueness and is the basis of his striving and aspiration. Out of it he can either turn his face in love and joy to the creator or reject true selfhood and God. A sparrow has no such native tension and accordingly has no possibility either of dedication or of nervous breakdown, of integrity or of sin. When man wills to be himself, accepting himself as a mixture of finite and infinite, he also wills to be what God ordained and so is in relationship to God; and when he refuses to be himself he is disobedient to God. (P. 19) The self 'is a relation' between earth and heaven, between time and eternity, and more specifically is a relation which willingly accepts itself in this strange and burdensome tension. Thus man is a relation which 'relates itself to its own self'. (P. 17) The self is not only a synthesis but a synthesis which rests upon choice. Such other concepts as of existence and of the stages on life's way take this view of man as a presupposition.*

In the notion of an interplay between temporal and eternal in the life of man, there is evident an important agreement between S.K. and the philosophical idealism and romanticism of his age. This is the more interesting in the light of his usual radical and outspoken opposition to such thought. The thought is that man can never be understood in terms of his animal cousins, for to be human is to be the strange creature which awkwardly and perilously compounds time and eternity. The decisive difference between S.K. and the romanticists is that whereas they regarded this contact of man with the eternal as constituting religion, he viewed it not as religion but simply as the mark of humanness. He agreed that God works 'through the slightest movement' of one's consciousness in even its solitary communion with itself, yet insists that this only tells what it is to be a human being. To become religious requires in addition a radical and dramatic alteration of this normal human consciousness.[59]

* Although Kierkegaard never abandoned the notion of man as a synthesis of the earthly and the spiritual in which the spiritual ought to dominate, in the closing period of his life he increasingly emphasized the bitter conflict between the natural man and the spirit. Born in sin, man 'is a cunning animal creation', bewitched and under a spell, infatuated with the world of sense, *loving rest*. Then Christianity presents eternity as 'the most intense unrest, in order to save man from this bewitchment...' (*Papirer*, XI² A 395.) Accordingly, to be spirit came to be thought of as living as though one were dead to the world. (*Ibid.*, XI¹ A 279.) The goal of existence as spirit is to be an 'I', for only a true self can fulfil God's desire to be loved. (*Ibid.*, XI¹ A 487.)

THE CHRISTIAN WRITINGS

If the finite and temporal in man is easily recognized, what is the nature of the eternal element in which the human synthesis is also rooted? It has to do with disillusionment over all anxious striving in time, a dissatisfaction with earthly values, and a spirit of peace, fulfilment, and calmness based on a firm expectation of the eternal. Yet Kierkegaard is loathe to attempt any descriptive reference. Perhaps the most illustrative and most indicative characterization which he gives, as one might expect from his Christian grounding, pertains to love. 'As the quiet lake is fed deep down by the hidden springs, which no eye sees, so a human being's love is grounded, still more deeply, in God's love. If there were no spring at the bottom, if God were not love, then there would be neither a little lake nor a man's love. As the still waters begin obscurely in the deep spring, so a man's love mysteriously begins in God's love.'[60] There is not the faintest whisper of romanticism's pantheism in this, but there is an agreement with romanticism that to be human is to draw mysteriously from divine resources in one's value experience. S.K.'s treatment of moral consciousness bears this out. He does not confuse the ethical with the religious. Nevertheless, he views the ethical consciousness as rooted in God; to be ethical is for one to relate himself to God in dutiful response to the divinely established universal law. In his reflections on the eternal, there are evident personalistic strains which emerge in S.K.'s doctrine. God is indeed creator, but he cannot be comprehended in terms of cosmological involvements. He is instead a person or subject, never an object, and can be understood only with reference to personhood or subjectivity and the experience of such.

Most fundamentally, S.K. identifies the self as spirit. By nature man is soul (mind) and body. However, through his relationship to the eternal man acquires a third factor in his make-up, 'spirit', which becomes the sovereign self and assimilates body and soul to itself in its concern for the eternal.[61] The very nature of spirit is responsible freedom. To 'choose oneself' is to become one's proper self because only by the act of freedom (in choice) is there a free self to be chosen.[62] The more one wills, the more selfhood he possesses, and a man who does not choose is not truly a self. (P. 43) Existence is radically subjective and voluntary, yet the charge that Kierkegaard loses himself in subjectivity is quite erroneous because he holds that man can freely choose and become himself only by relating himself to God.

Although differing with Hegel on the specific nature of man's selfhood and involvement with the eternal (Absolute), Kierkegaard here reflects something of the Hegelian notion of spirit. He explains that a self is that which actively relates itself to itself. Thus it exists inwardly and is controlled from within rather than from without—recalling Hegel's view of freedom (self-determination) as the characterization of spirit, whereas external determination (as gravity) is the reigning principle of matter. To exist humanly, as spirit, is to assume responsibility for oneself. It also follows that despair can never result solely from tragic external circumstances; despair is an internal dis-relationship, a malady of spirit itself.

S.K.'s account of the emergence of spirit makes it clear that the doctrine is more philosophical than psychological. He is not wanting to give an analysis of body-mind functions but to describe existence in a new dimension, that of value. It is primarily in value experience that the eternal discloses itself, although S.K. would cautiously agree with Hegel—or Pascal—that even in man's intellect there is a hint of the eternal. For example, a map maker has an experience of a sort of timelessness. Glancing at the map, he is at the destination in the same moment as that of departure. Yet this is a 'spurious' or 'falsified' kind of eternity, a kind of self-deception which professes to contemplate all things as seen by a divine mind but which in doing so destroys the temporal road man must walk in moving from place to place, and his responsibility in it.* If the eternal discloses itself properly, it cannot do so merely by contemplation which too often tries to take the place of an actual struggle in time. Rather, the eternal must break into time, identify itself with a truly historical moment —which remains historical—and transfigure the moment.

* *Purity of Heart*, p. 114. Man's finitude is obvious but that he is stretched towards the infinite is less clear. S.K. means that man can be fully understood only in the strain of a God-relationship. Then his contradictions are evident. Relative immortality is replaced by sin. Anxiety is understood. Eternal hope is meaningful. Thus, existence is fully possible only before God. The contrast between finite and infinite has led some to the error of supposing that S.K. adopted the Greek view that sin is finitude rather than an evil act of will. On this see Martin J. Heinecken, *The Moment Before God*, Philadelphia: Muhlenberg Press (1956), pp. 183 ff.

Basically then, for S.K., the self is spirit, that which freely, responsibly, and inwardly selects values and sets the course of life. A self is not a being, but an 'existing' *becoming* (lacking the static self-identity of things), in which the relation between finitude and infinitude perpetuates itself. In language reminiscent of Plato's myth of the charioteer, S.K. elsewhere describes the three-fold nature of existence: 'Eternity [infinitude] is a winged horse, infinitely fast; time [finitude] is a worn-out jade. The existing individual is the driver; and both horses are yoked together. Only by God's help can we succeed in the difficult task of "existing".'[63] The genuine self is not merely psychical (the psychic being rather referred to the 'soul'), or even mind and body. The true self is 'spirit', an eternal factor by which man is destined for fellowship with God and which binds body and soul to one another and to itself. (P. 17) Whereas the natural man must find his *telos* and measure within himself—just as Confucius insisted that man's measure must be patterned after *man* and not after heaven—the Christian finds in Christ the proper pattern of ideal humanness, so that in Christ the goal and measure of man are set forth by God. Similarly, sin is a refusal to accept Christ's measure of a man. (P. 186)

Spirit comes into being in the act whereby man relates himself to himself (and to God), for it is only by willing to be oneself that personal values are generated.* Yet, as for Saint Augustine, when man struggles to become a true self, he finds himself to be a dependent one and only by acknowledging his relationship to God can he properly relate himself to himself. Then the eternal relieves him of the dread successiveness of time in which the self perishes in each moment, each momentary self being replaced by a new transitory self. Without relating himself to God, man is not yet spirit but a kind of intellectual animal, trapped in the fleetingness of time. Only the religious man can become true man, as the eternal enters into his experience of time so as to transform his quasi-permanence into a genuine present, focusing on changeless

---

* Man's becoming spirit does not mean that prior to this becoming he is only soul and body. Spirit as self is always present but in a kind of dream state in which there may be contemplated the possibilities open for choice, but without seizing any of them. No Nietzschean animal ever yearned to become the super-animal nor did it dread the unknown outcomes of its free choice. But man is torn between such restless craving and anxiety.

goals rather than on momentary pleasures.[64] Just as personal existence thus takes on a new character as seen from the Christian standpoint, so too human despair is seen in a new light. The natural man fears death and clings to the fleeting moments. The Christian, in contrast, is in despair over the fleeting moments, knowing that within them he has not yet gained real selfhood.

What is the nature of the sickness unto death to which the self is subject? It roots in man's being a mixture and free, yet it is not this. Man is tense because he has been created a mixture and responsible before the eternal, but tautness or mixture is not as such a sickness, and even 'despair' is not as such sin. To be human is to possess the imprint of the image of God, and to have a foundation for eternal blessedness. To fall into sin consists of man's letting the mixture of his being become ill-proportioned. In this conception there are interesting parallels to Nietzsche and to Saint Augustine. Nietzsche thinks of man as a rope stretched to near the breaking point between earthiness and lovely dream. The difference for Kierkegaard is that the lovely dream is not self-created fantasy but, as for Augustine, the image of God which requires that one live before God and aspire towards the eternal. Consequently, sin is a disorientation towards God.

The disruption of the self can take many forms, as disproportion occurs among the dualities in which man is involved, soul and body, finitude and infinitude, time and eternity, and possibility and necessity. When man is not content to be such a mixture he may pretend, for example, either that he is plain beast or else pure angelic being. Man can despair by seeking to abandon either spirit or body. In these instances or in any other case, despair is a disrelationship between factors and an unwillingness to be the kind of creature which God ordained. To be human is to be dual, though with spirit in a dominant role, and the human sickness is a wilful imbalance within this duality.

Sickness unto death must be sharply differentiated from maladjustment. Some commentators have taken it to be a loss of 'integrated personality' but this is far too simple and superficial an account of it. The sickness does indeed root in 'not willing to be one's self', but it is a loss of a quite specific form of integration, that which reflects the will of God. Man has not created himself.

When he refuses to be himself he is also rebelling against his maker. Since despair is thus a disease of the will it is, in the deepest sense, not a deed but a state or condition in which one guiltily remains. In despair man returns to disobedience—or remains in disobedience—just as in faith one has a *repetition* of fellowship with God. (Pp. 173 f.)

Despair is a strange disease, quite unlike bodily ailments. Every physical disease runs its course and becomes a cause of its later stages, and, perhaps, of death. On the contrary, sickness unto death is not the cause of its later stages; each moment the soul is responsible for contracting the disease anew by not willing to be itself. Furthermore, in a paradoxical sense, despair is not sickness *unto* (into) death. If one is in total despair he may desire a release, but unlike physical illness despair does not culminate in death but only in a kind of existence which is a mockery of authentic life.

How strange the despair of being oneself can be is demonstrated by the fact that it is 'man's advantage over the beast'. No animal can be other than itself, whereas man alone can choose his destiny, and, doing so, foolishly betray himself. Further, to be clearly conscious of this sickness is 'the Christian's advantage over the natural man'. The natural man or pagan is in ignorance, a despairing unawareness of existing 'before God', whereas the Christian and he alone is fully conscious of the nature of sin. (P. 20) Correspondingly, the Christian is most aware of his guilt in rejection of the good. He knows most immediately the sickness which is *unto death*, which is 'perdition'. Even though the sickness is so radical it is nevertheless uplifting and ennobling. It calls attention to the fact that man is not a pawn of circumstance in that the sickness originates freely from within. Further, the sickness makes it evident that the supposition of a simple natural happiness resulting from pleasant circumstance is an illusion since spiritual health can only result from a proper relation of the self to its self. (Pp. 155, 33, 19) Indeed, despair is the spiritual prod which stirs one out of animalistic contentment and awakens one to the possibilities of selfhood. (Pp. 39 f.) It also makes evident the enduring nature of spiritual opportunity because the sickness does not issue in death, thus giving an opportune if bitter duration.

It should be evident that there will occur gradations of this despair, which is universally present in spite of the fact that it is sometimes supposed to be a rare ailment. The omnipresence of the disease is not readily recognized because people tend to confuse externally caused grief with the inward disease of the will. Also, in some instances, the public show of not giving way to despair may be a sheer pretence of spiritual health.

That it is the self which man despairs of, and is the sourse of his sickness, is an insistent Kierkegaardian point, and one which will seem strange, since most people in despair appear to be suffering from loss of love or some external treasure. If one despairs over loss of an external blessing this actually signifies that he cannot endure his own self and requires some external means of spiritual support. Despair of self is most fundamentally conceived in terms of ethical and religious self-betrayal. However, a self can be sick (indeed, can be 'fantastic') by disproportion of knowledge, of volition, or even of the life of feeling—none of which are necessarily and immediately of moral or religious significance. Thus a scientist who is so intent on understanding microbes that he forgets to grow in self-awareness is sick. Similarly, a dreamy utopian may will infinite good for all mankind but be blind to the daily duties for which he ought to be responsible. In such instances man also betrays his proper self, but does so more or less unconsciously, by permitting an improper balance within his nature.

Kierkegaard is particularly concerned with the variety of ways in which a self may lose itself or fail to possess itself. Although there is a common human spiritual sickness, there are the most varied manifestations, and it is in the analysis of these that S.K. manifests his psychological acumen. The form of one's sickness varies with the kind of imbalance in the self, and the degree of one's awareness—from almost inhuman worldliness to dreamy pre-occupation with ideals, and from the most insensitive obtuseness to self-conscious and demonic despair.

Because sin deforms the self it alienates one from his fellows. As dead men in a cemetery do not form a social club, so sin-sick men are isolated. (P. 197) Yet the very lack of true selfhood causes one to seek the anonymity of the crowd. This is a vulgar form of despair, for one to be a mere thing, a 'cipher in the crowd', scarcely a person at all except in a physical way. S.K. finds such a man—who is little more than a thing—'infinitely comic', though in a rather ghastly way. Imagine such a thing-person being introduced into eternity by the parson for the price of ten dollars, although 'a self he was not, and a self he did not become'. An amusing story is told of a peasant who came to town with 'so much money that he could buy himself a pair of shoes and stockings and still had enough left to get drunk on'. Staggering homewards, he fell in a drunken stupor in the middle of the road and went to sleep. A wagon came by and the driver shouted to the peasant to get out of the way or he would run over his legs. 'Then the drunken peasant awoke, looked at his legs, and since by reason of the shoes and stockings he didn't recognize them, he said to the driver, "Drive on, they are not my legs".' (P. 85) Kierkegaard never tires of ironical comment on the folly and the humour involved in the attempt to transform the worldly man who has little more identity or continuity than of the physical body ('an inhuman centipede') into a real self, having an eternal identity.*

Is it possible that the comic-pathetic 'man', who might recognize his legs—if they had the right shoes and stockings—but not his self, could be strictly nothing but a thing, and not in any sense a self? Surely not. Just as Plato holds that one can desire only that which in some slight measure he possesses (else he would not know what to desire), so too for S.K. man is never totally devoid of selfhood. In fact he argued that the very fact that 'despair cannot consume the self' is a demonstration of the presence of the eternal in man. (P. 30) In spite of man's dreadful deformity, he is still in the image of God, and never a mere thing.

The most common form of despair is worldliness, i.e. being unconscious of oneself *as spirit* and failing to sense responsibility to God. Worldliness is a moral weakness and is typified by drunken revellers or gay pleasure seekers. They are unconscious of ideal goals and therefore are also unconscious of falling short, so that their despair is likewise unconscious. They have no larger in-

---

* *Postscript*, p. 157. Kierkegaard nevertheless recognizes a serious difficulty in his own thought at this point, in that he dangerously seems to be asserting that one becomes spirit only by existential decision instead of being spirit by virtue of divine creation. Therefore, he not only qualifies the existential view by declaring that, at least potentially, men are all immortal (cf. G. Malantschuk, *Kierkegaard's Way to the Truth*, p. 85; also, *Papirer*, VIII B 81, 8), but also supports the view of general immortality by denying that anyone can spiritually die; there is only sickness *unto* death, not into death.

finitude or universality than the family or nation. Where man fails to sense his spiritual possibility, all may appear as necessary, and he may sink in a despair of fatalism. However, worldliness, even though the commonest type of despair, is not the most intense, for it is marked by relative unawareness.

Perhaps the most surprising form of despair is that in which the self seeks to be too 'spiritual', volatilizing itself in possibility, thus betraying its earthly and bodily nature. It can thus lose itself in an infinitude of dreams and have no concrete actuality. This would involve a failure of the self to relate itself appropriately to life's necessities, whereas to be properly human is freely to introduce purpose into earthly necessity. To take this imaginative or poetic approach to existence is a form of despair which S.K. knew intimately. The poet understands existence and glorifies it but lets his imagination serve as a substitute for reality. As demonstrated by S.K.'s own life, the poet loves the good and the holy but cannot accept all of concrete reality, in particular everything about the actual self which God has given him. He will not submit everything to God, e.g. a 'thorn in the flesh' which causes him suffering. Accordingly, he poetically transforms God into an over-indulgent grandfather who will change reality to suit men's wishes.

As despair varies with the nature of one's imbalance, it also changes with the extent of one's awareness. At one extreme it may manifest itself in an unawareness of having any personal problems, which unconsciousness is, however, somewhat a matter of pretence since in fact it involves an unwillingness to face the truth about oneself. Thus persons who seem literally blind to values other than pleasure are more or less unconsciously despairing of their higher possibilities. On the other hand, as clarity of consciousness increases despair deepens into either a state of broken weakness or of defiance.

When all obscurity is eliminated, an unwillingness to be oneself becomes genuine defiance and is demoniacal.* If one is defiant, of himself and of God, it is as if an author made a slip of the pen, which typographical error became a kind of self defying its maker,

* Rather than amounting to mere hypothesis, despair-as-defiance seems to reflect something of S.K.'s own youthful defiance of his father and his father's God. In this spirit he complained that he could not get along so well with Christ as with the Father because Christ is an example who must be followed. (W. Lowrie, *Kierkegaard*, Vol. I, p. 123.)

refusing to be erased, and attempting thereby to prove that its author was himself defective. In this form despair becomes at last true sin. S.K.'s concept of the demonic cannot be disposed of by comical allusions to devils with cow's hoofs, tails and horns. The demonic individual, as S.K. conceives him, is well concealed and well groomed. Subtle devilishness may appear in the seemingly innocent impulse to postpone the good until the morrow, or in an intellectual curiosity about the good which subtly avoids commitment by being academic, or, again, as a soft moral fibre which leaves moral strenuosity to someone else.[65] 'The devil's despair is the most intense despair, for the devil is sheer spirit, and therefore absolute consciousness and transparency...' (P. 65) That demoniacal despair is sin is evident when and because it is evident that the self exists in rebelliousness *before God*. Such sin can itself take various forms, as a despairing over sin, over forgiveness, or—most radically—taking offence at God's love in Christ. The latter is the sin against the Holy Ghost. (Pp. 190 f., 216)

Kierkegaard's solution for despair is of course not a personal victory over one's faults, but the grace of God received in humble faith, for 'salvation is humanly speaking the most impossible thing of all; but for God all things are possible'. (P. 59) Faith in God's working the impossible cannot be rational confidence. To believe is 'precisely to lose one's understanding in order to win God'. (P. 58) Faith begins when one is in the 'utmost extremity, so that humanly speaking no possibility exists'. (P. 58) Without God man has no enduring self, and is without the possibility of spirit.

A certain paradox is to be noted in the healing of the sickness unto death, just as it is present in the meaning of God, of Christ, and of the Christian life. Whereas in the natural order, the opposite of unrighteousness is virtue, in the religious life the opposite of sin is not virtue but faith. Genuine virtue is humanly impossible. Therefore Christian 'excellence' can only mean trust in God to heal man's sickness. The 'pagan view' that the opposite of sin is virtue overlooks the fact that 'all sin is *before God*'.*

---

* P. 132. Regis Jolivet intriguingly suggests that what S.K. really meant was not that faith is the opposite of sin but that *charity* is the opposite of sin, a Christian love which issues from faith-and-grace. (*Introduction to Kierkegaard*, p. 149.) The *Works of Love* somewhat supports this notion, although S.K.'s language here is defensible in that faith remains the initial Christian act.

Finally it should be noted that the solution of man's sickness is in no sense an *intellectual* solution of doubt. To 'defend' Christianity is to be 'Judas No. 2', once more betraying Christ with a kiss. (P. 140) Doubt is not uncertain because of lack of evidence; it is really sin, and no intellectual manoeuvres will heal this disease, nor will they make *rationally* acceptable God's strange attack upon sin. Eduard Geismar's biting words exactly summarize S.K.'s point: 'The only effective weapon against doubt is a stress upon the righteousness of God, the unrighteousness of human life. When theologians develop a system of apologetics...they make a fatal mistake. There can be nothing worse than a shuffling defence for something valuable, to say nothing then of an apology for something so infinitely valuable that men cannot do without it....Christianity is God's attack upon men; it is accusation upon accusation.'[66]

One concept developed in *Sickness* needs special comment, viz. that of 'possibility'. As a synthesis, man blends possibility which S.K. identifies with freedom (because in freedom one chooses a possibility), with necessity which he identifies with the eternal (in the sense of necessary or fixed meanings and life goals which are given by God). However, Kierkegaard deliberately oversimplified this thought in that possibility as well as necessity will be 'reduplicated' in the heavenly state. Not only will man share in the unchanging essences of godly goals; he will also retain freedom (possibility), but in an infinite form.[67] Furthermore, in spite of his emphasis on necessity as the quality of the eternal and of fixed divine purposes, there is a sense in which S.K. gives possibility a central role in the eternal itself. Possibility is the opposite of deterministic necessity and is akin to Hegel's 'freedom' which is precisely definitive of spirit. Indeed, possibility thus signifies God, by whom all things are possible. This substitution of an existential definition of God (possibility) for a metaphysical definition (as Substance, Form, or Being) is not only a recognition of man's limited metaphysical capacities. It is even more an expression of the conviction that a speculative definition of God is *evil*. As a lover will not busy himself trying to define love, so one who takes God seriously will hardly spend himself 'piecing together a definition of what God is'.[68]

THE CHRISTIAN WRITINGS

Not fully explicit here is the relationship of human possibility to that of divinity. There is no simple gradation from man to God so that in man there is limited possibility whereas in God there is supreme possibility. Man's freedom does not make him to that extent divine, nor does it of itself assure man a share in the divine or a return to the eternal. God's meaning is total possibility, while man is a fantastic mixture of thingness and spirit, of determinism and freedom. He is stretched taut between the temporal realm and the eternal toward which he must strive but which as a goal he cannot attain by his own efforts. Man's possibility only enables him to live humanly before God, and to grasp in faith the power of God, which in its unlimited possibility not only creates and redeems but also forever remains sovereign over man. Man's possibility is to be freely responsible and responsive to God—or rebellious before him—but certainly not to be in any sense divine.[69]

Kierkegaard does not present a comprehensive account of possibility since his more modest purpose is to explain the role of human possibility in earthly existence and existential fulfilment. Even here some of its significance remains largely implicit; yet S.K. is clear enough to present a striking contrast with a naturalistic existentialist like Sartre. The latter sees man flung meaninglessly into a purposeless world, seeking and even exercising an almost absolute freedom, but progressively losing it. S.K. sees man functioning not within the absolute freedom of meaninglessness, but rather placed in a meaningful and responsible situation by creation, and, even in his fallen state, having the possibility of choosing to accept or reject a God-given restoration to his spiritual home which, as a prodigal, he had abandoned. Both human possibility and sickness or despair are before God, and within the context of his purposes.

35. THE HIGH PRIEST—THE PUBLICAN—THE WOMAN THAT WAS A SINNER

'The High Priest'—'The Publican'—'The Woman that was a Sinner.' Three Discourses at the Communion on Fridays. By S. Kierkegaard. November 13, 1849. Translated by Walter Lowrie and published as an addition to the *Christian Discourses*.

These discourses are beautiful in their simplicity, and are very sensitive to the meaning of scripture. One scholar has argued that Christ only 'revealed' what all men should have known, viz. that God is love, a position which actually makes 'revelation' superfluous. For S.K. scripture is not so obvious; it does not reveal what the natural man can apprehend. He seeks therefore to let a text vividly express the message, the news, that it contains. It has been suggested that in this tiny book Kierkegaard is an artist who sets forth in sculptured form the High Priest, the publican, and the sinful woman. This is certainly his intention—to combine an artistic and arresting, with an accurate and revealing interpretation of these scriptural figures.

'The High Priest.' (Hebrews 4:15) Is Christ a High Priest? How does he assume a priestly relation to men in their need? S.K. notes that sufferers seldom find much consolation in the sympathy of friends. How can a friend understand the torment when he is not in the place of affliction? Yet there is One who puts himself in every sufferer's place. Christ understands, for 'he was absolutely the greatest sufferer'. All forsook him. The very disciples who had asked to sit at his right and left fled when the throne he occupied was a cross. Thereupon two robbers were compelled to occupy their empty places of honour. The only consolation which Christ knew was not consolation which he received but that which he bestowed on others. Now at the altar bread is given, and wine, as a pledge that by his sufferings Christ, as the High Priest, put himself entirely in the believer's place.

In Kierkegaard's view of atonement, Christ becomes a substitute for the sinner, so that judgment no longer falls on the sinner whom Christ loves. Yet S.K. adds that Christ no sooner brings release to the sinner than he imposes upon him a new pattern of holiness, in the form of his own sacrificial love. Many have felt that S.K.'s doctrine of atonement is excessively gloomy and negative. In any event, it is interesting to find in the thought of Dag Hammarskjöld a certain harmonious ring: 'How proper it is that Christmas should follow Advent.—For him who looks towards the future, the Manger is situated on Golgotha, and the Cross has already been raised in Bethlehem.'[70]

'The Publican.' The humble publican has now become the model of piety; yet unfortunately even this model is subject to distortion. In Christendom hypocrisy has come to the point of taking pride, of all things, in humility. Pride was soon 'sitting vainly in the lowest seats'. Surely the stance of true humility remains difficult to assume, yet it is the appropriate one for the man who will approach God. By standing afar off the publican was paradoxically close to God—if also he remained far away from God before whose holiness he could only cast down his eyes. By the miracle of faith it is the downcast eyes which see God. The natural man proudly stands erect, while the believer 'finds blessedness only in falling upon his knees, kneeling in adoration when he thinks of God, and in penitence when he thinks of himself.

'The Woman that was a Sinner.' A sinner! There was no hiding it. She sat at the feet of Jesus and wept, to the embarrassment of all at the table. 'In truth the banquet is disturbed by this woman.' She placed this torture of public shame on herself and was cruel to herself. Nevertheless, in truth, it was not cruelty or shame which she experienced because she loved much and thereby forgot herself in utter simplicity of confession and devotion. 'The true expression for loving much is precisely this: to forget oneself entirely.' (P. 382) The woman sits at Jesus' feet. Jesus does not even speak *to* her, but *about* her, that her sins are forgiven because she loved much. By the power of such love she entered in where the holy One was.

36. THE POINT OF VIEW

The Point of View for My Work as an Author. Written by Kierkegaard in 1848, published by his brother in 1859, four years after his death. Translated by Walter Lowrie, in a volume which contains also *The Individual* and *My Activity as a Writer.* New York: Oxford University Press, 1939. New edition with a Preface by Benjamin Nelson. New York: Harper & Brothers, 1962, Torchbook paperback TB 88. See separate headings for treatments of *The Individual* and *My Activity.* (Page references are to the Torchbook edition.)

In 1848, in the midst of tremendous social upheavals, and probably with a sense of urgency resting on his having already lived longer than he had expected, Kierkegaard felt the necessity for correcting various misunderstandings of his writings. It seemed to be his responsibility—for no one else could accomplish it—to undo his earlier deliberate mystification, and to unravel the intricacies of his vast and multiform literature. The perplexing subtlety of some works called for sheer explication, while his pseudonymous authors with their dubious personalities called for forthright clarification of purpose. The immediate occasion for this book was that at the time S.K. had reluctantly agreed to issue a second edition of *Either/Or,* and felt that he must make it evident how far that famous work was from his genuine point of view. Yet it is a striking fact that S.K., after he had written his little book, could not bring himself to publish it, lest he appear to be claiming to be especially virtuous. Therefore he left the document as a 'report to history'.

To correct the impression that a literary artist had gone astray and lapsed into religion only in his later years, Kierkegaard found it necessary to insist here that his purpose had been religious from the beginning. He pointed out that when he offered aesthetic writings with the one hand, he had invariably presented religious discourses with the other (often on identical dates), which discourses often answered the exact dilemmas of the secular literature.

Kierkegaard acknowledged that he had not possessed a complete prevision of the entire authorship, and, further, that his spiritual insight and purpose had not been adequate at the outset. Indeed, the authorship constituted his own education, and in the process of creating it he came to greater religious clarity and personal commitment. It is also evident, however—and is very important—that while the aesthetic literature indirectly served central religious purposes, that it also served personal aims such as reconciliation with Regine, and a legitimate aesthetic end. In view of this, it appears that even though S.K.'s explanation of his religious purpose is undoubtedly correct, in a measure it represents an over-simplification of his motives.

In what light does Kierkegaard himself appear in *The Point of View*? Was he a prophet, apostle, teacher? He was horrified by such thoughts. He could not claim to be a teacher, but only a fellow-searcher. In fact, he insisted that he had never succeeded in being a true 'witness', whose life might adequately express his truth. Yet using a deliberately cautious term to designate it, he did claim to be able to recognize a divine 'Governance' in his life. This Governance did not inspire him as the muses might inspire a poet, but instead shielded him from 'too great a wealth' of tumbling thoughts. More important, it did not bestow on him the authority of an apostle or prophet. Thus, in his own judgment, Kierkegaard was a poet, only an uninspired poet, but a poet so restrained by the hand of God as to grow in edification. 'I am he who himself has been educated, or whose authorship expresses what it is to be educated to the point of becoming a Christian.' (P. 75)

In general the facts indicated in the *Point of View* emerge and are evident in the treatment of other writings and therefore need not be repeated here—except perhaps for one essential thought. If S.K. was to succeed in leading his reader to Christianity he had first to gain his interest, and to do that it was necessary to 'take pains to find HIM where he is and begin there', viz. in the realm of pleasure and of the aesthetic, then to lead through the pathos of the aesthetic (in its most exalted or least deficient form) in order to draw that line—indeed, a fine line—over which one can pass to the spiritual life. It is a fateful passing as Kierkegaard describes it, a passing which can be made only by an act of will, a leap, a choice all one's own. No saintly benefactor or wise tutor can chart one's spiritual course for him. And so, however great the misunderstandings which S.K. occasioned, his perhaps overly subtle and indirect existential prodding had its method, and his bewildering flood of books was not without a consistent purpose.

37. ARMED NEUTRALITY

> *Armed Neutrality*, or My Position as a Christian author in Christendom; an addition to 'The Point of View for my work as an author'. By S. Kierkegaard. Notes for a book written in 1849. Not published, this material appears in *Papirer*, X^5 B 107–110. A significant fragment is translated as item 1029 in *The Journals*.

Intended to be a kind of addition to the *Point of View*, this fragmentary material was written by S.K. a year after the *Point of View*, and like it was left unpublished. It throws considerable light on the humble view that he took of his own role in the authorship, and was clearly an attempt to avoid any appearance of spiritual pretension.

Kierkegaard here defines his task as one of presenting the 'ideal picture' of what it is to be a Christian. Yet who dares to hold up this rigorous ideal? Is there not danger of some enthusiast asserting in pious self-assurance, 'I myself am the ideal Christian?' Kierkegaard quickly points out that nothing is more foreign to his own soul than such frenzied enthusiasm. Perhaps some of his sympathizers had been waiting for him to thus identify himself with the ideal and then become his frenzied disciples. As a matter of fact, the violent disturbance created by fanatical followers of S.K. at his funeral reveals how correct this anticipation was.*

Kierkegaard believes that 'the ideal picture of a Christian' must be held up afresh in every generation, but not with the supposition of everyone attaining it, indeed not even with the supposition that the man who presents the picture himself achieves it. The ideal must be presented anew simply to make certain that there is no confusion as to what is genuine and ideal in contrast to confusion, compromise and hypocrisy.

Why the strange title of the book? Wherein is Kierkegaard's position an 'armed neutrality?' He means to indicate that he is *armed*, militant, and uncompromising in setting forth with biting

---

* Cf. below, the treatment of *The Instant*.

clarity what it means to be a Christian. For this reason, although he felt that he would fail in his duty if he exposed himself to persecution, thus drawing attention away from the message and to himself, still he thought it not impossible that in one way or another he 'should have suffered martyrdom'. On the other hand, S.K. also professes to take the role of a 'neutral', i.e. of one who only accurately defines Christianity rather than of one who personally professes to be a Christian. Above all he does not mean to pronounce judgment in the role of a superlative Christian. In speaking to Christians he thinks it would only confuse the issues if he in any way diverted attention to himself.

What, however, if Kierkegaard had been living among pagans? Then, he says, he could not have so remained neutral, and would have witnessed for the faith *as a Christian*. In that case he would not have been guilty of presenting himself as being *more* Christian than others—since none of his hearers would claim to be Christians at all. He would then have appeared as a representative of Christian life and truth.

To the contemporary critic it appears that S.K. understood his own role very well. He was not, and did not choose to be either martyr or apostle, but only sought to express the true Christianity in his gifted capacity of poet and dialectical thinker.

38. THE INDIVIDUAL

> '*The Individual*'. Two 'notes' concerning my Work as an Author. By S. Kierkegaard. Written in 1846, revised and enlarged to accompany *Edifying Discourses in Various Spirits* (Spring, 1847), but finally left unpublished until after the author's death when it appeared in 1859 with *The Point of View*, with which it also appears in English.

This tiny book, quite important for Kierkegaard's doctrine of the individual in his relation to society, was written as a commentary on S.K.'s life work two years before the *Point of View*. Pertaining to the authorship, it does not explain the writings. What it does is to reveal the heart of the author and his passionate earnestness. In it S.K. dared at last to call himself 'That Individual' (i.e. a real Christian) and expressed the wish that this designation might be inscribed on his tombstone. Having written so frankly, however, he feared that he might seem to be posing as a martyr, saint or reformer, and therefore decided not to publish these candid 'notes' but to remain a 'poet', in whom there is permitted an element of mystery. In consequence, this writing did not appear until four years after S.K.'s death.

In the twentieth century, with the frequent submergence of the individual in the mass of humanity, and with the recurrent revolts—often violent and senseless—of oppressed individuals against the provocative mass, S.K.'s analysis of the situation of the individual will be of greater interest than his personal involvement in his authorship. At the beginning of S.K.'s authorship, by 'individual' he had referred to Regine, but quickly the term came to refer to every authentic person. In similarity to Nietzsche's Zarathrustra who first sought vainly to win the populace but finally turned aristocratically to those rare persons who had ears for his truth, so too S.K. wrote for the individual. 'Who thou art I know not.... Yet thou art my hope, my joy, my pride; although unknown thou art an honour to me.' (P. 109) Nevertheless, there is a profound unlikeness between S.K. and Nietzsche at this point. Kierkegaard did not really turn away from the masses, although he scorned their collective judgment in matters of existential importance. In fact, he even wrote in newspapers in order to reach the common man, and he wished to preach on street corners—not in a quiet church. He admits that 'the crowd' can be responsible, showing even 'decisive competency as a court of last resort' for ordinary matters of truth. It is then only in the ethical and religious spheres that, for S.K., the crowd is 'untruth'.

The 'crowd' against which S.K. protests is not the 'masses' as opposed to the aristocracy. Aristocrats too could form a crowd. The crowd is any group which takes its mere numerical frequency to be somehow significant for truth or value. (P. 112) In the realm of conscience there is no strength in numbers. No mob is guilty or does anything, although an individual in a mob may delude himself by thinking that the crowd is responsible for his actions. (P. 115)

Existential thinking is clearly evident in this outlook; that the crowd is 'untruth' is such an existential notion. This assertion does not mean that the many people working together are more likely to arrive at a wrong doctrine than they would individually.

It does mean that in the crowd men tend to lose their responsible relationship to truth and reality. They impulsively and immorally betray themselves and the very principles to which their intellects may still give lip service. It is not difficult to delude the crowd. 'All that is needed is some talent, a certain dose of falsehood.' (P. 112) Elsewhere, S.K. comments that truth is more likely to be served by a minority than by a majority, because the persons in the minority are more likely to have their own rather than borrowed opinions.[55]

The essential point is that in faith 'only *one* attains the goal'. However, *every* man can be that one, not as a mere specimen of the species but rather as a unique and responsible person. In a sense there cannot be a human 'race' but only individuals, for when any man loves, marries, or dies, whatever joy, suffering or responsibility is involved is entirely personal even though it is duplicated in the lives of other men. Christ 'would have no dealings with the crowd', but was 'the Truth, which relates itself to the individual'. Therefore he was crucified, by the *crowd*. Man is to love his *individual* neighbour; Scripture never enjoins, 'Thou shalt love the crowd', for if one does this then he has dehumanized each person in the group, making each one indeed equal to the others but only as a faceless numerical instance.

This should make it clear that there was nothing unsocial or haughty in S.K.'s emphasis on the individual. The issue is rather the nature of the authority to which the individual is responsible. Hegel, for example, had argued that the rights of the individual derive from the state. For Hegel, freedom meant to live in conformity with the public will which in turn enables the person to be himself. S.K. sets his doctrine of the individual in radical opposition to this. His individual has no less of social concern, nor any more of self-seeking. The difference is that for Kierkegaard man is an authentic individual only as he is responsible to God. In the eyes of God all the host of mankind do not constitute a crowd, for God sees each individual within society.[71] There is then no haughtiness in one who is a true individual, a single one,* because

---

* Ronald G. Smith has suggested 'the Single One' as a better expression for the meaning of 'the Individual'. Every person might claim to be an individual but only a unique and authentic self is a 'single one'. Cf. Martin Buber, *Between Man and Man*, New York: Macmillan Co. (1948), p. 207.

his being singled out of the mass is not really a personal achievement but ultimately the result of his being separately encountered by God, but this opportunity is not offered to one alone. Marjorie Grene's comment that Soren Kierkegaard was unaffected by public criticism because 'he hated the crowd as cordially as a "subjective thinker" was bound to do' is both false and cruel.[72] In fact, Kierkegaard loved the common man, and when on occasion he was under the abuse of public misunderstanding and ridicule he suffered bitterly. Further, his being a 'subjective thinker' actually helped him to view every individual as being capable of release from domination by the crowd.

Finally, S.K. is most anxious to make clear that while initially, in the edifying literature, he had wanted only to portray the individual as an authentic *man*, i.e. 'what every man is or can be', that the ultimate goal is to treat the 'individual' as 'the decisive Christian category'. An authentic man would be an individual even if he were identical with all others, eating, working, loving like them. Yet he is not like them. As implied in *Fear and Trembling*, every person is an 'exception', even though he acknowledges the sovereignty of the universal (ethical law). Every person is unique, with special opportunity and responsibility. Yet in a still deeper, essentially Christian, sense, one can be an individual. This is to overcome the splitting or division of the self so as not to be possessed by evil (which is still *other* even when it holds power over him), but instead to be so unified as to be able to 'will one thing', viz. the good. Whereas every animal is little more than an identical instance of the species, no man is really a man unless he differentiates himself out of and above the species in a process of self-becoming.[73] Since the race is lost, the 'individual' takes on the character of the redeemed person, restored to wholeness.[74] 'It is the peculiarity of the human race that just because the individual is created in the image of God, the "individual" is above the race.' In the crowd each man is anonymous but as an individual he grasps his responsibility before God.[75] In its pretentious concern for 'equality', society can grant it only by robbing each man of that which is unique, reducing all to a drab similarity. Only in relation to God, before whom all are on the same footing, do unequals become genuinely equal while remaining individuals. Christianity is thus the most genuine humanism.

THE CHRISTIAN WRITINGS

As an individual, the soul comes to God naked, stripped bare of trappings and without benefit of influential friends. As in S.K.'s own personal life, being an individual involves obedience to God and imitation of Christ, to the point of suffering, and even of martyrdom. This focus on obedience to God constitutes a rejection of ordinary humanism which seeks the norms of human life within man himself rather than in the divine will. Such humanism is a tragic pantheism. It is 'an acoustic illusion which confounds *vox populi* with *vox dei*'. (P. 135) Against such, Christianity is the only authentic humanism.

In a peculiar sense 'the individual' eventually seemed to tend to replace the 'church' in S.K.'s thought. If the Christian is one who suffers self-sacrificially for righteousness then he does so all alone. Martyrdom is scarcely a fellowship, and each martyr chooses to enter in at this door in solitude. As indicated above, this meaning certainly does not interfere with the emphasis on love for neighbour, but it focuses on the fact that each one must do his own loving, willing, and entering in. Religion is a God-relatedness, not a brotherhood, although the God-relation evokes brotherly love. Even this tendency to stress the individual rather than the church must be cautiously interpreted however. Just as S.K. glorified 'the monastery' as a corrective but did not wish to re-establish it, so his attack on the church did not imply an ignoring of its function. Neither does insistence on personal faith rather than acceptance of churchly doctrine represent a discounting of the importance of doctrine. Thus S.K. bitterly assails Catholic work-righteousness and enthusiastically endorses 'excellent' Lutheran *doctrine*. His practical purpose, however, was not to evaluate doctrine, but to insist on personal commitment.

It is God's revelation of sin which above all requires that man come before him as an individual. To face God is not a mystical communion but a standing in fear and trembling, unshielded and naked. It is against the truth of sin—which is always an individual matter—that man seeks refuge in the mob or crowd. 'If only there are many of us engaged in it, it is not wrong.... Then we are secured against the judgment of eternity.'[76] Not only sin, but forgiveness, faith, discipleship, love and grace are all solitary matters in the believer's relation to God. Christ takes one aside from the herd to turn him into spirit, but this blessing involves suffering. 'And this in itself is enough to make a man fearful and anxious—more than in the face of death. For man is a social animal—only in the herd is he happy. It is all one to him whether it is the profoundest nonsense or the greatest villainy—he feels completely at ease with it, so long as it is the view of the herd...'[77]

A positive correlate to the principle that sin imposes on man the necessity of individuality is that individuality seems to be that in man which is the image of God, and which puts man in a personal relation to God instead of leaving him a mere instance of a species.[78] Because of this very fundamental meaning attached to the term some have wished that S.K. had used a different word for the idea, such as selfhood or personality.[79] Nevertheless, the term 'individual' seems preferable in that it recognizes the radical solitude in which one makes his fateful choice as to the kind of self he is to be. 'Personality' represents too socialized and even incidental a concept, with affableness and indecisive responsiveness commonly prominent in it. If 'self' were used to capture the idea, at least it would be necessary to fix in mind that the self is individuated as it stands before God. Such an 'image of God' leaves no ground for pantheism or mysticism because the self finds itself as an individual in confrontation with God.

39. MY ACTIVITY AS A WRITER

My Activity as a Writer. By S. Kierkegaard. August 1851. In English appended to *The Point of View*; in the 1939 edition given the title *On My Work as an Author*. (Page reference is to the 1962 edition.)

How disappointing Kierkegaard was to the sophisticated! First he created a sensation with *Either/Or* and was the epitome of wit, perceptiveness and irony. Then he grew older—and religious. Had age soured his humour, spoiled his realism, made him take refuge in piety?

Having argued against this monstrous misunderstanding in both *The Point of View* and *The Individual*, S.K. was still undefended, for he had not been able to publish them for fear of seeming to glorify himself. Finally he had to declare himself, and did so in this 'accounting'. In his Journal S.K. wrote of this tiny booklet that it was not 'a kind of authorship...but a deed', which therefore had to be as short as possible (less than twenty pages). Here he successfully avoided any appearance of spiritual vanity by characterizing himself as a humble *reader* of his own writings, gaining through them his own spiritual upbringing.

The artfulness of the authorship, he explains, was first to charm and interest the public, 'to stir up the "crowd" in order to get hold of "the individual"'. In the crowd men are irresponsible and even detestable, but as individuals they can possess truth and loveliness. The aim was, by indirect means to 'beguile a person into the truth'. The authorship moved from the aesthetic and philosophical to the authentic (therefore not pseudonymous) Christian writings. This procedure was made necessary by the fact that S.K. wanted to make Christians out of 'Christians', and it seemed that this could best be accomplished by first securing the attention of deluded men with that which is interesting and attractive, and then subtly and indirectly divesting them of their illusions.

Insisting that he did not turn to the religious only after he had wearied of the aesthetic, Kierkegaard pointed out that he had used a measure of religious directness throughout the entire authorship. In discourses which were made to literally accompany the aesthetic works he had written plainly and penetratingly on the great Christian issues and themes. This writing, he humbly insisted, was 'without authority', a fact which did not however minimize its message, and also indicated the *responsibility of the reader in his reaction* to it.

In an age of actual revolution and of revolutionary ideas and turmoil, when Marx and Mill—so differently—were reflecting on the need for social reform, S.K. decried the social gospel which thought to solve mankind's problems by either law or revolution. Utopia is not to be found in a classless society which reduces all to selfless uniformity. What can and ought to be hoped for is an inward transformation of individuals who gain responsibility by standing consciously before God. In the concluding 'Supplement' S.K. takes note of the revolutions in Denmark and elsewhere which occurred in 1848, just prior to this writing, and makes it clear that the solution to mankind's problems is not revolution but responsibility on the part of the individual. 'With regard to the "established order", then, seeing that my special concern was "the individual", which was the point of my polemic against the numerical, the crowd, &c., I have always done the very opposite of attacking it; I have never been in or with the "opposition" which wants to get rid of the "government", nor have I been allied with it; but I have furnished what may be called a "corrective", the intent of which was: For God's sake let us continue to be ruled by those who are appointed and called to this task, and that they should stand fast in the fear of God, willing only one thing, the Good. And thereby I have managed to fall out with the opposition and the public...' (P. 156) This does not mean that S.K. was a docile conformist, although it does suggest that his primary concern was elsewhere than with collective social and political issues. His 'correction' from within was, in at least one instance, a great public disturbance, viz. his uncompromising attack on the church. Nevertheless, even here his primary concern was the individual's spiritual reorientation rather than social action.

This then is the 'deed'. It is an 'accounting' which spells out in inescapable simplicity the guiding thread of the intricate authorship. The whole purpose was to disturbingly demonstrate 'how to become a Christian'.

40. TRAINING IN CHRISTIANITY

Training in Christianity. By Anti-Climacus. Edited by S. Kierkegaard. September 27, 1850. Translated by Walter Lowrie. The translated work includes *An Edifying Discourse* (1850), which is here treated separately. New York: Oxford University Press, 1941. Princeton: Princeton University Press, 1944. (Page references are to the 1941 edition.)

In *Training in Christianity*, Kierkegaard speaks out at last with devastating clarity against the confusions of modern Christendom. As opposed to the common cautious reference to 'the Christian tradition' and 'Christian culture', S.K. here seeks to make it dramatically clear that Christianity is not a tradition or culture to

THE CHRISTIAN WRITINGS

which one may be an involuntary heir, but a gospel and a Person by whom one must be personally either scandalized or moved to faith. Genuinely confronted, there is no third alternative, no comfortable middle ground. Being concerned with the grounds of faith, this book might be called 'The Evidence for Christianity', except that for S.K. there is no evidence, in the normal sense, no proof other than through the experience gained by submitting to its 'training' and following Jesus as a 'contemporary'. Modern man can and must seek to be a 'contemporary' of Jesus because otherwise a deceptive belief in him is too easy and the radical nature of discipleship is obscured. Whereas most people suppose that it was easier for people of the first century to accept Christ, in actuality the accretions of pious sentiment and the 'successes' of Christian history now conceal the severity of Christ's claims and conceal the offensiveness of a professed saviour whose followers were herring fishermen, dubious tax collectors, and sick people, and whose kingdom ended with a cross for a throne and a mocking crown made of thorns.

Although written in 1848, the publication of this book was postponed until 1850 because it involved a severe attack on the established church. Filled with bitter irony, it begins with deceptive gentleness, stressing Christ's compassionate invitation: 'Come hither to me, all ye that labour and are heavy laden, and I will give you rest.' Then, when the complacent Christians have come comfortably assuming that all is well, S.K. presents the shock of genuine Christianity as he understands it. That the pseudonymous author of the book is 'Anti-Climacus' relates to the severity of the attack. S.K. in this case had no intention of concealing his identity as author, and in fact listed himself as editor. The use of the pseudonym was Kierkegaard's way of acknowledging that he, being only a 'poet' or Socratic teacher, felt that he had no right to speak in the name of Christ in an attack on a degenerate Christendom. The fictitious Anti-Climacus could speak with bold authority and without a suggestion of arrogant self-esteem. After this work S.K. hoped that no further attack on the church would be needed. He even reported to a friend that his writing was finished.[80]

It may be noted that the closing third of the book, and its accompanying edifying discourse, while not in the least weakening the dreadful earnestness of the approach, do speak in milder, more 'edifying', and winsome fashion, showing that 'He will draw all' unto himself.

To be trained in Christianity one must first recognize that the real Christ is offensive. Men want a magnificent and benevolent King, but God will not cater to their wishes, and insults them by being a mere carpenter. Whereas Socrates was accidentally persecuted, Christ invited men to despise him. He abased himself, demonstrating that (men being what they are) love must always suffer, and yet that only dying love is beyond death's annihilation. Confronted by such a lowly peasant Lord, man's only alternatives are, on the one hand, faith, and, on the other, offence. Most decidedly, they are not knowledge as opposed to ignorance. When John the Baptist doubted, Jesus pointed to all his blessed works, but *not as proofs*. Faith is a response to Christ as a person, not a response to evidence. Miracles may compel one to look at Christ but cannot compel the requisite leap of faith and love. Their function is to force man to face and answer the question, 'What think ye of Christ?' (P. 116 f.) It is a Christ who perfectly understands that he is an 'essential offence' who proclaims, 'Blessed is he who is not offended in me'. (P. 139) Only pagan gods claim outright recognizableness. Christ's divinity is so hidden that only his *love* discloses the transcendent God. (P. 135) It may be noted that S.K.'s emphasis on the principle of offence is not exclusively theoretical. In his youth he himself rebelled against the severe requirements of Christianity as interpreted by his legalistic father. Furthermore, the religious life tended to remain unhappy for him in an earthly sense, an unpalatable option, even though he eventually gave himself to it in an abandon of self-renunciation and religious joy.[81]

Recognizing the prominence of offence in *Training*, one must not gather the impression that it is a negative work. In fact, it was *Sickness Unto Death* which developed the concept of the various disturbances of the temporal-eternal synthesis, with rebellion against God as the ultimate sickness, while *Training* develops the antithetical concept, viz. that of the complete submission of the temporal life to the eternal, and thus of perfect spirituality.

The three parts into which *Training* is divided represent three phases of the Christian life, first, Christ's invitation, second, the believer's response, and third, the life of discipleship. The second section indicates the unavoidable alternative of faith or offence in response to the invitation. Because Christ is a plain man who claims to be God and declares himself only indirectly, he can be received only by the personal response of love and faith rather than by comprehension and with good evidence. In accordance with this it develops that whereas in paganism truth is a doctrine, in Christianity it is Christ himself who occupies the role of truth. (P. 134) The third section interprets the life of discipleship for those who enter into the fellowship of Christ's suffering. The martyr—so far removed from the comfortable 'Christian'—represents the ultimate ideal.

In *Training*, S.K. is caustic about the deceit and complacency with which Christendom evades the spiritual life of Christianity. Indeed, no one can be altogether a successful Christian but can only be a 'becoming' one, i.e. be on the way to the goal. Yet to S.K. it seemed that everyone carelessly assumed himself to be a Christian as a matter of course. Thus Christendom was actually in the process of destroying Christianity, although in all probability its members were not clearly aware of what they were doing. In his journal S.K. paints a telling word-picture to portray the confusion of Christianity with culture and even with sensuality. 'On one pedestal one sees a naked Venus, on another the crucified Saviour, and a young lady and a speculative priest (both, of course, true Christians) discuss which is the more beautiful of the two figures.'[82] It is imperative for the confused and worldly church to acknowledge that it is worldly. The difficulty is that men are unwilling to take Christ as he is, and have completely 'poetized' him so that he becomes a fairy-tale figure. Humanity has made of him an 'extraordinary figure', perhaps even acknowledging that he is very extraordinary. Further, he is offered misguided sympathy, as one who was supposedly abused by the impiety or foolish misunderstanding of his age. But by this view of Christ as a misunderstood genius, his humiliation becomes a mere accident of fate and circumstance, comparable to the persecution of Socrates or other great men. Far from it, Christ's humiliation was *essential*; it sprang from the fact that Christ cannot be known but can only be trusted in and responded to, so that there always remains the possibility of offence.

Like Nietzsche, Kierkegaard understood that nothing can

touch to the quick as humour can. Therefore where he wanted to strike the hardest blows he turned to humour, drawing caricatures of the 'Christians' of his own city of Copenhagen, portraying them as rejecting Jesus by offering him hollow praise. He imagined Christ actually coming to Copenhagen, and he dramatized the tumult which resulted. All classes of society join in giving cautious (blasphemous) tribute to this extraordinary man, but for all their professed piety they make it quite evident that they do not really desire a Christ.

The philosopher, for example, appreciates the 'aphoristic utterances' of Jesus (nevertheless lacking system, and unfortunately leading people to 'believe in Him' rather than giving them rational understanding). The pious man, in turn, puts a halo on Jesus' head (to make him more recognizable), and perhaps even puts one on the head of each apostle (possibly in order to forget that the apostles were herring fishermen). Some persons speculatively reflect on the natural 'unity of God and man', thereby denying the paradox and sacrifice of God in coming to them indirectly as one who is unrecognizable, a servant, and crucified. This unity of God and man is not natural, S.K. intimates. Indeed it was only to evoke faith, yet permitting offence, that God did the absurd thing of becoming a lowly man. S.K.'s cutting sarcasm is well illustrated by the comments of the 'solid citizen', who appreciates Christ's idealism (but wishes there were more of moderation in it!), and who cannot help but observe that it is not the wise or well-to-do, but only the idle and unstable persons who are running after Jesus. In fact, he notes that Pastor Green, who is even better at the club than in his sermons, predicts a terrible end for Jesus. And why does anyone run after him? Only because of a few miracles, and after all a miracle is a mighty uncertain thing. (P. 54 f.)

One of the most interesting of Christ's critics in this story is a clergyman who observes that, for an impostor, Jesus is uncommonly honest, since he does not even try to make himself resemble the Messiah whom he pretends to be. This is 'the sort of honesty one can detect in a person who would issue false bank notes and make them so badly that everyone who has any intelligence can easily detect the fraud'. (P. 50) Everyone, indeed, expects a Messiah, but not one like Jesus, for the world process does not move forward by revolution but by evolution (Hegel). The Messiah 'will act in a totally different way, He will recognize the established order as an authority, He will summon all the clergy to a council...' (P. 50)

How many different kinds of pagan admirers there are, who refuse—perhaps scarcely realizing it—to be *followers*! Such paganism is strangely but vividly symbolized by 'Christian art'. Perhaps the artist paints a pretty Christ, and then 'the artist admires himself, and all admire the artist'. Or is it the suffering Christ who is depicted on a cross? Are then the shadows just right, and does the blood look just like this? The admirer who paints thus is perhaps no longer admiring Christ at all, but only his own artistry. Is it not quite possible that the Crucified does not want to be painted or sculptured, neither contemplated nor admired, but followed? (P. 248) Such following is possible only through worship—not in place of worship—for imitation of Christ is not ethical but is a religious discipleship. The follower walks where Jesus walked but not as he walked, for he came to bring atonement.[83] True following will cause the disciple to be persecuted for godliness, but men have obviously learned the lesson well that persecution can be avoided by compromise. (P. 173)

Kierkegaard's portrayal of false tributes to Christ may seem extreme. Historically it must be understood that his protest was a clear-minded reaction not only to a bourgeois complacency but more specifically to the Hegelian tendencies in Danish theology. This theology tried to identify Christ with culture and with world history, and tended to think of his divinity as consisting of a nobler sort of humanity. Opposed to this, S.K. argued that either Christ is unique, heterogeneous, or else Christianity is simply false. This insistence in no sense repudiates the humanity of Jesus; in fact, Kierkegaard is articulate on the point that in Christ the eternal and the temporal meet and, paradoxically, intertwine. But Christ is not to be assimilated into mere earthly events, and his teaching is still 'an eternity older' than all systems of thought, even that of Hegel. (P. 206) Accordingly, Christian life is not good citizenship but a responsiveness to a Christ who comes with transcendent claims and absolute requirements.

Intimately related to Kierkegaard's insistence on Christ's unique and divine character and on a discipleship oriented to the eternal is his defiance of all rationalistic attempts to escape from the difficulties of the incarnation. In contrast, he characterizes the incarnation of Christ as the 'insane combination' of the infinite God and the lowly man. As opposed to paganism which looks wistfully for some shining theophany, Christianity teaches that the divine cannot be directly seen. It is only the hidden God who can be known, and he is revealed by and through his hiddenness. Christ is no visible mixture of God and man, for the transcendent God does not qualify or lose his transcendence in incarnation. Christ is *visibly* a man who claims to be God. The gravity of incarnation is found in the fact that the lowly form is no cloak which the king can lay aside. Christ's divinity cannot be separated from his lowliness.* The true humanity of Jesus is a sign of contradiction (to be spoken against—Luke 2:34), which points away from itself to that which it cannot be, viz. God. (P. 125) Parable and miracle alike astonished men. That is, they were not simple expositions of truth or manifestations of divine love, nor rational evidence, but *signs*, pointing beyond themselves to the hidden God who revealed himself by indirectness. It follows also that since the incognito of Christ is impenetrable, man cannot escape the very real choice of being offended by such a Christ or else accepting him in faith. (P. 126) That the opposite of faith is not mere disbelief but an attitude of offence (stressed in *Fragments*, *Judge for Yourselves* and elsewhere) is shown by the fact that those who crucified Jesus complained that he made himself equal to God, which is the identical assertion of faith except that it is made with assent. This entire matter of the hiddenness of God is summed up in S.K.'s doctrine of indirect communication.

Kierkegaard goes to radical and inflammatory ends to make it clear that Christianity is not to be established as having a degree of probability by means of devious arguments and shreds of evidence. It has no objective probability and, seen clearly, may well repulse men. Even miracles do not tend to prove the divinity of Christ. They play instead an existential role, confronting man with the alternatives of responding in faith or by taking offence.

* *Journals*, 14. Arland Ussher is grossly in error when he says that for S.K. the incarnation is not a bridge but a barrier between God and man, since it is offensive. Indeed, it is *the* bridge, but it can be so to men who are both free and sinful only if it permits both rejection and faith. (*Journey Through Dread*, p. 34.)

(P. 79) Does it follow from this that faith is literally in every sense absurd? At this point it appears that the heat of battle with the apologists and the rationalizers of faith led S.K. to a deficient exposition of his position. He did eventually, cautiously, make it clear that Christianity is not really absurd to the Christian—although still a matter of faith rather than demonstrable probability.[84] Faith has its own winsomeness and does not act in a vacuum. It recognizes the wonders of divine love in the same moment that it comprehends the strangeness of *agape*. It senses the beauty of holiness which is affirmed in the very transcending of the divine law in God's redemptive act. There is a certain naturalness and appropriateness in its yielding in worship before a God who does the 'impossible' of coming as a suffering servant, manifesting a new and creative holiness which common sense and moral sensitivity have no right to expect of God. S.K. is intent on making it clear that faith does not rest on objective evidence or reason, but he certainly does not think of it, as suggested by Zuidema, as an 'infinite existential passion' which is triggered by an ultimate Absurdity.[85] There is a persuasiveness in the 'signs' which point to God. The critical issue in the entire argument is that S.K. will not permit Christianity to be reduced to the role of one element in human culture. To be Christian is to be lifted out of the realm of reasonableness, comfortableness and complacency and to respond to a divine encounter which dethrones customary and relative values.

One famous doctrine enunciated in *Training* is that of Christ as man's *eternal contemporary*. It springs unavoidably from the understanding of the incarnation. God has broken into time, has become an historical event, an event which indeed is growing more dated with each passing year. Yet if it is the eternal which has entered into time it surely follows that passing time does not diminish its significance. Despite its special appearance in a moment of time, the eternal is contemporary with every age. Jesus confronts every age with the same invitation as that which was given centuries ago, 'Come hither unto me, all ye that labour and are heavy laden'. Christ is 'the same yesterday, today, and for ever', and gives a timeless invitation in time. It is not man who somehow succeeds in being contemporary with Christ, but Christ who makes himself every man's contemporary in that he is not subject to historical accidents even though being in history. 'In relation to the absolute there is only one tense: the present.' (P. 67) The issue of contemporaneity is critical and possible for the reason that Christianity is not a doctrine to be accepted but a Person to be loved and trusted, and plainly a past non-contemporary (i.e. dead) person is not a power on which to rely.

With this emphasis there goes a protest against replacing the contemporary God with an institution, a contemporary church. S.K. severely criticizes Judaism as 'a self-complacent, self-deified establishment', but within this accusation is an identical protest against the pretentious Christian church which tries to play the role of God. The churchly establishment is guilty of compromise and seeks worldly prestige by a pretence of intellectuality. 'Ah! Now everything is all right!... In case Christ were to come into the world, He would first of all be Professor....!' (P. 90)

The theme of contemporaneity is often wrongly located by critics of Kierkegaard, if not totally misunderstood. At times it has been thought to be a near-Hegelian issue of how the finite can be contemporaneous with the infinite. Actually, the matter is simple and the concern is essentially religious; the insistence is simply that the relationship of a believer in the nineteenth (or twenty-first) century to the Christ of the first century is neither made any easier nor more difficult by the passing of the centuries. Nothing can be learned about Christ from history (i.e. other than the historical Christ himself) because Christ is not 'a simple historical fact' but became historical only by God becoming man —doing the absurd. (P. 28) The most that history could offer would be probability about the historical Jesus and such probable 'knowledge' could never affirm that it was actually God who thus existed as a man. Only faith can deal with this ultimate issue. If Christ were not contemporaneous with every generation, then Gailieans of the first century would have a very special advantage, for only they could have any direct relationship with him. For the rest it would be hearsay and recollection. Contemporaneousness, on the part of the disciple, is faith itself, for it is the very act of receiving this individual man as God. (P. 9) Christianity had by S.K.'s time become well established. This supposedly made the Christian life easier, for it sought and claimed to make faith reasonable, easily available, and spiritually comfortable. Its objectification of faith is marked by its replacing Jesus' shameful crown of thorns by an easily discernible halo. S.K. retorts that all of this is distortion and that the faith relation of a believer to Christ is identical in every age.

It is only by truly being contemporary that one can recover perspective and see Jesus as he truly was, as a pretentious carpenter, mocked and crucified, but making absolute claims upon the disciple. Further, in S.K.'s judgment, it is not difficult to avoid being trapped in one's own age and its misconceptions, but one must rid himself of the pious accretions of the centuries. By being contemporary with Christ—rid of the historical—one can believe in Christ as he was, finding him to be true Lord in spite of the stable, in spite of the queer crowd which followed him, and in spite of the failure of his cause. By being contemporary one can genuinely believe. And there is another momentous consequence. It is that if one 'follows' this real Christ, then the believer's life, like that of the Lord, will involve lowliness, suffering, and will result in imitation.

Some critics have deplored the fact that in this treatment of Christ as an eternal contemporary S.K. did not appeal to the contemporaneity of the kingship which followed Christ's ascension.[86] It is true that here, as often, S.K. uses a language which is strangely his own, yet the supposed deficiency is more linguistic than actual. Thus he does note that the modern Christian, through his knowledge of the power and glory of the *resurrected Lord*, has a comfort which was not so available to the early disciples.[87] Yet his fundamental and impressive reply to this complaint would be that the eternal contemporary is always kingly and lordly, and that it is a tragic error to suppose that either the disciple of the first or of the twenty-first century is at a disadvantage in this regard.

Certain other concepts which are related to that of contemporaneity may be noted, particularly those of the 'instant' and of 'repetition'. Regarding the instant the thought is that although the believer is in *time*, his relation to God is not a process. There is a disjunctive situation such that either one *is* in faith or else *is not* in faith. Thus the Christian—if truly Christian at all—does not move forward or backward but instead *as Christian* exists in the *instant* fully in God's fellowship. Most fundamentally, the instant is the point at which the eternal is added to the temporal in an act of freedom, thus the point at which man becomes 'spirit', or the point at which one *chooses himself* before God. There is also a durational 'becoming' in Christian life, but this is in the quest for repetition or continual return to the fullness of faith. When faith is present then one is not merely recalling sacred history or anticipating future bliss, but contemporaneous with Christ and bound to him as a disciple. Repetition has essentially this same significance of maintaining or recovering one's true selfhood in spite of change.

Is it not necessary to ask what Kierkegaard hoped to accomplish by this devastating attack on the church? Did he aim to destroy it? Certainly not, but he did want to inject more of Christianity into 'Christendom'. In his journal he makes it clear that his aim was not to replace the state church by a 'people's Church', nor indeed by any kind of church, but to 'work towards dispersion into the "single person"'.[88] Obviously there will continue to be a church, with preaching and sacraments, but it must foster Christian singleness. Moreover, S.K. did not hope for the church to become perfectly Christian, any more than he expected any individual to be a perfect disciple. Nevertheless, he felt that there was one absolute essential confronting the church, viz. to realize the truth about itself, and then to confess that it was not a genuine and adequate expression of Christian faith and life.

In face of the mockery and irony in the supposition that, with scarcely any choice or concern, everyone was Christian—yet never taking Christianity seriously—Kierkegaard pleads his case. In the Preface to Part I and in the 'Moral' (at the end of Part I) of the book he stated that it was incumbent upon all men to humbly confess that they were in fact not ideal Christians; then, in humility, to turn to grace. What was needed was not the abolition of Christendom, but instead for humble confession and personal faith to spring up within it. At a later time, S.K. came to feel that until such confession were made that an individual ought not contribute to the mockery by participating in the public 'worship'.

41. REPLY TO THEOPHILUS NICOLAUS (FAITH AND PARADOX)

> Unpublished fragments of an intended reply to an attack by Magnus Eiriksson who had published a pseudonymous work: *Can Faith Ever be a Paradox? And This Because of the Absurd?...by a Brother of the Knight of Faith, Theophilus Nicolaus*. The important parts of the fragments are translated, with commentary, in C. Fabro's essay, 'Faith and Reason in Kierkegaard's Dialectic', *A Kierkegaard Critique*, ed. by H. Johnson and N. Thulstrup, pp. 178 ff.

These fragments, although sketchy and difficult to interpret, are nevertheless extremely important in that they help to clarify Kierkegaard's position as to the relation of faith and reason, and his real meaning of 'paradox', 'faith', and 'the absurd'. In particular, they demonstrate that the frequent and easy charges of his being an irrationalist must be severely qualified. What makes these fragments particularly important is that they were not written until after 1850, in response to an attack published in that year. Thus they stand near the end of the authorship and represent a careful re-examination of this cluster of issues.[89]

An Icelandic theologian named Magnus Eiriksson wrote a pamphlet which attacked Kierkegaard's position. Perhaps in ironical humour he wrote it pseudonymously and under the rather astonishing title: *Can Faith Ever Be a Paradox? And This Because of the Absurd? A Problem Occasioned by the Book, Fear and Trembling by Johannes de Silentio, Who Is Answered through Private Communications of a Knight of Faith, a Brother of the Knight of Faith, Theophilus Nicolaus*. Eiriksson accused S.K. of treating faith as a response to the absurd *qua* absurd, so that a person ought to believe anything which appears absurd.[90] Further, he argued that 'the absurd' as treated in *Fear and Trembling* is different from 'the paradox' in the *Postscript*. Kierkegaard's reply is that this is essentially wrong even though superficially correct. He says that, in *Fear and Trembling*, believing 'by virtue of the absurd' expresses the bare principle of faith whereas in the *Postscript* paradox expresses the relation of faith to concrete Christian revelation.[91]

Properly considered, 'the Absurd' is to be viewed as identical with Christian paradox. It is a unique category, not at all to be put in a general class of absurdities. It is a Christian category, distinct, having a quality which lays claim upon one with authority. In its essence it is not nonsense but offence. In contrast, if God had become a carpenter, had married and had done nothing but pursue his earthly trade, that would not have constituted paradox. Instead, it would have been a different and meaningless kind of irony or paradox, for in such a case there would have been no evidence or manifestation of the divine but a simple absence of it. In Christ, however, there is paradoxical clashing between revealment and concealment. On the one hand, Christ claims authority and signifies it by miracles. On the other hand this divine claim and demonstration are an *offence* in that God appears as a servant, is humiliated, speaks only indirectly, and does not call upon legions of angels for aid but submits to suffering. He presents himself in such fashion that he cannot be simply *known* but can evoke either faith or offence.

In part, Kierkegaard objects that Eiriksson had identified S.K.'s own views with those of his pseudonyms, a somewhat understandable error. Yet he does acknowledge a kind of validity in the attack in that he agrees that Johannes de Silentio (not really a man of faith but one who, in *Fear and Trembling*, describes faith from the outside) had given too extreme a characterization of faith.[92] Far from saying what Johannes had declared, viz. that a Christian believes 'by virtue of the absurd', S.K. now argues that in a limited sense the Paradox is absurd only to the unbeliever and not to the believer, even though for him too it is incomprehensible.[93] It is suggested that this is so because faith makes one blind to the absurdity of God's love just as human love makes a person blind. Yet such blindness is no misfortune but the source of life and health.[94] The absurdity of Christianity thus remains—though hidden by faith—but it seems to emerge as a special category which is transformed by faith into the true though incomprehensible revelation.

Kierkegaard makes it clear that faith in its purest form does not rest upon miracles even though miracles are indicative of divine authority. If faith were to rest on miracles, it would be a kind of incomplete knowledge (i.e. an acceptance of miracles as *evidence* establishing probability). S.K. argues that, instead of this, miracles serve to arrest the attention, deliberately outraging reason with a violation of the natural order in order to show the necessity for a non-rational foundation for faith, viz. the authority of Christ. At its best, faith senses the divine authority without any necessity for prompting by miracles.[95] Any attempt to explain miracles as events of a higher order which do not violate nature or reason would miss the whole point to the miraculous, which is that it arrests reason and points to faith as a unique sphere of experience.

Kierkegaard argues that if anyone wishes to go beyond faith he must proceed not to speculative science or philosophy but (ironically?) to martyrdom (the restriction upon martyrdom in 'On the Difference Between a Genius and an Apostle' notwithstanding), which is indeed exalted. Nevertheless, there is a function for reason in relation to faith; the function is not to go beyond faith, nor to justify it, nor to make it probable, but to *comprehend that faith cannot be comprehended* (since it is meta-rational). 'The Absurd, the Paradox, is so constructed that the reason is by no means able of itself to resolve it into nonsense and show that it is nonsense. No, it is a sign, an enigma, a composite enigma, of which reason must say, "I cannot solve it, it is not for me to understand it".'[96] The Absurd is thus an *actual* concept (not nonsense), albeit a problematic one, the function of which is to determine boundaries, so that faith is above reason rather than against it.* Accordingly to Søe, S.K.'s statement that reason's function is to understand that faith cannot be understood does not mean that it lacks clarity of meaning, but that—as opposed to rationalistic theology—faith's object cannot be proved to be necessary or true, as, for example, one might try to 'prove' the necessity of the incarnation or atonement.[97]

Kierkegaard now explicitly adopts the view that while Christianity is a scandal or offence to reason it does *not* offend the believer and is not absurd to the man of faith who understands that with God all things are possible. True faith 'breathes healthfully and blissfully in the Absurd', just as true love makes one truly blind to that which contradicts it. For the pagan, the paradox of Christian-

---

* S.K. here seems to be referring to speculative rationality. Although he does not focus upon, he undoubtedly assumed the legitimacy of reason in cognizing —though not accounting for—the content of faith.

ity offends, but for the believer it is a 'call from on high'. It functions as a 'negative criterion' (perhaps being somewhat analogous to the *via negativa* of Neoplatonism) for what is higher than human comprehension.

Torsten Bohlin took the reference to 'blind love' to indicate that faith is viewed as a passion which clings to the element of grace in the paradox and therefore takes no offence at the intellectual absurdity, which it nevertheless recognizes. Søe's protest against this seems correct, in view of S.K.'s insistence that there is no self-contradiction in the *idea* (*qua* idea) of Christ as servant. The absurdity which faith, as 'blind love', overcomes is not meaninglessness but improbability, implausibility, and offensiveness. Søe and Fabro are in impressive agreement that for S.K. faith is *not contrary* to reason but above it, venturing where reason is beyond its depth. Kierkegaard plainly indicates in the *Postscript* that whatever is essentially irrational or nonsensical *cannot be believed*.[98] From this it seems obvious that at times S.K. was carried into exaggeration in thinking of reason being 'set aside' by faith. The fundamental point to 'blind love' seems to be that faith *does not look to reasons* because man exists primarily at the level of value (as moral will) rather than of cognitive awareness.

Finally, it may be added that very many, including some who are profoundly appreciative of Kierkegaard, have insisted that he should never have used the term 'absurd' since it seems to imply an irrationality, and that even 'paradox', even though it is a natural form of Christian expression, should have been used less indiscriminately. Some would prefer such a word as 'mystery'. Thus Theodor Haecker thought that even 'paradox' should be employed with 'a strong sense of responsibility'. For example, rather than to say that God allows evil in order that good might come of it, which seemingly must be said but nevertheless says too much, Haecker would 'remain silent' in abysmal ignorance 'and adore'.[99]

42. AN EDIFYING DISCOURSE
THE WOMAN THAT WAS A SINNER

An Edifying Discourse. The Woman that was a Sinner. By S. Kierkegaard. December 12, 1850. Published in English with *Training in Christianity*, which it was intended to accompany.

Referring to the 'woman that was a sinner', the discourse reflects Kierkegaard's idealization of Regine and gives a delicate tribute to womankind. Walter Lowrie wrote of it: 'It is the most striking expression of the religious sublimation of his earthly love. At the same time it is the loftiest eulogy of woman we have from his pen. He shows how this woman was fit to be a teacher of men, and from her he passes on to the example of Mary the Mother of our Lord, extolling her as perhaps few Protestant writers have done.'[100]

In some of Kierkegaard's writings there is a seeming harshness in his reference to woman, although usually in a strange blend of respect and melancholy, e.g. in this comment written not long before his death: 'When a youth...runs wild in debauchery there are two powers watching to save him: a loving woman and God in heaven. If he is saved by the first he will still have a finite aim. If, on the other hand, he is not saved by a woman...but...by God: then his will be a significant life.'[101]

In an impressive contrast to his usual reserve, Kierkegaard here exalts not only the penitent sinner who wept at Jesus' feet but takes note of certain common glories of womanly piety. From Mary, mother of the Lord, one can learn how to accept God's will. From the sister of Lazarus who sat silently and listened to Jesus' words one can learn to hear the Word of God rightly, i.e. to hear it silently and keep it in the heart, and from this sinful woman one can learn the nature of utter devotion. By comparison, man is manifold, has *many* thoughts (and half-thoughts), but *oneness* is woman's element. Whether in learning the one thing needful (as Mary), or in learning how to sorrow over sin (as the woman that was a sinner), women manifest a unity and seriousness of feeling which is spiritually essential.

Three lessons are evident in the strange heroine of the discourse. (1) In sorrow over sin one should become indifferent to all else. Who but this penitent woman would be willing to have all mankind be witness to one's shame and see every secret of the heart bared, even if thereby forgiveness might be obtained. It was suffering which enabled her to ignore her public humiliation in order to gain the one thing needful—forgiveness. (P. 265) In the abandon of humility she may not even have heard the Saviour say that she had been forgiven much because she loved much. 'Or perhaps she heard it but...thought He said, "because He loved much", so that what was said had reference to His infinite love, that because it was so infinite, therefore her many sins were forgiven.' (P. 268) (2) The second lesson which men can learn from this woman is that by one's own power one can do nothing to gain reconciliation with God. Although this woman wept at Jesus' feet she did not do so in order to gain merit, but instead poured out her tears as she poured out her precious ointment, in frivolously wasteful festivity. She did not even presumptuously enter into the conversation, no, not even when it honoured her or praised God. Instead, she dried Jesus' feet with the hair of her head. 'So she goes home—a dumb person in the whole scene.' (P. 268) From such selfless devotion the disciple can learn *to do nothing* for salvation, but instead to lovingly welcome the Lord.

(3) The modern Christian ought also to understand that he has a source of comfort which this woman did not possess. There is a kingly power and atoning victory which is evident to the later Christian who can behold the completed life of Jesus. For the modern Christian there is a sense of consolation in Christ's dying and resurrection which was less available to his contemporaries who, unavoidably, viewed him more as Pattern than as Redeemer. These facts make the infinite trust of the remorseful woman the more beautiful. Is any believer tempted to doubt whether his own sins can be so covered? Christ's reply might be: 'Believe it, nevertheless, for I have laid down my life to procure the forgiveness of thy sins...' (P. 271) In the finished deed of Christ's life there is ultimate consolation.

In view of the stress which S.K. placed on Christ as *pattern*, and the tendency on the part of some interpreters to believe that in his later period S.K. was moving to a concept of *imitation* of Christ as the proper Christian life, this discourse is very important. It plainly regards the thought of the pattern as based on incomplete awareness. Absolute trust, doing nothing for salvation, rather than imitation, is here glorified.

43. TWO DISCOURSES AT THE COMMUNION ON FRIDAYS

Two Discourses at the Communion on Fridays. By S. Kierkegaard. August 1851. Dedicated to 'One unnamed' (i.e. Regine). Translated by Walter Lowrie and included in *For Self-Examination,* 1941 edition.

This little work was the religious accompaniment of *My Activity as a Writer,* a work which hardly needed accompanying discourses since *My Activity* itself was intensely religious. Kierkegaard viewed these discourses as a culmination of his work, a quest which began in *Either/Or* and which finally came to rest at the foot of the altar. It was more than traditional piety, which, for S.K., causes the trail of existence to end in penitence at the altar. Faith never leaves repentance behind. Repentance is not preparation for Christian life; it *is* Christian life in the act of receiving the communion of compassion.

This explains why Kierkegaard never left behind the earnest concern over 'becoming' a Christian, a straining process. This has seemed strange to some. For example, Theodor Haecker, a Thomist, surmised that S.K.'s concern rested on 'preoccupation with trifles', since—as Haecker viewed the matter—it is so simple to be a Christian, i.e. by baptism, obedience and love of God and man.[102] It is rather astonishing that Haecker, who understood S.K. very well, should miss his point that even in faith the Christian is a forgiven *sinner,* and that man is always guilty before God.

The themes of the discourses, particularly evident in the second discourse (Love Covers the Multitude of Sins), are the elemental Christian messages of love, grace, and forgiveness. Nevertheless, there is something new and strange in this work. The first discourse (a 'disquieting' one) is a rather surprising challenge to conscience, hardly in keeping with the occasion of the Lord's Supper. The discourse seems given to judgment, if not being actually polemical. Yet the challenge of the discourse is authentic, for it is found in the words of Jesus, 'To whom little is forgiven, the same loveth little'. (Luke 7:47)

S.K. gives the remarkable, and not inappropriate, suggestion that whereas 'Come Unto Me' might properly be posted as an invitation on the outside wall of the church, that on the inside there might rather be placed the above words from Luke, to encourage self-examination, indicating how it might come about that little would be forgiven. Does one perhaps scarcely feel forgiven, even at the altar? Then let him reflect on how little he has loved. It is obviously true that love is full of compassion, in contrast to justice which never graciously gives anything but only acknowledges what is one's due. Yet it is paradoxically true that compassionate love has its own peculiar kind of severity. Love is not gentle, for love will not be mocked. The severest of all judgments was Jesus' death, which lovingly demonstrated the hatred of the 'good men' who crucified. 'It is not justice which sternly denies pardon...; it is love which says gently and compassionately, "I forgive thee all; if but little is forgiven thee, it is because thou dost love but little".' (P. 11) Thus it is that forgiveness is *merited*, not indeed, by works, but by love.

The second discourse is intended to console the penitent. Christ covers one's sins, covers them even more with his loving death than with his life; therefore sins are securely hidden, for 'a dead man cannot possibly be...disposed of'. As a hen 'gathers her chickens under her wing at the instant of danger', sheltering them with her living body, so Christ gives shelter. Yet when the hen has given her life for her brood she can no longer shelter them, while Christ covers the sin 'just by covering it with His death'.

These discourses are particularly important in showing that the severity of Kierkegaard's last writings are in no sense a reversion from grace and love to legalism. They demonstrate that love mysteriously has judgment hidden within it as truth about the sinner, truth which divine love discloses in the very act of grace.

THE CHRISTIAN WRITINGS

44. FOR SELF-EXAMINATION

For Self-Examination Commended to This Age. By S. Kierkegaard. September 10, 1851. Translated by Walter Lowrie and published with other items in *For Self-Examination* and *Judge for Yourselves!* New York: Oxford University Press, 1941. The volume includes: *Two Discourses at the Communion on Fridays* and *The Unchangeableness of God* (both treated separately). Also translated in *For Self-Examination and Judge for Yourselves!* by Edna and Howard Hong. Minneapolis: Augsburg Publishing House, 1940. Subsequent printing includes only *For Self-Examination*. (Page references are to the 1941 edition.)

This volume marks the initiation of the 'attack on Christendom', which was to grow in intensity to a fearful crescendo. Previously Kierkegaard had in large measure conceived of himself as a Socrates, who, mostly by indirect methods, could draw forth into clear consciousness the Christian truth which believers had allowed to be obscured by worldliness. At last he came to the conclusion that Christendom had become too unfaithful to benefit by the prompting of a Socratic teacher. The teacher must become a witness, one who by his willingness to attack error and suffer for the truth compels his hearers to make a clear choice.[103] In this closing period of his life Kierkegaard came increasingly to think of his work—and Luther's—as a corrective, a protest, and witness. For this reason he not only concluded that he might aspire to martyrdom (perhaps a living martyrdom rather than actual loss of life), but also concluded that Luther did great harm by not becoming a martyr.[104]

From this standpoint, the genius of Protestantism is that it should protest against the corruption evident in churchianity. It betrays its genius if it proceeds to establish another (corrupted) form of churchianity. The goal is not, however, the reformation of the Catholic church, but a protest against the more or less inevitable diseases of any form of Christendom. The protest is in behalf of authentic Christianity which is a fellowship of believers (single ones), which fellowship may be identified with or separated from the variable forms of Christendom. The nature and degree of any protest will depend upon how that protest is received. S.K.

clearly entertained the possibility of any form of Christendom accepting the corrective so that true Christianity could express itself more effectively within it.

The first discourse, 'The Mirror of the Word', pleads for men to earnestly behold themselves in the mirror of the Word of God, in order to silently apprehend their need of grace. S.K. deplores the fact that his fellow Lutherans seem to take salvation 'by faith alone' to mean that they might live as carelessly and vulgarly as they pleased. Then, is one free to live as he pleases? 'Capital! That suits us exactly', the worldly Christians exclaim. (P. 41) Kierkegaard protests that Luther's own mighty works and earnest strivings give a silent rebuke to worldliness. 'Thy life shall as strenuously as possible give expression to works—and then one thing more is required: that thou humble thyself and admit, "But none the less I am saved by grace".' (P. 42) S.K. notes that Luther himself insisted that 'faith is a perturbing thing', so that it would make a recognizable difference in one's living. With a sense of the dramatic he imagines Luther coming back to life to pester people with Socratic questioning: 'To what effect has faith, which thou sayest thou hast, perturbed thee?...What sacrifices hast thou made, what persecutions hast thou endured for Christianity?' (P. 42 f.) S.K. makes this interesting personal comment: 'I have only one misgiving about this excellent Lutheran doctrine. That does not apply to the Lutheran doctrine, but it applies to me: I have reason to know that I am not an upright soul, but a crafty fellow. So it doubtless would be well to examine...works of love, etc.' (P. 49) It follows that one ought not look into the mirror of the Word of God in order to admire the mirror but in order to see oneself in honesty, reminding oneself all the while, as the prophet Nathan said in dreadful judgment to King David, 'Thou art the man'. Further, in turning away from the mirror one must not deceitfully forget what manner of man he was.

It is rather astonishing that Kierkegaard's reliance upon Scripture should ever have been questioned—which nevertheless is the case—because of his insistence on subjectivity in Christian experience. His invariable use of Scripture in all of his writing should be sufficient to correct this doubt. The correction is impressively reinforced in *For Self-Examination* as he makes

Scripture not only the disclosure of God but also the mirror in which the believer puts his own subjectivity to the test. Only when read as a love letter, however, does it serve this purpose. (P. 51) What is needed is not to guarantee the certitude of scripture—which can never be objectively accomplished—but to use scripture as 'a profitable schoolmaster in the existing uncertainty'.[105]

True, S.K. is unwilling to let Scripture be a wordy assemblage of revelatory facts. It has its centrality in the meaning of Christ, and its 'truth' is available only to the man of faith. Yet, while S.K. daringly asserts that its essence could possibly have been reduced to the simplest apostolic witness to Christ he recognizes that much more than this minimum essential is available and he faithfully accepts it. His acceptance plainly ranges from miracle and parable, through law and gospel, to hope and love, but most of all it recognizes the disclosure of Christ himself. In view of this the assertion of a scholar like Zuidema that S.K. eliminates all of Biblical revelation except the mythological notion of the Absolute Paradox seems utterly groundless.[106] In fact S.K. explained that the reason he used the language of 'the Absolute Paradox' in the Fragments was that he felt it necessary to avoid typical ecclesiastical terms because these had become so fuzzy with over-familiarity and so distorted by speculative usage. He wished to present Christianity without naming it, thereby letting it make a fresh impact.[107]

Men give pious tribute to the Bible, says Kierkegaard, but in truth they fear to use it as a mirror. They may look at the lovely frame about the mirror or notice cracks in the glass or smudges on its surface. They may wish to treat the Bible as *literature*, referring to its antiquity, may reflect on the problem of the Bible's authenticity, or ponder its subtle meanings. However, all such pre-occupations suggest an actual rejection of the Word. To spiritually benefit by reading one must forever remind himself that the Word is speaking *to him*, and this is no mark of vanity but of earnestness.*

---

* S.K.'s friend Hans Brøchner noted that Kierkegaard could not make Scripture a matter of *scientific* study since that would be to concern oneself about knowledge rather than faith, and to look at the incidental rather than at what is central. (Cf. T. H. Croxall, *Glimpses and Impressions of Kierkegaard*, p. 32.) Granted that the Bible may also be objectively studied and analysed, yet this is not, for S.K., what is spiritually needed.

'To be alone with the Holy Scriptures! I dare not! When I turn up a passage in it, whatever comes to hand—it catches me instantly, it questions me (indeed it is as if it were God Himself that questioned me), "Hast thou done what thou readest there?" And then, then...yes, then I am caught. So then it is action at once, or instantly a humiliating admission.' (P. 56) It is not really difficult to understand the Bible when it says 'Turn the other cheek'. What is difficult is to accept its injunction resolutely. To polish the mirror as a notable antique is insincerity, but to be goaded into action by one's unfavourable image in the mirror is Christian living. Far from constituting work-righteousness, this is a recognition of the natural quality of the life of faith and grace. As with Luther, one is saved by faith and then lives a life full of good works as the embodiment of love.

May the critic complain that in all of this Kierkegaard has still not escaped from the perils of subjectivity? If Scripture is only a mirror then one discovers only himself, albeit his true self, within it. Nothing could be farther from S.K.'s meaning. Scripture is a mirror because one truly sees himself only when he sees himself before God. What one must seek to behold in the mirror is what God's way is and whether one is walking in that way.

The second discourse, 'Christ is the Way', sets forth the way as disclosed in the mirror of Scripture, and does so in powerful language. Christ as the Way leads to heaven, but the way is narrow. That the ascended Christ leads to glory no true believer doubts, but that One who suffers and is ridiculed is the Way seems odd. Nevertheless, this fact is essential to faith. This Way—Christ—is 'narrow' from the beginning—born in a stable (almost as if he were not human), plotted against by the mighty. Certainly his coming was strange. 'One would have expected that the Lord would at least have waited to let himself be born until the art of printing had been invented, that until then the fullness of time had not arrived.'[108] His whole life, like the forty days, was a temptation to abandon his lowly calling. The way became progressively narrower, and led to death, by way of a friend's kiss. Finally it became evident that he *was the Way*, for he ascended into heaven (the discourse is for Ascension Day). Yet there is a fearful temptation for a disciple to begin at the end of the way (glory), and not walk through the narrowness by which alone he can approach the ascension. If one does this he will even doubt the ascension, but true believers will not doubt. 'It is like a warrior who possesses a gorgeous robe; he knows well that he has it, but he almost never looks at it, for his whole life is passed in daily combat and peril, and therefore he wears an everyday dress which gives him freedom of movement.' (P. 89) If one is troubled by doubt, let him become a *follower*; a follower does not doubt.

Lest the much publicized melancholy of Kierkegaard cause one to suspect that he is here giving a gloomy glorification of suffering *qua* suffering it is to be noted that S.K. specifically points out that not every 'narrow way' is Christian. There are many sufferings which do not result from service to the good. Yet even in these circumstantial or accidental sufferings the believer should strive to 'walk Christianly', and if he does so his path will then be the path which leads to heaven. (P. 87) Kierkegaard's view of suffering undoubtedly rested on his own afflictions and perhaps included an element of egocentrism and self-pity. In like manner had his view of the New Testament been influenced, by his conceiving God in terms of his own father, who through love had brought suffering on his children.[109] Yet for everyone understanding is always gained against a background of personal experience, and the nature of Christian suffering is here illumined more than it is distorted by such subjective experiences. There is a realism about S.K.'s view of life which perhaps the twentieth century can begin to comprehend better than could his contemporaries. S.K. was vividly conscious of the sufferings of the martyrs. The Roman arena was to him not an oddity of history but a natural response of the evil world to dynamic godliness. The security of 'Christendom' within its cathedrals—monuments to a piety which *once* was vigorous—was perhaps largely due to the spiritual drowsiness and unconcern of the multitudes who supposed themselves to be Christian. Twentieth-century torture of Christians and others in a new age of hate, although no simple response of satanical man to evident godliness, has made S.K.'s outlook more meaningful and plausible.

Finally, what is the nature of the Christian life? A careful answer is formulated in the last discourse, 'The Spirit Giveth

Life', which is a meditation for Pentecost. Every worldly man believes in spirit, S.K. complains, but only in the 'spirit' of the age, or of humanity, or of the race. The worldly man is in fact reluctant to believe in a Holy Ghost because a *holy* spirit makes heavy demands upon him. Men forever seek to take Christianity in vain, trying, since the Spirit giveth life, to make it some gentle thing. Christianity does indeed offer consolation, but only if a man first dies; that is not so gentle! The Spirit does give life, yet it was only after the apostles had died unto the world and unto themselves—died to every earthly hope—that the Spirit changed despair to life. Just here lies the problem, for men do not want to die unto selfishness. It is blasphemy to ignore the fact that it is *new* life which the Spirit gives, not 'a direct increment of the natural life'. (P. 96) Merely more of the same life, with its lusts and frustrations? That might be a nightmarish prospect.

Mankind confuses Christianity with natural goodness, but this too is subtle blasphemy, for it is *spiritual* life which is given by the Spirit. Christianity is not quackery; 'it does not heal every wretched little ailment by means of eternity'. (P. 99) Rather, the three gifts of the Spirit are *faith* (when human confidence is gone), *hope* (but not until one has tasted of despair), and *love* (generous giving, like God's grace, rather than possessive cherishing). The conclusion of this trenchant work makes it clear that S.K. is precisely repeating what he had learned from Luther. Christianity is not a righteous walking in the way, but is instead a turning by faith to the grace of God when one discovers how pathetically incapable he is of walking in the way.

45. JUDGE FOR YOURSELVES!

> *Judge for Yourselves!* For Self-Examination Commended to this Age. Second Series. Written in 1851–52. Published in 1876, not having been published by Kierkegaard himself because of its severity, being printed 21 years after his death. This sequel to For Self-Examination appears in English in *For Self-Examination* and *Judge for Yourselves!* Translated by Walter Lowrie. New York: Oxford University Press, 1941. Also translated by Edna and Howard Hong in *For Self-Examination* and *Judge for Yourselves!* Minneapolis: Augsburg Publishing House, 1940. (Page references are to the 1941 edition.)

This sequel ('Second Series') to *For Self-Examination* is much more drastic than its predecessor and is at least equally powerful. It begins with 'Becoming Sober', which is a challenge to flabby, common-sense Christians to take their religion earnestly. On Pentecost the mockers thought Simon Peter and the other apostles to be drunk—already at nine o'clock in the morning—but the apostles were 'drunk' every morning from then on, with the wine of the Spirit. Genuine soberness requires exactly such intoxication with the Spirit. Christian soberness is not worldly prudence; indeed, it calls for a kind of passion which knows that not only the murderer is excluded from the Kingdom of God but also the flabby one. To be sober is to know oneself as being nothing before God, yet under absolute obligation.

Kierkegaard includes a masterpiece of irony, which is one of the great satires of literature. It is a short story about a theological student who seeks, no, not the Kingdom of God, but a fat living. (Pp. 126 ff.) He wore himself out 'running and seeking, which can hardly be said to be in the service of the absolute, except... that he seeks "absolutely everything"'. (P. 127) Finally, the Scriptural assurance 'Seek and ye shall find' was fulfilled, 'but the absolute he did not find, it was only a small living—but after all it was not the absolute he was seeking'. (P. 127) Dismayed at the salary and at how much his wife might expect—more each year—he nearly resigned, but finally he became a parson and the text for the day on which he had to preach at his installation was 'Seek ye first the kingdom of God'. The sermon was an oratorical masterpiece, with thrilling effect, but good heavens! 'This represents about the way Christendom stands related to Christianity, the absolute.' (P. 128)

Does Kierkegaard then believe that a pastor should live on thin air? Nonsense! Pastors should in fact be rewarded more liberally than they are; it is the most honourable thing in the world for a man to work for his living, and this includes the pastor. Moreover, it is wretched meanness for congregations to want to 'scrape something off' the pastors' salaries in miserly fashion. (P. 143) Yet the necessity remains for the pastor to make it clearly evident what he is asking for *his* sake and, on the other hand, wherein he is working for a cause. There can be no harm and indeed much benefit in informing the congregation of what it already knows, viz. that a pastor requires a living. He need not hypocritically hide his need under the pretext of need for the gospel. Again, consider the 'honour' of the ministerial office, and its deceits. What ambiguity there is in calling the pastor 'his Right Reverend Reverence!' If he lives nobly he may indeed be revered and reverend, and as one who ably ministers he may be 'Worthy' (Vaerdig—Danish reference to a clergyman), but there must be no appropriation of God's holiness in such titles.

In actuality then the crying need is not for church people to become really 'sober', for no one can ever be truly sober, i.e. Christian. What is imperative is that they understand the demand for soberness and make no false pretence as to how close their straining 'Christendom' stands in relation to the ideal goal of Christianity. 'We extol our age for the fact that Christianity is no longer persecuted. That I can well believe: Christianity doesn't exist [and indeed never can fully, in a world of sin]. If it existed in its true form, persecution would instantly persecute this treason against humanity.' (P. 155) It is to be observed here that S.K. expresses a kind of agreement with Nietzsche in viewing Christianity as 'treason against humanity', in that it glorifies humility rather than mastery and repudiates honour, power, comfort and common sense.*

---

* S.K. endorses the 'treason' whereas Nietzsche deplores it. Yet the antithesis is unclear. What infuriated Nietzsche was the hypocritical humility of insincere Christians, not humility itself. Further, despite his glorification of mastery, Nietzsche manifested a remarkably Christian-like sympathy.

The more formidable discourse is 'Christ as the Pattern'. Christianity offers a pattern and Kierkegaard insists that it must be taken seriously. No man can serve two masters, even though only One has fulfilled the pattern absolutely. Christ is the pattern. He showed what it is to serve only one Master, serving neither parents nor disciples but serving God by obeying parents and by loving his disciples. 'With the resources of omnipotence He assures Himself of becoming nothing.'

Christ did not come to the world to teach or explain a doctrine. He was not a professor! His teaching was his life and this can be learned only by imitation. 'The professor!' This person, never mentioned in the New Testament (so Christianity must have been able to come into being without his help), changes Christianity from actual existence to mere idea, from life to doctrine. Moreover, while honoured professors do not suffer, anyone who lives in imitation of Christ will be called on to suffer. The Pattern must be held aloft, 'to get Christianity transferred from learned discussion and doubt and twaddle (the objective) into the subjective sphere, where it belongs'. (P. 217) If S.K.'s violent and effective satire seems exaggerated there nevertheless certainly is a ground for his protest. The professorial mentality is forever in danger of committing the unpardonable sin of converting Christianity (or any way of life) into something to reflect on rather than to live by.

In a rather extended lyrical statement, Kierkegaard proceeds to state the nature of the Pattern which is to be observed in Christ. All of his life Jesus was the example of a person living but to serve one Master. Without earthly father, and without a home whereas even foxes have holes and birds their nests, his entering into the calloused world was little noticed, but the heavens were rapturous. Then he was without a country; there were no strong earthly ties as to brother, mother. He seemed decidedly queer. He did not seek wealth or influential friends. He could have been a king but turned away. He offended the leaders. True, he had his disciples, but in his decisive moment, when he struggled in anguish, they were without anguish. They were sleeping. Only one of them did not sleep. He grasped that decisive moment to betray him. Then was Christ condemned to death. When it was too late he made his declaration—he was a king. But he was killed and his crime was that he had served only one master. To do good and have to suffer for it, this then is what the Pattern expresses.

'The Moral', at the end of the book, is extremely important for an understanding of Kierkegaard's goal. He states plainly that his purpose is *not* to reform the Danish church, for bungling efforts at reform are more pernicious than the most pernicious establishment. What he hoped for instead of this was for churchianity to humbly acknowledge how far it was from imitating the Pattern, in view of the obvious fact that 'becoming' Christians can hardly constitute more than a 'becoming' church. All of this is extremely important because S.K.'s aim is easily misunderstood. He could be taken to be a moralist, disgusted by the failure of Christians to live according to their principles. In fact, nothing could be farther from the truth. To be a Christian is instead to know that one cannot live according to his principles, and to feel the dread weight of sin, then to rely on grace. However S.K. insists that if one does not even try to bear his cross he cannot be conscious of his failure and cannot understand what divine love and forgiveness signify. The essentials are therefore to hold high the absolute character of God's requirements, then to make confession and undertake the venture of faith.

At this point we may review the entire concept of 'imitation of Christ' which looms larger and larger in Kierkegaard's later thought. In sharp contrast to the medieval understanding of imitation, S.K. points out that man cannot literally imitate God. Like Luther, he thinks of any human attempt at being a kind of duplicate of Christ as a dangerous presumption which necessarily ends in despair. Thus the attempt at imitation, even though essential to discipleship, leads properly to a realization of the need for divine grace and an appreciation for what God in Christ has done for man.[110] Even the required effort of denying self and following Christ as Pattern does not consist of deeds legally performed, but of love naturally expressed (cf. treatment of *Works of Love*). Following Christ is the external manifestation of the life of prayer and faith, and obedience is therefore not the means of salvation but an act of worship.[111] Good works are indeed dead unless they are natural expressions of love. S.K. rejected any notion of merit gained by self-denial. The life of righteousness is a response to the favour of God which has already been received. Nevertheless, the gospel does demand that the believer forsake the world—even though gaining no merit by doing so.

In view of Kierkegaard's final accent on suffering and world-renunciation, it is of special importance to note that he did not hold these to be ends in themselves. Given the world in which man finds himself, suffering is a means of witness to the truth, a witness which is not grudging but which expresses love for God. The earnest recipients of grace can joyously follow Christ and can proclaim the grace of God, which for them is a transforming reality.[112]

God's forgiveness eliminates man's guilt and establishes a God-man relationship but it does not eliminate the sorrowful consequences of guilt in human life—interpreted by S.K. in terms of his own deep melancholy.[113] The state of forgiveness is another expression for religious 'repetition', and for the 'infinite double movement' of resignation and faith.[114] It is also somewhat expressed by the thought of being contemporaneous with Christ or by having the immediacy (awareness of God) which occurs after reflection. Involved in all such expressions is the dual conviction that Christian life is a new birth of the Spirit and that it requires a dying to the world in order to love the holy, not an actual abandonment of the world but a release from its domination. Faith, love and hope are the new gifts of the Spirit, but, as demonstrated by the martyrs and by the life of Christ himself, dedication to the good does not remove suffering from existence.

Kierkegaard is outraged because modern churchmen seem unconcerned about attempting to model their lives after the 'pattern' given by Christ. He regards most Christians as manifesting a 'Jewish piety', which expects things to go well in earthly life if one keeps close to God. In the strict sense, he held that to be a Christian and follow the pattern means 'to die to the world', and then to be cursed by men and seemingly even abandoned by God.[115] The folly of confused and corrupted 'Christians' is evident in the fact that when the sceptics attack the faith and call it mythology or poetry, the church's rescue squad rushes to the defence by treating it as a pretty doctrine rather than a way of existence, thereby proving that to the defenders as well that Christianity is only mythology and poetry.[116]

At this point, where world-renunciation becomes so prominent, it is imperative that the quest for the eternal and the corresponding renunciation of the temporal be placed in their existential framework. The grossest misunderstanding of the eternal as treated by S.K. is to think of it as a sheer replacement, a substitute for the temporal. Instead, it introduces a norm whereby the temporal may be judged and held fast. In *Sickness Unto Death* the eternal has so central a role for one's existing *in the world* that there can be no human existence without a relationship to it. David Swenson notes that Kierkegaard viewed faith in the eternal as giving man-in-the-world the needed courage to be himself in spite of the pressures of transitory moods. 'He is relieved of the necessity of being "modern"; he is permitted to reflect that every error and aberration which we now condemn as belonging to the past, was once "the very latest thing out".' For Kierkegaard as for Socrates, the hope of better judges in another world enables one to cling more tenaciously to the right.[117] The eternal is for S.K. both the compass and the anchor of earthly existence, no simple flight from it.

How far will following Christ involve one in sacrifice? Kierkegaard's views wavered on this. In *Judge for Yourselves* he seemed to feel that the requirements of discipleship should be made dramatically evident to all but that their full severity is binding only on the few who voluntarily commit themselves to sacrifice and suffering. It is the person who has an unusual God-relationship, e.g. an apostle, who has the more severe duty of imitation. Others are not even permitted to commit themselves to a life of radical world-renunciation such as martyrdom.[118] Subsequently, however, S.K. became radically uncompromising, and seemed to impose world-renunciation on all.

46. ATTACK UPON 'CHRISTENDOM'

Kierkegaard's Attack Upon 'Christendom'. Scattered items, written in 1854–55, translated under this title by Walter Lowrie. Princeton: Princeton University Press, 1944. Boston: Beacon Press paperback, 1956.

The man on the street will hardly read a book on theology, but he will listen for a moment to someone preaching on the street corner, and his wife will take note of an explosive editorial in a newspaper. To reach these common people, when the church leaders would not take heed, Kierkegaard used such tactics. His attack (Marie M. Thulstrup prefers to call it a 'challenge')[119] is thus not really a book. Instead, it is a large collection of newspaper articles and tiny polemical tracts which represent the final dramatic conflict of his life, a struggle with the established church which ended at his death.

Two points need to be made by way of clarification: (1) The 'attack' was well under way before the writing of the materials assembled in this volume. Already in the *Postscript* (p. 43) the church had been accused of substituting impersonal externalities for spiritual inwardness: 'My father has told me so, the church records attest it, I have a certificate, and so forth. Oh, yes, my mind is at rest.' (2) In these writings the positive and constructive significance of the attack is often obscured by the violently negative and deliberately exaggerated criticisms. 'The Moral' at the end of *Judge for Yourselves*, aiming at repentance, should be fixed in mind as the implicit purpose, even though S.K. seemed to eventually despair of repentance. He insisted that his 'corrective' had to be one-sided. 'Ye gods! Nothing is easier for him who applies the corrective than to supply the other side; but then it ceases to be the corrective...' (P. 90)

As pointed out in the treatment of *Judge for Yourselves*, S.K.'s purpose was not to reform the church but to bring it to repentance. It is not the state church which he attacks—although he also bluntly criticizes it. Instead, it is 'Christendom' which is guilty of apostasy, pretending to be Christian when it is actually worldly.[120] No community, including the state, has a right to set itself between a man and God or charge for providing 'religion'. Nor does it have the right to impose religion on a man. For the church the minimum essential is to honestly confess what it is and what it cannot be.[121] S.K.'s calling the church to repentance can be understood only by recalling his view of the role of repentance in the individual Christian's life. The walk of faith culminates when the believer *repents*, repents even of his neglect of grace, and when communion is possessed through renewal of forgiveness. That which is essential for the individual is essential for believers, i.e. for Christendom. The goal is not to establish a new Christendom, nor to destroy the smug churchianity, but to bring all who profess Christ to repentance and grace. Repentance is thus not a means to some other end but is the existential goal. Only such radical sincerity can relieve Christians of the guilt of betrayal.

Contrary to this interpretation, there has been a common supposition that Kierkegaard did wish to introduce a truer, ascetic kind of Christianity. However, his fundamental insistence is that no one can be a true Christian, and certainly he made no pretence of having personally succeeded. Moreover, he took comfort in the thought that the requirements of discipleship might be less severe for others than for himself.[122] In this light, the attack was not only the culmination of S.K.'s entire religious outlook, but also might seem a virtual necessity in view of the complacent religiosity of the age. Complacency needed to give way to fear and trembling. S.K.'s religious attack seems to have been somewhat complicated by his more philosophical notion of a degenerating society. When men have once been thus far 'levelled' to a corrupt state within the mass of society, it is too much to hope that the levelling can be arrested or corrected. The most that can be hoped for is to press the levelling to its bitter conclusion, by challenging it and suffering under it, and thus also bring judgment upon it.[123] In consequence, the contemporary church cannot well hope to manifest the commitment of the ancient martyrs, but it can at least confess that it is a watered down version of Christianity and encourage men to humbly examine their *existence*—not their intellectual comprehension.

In all of this literature, which consists of short, violent outbursts, Kierkegaard abandons his indirectness. His artistry is here less in evidence, and he is often bitter, indulging in painful satire. He consciously uses exaggeration, having come to the conviction that only the most dramatic statement could make men confess that in their self-indulgent lives they are not really following the Man of Sorrows. Also, as S.K. repeatedly points out, he is writing to Protestants, more specifically to Lutherans, and still more precisely to cultured, pleasure-seeking Danes who, as he saw it, tried to bless their selfishness with a sanctimonious prayer.* In

* The fault of Danish Lutheranism, says S.K., is not wild excess or indulgent hypocrisy, but being ridiculous by giving lip service to ideality while in fact

reality Kierkegaard therefore referred approvingly to the earnestness of the monk and self-sacrifice of the priest.

Some interpreters, in particular Roman Catholics, have taken this to imply that if S.K. had lived longer he might have become a Catholic. This is surely a mis-reading of the case. He is equally pointed in his criticism of the monk. Entering the monastery, he says, gives no spiritual inwardness; being a monk is 'just as truly external as being an alderman'.[124] Had he been living in Rome and writing for a different audience, he would surely have written newspaper articles in the Roman press satirizing the fat and self-indulgent monk, or the priest who dares to assume that by giving up a wife—but not cigarettes, wine, honour and titles ('Right Reverend Reverence')—that he is actually imitating Christ. Further, S.K. would have satirized the 'building' of the Kingdom of grace and faith (always individual) by priestly acts and official pomp and ceremony. As opposed to the 'establishment', whether Jewish, Protestant, or Catholic, S.K. is vehemently protesting against institutional and official religion.

On Luther's central thesis of grace and justification, Kierkegaard is clear and blunt: 'A man is justified only by faith. And therefore, in God's name, to hell with the Pope and all his auxiliary assistants, along with all your fasting, flagellation, and all the monkeyshines which are resorted to under the name of following.'[125] Similarly, S.K. held tenaciously to most other Lutheran views on such matters as the radical character of sin, religious authority, the church, and priesthood. On the other hand, S.K. was critical of Luther's emphasis on the peace which Christ gives to an anxious conscience. That was well enough for Luther himself, he thought, for Luther had an earnest and anxious conscience, but it is not good enough for careless Christians who take salvation lightly. For them, it should be reiterated that Christ came to give an anxious conscience to a world which is content in its sin.[126] S.K. felt that the monastic ideal should be added to Luther's understanding of grace, not, however, in the familiar form of self-discipline for obtaining merit. The 'asceticism' he had in mind is the submission of the soul to God's absolute claim to disciple-

clinging to the worldly. (*Papirer*, XI² A 398.) His protest finds an impressive parallel in Dietrich Bonhoeffer's protest against 'cheap grace' and in his demand for costly discipleship. (*The Cost of Discipleship*, Macmillan (1959).)

ship. It is no medieval monastery which S.K. seeks. What he desires is a symbol—best found in the lives of apostles and martyrs—of what 'following Christ' means. '"The Monastery" is an essential dialectical fact in Christianity, and we need to have it there like a light-house, in order to gauge where we are.'[127] S.K.'s slogan 'back to the monastery' must not then be taken with literalism. He intended it only as a corrective ideal. He states plainly that he does not propose to reintroduce the monastery, but wanted men to understand it and admit what sound principles could be represented by the monastery if removed from the errors of Catholicism.[128]

Kierkegaard remains severely critical of Catholicism. 'Of course everything that Catholicism has invented concerning the merit of works is absolutely to be rejected.'[129] What is more, Catholicism is particularly guilty of attempting to turn Christianity, 'which is not of this world', into a kingdom of this world, with 'straightforward recognizability', objectivity, and externality.[130] If the state (as Protestant Denmark) is guilty of trying to use Christianity as a means of producing good citizens (doing so in good faith but in confusion), it is the Pope who is most guilty of usurping divine authority as he seeks 'to rule men with the help of eternity'.[131]

There is only one feature of Catholicism which pleases S.K., and even it is of a mixed value, that of ascetic renunciation. He is critical of Luther's lack of the ascetic, feeling that he thereby loses the severe requirements of true Christianity.[132] The error of Catholicism is not the celibacy of the priest, for in these later writings he asserts that every Christian ought to be celibate; the Catholic error is to make a distinction between the layman and the more 'religious', so that the asceticism of the priest becomes a unique virtue.[133] Indeed, Luther should perhaps have married in order to correct the false concept of a priesthood which is set aside but he should have married 'say, an ironing board' so as not to encourage a 'throng of philoprogenitive men'.[134] Catholicism has perverted simple obedience to God's will into the sinful notion of the proud priest being an intermediary between God and man.[135]

The Catholic theologian Louis Dupre is one of the most discerning interpreters of these issues. He notes certain remarkable contributions which S.K. makes 'to the Catholic-Protestant dialogue', e.g. in his reintegration of asceticism in the *sola fide* doctrine of the reformation and his paradoxical addition of freedom to grace. Yet Dupre concludes that Kierkegaard's essential position is 'perhaps the most consistent application of the Reformation principle that has ever been made'.[136] The core of this principle is subjectivity, which for S.K. involves a unique kind of objectivity. Dupre concludes that, even as S.K. removed himself from the Protestant 'establishment', he 'never abandoned the Protestant principle'. With an unyielding protest against any attempt at institution or external security, Kierkegaard insisted that Christianity must be a relationship of the individual to God, which relationship then requires a fellowship of believers in the grace of love.[137] This 'Protestant principle' in Kierkegaard involved a rejection of any external authority. Whereas the Catholic needs no evidence of authority (the Pope *is* authority), S.K. insisted that there must be personal evidence of authority, and that this evidence is willingness to suffer for Christ. Further whereas the bishop can never, from the Catholic viewpoint, jeopardize the authority of the church, no matter how depraved he may be, for S.K. such betrayal can end in loss of true Christianity.[138]

The separately published items which are assembled in the *Attack* are reviewed below separately. For treatment of contents, see:
Articles in the Fatherland.
This Has to be Said—So Be it Now Said.
The Instant.
What Christ's Judgment is About Official Christianity.
The Unchangeableness of God.

47. ARTICLES IN *THE FATHERLAND*

Twenty-one articles in *The Fatherland*, a political newspaper. December 18, 1854–May 26, 1855. Translated by Walter Lowrie in *Attack Upon 'Christendom'*.

With a passionate concern for reaching people's hearts, Kierkegaard wished that he could preach on the street corner, remembering what Luther had said, that sermons ought not be preached in meditation chapels but in the midst of life. Unable to do this because of his physical frailty, he wrote in a secular newspaper of wide circulation.

Towards the end of his life Kierkegaard found it increasingly difficult to restrain himself from making a violent protest against the confusion of gospel and worldliness, but did so until his honoured friend, and the friend of his late father, Bishop Mynster, died. Then he was strangely prodded into making his attack. Unwittingly, Professor Martensen, who was soon to succeed Mynster as bishop, referred in a sermon to the dead leader as a genuine witness to the truth. In a running battle with Martensen, carried on in the newspapers, S.K. bitterly objected to this careless tribute to the bishop, and also extended the attack to related matters. In spite of the critical differences between them, Martensen subsequently acknowledged his former pupil's 'keen insight', and 'the dexterity in psychological experiment' by which he probed 'the mysteries of existence, both actual and possible, which but few ever know, and fewer still are in a condition to express'.[139]

Kierkegaard had come to think of a 'witness' as one who is willing to face sacrifice and who inevitably suffers in following a Lord who was despised, mocked, scourged and crucified. Martensen objected, persuasively, that not every witness to the truth is a martyr, but he underestimated the force of S.K.'s argument. Kierkegaard did not at all maintain that every true witness will be a martyr but only that a true witness will inevitably be called on to suffer for the truth. He did not in fact expect all Christians to be witnesses but it shocked him to hear a man called a witness (one who is at least *like* a martyr) who had lived a life of luxury and honour.

A particularly important article is that entitled 'What do I want?'[140] It is significant because even in the twentieth century some scholars are asking what it was that Kierkegaard really wanted. The earnest answer found here should probably be taken at face value. He wanted honesty and sincerity; he did not want to institute a new (severe) form of piety, nor to lower pastors' salaries, but simply to have people frankly recognize that the modern church is far from identical with New Testament Christianity. Inasmuch as the latter calls for giving away one's wealth and following the lowly Jesus, Christians ought to realize and admit that there are special hazards for high-salaried, cultured and worldly-secure Christians, whether they be laymen or pastors. What S.K. sought and what he did not seek become even more clear in the journals of this last period than in the published articles. He wanted no one to do as he did, for each has his own function. His own task was to 'scatter' men, making them single persons.[141] He wanted no 'followers', did not wish to establish a party or sect, and did not want 'academic' discussion but instead wished to be a voice for conscience.[142] He hoped more to bring mediocrity to a stop than to begin something new. Above all he wished to take from men the illusion that they were Christians.[143]

Kierkegaard's personal relationship to Mynster deserves special mention. He honoured and loved the old bishop, so that even in the midst of his terrible attack he was still captivated by 'this enchanting and admirable figure'. He recognized the bishop to be religiously well-intentioned even though he believed him to be leading the church to self-destruction.[144] S.K. had previously gladly defended Mynster and now indicated that he could do so again. What was even more important was that he had in that instance argued that there was no imperative need for change in the outward church. What was needed was a deepening of sincerity. His plea was for genuine Christian inwardness.[145] He would even have liked to have been Mynster's ultimate defence, but could not bring himself honestly to be this because of Mynster's worldliness.[146] Quaintly, S.K. said that he himself was the bishop's 'sermon' on Monday, i.e. taking or exemplifying the latter with intense seriousness. This ambivalent devotion and bitter condemnation can better be understood by noting Mynster's close identification with S.K.'s father. As S.K. deeply loved his father but harshly resented his sins, so too he took this dual attitude towards his father's spiritual counsellor, ambivalently referring to him as 'that liar of blessed memory'.[147] Yet if the bitterness of the great public attack on Mynster and the church seems to reflect a personal and emotional ambivalence in S.K. which recognized serious fault in the objects of love, it was based more on principle than past association. The fact that the attack had its focus on Mynster rather than Martensen, the clergy, or the government, seems to have had real point. It was Mynster's very spiritual earnestness which made his compromise with worldly pleasure the more alarming. Further, his failure to give S.K. support during the ordeal with the *Corsair*, and his even making veiled attacks on S.K. made it clear that he did not intend to persuade casual church 'members' to take godly living more seriously.

Kierkegaard points out in these newspaper articles that there are many respectable, competent and worthy pastors, who as a group are as 'estimable' a class of people as any other, but that these must not be confused with 'witnesses', martyrs, or real 'followers'. They are, of course, *related* to Christianity but they cannot claim to be completely dedicated Christians. They have made the blood of Christ the 'greatest source of revenue', doing much better in fact financially than Judas who got only thirty pieces of silver for his betrayal. To talk of such a minister as a 'witness' is like talking about a 'maiden who is surrounded by her numerous troop of children'. S.K. did not demand that the clergy live as witnesses, but he did insist that the 'signboard must be taken down', so that pastors do not profess to be more than they are. By failing to confess that they compromise the Christian life with worldliness, such ministers forfeit their right to speak for Christianity and indeed make it necessary for the state church to be dis-established. Whereas before, S.K. had thought that the church could defend and validate itself by confessing its faults, now he comes to view the establishment as beyond purification. It seemingly will not repent and therefore he abandons his call to repentance which had been the goal (in the 'Moral') of *Training in Christianity*. (P. 55)

48. THIS HAS TO BE SAID; SO BE IT NOW SAID

This Has to be Said; So Be it Now Said. By S. Kierkegaard. May 16, 1855. This tiny 'midnight cry' against the established church now appears in *Attack Upon 'Christendom'*.

What utterance could be so radical as to justify such a title? The dreadful thing which had to be said was that a Christian should cease taking part in 'official' Christendom's worship, waiting for the church's confession and its cleansing. In particular, Kierkegaard attacked the union of church and state. The church wanted to enjoy aid and comforts from the government and it demonstrated thereby that it was not Christian. Through the ages, the church has become worldly, 'exactly the opposite of what it is in the New Testament'. As a punishment for the worldly pastors, S.K. wishes that they could be given what they want, ten times the salary—but without a single man in church.[148] Might not S.K.'s cure be as dangerous as the malady? If people quit the church may they not also, at least eventually, be abandoning God? S.K. would probably acknowledge the peril. On another occasion he insisted that man is *always guilty* before God, whatever he does. There is therefore no sure or complete cure, and S.K. is not proposing one; what he is saying is that the guilt of hypocrisy is the deadliest sin.

To comfortable people—and who wants to be disturbed?—S.K.'s attack must seem fanatical. What nonsense—a plea to Christians to be Christian! Even more, his urging them to quit the church! Was he serious? And did he expect the whole church to reform itself? No, he was not at all assured that churchmen would reform themselves. Nevertheless he was quite certain that they would be reformed in spite of themselves through the terrible outcomes of their folly and hypocrisy. Near the end of his life he wrote these appallingly prophetic words:

'Certainly things will be reformed; and it will be a frightful reformation compared with which the Lutheran reformation will be almost a joke, a frightful reformation that will have as its battle cry "Whether faith will be found upon earth?" and it will be recognizable by the fact that millions will fall away from Christianity . . . and it is terrible when a generation which has been molly-coddled by a childish Christianity, fooled into thinking it is Christianity, when it has to receive the death blow of learning once again what it means to be a Christian...'[149]

A century or more later, Christians who concede that at times Kierkegaard was fanatical nevertheless ponder with anxious sorrow the fulfilment or near-fulfilment of this prophecy. In Russia where nearly 100 per cent of the people were 'Christians' in S.K.'s time nearly 100 per cent have become atheists. Is there not even more of conscience-stirring anxiety for believers over the still 'Christian' nations where almost all 'belong to the church' and where nevertheless the cathedrals are little more than aesthetic monuments to a spiritual life which once was? And, is there possibly the greatest cause of all for Christian concern in America where—as in S.K.'s Denmark—the church seems to be a thriving success, but is such largely because of its perilous mixture with the world—culture, music, socializing, coffee, and status? 'Millions will fall away.' 'A frightful reformation that will have as its battlecry "Whether faith will be found upon earth".'

The question may reasonably be raised whether Kierkegaard in his last days was not grossly inconsistent, on the one hand calling on Christians to repent and on the other denying that there were any longer Christians (or church). Yet there is no self-contradiction. S.K. understood perfectly that a Christian is a forgiven sinner and that hypocrisy is always present. It then becomes a matter of practical judgment to decide when a given form of churchianity must be rejected as a betrayal of true Christianity. There must for ever be protest and a demand for penitence.

In his journals Kierkegaard recorded that he considered it conceivable and desirable, but unlikely, that because of this denunciation of public worship as a crime he might be arrested and even executed.[150]

49. THE INSTANT

> *The Instant*, Numbers 1 to 10. May 10–October 1855.
> Ten small tracts which attacked the established church.
> Translated into English in *Attack Upon 'Christendom'*.

In *Training in Christianity* and *For Self-Examination* Kierkegaard had sought to show that the church was not authentic Christianity. Nor did he expect it to be. However, he felt that the minimum essential was for it to confess its faults. In growing impatience he waited for three long years for such confession. In the meantime, in his Journal, he gave vent to his feelings. For example, he commented that even though Christendom was 'respectable' and free of many vices, it was like a certain medical case: the fever has entirely vanished—but the patient is dead.[151]

On May 24, 1855, six months before he died, S.K. issued the first copy of an occasional pamphlet, *The Instant*, which was an expanded continuation of the articles in *The Fatherland*.* In *The Instant* he could speak to the very moment, could write at much greater length than in the newspaper, and could develop broader themes. Each issue of the pamphlet contained several little articles. The copy of the tenth issue was ready for printing at the time of S.K.'s final illness. During its brief existence *The Instant* gained a wide circulation and had a profound effect.

There are two illusions which are endlessly under attack in *The Instant*: the first, that all people in Denmark, regardless of what they believe or do, are Christians because they have had a drop of water on their heads and live in a 'Christian' land; the second, that the state can 'establish' Christianity and assist it. The corrective for the first illusion is to make men recognize and honestly admit what 'being a Christian' means. The corrective for the second is to get the state to dis-establish the church, on the realization that while furnishing water, roads and bridges may be a proper function for a state, furnishing eternal life is not. Yet, says S.K., it is not the King who is a fool. Rather, the clergy have made a fool of him, for the sake of the fat 'livings', honour, and official status they get from the state church. Privately, S.K. recognized a one-sidedness and distortion in these charges, but he insisted that this was necessary to accomplish a correction. (P. 90)

It must have been obvious to Kierkegaard that a 'free church' could be as subject to worldliness, concern for numbers, and fat salaries as a state church. His underlying concern was with any adulteration of Christianity, any accommodation of it to the culture in which it existed, and in Denmark this happened to mean the established Lutheran church. Here he addressed himself specifically to the monstrous notion that by just being a citizen one was already taken care of spiritually. Indeed, he said ironically that the question might be raised whether in such a Christian land

* The title of the pamphlet is taken from a concept developed earlier, as in *Dread*, viz. that the leap of faith occurs in an *instant*. The instant is not a mere passing moment but a moment which is given identity by being transfused with the eternal. In the instant when forgiveness is accepted the flow of temporal duration is broken by the introduction of an absolute quality, the miracle of God's fellowship, which is given ni spite of sin. 'Such a moment ought to have a distinctive name; let us call it the *Fullness of Time*.' (*Fragments*, p. 22.)

'among the domestic animals, the nobler ones, the horse, the dog, the cow' may not be a little bit Christian. (P. 105) In contrast to such a church, how unsuccessful Jesus appears to have been! God did assure himself that at least One—the Teacher—would become Christian, yet it almost seemed that the whole project would end with the Teacher, since he was put to death. Still, he managed to win eleven (for a while it seemed twelve). Then matters improved. One apostle, perhaps 'a little too hasty in the direction of extension', won 3,000 genuine (?) disciples in an hour. (P. 160) In the modern world, better still, men do not even need to be won; they are *born* into Christendom. Yet may it not be possible that God is 'too great a connoisseur of love' to want to be attached to unconcerned battalions or nations rather than to be loved by individuals? (P. 167)

In this flow of sarcasm S.K. was not inclined to interject practical suggestions, but only to wound the conscience. However, he did acknowledge that the dis-establishment of the church could not be accomplished in a day. The state should continue its support of pastors to whom it was committed, but after a designated year it should make no more appointments. In the meantime, all should acknowledge that inasmuch as Christianity is not of this world, it is mockery to make it 'official', and that to do so seduces ministers into false motives. To illustrate, S.K. satirizes an imaginary theological student, Frederick, who develops doubts about Christianity. Quite disturbed at the prospect of losing the comforts and honours of the parsonage, Juliana, his sweetheart, persuades him: 'Sweet Frederick, only let us manage to come together, Why go and torment thyself with such thoughts? There are surely 1000 priests like thee.' And so he is seduced. He preaches against vain honours and 'is tickled to death when he himself is decorated with...the Cross. The Cross!' (Pp. 145, 165) When a still more fat church is offered him he nearly faints in anguish in accepting it, doing so, of course, only from a sense of *duty*. (P. 176)

As Kierkegaard sees it, the identification of Christianity with culture is the background for a Frederick's hypocrisy. If Christianity is an epoch in world history, as Hegel thought, then it requires no absolute commitment since its validity is confined to the epoch. Moreover, even if literally everyone of the epoch were a Christian it would be equally true that literally no one would be a Christian in some ensuing era. Any Frederick need have little concern except for the practicalities of the moment.

The people of the parish are also infected by worldliness. Worldliness and piety, gospel and poetry, time and eternity are all evilly blended. The way of the cross is treated with poetic licence and becomes 'a lovely idyl, with procreating of children and waltzes, where everything is "so joyful"'. (P. 158) In all history, says Kierkegaard, there is no analogy to this, a religion destroying itself by flourishing.

The Catholic scholar Louis Dupré objects that this impetuous attack on Christendom leads to an unintended attack on Christianity itself. 'From his own principles it will appear that no form of established Christianity will ever find favour in his eyes, and therefore, it is after all Christianity itself that he attacks in the name of Christianity.'[152] However, S.K. would challenge Dupré's underlying assumption that Christianity cannot exist except in some 'established' form. He believed that although the Christian life can work through any form, yet that it is not dependent on such, and some forms are positively harmful. From his standpoint he is not attacking Christianity, but rather, its secular facsimile, 'Christendom'. In spite of the deliberate vagueness it is clear that S.K. expected the external church, in one form or another, properly to continue, with congregations, pastors, preaching and sacraments—perhaps even in the form of a state church. But it must not identify itself as the Kingdom of God which is the invisible church. Thus the sacraments do not belong to the organized church even though the organized church will perhaps normally administer them (note S.K.'s desire on his deathbed to receive the Lord's Supper from a layman). Further, while external 'congregations' are needed, they are 'an impatient anticipation of eternity', a mere church militant as contrasted with heaven's fellowship of peace and love.[153]

There is special reason for carefully reflecting on the true impact and message of the *Instant* because its extreme positions have raised grave doubts and have stirred much controversy. Often the painful thrusts may be somewhat discounted as ironic. An example is the description of the church as a big fish net set up for catching human herring, an efficient application of Jesus' promise, 'I will make you fishers of men'. (P. 203) Still more cutting instances of irony may be cited. 'In the magnificent cathedral the Honourable and Right Reverend Geheime-General-Ober-Hof-Prädikant, the elect favourite of the fashionable world, appears before an elect company and preaches *with emotion* upon the text he himself elected: "God hath elected the base things of the world, and the things that are despised"—and nobody laughs.' (P. 181) Again: 'It is related of a Swedish priest that, profoundly disturbed by the sight of the effect his address produced upon the auditors, who were dissolved in tears, he said soothingly, "Children, do not weep; the whole thing might be a lie".' (P. 181)

Nevertheless, not all is exaggeration and sarcasm; plainly Kierkegaard is in bitterness. Whatever justification he may have, he seems here to be in danger of neglecting his own thesis that the Christ-Pattern of sacrifice is not a pattern to be simply and literally emulated, being a *paradox*, a strangeness in the world. He is in danger of making the paradox a simple transvaluation of values, whereby the created order is renounced and replaced in the interest of other-worldliness.

The very language at times becomes slanderous, even repetitiously so. Yet there is some justification, or at least an explanation. S.K., to use his own illustration, is like a man who has discovered a house on fire and screams 'Fire!' at the top of his lungs. No one pays the slightest attention, and so he keeps on screaming 'Fire'. He claims, in fact, to be the Fire Chief. Indeed, the people of the neighbourhood have noticed that there is a fire, only a *little* fire, and so they run with pitchers and basins of water to save the place. 'But what says the Fire Chief? The Fire Chief, he says—yes, generally the Fire Chief is a very pleasant and polite man; but at a fire he is what one calls coarse-mouthed—he says, or rather he bawls, "Oh, go to hell with all your pitchers and squirts".' (P. 193) The blazing sins of Christendom call for more furious fire-fighting. It ought to be noted that of the many personalities which are Søren Kierkegaard, neither this strident voice nor the satirical tones of the aesthetic writings is truest. S.K.'s truly gentle soul—gentle with people but not with falsehood—shines forth best in the beautiful discourses.

At times the argument of the *Instant* seems fanatical and almost nihilistic. Whereas Jesus honoured a wedding by his presence, and even—to the chagrin of many—changed water into wine for the feasting, Kierkegaard here goes so far as to argue that it 'is egoism in the highest degree that because a man and a woman cannot control their lust another being must therefore sigh, perhaps for seventy years, in this prisonhouse and vale of tears, and perhaps be lost eternally'. (P. 223) Christianity, it now seems, should be all renunciation, with an end to the begetting of potentially lost souls. Infant baptism (apparently not really rejected), confirmation, the wedding, and Christian 'education' all fall under the same tirade. Infant baptism, for example, is criticized because of the impression it leaves that ready-made Christians can be produced by it.[154] People have so misconstrued the sacraments as to believe that simply by the perfunctory use of them, as objective devices, one becomes Christian.[155]

In his later works Kierkegaard progressively tended to view the religious life as a battle against sensuousness and in particular against sexuality. This contradicts much of his own thought (as his glorification of motherhood and of marriage as godly duty, and even more his view that renunciation is only ethical whereas by means of religious faith one is able to recover that which has been renounced—cf. treatment of *Fear and Trembling*). It must never be forgotten that S.K. not only insisted that man is a synthesis of earthly and eternal but further that he protested as vehemently over the neglect of the earthly as of the eternal (cf. Introduction, above, p. 32). Whatever view one takes of this later development, it should at least be understood that S.K.'s challenge is not superficial or a merely negative asceticism. Even here he is not so much objecting to the sensuous life or to sexuality as to the widespread unconcern about eternal life. Judging from common behaviour, it seems that so long as men can satisfy their passions they have little thought of eternal life. Kierkegaard charges, as many a pagan would agree, that reproduction functions as a kind of 'biological immortality', a tenaciously sought substitute for eternal life.[156] This, he says, is particularly evident in Judaism where the emphasis is on the growth of Israel rather than on the eternal life of the person.[157]

What particularly outrages Kierkegaard is that avowed Christians themselves now hold eternal life so lightly. It had been his position that while it is perfectly appropriate to wish for aesthetic satisfactions, 'eternal happiness' is not one of these goodies, 'included among other bon-bons'. Pleasures are unequally distributed but eternal happiness, because it is spiritually essential, is available to all. In ordinary living the human spirit is in a state of dispersion, scattered among the things with which it identifies itself. It needs to 'collect itself' to begin to sense its eternal validity, and to move out of irresponsibility to constancy.[158] Once men understood all this and viewed eternal life as the goal towards which all their serious strivings should be directed. They understood that one could not gain immortality by virtue of others having done so, there being no immortality 'in the third person'.[159] Now, ironically, it appears to be much easier to produce immortal souls and eternal blessedness. 'Now, if males and females merely copulate—there immediately results an immortal creature, and with a drop of water on the head—A Christian, with the expectation of eternal blessedness.'[160] As a violent protest against worldliness, S.K.'s words are a stern and legitimate reminder of the New Testament's injunction to seek first the Kingdom of God. On the other hand, if the Christian attempts to develop S.K.'s requirement (to 'die to the world' in order to gain the eternal) into a consistent doctrine, he must beware of the peril of repudiating the legitimacy of creation itself. This tendency, manifest in S.K.'s later work, nevertheless conflicts with much of his own thought, as when he expresses the very hope which he questions, viz. that *all* will be saved, and not merely the ascetics and martyrs.[161]

The emphasis on suffering here takes on a new and discordant tone. In his earlier writings Kierkegaard had held that suffering is a mark of Christian life, in spite of the fact that God is gentle and loving, on the ground that the believer is called to live in the world but not of the world.[162] Suffering was then viewed as evil though God's grace could use and redeem it. Therefore it had seemed a daring presumption to wish to suffer for the good. In *The Instant* S.K. seems no longer troubled about such presumption. In effect, overwhelmed by the sin of gluttony, he is prone to stop eating and to abhor the pleasant taste of food. S.K.'s courageous echo of the New Testament in condemning the worship of mammon is surely in danger of falling into self-righteousness.

THE CHRISTIAN WRITINGS

Many other changes appear in these last writings. Whereas earlier S.K. indicated that the established church could make itself legitimate *if* it confessed that it did not measure up to New Testament Christianity, here (fifth issue of the *Instant*) he seems to insist that there can be only one kind of Christianity, the radically ascetic, celibate, other-worldly and individualistic following of Christ. His much debated view of marriage is also focal. In all the last writings there is much negativism expressed towards it. S.K. states that whereas he once thought of marriage as the normal rule and his own singleness as a permitted exception he has now come to regard celibacy as the normal Christian rule to which marriage is a permitted exception. Sinners are tricked by the very nobility of marital love into a subtle egoism.[163] Family life threatens the concern for the eternal by its focus on the immortality of the race,[164] and at that of a 'sinful species'.[165] Procreation is 'the fall' whereby one is born in the prison of this world.[166] Moreover, while atonement overcomes the parents' guilt in procreation, it also calls for celibacy on the part of the child.[167] Lovers should be first admonished by the church that 'the solitary life pleases God more', even though it is better to marry than to sin, aflame with passion.[168]

Geismar suggests that Kierkegaard's attack on marriage, procreation, earning a livelihood, etc., are related to his inherent idealism, whereby (in his aesthetic writings) he idealized love rather than sex or marriage, and glorified inwardness rather than the practicalities of the temporal world.[169] If this be so, which is quite uncertain, then it follows that in the fury of his attack on hypocrisy, S.K. failed to separate the aesthetic idealism with its abstract dreams and asceticism from Christianity with its forgiveness and its redemption of the whole life of man.

Contrary to all such interpretation, and the apparent and literal meaning of many of S.K.'s later statements on the perils of marriage, there is considerable evidence for concluding that S.K. never literally opposed marriage but rather its abuse by the sinner. He acknowledged that it was his 'wretchedness' which prevented his own marriage, but trusted that his atypical existence gave him the opportunity to praise the unmarried state as a standpoint from which to reflect on the meaning of Christianity and its severe demands.[170] To the end Kierkegaard continued to think of himself as one of those rare individuals who, solitary and without comfort of wife or child, are called on to take a historic lead into new paths of the spirit, able by virtue of strangeness to throw a unique light on the different but related duties and problems of all men.[171] Thus as a celibate critic Kierkegaard is able to point out how the very beauty of familial devotion, the very nobility of patriotism, and the very God-given glory of the moral life threaten to lead men into self-righteous hypocrisy, making them fail to recognize the deep despair which infects the moral consciousness.

To the authors, the only legitimate interpretation of Kierkegaard is one which at least recognizes that the man who praised asceticism and uttered the cry of 'Back to the cloister', also glorified such things as family life and an outing in the park *as religious duties*, to be *really enjoyed*. In fact, the Christian dare *not* 'choose the way to the cloister'; the monk sinfully rejects humanness as God created it.[172] The crucial need is to make people face the issue of how they stand with God—which in every way they seek to avoid—and if they will do this then they can joyously continue with work, happy family life, and companionship. The difficulty is that pseudo-Christians try to place the world on the throne of God.[173]

The violence of Kierkegaard's attack on Christendom is then probably not an abandonment of an earlier position. It rather represents a practical realization that whereas monastic and ascetic individualism was the peril of medieval Christianity, the present danger is the obliteration of personal Christianity in worldly social life. Therefore S.K. emphasizes that, although the individual is a reproductive means for the race and a contributor to society, the individual is basically an end in himself. In speaking as a corrective to his own age S.K. makes his primary concern the eternal destiny of the self, even to the extent that this concern might impair or nullify the individual's function in the temporal order. This position is not a manifestation of a selfish concern of the individual for his own eternal welfare at the expense of the rest of society. As pointed out repeatedly elsewhere, a true individual is naturally and joyfully socially responsible. Yet there are times when one must ask of himself whether he will first and foremost strive to be an authentic self, fundamentally responsible to the eternal, or whether he will let himself be trapped in a worldly order.

THE CHRISTIAN WRITINGS

On October 2, 1855, Kierkegaard fell paralysed on the street, and was taken to the hospital where he died six weeks later, his funds largely exhausted. He had never been anxious about money, nor miserly. He lived well, 'shared quietly with many a needy person', and slowly used up his fortune.[174] On his desk, at the time of his final illness, was found the complete text of the tenth issue of *The Instant*. S.K. failed to have it printed, or perhaps chose not to do so. Certainly this was not due to a change of heart, for while he acknowledged that he had written with exaggeration, he insisted that this could not be avoided. He would not retract. He died with a sense of spiritual peace and with some feeling of mission accomplished. Possibly he had sensed his approaching death for some time, for he had seemed to write as a dying man.

Friedrich Nietzsche has suggested that a man ought to die at the right time. It almost seems that Kierkegaard did just this. Presumably everything which he had to say had been said.* Certainly, Kierkegaard himself thought he was dying at the right time. He made it clear to his physician that he felt that he had expressed himself fully in the religious struggle; any continuation would become enfeebled. On the other hand, his death, while something less than that of a martyr, would place a final seal upon his work and bring it a measure of victory.[175] His feeling had been that Providence had put him in the world to serve for a few years and was now taking him back. 'That is always the life and fate of the extraordinary messenger.'[176] He also stressed the point that he was 'the exception', unable to marry or to serve as a pastor because of his 'thorn in the flesh'. Although in the last weeks his legs seemed paralysed, he appeared fresh and confident, yet humble. He hoped soon to sing with the angels, 'Alleluia, alleluia, alleluia'.[177] Thus he made it clear that while it was incumbent on every person to be an authentic individual, steering a perilous middle course between self-indulgence and self-sacrifice, he felt

---

* Marie M. Thulstrup disagrees, holding that S.K.'s death was premature. She thinks he would soon have explicitly taken the next step of demanding that Christians renounce the world, avoiding marriage, possession of property, etc. (Marie M. Thulstrup, *op. cit.*, p. 279.) If this highly debatable inference is correct, then S.K. could no longer have said that his position was a deliberately unbalanced 'corrective'. He would have had to say the extreme 'imitation' of Christ is the only legitimate Christian life. Even granting a growing fanaticism, this is unlikely.

that he was called on to be not only an individual but an exception, whose exceptionality would serve as a unique warning to others, even though not constituting a model for them.

Even from the practical standpoint, S.K.'s death seems timely, for his funds were now largely exhausted. More notable however, he was becoming famous and even popular, and how ironical it would have been for one to become honoured and popular by seeking to suffer for the truth! No. 10 of *The Instant* seems to be a fitting last word. There are three thoughts in it which are especially memorable.

First, when is 'the Instant' which has been brought into focus? When does temporally distracted man encounter eternity? Regarding this, all men are prone to procrastinate and deceive themselves, wanting to think that they can hardly be held responsible in relation to the eternal. Worldly shrewdness wants to blame human failings on unfavourable circumstances. In truth, however, the Instant is that moment which does not depend on circumstances but on faith. Any instant can become *the* Instant, if a man willingly ventures into it. Then the instant becomes 'the woof' of eternity which is woven into the warp of his life.

Second, what was Kierkegaard's own religious task? He replies that in the entire history of Christendom there is nothing corresponding to him. 'The only analogy I have before me is Socrates. My task is a Socratic task, to revise the definition of what it is to be a Christian.' (P. 283) As Socrates did not claim to be wise but only demonstrated that those who claimed to be such were even less entitled to the designation than he, so S.K. does not claim to be a true Christian but reveals that those who accept the name lightly have falsified it.

Third, in impressive but pathetic simplicity, S.K. here again addressed himself to the 'plain man', assuring him that while the requirements of Christianity are very high they are no more difficult for the plain man than for the intellectual. 'Thou plain man! I have not separated my life from thine; thou knowest it, I have lived in the street...; moreover I have not attained to any importance, do not belong to any class egoism, so if I belong anywhere, I must belong to thee, thou plain man...' (P. 287) This is a dramatic negative instance of what Marjorie Grene dares to refer to as Kierkegaard's 'anti-social temper'.[178] Hans

THE CHRISTIAN WRITINGS

Brøchner, who sharply disagreed with S.K. on many points, nevertheless observed that in the tragic conflict with the church S.K. 'maintained his loving sympathy for others..., his gentleness and friendliness, even his sense of fun; maintained his equanimity and clarity of thought; above all, maintained, through faith, a peacefulness and repose which did not desert him, even in the terrible sufferings of his deathbed'.[179] It is true that during his final illness S.K. would not see his brother lest their religious differences re-emerge. He did, however, with deep feeling, greet his brother by means of a brother-in-law.[180]

Finally, in a strange manner, Kierkegaard had the last word; at least, his own words were the last words at his burial. In spite of all that he had said against it, the official church buried him, from the cathedral. His brother, who neither understood him very well nor had much sympathy for him, preached a sermon which succeeded in preventing S.K.'s youthful disciples from rioting. However, at the grave, his nephew Henrik Lund, a young physician who had helped care for him in his last illness, boldly broke into the service in order to shame the official church for claiming a man in death who had rejected it in life. He read from *The Instant*, heaping insults on the church. To this, one wonders, if S.K. himself, like his hero Socrates, might not have replied that a man ought to be allowed to die in peace.

Shortly afterwards Lund published a sequel to *The Instant*, 'The Next Instant; What Now?' but it was of no consequence. Terribly disturbed, he tried to commit suicide but eventually recovered his equanimity.[181] There was a profound and widespread soul-searching which followed S.K.'s death. Even the clergy whom he so violently attacked and who in turn attacked him were inclined to acknowledge a great debt to him for his conscience-stirring writings.[182]

50. WHAT CHRIST'S JUDGMENT IS ABOUT OFFICIAL CHRISTIANITY

What Christ's Judgment is About Official Christianity. By S. Kierkegaard. June 16, 1855. This small tract, related to *The Instant*, appears in *Attack Upon 'Christendom'*.

Kierkegaard here reminds the reader how he came to pronounce judgment on Christendom. At the outset he was on the best terms with the 'perjured' churchmen who refused to take Christianity seriously. Although as a poet he began to draw forth ideals out of the sodden mass of pleasure-seeking and confusion, the religious functionaries did not even suspect at that time that they were under attack for converting Christianity from earnestness to pretty sentiment and fantasy.

'Then this poet suddenly transformed himself, threw away the guitar..., [and] brought out a book which is called *The New Testament of our Lord*...' (P. 118) Embarrassed by the severity of the New Testament, to which they were supposedly committed, the churchmen fell into strange silence. In this situation S.K. claims it is important to hear, not the judgment of the poet, but Christ's own judgment on official Christianity: 'Woe unto you... hypocrites!' What Christ wants is a *follower*, but men do not want to follow into suffering, so they refuse to follow. They only play at and talk Christianity.

At this point the logic of the 'imitation of Christ' is given a literal and unparadoxical interpretation, and is carried to the extreme. In contrast to his earlier views, S.K. here describes Christianity as requiring renunciation of the world. He does not mean that the world as world is evil, but that in actual fact earthly life is sinful. It is therefore unavoidable that the true witness for Christ will suffer in the world. If there is joy in such suffering, it is not because suffering is joyous, but because godliness is always such, even when it ends in persecution.

S.K. notes that evil is lodged within the self as well as in the world. Accordingly, spirit must rebel against the egoistic and animalistic impulses, including sex and its fulfilment in marriage. Whereas Judaism was concerned with multiplying and with earthly happiness, Christianity, it is claimed, seeks the end of reproduction and the replacing of earthly by heavenly happiness. Earlier, S.K. had viewed marriage as a holy duty, and had thought of it properly as a stewardship. In his later thinking world renunciation leads him to charge that the church has becomed a refined Judaism, having an earthly rather than a spiritual orientation.[183] To see how great is the shift in emphasis, one might compare S.K.'s attack on mysticism in *Either/Or*. There he objected that for the mystic the whole world is 'dead', in that the mystic neglects personal virtues and 'disdains the reality of existence' in the world where God has placed him. To thus renounce the world was claimed to be disobedience to God, and the only purposeful prayer is one which is grounded in earthly duties.[184]

The defence of the severely ascetic life in the present work is not necessarily in contradiction with S.K.'s earlier view, but the emphasis is totally different. Even here the ascetic way is presumably *not* intended to be definitive of Christian life, but rather a lofty ideal, not generally attainable, but having the benefit of clarifying for everyone the nature of spirituality. This severe form of the religious life is depicted as properly available only to men. It 'is not really for children' even though Christ objected to the disciples turning children away, and commanded the disciple (who is *not* a child) to become like a child.[185] What is more, woman lacks the hardness and strength which are required to endure the severity of Christianity. It is 'sheer nonsense' that children should be Christians; they must wait until maturity, whereas woman 'participates in religion in a secondary way, through the man'.[186] In 'the scale of directness' woman is superior in 'fineness, depth and inwardness' but is deficient in the dialectic which Christianity always involves.[187] In another journal entry S.K. goes farther in recognizing woman's spirituality, stating that she is 'better suited' to religious service because it is her nature 'to give herself entirely'. 'Strong masculine intellectuality, joined to feminine submission: this gives true religiosity'.[188] From no point of interpretation can S.K. be viewed as questioning any person's access to the grace of God either because of a deficiency of dialectic, or immaturity, although for such reasons one may be incapable of 'assimilating what Christianity really is'.[189]

In spite of a fairly consistent and increasingly manifest pattern of world-renunciation, there is clear evidence that this never came to truly dominate Kierkegaard's outlook. His death-bed statement that it was only his physical infirmity which kept him from entering 'the usual relations of life', such as marriage, makes it clear that the other-worldly expressions must be cautiously evaluated. To the end, S.K. 'loved the universal' or natural order of life, even though bitterly assailing its distortion by sin.[190] Far from thinking that all men should follow him in a life of sacrifice, suffering, loneliness and semi-renunciation, Kierkegaard repeatedly stressed the point that he was a strange exception who might be erased by God as an unsuccessful experiment, one of those two or three persons in any generation who are doomed to suffer in order that others might profit by it, a concept already intimated in his definition of a poet in *Either/Or*.[191]

51. THE UNCHANGEABLENESS OF GOD

> *The Unchangeableness of God*. A Discourse. By S. Kierkegaard. August 1, 1855. Translated by Walter Lowrie and included in *For Self-Examination*; reprinted in *Edifying Discourses, A Selection*, edited by Paul L. Holmer, New York: Harper & Brothers, 1958, Harper TB 32. Page reference is to *For Self-Examination*.

This sermon is quite important as a reminder that even in his fierce 'attack on Christendom', Kierkegaard's sole purpose was to give Christian edification. The sermon was preached by him in the midst of his conflict with the church, on May 18, 1851. Its text is James 1:17, 'Every good gift and every perfect gift is from above, coming down from the Father of Lights, with whom can be no variation, neither shadow that is cast by turning.'

The discourse warns that there is sheer fear and trembling for frivolous men in the thought of God's unchangeableness. How frightening that the silent, changeless God cannot even be moved into striking back at those who mock him! If one screams at God in challenge or derision he hears nothing in reply but the echoes of his own blasphemous voice. Of the unmoved God S.K. comments: 'He gives men time, and He can afford to give them time, since He has eternity...' (Pp. 233 f.)

However, when a man has wearied of earthly mutability and is willing to be disciplined by God's unchangeable will, then such horror is replaced by joy. When man himself is willing to renounce inconstancy and caprice, then he can find peace and repose in a God who is dependably and steadfastly the same. This duality of a God who is immovably stern yet unchangeably gracious reflects the sin-grace duality of S.K.'s attack on the church, which recognized divine forgiveness and compassion but only after the sinner came to penitence. In this regard this sermon loses some of the gentleness of earlier discourses.

Imagine some distraught person confiding a folly to a wise friend, and his subsequent alarmed realization that the friend has not forgotten it even though it has become vague in his own recollection. How ironical that perhaps the wise friend recalls the other's folly even when the guilty person has managed to forget it! To such a fool the eyes of others seem to say, 'I know something about you'. In this way the human heart is a graveyard in which are buried, as men carelessly but truly say, 'God knows what'. In eternity one must give an accounting for all his buried secrets because nothing which he does will ever be anything but veritably his own deed (cf. Josiah Royce's similar treatment of the eternity of the deed). Furthermore, one's accounting will not need to be dug out of musty account books, for 'the account is every moment complete' in the memory of the unchangeable God.

Even though the unchangeableness of God properly evokes fear at the prospect of facing the awesome truth, there is still more of rest and happiness in God's fixity *if* one will let himself be disciplined by it so as to renounce caprice and inconstancy. Then the balm of God is like the coolness of a desert spring, but with the wonderful difference that it may be found everywhere. Indeed, it need not be searched for because it seeks out the thirsty soul with its unfailing gifts.

Finally, it should be observed that in this discourse S.K. has in mind eternality as spiritual steadfastness or constancy in God, not the manner in which the Eternal acts *in time*. The latter he treats elsewhere in some interesting but vague hints of ontological views which are reflected in the sermon only in the notion of *constancy* as a quality of the eternal. God is also defined as 'pure subjectivity' and is therefore said to have pure freedom (the quality of subjectivity) for actualizing the good in which he unchangingly remains. There is no shadow of darkness nor of deforming externality which can change this.

CHAPTER IV

MISCELLANEOUS WRITINGS

In addition to the many books which Kierkegaard published, he also wrote about an equal amount of material which he failed to publish, but which eventually, after his death, did appear in the many volumes of *Papers*; or (as in the case of *The Point of View*) were published separately. Some of the incomplete works which appear only in the Papers, such as *On Authority and Revelation* and *Johannes Climacus* have already been reviewed.

The most important element of the Papers is the relatively autobiographical material of the *Journals*, and while these have been extensively referred to they require special comment.

One other item of miscellany consists of newspaper articles (other than those already treated (units 31, 47)), important because they pertain to the authorship.

Finally, there are reviewed here two collections of materials from S.K.'s writings—the one of brief meditations, and the other of prayers. Although these are not independent works, they merit attention because much of the material assembled in them is from the untranslated *Papers* and therefore is not elsewhere available in English.

52. JOURNALS

Three works in English contain extensive selections from the voluminous journals:

The Journals of Søren Kierkegaard. A Selection edited and translated by Alexander Dru. New York: Oxford University Press, 1938. A small selection from this is *The*

Journals of Kierkegaard, which includes a new introduction by Dru. New York: Harper & Brothers, Torchbook TB 52.

Søren Kierkegaard, *The Last Years*; Journals 1853-1855. Edited and translated by Ronald Gregor Smith. New York: Harper & Row, 1965. Almost none of this material is in Dru's large selection, chiefly because Dru's translation was made before the last volume of the Danish *Papirer* was published.

The Diary of Søren Kierkegaard. Edited by Peter P. Rohda and translated by Gerda M. Anderson. New York: Philosophical Library, 1960. This small selection supplements the other volumes, particularly with more biographical materials.

The Journals comprise about half of the twenty-volume set of *Søren Kierkegaard's Papirer*, the remainder being the book on Adler, note books, incomplete writings, etc. Although not all of the Journals have been translated in the three works cited, yet nearly all of their important elements do appear in them. They offer a wealth of materials without which it would never have been possible for scholars to gain an adequate understanding of Kierkegaard. Even for the casual reader the Journals are a revealing, moving and provocative work which in one sense can be compared to the *Confessions* of Saint Augustine and in another sense to the proverbs of Nietzsche.

The Journals do not constitute a true diary although they do include important biographical elements. For the most part, they consist of penetrating observations, judgments on the controversial issues with which S.K. was involved, disclosures of personal and literary plans, and important explanations of his views and purposes which help to break through both the mystery and the mystification surrounding the author. Frequently highly confidential, the entries are written in great and at times painful candour. However, the author himself thought that they might be published after his death and proposed a title for them, 'The Book of the Judge'. There is a rather sharp division between the early section (1834-46) which is more exploratory, and the later section which may be viewed as the basic journal (1846-55).

The journals of the very last years (1853-55) offer insight into the 'attack on Christendom', and serve as a passionate commentary on the controversy with the church. The issues here are much deeper than at first they appear to be. S.K. is not chiefly concerned with the worldliness of Danish Lutheranism nor the hypocrisy of Roman Catholicism, nor even with the faults of any or all of organized Christendom. Instead he is attacking that spiritual evasiveness which seeks to substitute some external crutch for an inward life of faith. The issue is between Christianity and Christendom.

The little so-called *Diary* (ed. P. P. Rohde) in which certain selections appear is obviously no diary. However, it does serve something of the function of a diary, allowing the personality and character of Kierkegaard to shine through in relation to his loved ones, associates, and antagonists. It illuminates his authorship and purposes, his judgments upon the culture, mentality and philosophy of his age, and once again reflects his understanding of Christianity and his dedication to its cause.

The extended materials of the Journals, rich in reflection, cannot well be characterized here, and, in fact, have been frequently referred to in connection with related thoughts in the published works, particularly in the appendix to the treatment of the *Gospel of Suffering*. However, to suggest the style and content, a few items are here reproduced or reviewed. The first two listed here indicate the common aphoristic form.

'I too have fused tragedy and comedy: I make jokes, people laugh—I weep.' (151)

'The early Christian dogmatic terminology is like a magic castle where the most beautiful princes and princesses lie in deep sleep—it only needs to be awakened in order to appear in all its glory.' (127)

Almost every facet of S.K.'s personality and thought finds expression in the Journals. For example, his familiar blend of pathos and the aesthetic is manifest, as in this earnest utterance: 'Whilst . . . the birds sang their evening prayer—the few that are dear to me came forth from their graves, or rather it seemed... they had not died.' (20) The following topical items will suggest the scope of the contents.

Irony—Guilt: 'A man walked along contemplating suicide; at that very moment a slate fell and killed him, and he died with the words: God be praised.' (52)

Irony—Speech: 'By means of speech every man participates in what is most exalted—but by means of speech to participate in what is most exalted, in the sense of chattering about it, is as ironical as being a spectator from the gallery of the king's banquet.' (XI² A 356)

Existence: 'It is perfectly true, as philosophers say, that life must be understood backwards. But they forget the other proposition, that it must be lived forwards...Life can never really be understood in time simply because at no particular moment can I find the necessary resting-place from which to understand it—backwards.' (456)

Hegel: 'If Hegel had written the whole of his logic and then said . . . it was merely an experiment in thought . . . then he would certainly have been the greatest thinker who had ever lived. As it is, he is merely comic.' (497)

Personal: 'I was born in 1813 [a year of financial panic], in that mad year when so many other mad bank-notes were put into circulation...' (477)

Prayer: '...The true relation... is not when God hears what is prayed for, but when *the person praying* continues to pray until he is *the one who hears*, who hears what God wills.' (572)

To love God: 'What Alcibiades said of Socrates, that in the end from being a lover he became the beloved, also expresses God's relation to a man: in the end God becomes the beloved.' (XI¹ A 356)

Freedom: 'The most tremendous thing which has been granted to man is: the choice, freedom. And if you desire it and preserve it there is only one way: in the very same second unconditionally and in complete resignation to give it back to God, and yourself with it.' (1051)

Philosophy: 'It is a positive starting point for philosophy when Aristotle says that philosophy begins with wonder, not as in our day with doubt.' (355)

Entrance and exit of life: 'Listen to the cry of woman giving birth—look upon the death struggle at its height: and then say whether what begins and ends thus can be intended to be pleasure. True enough, we men do everything we can in order to escape as quickly as possible from those two points, we forget the pangs of birth as quickly as we can and turn it into a pleasure to have given life to a being. And when someone is dead he is immediately described as having passed away peacefully, death is sleep—all of which we say . . . so as not to lose our *joie de vivre*...' (1390)

Father: When his father died, S.K. recorded in his Journal that he had found God to be his Father and his beloved earthly father to be his stepfather. (*Diary*, p. 33 f.)

Angels: St Stephan died as a martyr and his face was like that of an angel. But are there any angels? S.K. gives this harsh but characteristic existential reply: 'Nonsense, rubbish, shut up—just you see to it that *you* become like *Stephanus*, that your face resembles that of an angel; in that way the rest of us will get to see an angel!' (*Diary*, p. 162)

Following Christ: A bitter parable is told about Christian geese who waddled to their church every Sunday. When the old gander preached about their noble destiny, being winged creatures by the gift of God (here the lady geese would curtsey and the ganders bow), they would feel quite noble. But instead of using their wings for flying through the heavens in beauty and with purpose they continued to waddle and put on yellow fat. Man too has wings, but like the geese he listens to sermons which call for the high flight of the soul and then returns to his waddling, becoming quite 'successful' in the world. (XI^2 A 210)

S.K.'s Death: 'What Denmark needs is a dead man. At the very instant I shall be victorious as rarely any other human being has been. In that very second all about my spindly legs and my trousers and the nickname "Søren" will be forgotten—no, not forgotten, but interpreted differently, and it will give vast impetus to the cause.' (*Diary*, p. 119) To the reviewers this judgment appears generally accurate. S.K.'s sufferings and strangeness have tended to lend nobility to his image, and, as he trusted, also to his cause.

Historic Christendom: 'In Christ God offered to enter into relation with the human race. . . . Instead of entering into relation with God they transformed it into the *history* of how God in Christ entered into relation with the apostles...' (XI^1 A 388)

Christianity: 'Christianity is the good news which turns this earthly existence into the greatest misery, and then into the most anxious effort, in fear and trembling—and in this way Christianity is the good news about eternity.' (XI¹ A 363)

53. NEWSPAPER ARTICLES PERTAINING TO THE AUTHORSHIP

> Newspaper Articles Pertaining to the Authorship. Published in *The Fatherland* and reprinted in Vol. 18 of *Samlede Vaerker*. Not translated except in fragments. The authors are indebted to Dr Ernest Nielsen for assistance by way of translation.

Kierkegaard wrote a number of newspaper articles in addition to those of *The Crisis* and those of the 1854–55 attack on the church. A few of these, particularly numbers 6 and 8 below, are very important. Four articles were published (1835–36) in the *Copenhagen Flying Post*, expressing political conservatism. They pointed out that rule by the masses can degenerate into rule by a misguided mob, and that would-be reformers lacked both wisdom and courage. Also it was argued that institutions should be appropriate to the history and individuality of a people. An earlier article (1834) in the same paper, entitled 'Another Defender of Woman's Lofty Qualities', objected to the romantic exaltation of woman and insisted that she be honoured with an appreciation of her special function and role in society. The article was clever but was of no serious consequence.[1]

Nine articles appeared in *The Fatherland* (1842–45). They are of considerable importance in that they pertained to S.K.'s basic authorship. Briefly, their content and significance may be summarized as follows:

1. 'An Open Confession.' June 12, 1842. An ironical attack is made on Hegelianism, extending beyond this to a criticism of the age—its rival movements, factions, and parties.

2. 'Who is the Author of *Either/Or*?' February 27, 1843. Kierkegaard cleverly reviews the rival guesses about the authorship of *Either/Or*, noting that some of the suppositions are based on contents and some even on the size of the work and the cost of its publication. Among the varied guesses are: a wealthy man,

several authors collaborating, an old man, a profligate, a philosopher, a theologian. S.K. observes that most people are happy to leave the author anonymous. Then they can read without being distracted by his personality. S.K.'s purpose at the time was to mystify and intrigue—for a time, but certainly with no intent of continuing the 'polynymity' for long.[2]

3. 'Thanks to Professor Heiberg.' March 5, 1843. Kierkegaard registers a complaint about Heiberg's review of his writings, particularly with reference to his careless reading and failure to grasp the real point of *Repetition*. More broadly the article complains about the lack of discernment on the part of book reviewers generally.

4. 'A Brief Explanation.' May 16, 1843. An objection is raised against careless reviewing and a specific protest is made about someone having confusedly identified the sermon in *Either/Or* with a sermon which S.K. had preached in a class in homiletics.

5. 'A Declaration and a Slight Addition.' May 9, 1845. Here S.K. defends the anonymity of his authorship. 'If I am not the author, then the opinion (of others) is false; if on the contrary, I am the author, then I am the only one who has the right to say it.'

6. 'The Activity of an Itinerant Aesthete and how he paid for the Banquet.' December 27, 1845. This article was a reply to a criticism of 'Guilty'/'Not Guilty' in the *Stages*. P. L. Møller, the debauched but talented acquaintance who is also the model for 'seducer' of 'The Seducer's Diary', had included a criticism of S.K.'s work in an elegant volume entitled *Gaea*. Perhaps he had done this in order to even the score with S.K. The rather astonishing fact is that the rake Møller protested against Kierkegaard on moral grounds. He protested that Quidam's diary was guilty of experimenting with a person's life, dissecting the beloved alive. That Møller should praise the aesthetic element in his writing, which S.K. hoped people would transcend, and then morally protest against the morally earnest portion outraged Kierkegaard.[3] The latter's reply in this article ruined Møller's career, ending his chance of attaining a professorship by revealing that Møller was editing the slanderous *Corsair* which was feared and hated by the upper classes. S.K.'s article is in the nature of comments about a discussion of the Kierkegaard authorship at a dinner party where a Professor Hauch (a visiting writer and poet) was present along

with Møller. S.K. branded Møller's attack on him as spiteful self-defence. However, the crucial point was the disclosure of Møller's identification with the *Corsair*. In utter contempt and with a readiness to suffer a kind of martyrdom for the right, S.K. invited the *Corsair* to abuse him as it had many other prominent people. 'Would only that I might now shortly get into *The Corsair*. It is really hard on a poor author to be thus singled out in Danish literature as the only one...who is not abused there.'[4] Møller obliged him with an article, 'How the itinerant philosopher found the itinerant virtual editor of *The Corsair*'. Worse still he kept up a prolonged and cruel attack not only by word but by vicious caricatures, which played upon S.K.'s crippled body.

7. 'The Dialectical Outcome of a Literary-Political Business Concern.' January 10, 1846. In spite of intense suffering, and apart from many replies to *The Corsair* which he drafted but did not publish, this was S.K.'s single retort to the scurrilous attacks in that paper. He comments on the fact that the publisher, Goldsmith (who even gave the appearance of being his friend), had put irresponsible editors in charge of the *Corsair* in order to avoid legal responsibility in case of charges of slander against leading citizens. Not so much as an effect of this rejoinder but rather out of a growing sense of shame over the unchecked viciousness and vulgarity of the attack, Goldsmith severed his connection with the paper ten months later and for a time left Denmark. Møller likewise went to the continent and died in degradation.[5]

8. 'On the Occasion of a Statement About me by Dr Rudelbach.' January 31, 1851. S.K. expresses respect for Rudelbach, a religious leader, who, like himself, wished to reform the church. However he wants to correct Rudelbach's misunderstanding of the nature of his attack on Christendom. His aims are different than those of the divisive and sectarian Rudelbach in that his purpose is not to champion a new form of church organization as opposed to the established church. In effect, S.K. was here defending Bishop Mynster and the state church—in spite of his criticism of it—by showing that what was needed was not so much a different *external* form of Christendom but rather the re-introduction of inward Christianity into whatever form of Christendom may exist.[6] He is not seeking the 'emancipation' of Christianity and does not agree that the proper goal can be

reached by means of 'free institutions'. The reason is that it is the *solitary individual* rather than institutions of any kind with which Christianity is essentially concerned. S.K. nevertheless reiterates his protest, not clearly understood by Rudelbach, against the 'jumbling together of politics and Christianity' in the established church. 'Politics is that externalism, that tantalizing activity or business directed toward a change in the outer forms.'

9. 'A Passing Comment on a Detail in Don Juan.' May 19–20, 1845. This short essay on art criticism, an afterthought on Mozart's opera which had been impressively treated in *Either/Or*, was translated in *Crisis in the Life of an Actress*, where its content is treated (section 31).

54. MEDITATIONS FROM KIERKEGAARD

Meditations from Kierkegaard. Edited and translated by T. H. Croxall. Philadelphia: Westminster Press, 1955.

This is not a book written by Kierkegaard. It is instead a collection of scattered meditations which he wrote but left unpublished, and are therefore printed in the *Papirer* for the most part, and not elsewhere translated into English. However, in some instances the material is taken from translated books. Some of the meditations are single units, but most of them are composites of small items assembled from scattered sources. In a few cases the text has been slightly modified by the editor in order to clarify the meaning. Croxall has grouped the seventy very brief meditations under five headings: (1) For Times and Seasons, (2) The Sermon on the Mount, (3) Some Biblical Personalities, (4) Parables and Miracles, and (5) General. The little book of 165 pages is a notable contribution to devotional literature. Most of the following core ideas are from items not elsewhere translated.

Christmas. When Christ was born the angels sang for joy but mankind complained, 'Why do you do this?' Christmas is not joyous for worldlings. (P. 27)

Seriousness. With only a rumour to go by, the wise men made a long journey, but the scribes who told them where Christ should be born did not even accompany them to Bethlehem. 'Similarly a man may know the whole of Christianity and make no movement.' (P. 38)

Solitude. A man seldom achieves anything unless he has known the solitude in which one is confronted by the Absolute *and* by absolute danger. In society, by contrast, there are only relative perils but there is also 'the danger of missing the Absolute altogether'. (P. 42)

Peter. After Peter denied him, Jesus glanced at him. We may criticize Peter, but at least 'a glance was enough for him', to bring him to cleansing tears. (P. 48)

Judas. The Kingdom might so easily have been more 'of this world', and might thereby have 'succeeded'. Perhaps it was this that tempted Judas to betray, thinking to force Jesus 'to give the thing a different turn by that little push'. (P. 51)

Barabbas. This was the criminal who was chosen by the mob *to live* so that Jesus might be crucified. Did he later sense the wonder and the horror of his reprieve and become a believer? (P. 54)

Indirect Communication. There is much talk about God directly communicating. 'But really—that a person despised and cursed by all, condemned as a criminal, nailed to a cross—when he says, "Believe in me that I am God".—Good heavens! is this direct communication?' (P. 61)

'Come down from the cross.' Humanity's conclusions are topsy-turvy. 'It would conclude that he was the Son of God, if he came down from the cross.' (P. 65)

Easter. Jesus talked with the disciples on the way to Emmaus, but vanished as soon as they recognized him. The vanishing was the 'result of their recognizing him', for he cannot be known directly but only in faith. (P. 68)

Ascension. It was 'expedient' for Christ to go away. 'A disciple leads a kind of stunted existence so long as his master lives with him,' leaning too intimately upon him. (P. 70)

The Other Cheek. To turn the other cheek seems a cruel requirement. 'But can I honestly say that I wish Christianity did not demand so much...?' (P. 84)

Blessing Persecutors. If the persecuted Christian simply forgives his persecutors he is not creating a festive occasion. 'No, he must say "I bless them".' (P. 85)

'Seek first...' Usually men seek God not *first*, but last, after they have sought peace and joy every other way. (P. 87)

By Night. Because of danger Nicodemus came as a sneak by night. Christians who have no danger to excuse them are also guilty of hiddenness, refusing to confess Christ by their open deeds. (P. 104)

Isaac and Christ. 'He who spared Abraham's first-born, and only made trial of the patriarch's faith—he spared not his only begotten Son.' (P. 109)

Abraham. Let us imagine that Abraham pretended to Isaac that he meant to kill him out of idolatry, thinking it better for his son to curse him than perhaps to curse God. Faith can involve such dreadful collisions. (P. 110)

Job. The significance of Job is to show the cruelty men display by regarding misfortune as due to guilt. (P. 117)

Anointing Christ. Jesus displayed his divine dignity by making 'an insignificant event' to be eternally remembered; an unknown woman 'becomes immortal' merely because she one day anointed his head. (P. 118)

The Great Supper. A man asked to be excused because he had just married a wife. Is it not unkind of the gospel to issue its invitation at such an inconvenient moment? Yet the gospel allows no evasion; it presents an either/or. (P. 127)

Unmerciful Servant. God seems severe, treating us as we unmercifully treat our fellows. Yet God's severity is only as play, considering how great is our guilt against his holiness. (P. 130)

The Vineyard. Who are those called to work at the last moment, the eleventh hour? They are the multitudes of shipwrecked people who have stood waiting, without power to work or heart to pray, who even had lost the confidence that 'it was still possible to begin work'. (P. 131)

Lost Sheep. The lost sheep is guilty in leaving the herd. To stray in sin it 'can do something', but for its redemption 'it can do nothing'. (P. 133)

Ten Lepers. Usually the ingratitude of the lepers is stressed, overlooking the severe test they were subjected to. By acknowledging that Christ had healed them they might well have been persecuted by the priests. (P. 137)

Feeding the Thousands. The multitude did not ask food but only to be taught, but Christ who had personally known hunger gave bread as well as bread of life, not putting asunder the bodily and the spiritual which God had joined. (P. 142)

Wedding at Cana. The world pours out its best wine first, but the miracle in Christian life is that the best is reserved for last. (P. 143)

Unconditional Surrender. The fault in the man who wanted to be a disciple but only after he first went to bury his father is that he did not want to place God first. He would surrender to God *only on a condition.* (P. 155)

Venture of Faith. Every one in Christendom has enough information to act in faith, but the tendency is for a man 'to inquire, ponder, meditate, waste year after year of his life in trifles'. (P. 159)

55. THE PRAYERS OF KIERKEGAARD

The Prayers of Kierkegaard. Edited and with a New Introduction of His Life and Thought by P. D. LeFevre. Chicago: University of Chicago Press, 1956.

These prayers, never assembled by Kierkegaard, are to be found scattered throughout his writings. About half of the prayers included in this collection are not elsewhere available in English because they are taken from portions of the *Papirer* which are not included in the translations of the Journals. Somewhat arbitrarily the prayers are grouped by LeFevre under the headings of (1) Father, (2) Son, (3) Spirit, and (4) special occasions (chiefly the Lord's table).

The prayers are profoundly spiritual and remarkably beautiful. The personality of S.K. glows here with a warmth which is often lacking elsewhere, and his famed melancholy is here seen to be absorbed in joy. 'I have had more joy in the relation of obedience to God than in thoughts that I produced.... Even in prayer my *forte* is thanksgiving.' (169) The infinite transcendence of God does not make him remote and unapproachable. The gracious love of God enables lowly man to address him as a son. 'It is wonderful', writes Kierkegaard, 'how God's love overwhelms me—alas, ultimately I know of no truer prayer than what I pray over and over again, that God will allow me and not be angry with me because I continuously thank him for having done and for doing, yes, and for doing so indescribably much more than I ever expected.' (168)

Kierkegaard's view and practice of prayer resolve many a mystery. The man who addresses God as Father nevertheless remains in utter lowliness. If he 'conquers' in prayer, it is only because man's true victory consists in permitting God to conquer the human heart. To pray is not simply to ask in child-like fashion for blessings, because any and every gift from God is a blessing. Indeed, in a world of sin, those who are loved by God are called on to suffer with Christ. Yet the believer must not pray for suffering; that would be presumptuous. If then one can neither pray for happiness nor for suffering, prayer becomes instead a silent surrender, in which one turns in trust to God because he scarcely knows how to pray. (206)

Of philosophical interest is the fact that prayer was not, for S.K., a supplement to his thoughts and existence. Prayer is the epitome of existence for the reason that man gains full selfhood only in his God-relationship. Prayer is thus an ontological necessity; it furnishes the very being which in existence man seeks to possess. Paul S. Minear comments: 'A man does not exist and then become thankful. Rather, in and through his thankfulness he becomes a man. In gratitude his God-relationship gives birth to a self-awareness and a neighbour-awareness which together constitute him as a self.'[7]

Prayer establishes man's existence as *spirit*. Whereas *Sickness Unto Death* theoretically describes spirit as a tension between finite and infinite, it is prayer which enables man to properly engage or live in this relation.[8] In man's spiritual existence the finite remains finite (e.g. a cup of cold water or a loaf of bread), but this receives infinite meaning as the gift of God. There is no pantheistic or mystical blurring of God and man in the life of prayer. In fact, prayer celebrates the prior glory of incarnation and atonement by which the eternal God secured man's lowly life within his fellowship.⁹

Not all Kierkegaard scholars have arrived at precisely the same judgment on the issue of mysticism. Impressed by the 'magnificent spiritual intensity' of S.K.'s prayer life, the Catholic philosopher Regis Jolivet dared to identify him as a kind of mystic. This mysticism, he argued, is not the classical one, as in Neo-Platonism, in which the dazzling light of God is like an unutterable murk. Instead, it is marked by man's free choice of the eternal, in which faith is accompanied by inexpressible joy and at the same time by deep suffering because it rests on no certainty and acts with absolute risk.¹⁰ This characterization of the prayer life is accurate but it remains highly dubious whether it is in any way defensible to designate it as mystical.

While the prayers of Kierkegaard generally are highly expressive of his moods and point of view, the following, a prayer for the new year, may be taken as indicative of the spirit of his life and work.

> 'Another year has passed, O heavenly Father! We thank Thee that it was a time of grace, and we are not terrified by the thought that it was also a time for which we shall render an account; for we trust in Thy mercy. The new Year confronts us with its demands; and though we cannot enter upon it without humility and concern, because we cannot and will not forget the lusts of the eye that ensnared us, the sweets of revenge that seduced us, the wrath that made us irreconcilable, the coldness of heart in which we fled from Thee, yet we do not enter it altogether empty-handed. For we take with us the memory of fearful doubts which were set at rest, of anxieties which were solaced, of the downcast mind which was cheered and strengthened, of the glad hope which was not put to shame. Aye, and when in our melancholy moods we seek strength and encouragement in the thought of the great men, Thy chosen instruments, who in sharp trials and profound anxieties kept their souls free, their courage unbroken, the heavens open above them,

then we also wish to add to theirs our testimony, convinced that even if our courage is but discouragement in comparison with theirs, and our strength weakness, nevertheless, Thou art ever the same, the same mighty God who tries the spirits of men in combat, the same Father without whose knowledge no sparrow falls to the ground. Amen.' (Prayer 92, p. 113)

CHAPTER V

KIERKEGAARD AND EXISTENTIALISM

Kierkegaard is often referred to as the founder of existentialism. Actually he did not wish to father a school of thought, and he is more appropriately thought of as a Christian thinker than as an existential philosopher. Nevertheless, his relationship to existentialism is quite direct and needs characterization. Among earlier men of prominence who were greatly influenced by him were the Norwegian poet Ibsen and the Danish philosopher Høffding, and among the famous existentialists Miguel Unamuno, Karl Jaspers and Martin Heidegger.[1] At the same time as S.K.'s writings have been translated into all major languages, including Japanese, his influence on the general populace has mounted to monumental proportions.

Perhaps, most simply, existentialism may be described as an emphasis upon an attaining of the special kind of existence which human beings possess. Someone has, by contrast, paid glowing tribute to the existence of the brachiopod, rating it as one of the most successful of organisms because as a species it has survived unchanged for 500 million years. Obviously this is not the kind of success which existentialists envision. For them, if man is to succeed he must do so as an individual, not as a species. He must attain self-identity by choice rather than by some kind of stimulus-response mechanism, and such identity must be one of personal character and moral purpose rather than of natural function or external structure. As Dag Hammarskjöld phrased it, 'Only in man has the evolution of the creation reached the point where reality encounters itself in judgment and choice.'[2]

Existentialism is not, however, a single and consistent doctrine. There is a strange perversity in the history of thought whereby systems tend to change and eventually events contradict their meaning. Thus idealism began in Plato with a protest against those 'crude fellows', the materialists, who try to destroy mind, purpose, and freedom by reducing all to mechanism and matter. In time, idealism in some of its forms reverted to determinism, but within an Absolute rather than in matter. Existentialism began with Kierkegaard in the form of a Christian transcendent theism. It was later radically transformed by the prominent existentialist Heidegger, for example, who relocated transcendence *in man*. Heidegger recognized man's transcending things and even himself in some measure, but he saw no transcendence in God because by definition God could not change or *go beyond* his situation. Another existentialist, Sartre, replaced God with Nothing, and both of these secularists find the culmination of human existence not in Kierkegaard's eternal life, but in eternal death. With such perplexing disagreements to be found in existentialism, many persons sympathetic with phases of the doctrine (the same would of course apply to other schools, such as logical empiricism) are nevertheless reluctant to be identified by a name, now standing for much with which they are out of sympathy.

It may even be asked whether in principle there could be a system of thought appropriately called 'existentialism'. In a sense, perhaps, there can not. One of the cardinal tenets of existential thinkers is the impossibility of adequately characterizing human existence in any rational system, on the ground that man's life is more a matter of free volition and action than of rational pattern or intellectual comprehension. Thus Kierkegaard's famous rebellion against Hegel was not so much against Hegel *qua* Hegel but against Hegel as the systematist *par excellence*. S.K.'s point is that human existence cannot be explained by or understood in a system, and that such rational structures are therefore untrue to life. 'The case of most systematizers is as when a man builds a huge castle, and himself lives by the side of it in a hovel. They do not themselves live in that huge systematic building of theirs, but in a spiritual relationship, this is, and becomes, a decisive objection. Spiritually understood, a man's thought must be the building in which he lives—or all is mad.'[3]

Does it follow then that existentialism—Kierkegaardian or other—which so vehemently protests against system is guilty of self-contradiction by building a system around the concept of existence? Not in principle, for S.K., for example, is neither, on the one hand, essentially a system-builder, nor, on the other, does he make any objection to rational reflection. On the latter count, he sought with almost painful intensity for intellectual clarity about the nature of human existence and of Christian experience. His insistent point is that one is or ought already to be existing when he begins to rationally reflect and that existence and reflection dare not be confused with one another. What is wrong with the systematizers, from this point of view, is certainly not that they think, but that they tend to ignore features of life which reason can neither produce nor explain, e.g. faith, volition, and love. By concentrating all attention on rational understanding and accurate description, the systematizer forgets what it means to genuinely exist as a being with personal feelings and choices. The issue is not whether reason is of value, for S.K. points out that it furnishes needed ideality and system. It is rather that reason must not be thought to offer any kind of aid whatsoever at the point of one's making a leap of faith, or even an ethical commitment, such as promising to love a wife or honour an obligation. It appears clear that there can be an existential doctrine in the form of a rational and orderly characterization of existence as one finds it to be, but with the understanding that this characterization must not be used to dictate to, or deny the features of real existence (e.g. freedom). A satisfying rational comprehension of life must not be mistaken or subtly substituted for life itself. Of course, even though a doctrine of existence does not as such violate the objection to a 'system', it is obviously still possilbe that in given instances existential thinkers have violated their own principles by espousing systematic dogmas.

It is sometimes said that religion is a way of life and philosophy an attempt to understand it. From this point of view, S.K. must be thought of primarily as a religious person. He was not particularly interested in championing or proclaiming a doctrine—even one which was true to experience. He rather wished to challenge or provoke man to choose to exist at higher levels. He wanted to encourage men to exist nobly, not to understand noble existence.

A Kierkegaardian existential-*ism* will tend towards self-contradiction in so far as it becomes a theory rather than a personal persuasion. Knowing how the academic mind transforms life into systems of concepts, S.K. made scathing comments about professors. He correctly anticipated, with sorrow and resentment, that his own work would be taken over by the professors as an occasion for *reflection*, and furthermore that even his anticipation of this fact would become the occasion of a lecture. What would undoubtedly distress him above all is the way in which some of his concepts are taken out of context and transformed into intellectually curious or aesthetically interesting notions, rather than remaining the prods to choice or commitment which they were intended to be.

What then is the essence of existentialism? Because of its delicate relationship to doctrine, and because definition usually focuses on doctrine, it becomes difficult to offer a precise definition. Furthermore, largely because of its intentionally provocative goals and methods, peripheral and inconsequential features have often been given unfortunate prominence. Nevertheless, the most important features can be fairly certainly charted.

Pure existentialism can perhaps most clearly be viewed in relation to that against which it protests, i.e. the reduction of man to the status of thingness. Man has a unique kind of being (unlike that of sticks and stones, of animals, or even of God), viz. 'existence'. Thus to define man as essentially 'an animal'—even an unusually complex and rational animal—may lead one to ignore man's strivings to be an authentic self, which strivings presumably characterize no animal; and to identify him as an object in nature ignores his purposiveness and self-determination. Nevertheless, an existential thinker is perhaps even more distressed by the threat of an absolute idealism than by some naturalisms. In an idealistic system as that of Hegel, the individual person comes to be viewed as nothing but an exemplification or necessary manifestation of the Idea (the Absolute, or God). Even to concentrate on man's kinship to the divine, as do many mystics and some idealists, may be to grossly misunderstand the perilously free nature of human existence. According to existentialism, man must be viewed as a finite but self-determinative and responsible agent, not passively shaped and guided by circumstances or the transitory contents of experience. Man is responsibly (and perhaps pathetically) free even in his relationship to the whole of nature, the Absolute, or God.

What then is the kind of being which man possesses? One existential answer is that it is the sort of reality that is initiated by man's 'being there', a kind of bare being or mere being in the world. This means that the kind of being which man possesses *qua* man is no specific kind of being, no established nature, but that he experiences a confrontation by the world which leads him to choose for himself what he shall be. For simple contrast, we may think of Aristotle who held that there is a common essence, form or whatness of humanness which becomes particularized in given men. Thus the universal form 'man' is in Socrates and constitutes his essential nature. For the existentialist, on the other hand, the very being and nature of Socrates is the unique selfhood resulting from his remarkable decisions and deeds. The essence or whatness of a man is a product of his own existing. Thus for Sartre, a famous existentialist, man 'makes himself', determines his own essence, and is responsible to himself alone for the character (whatness or being) of his life.

In connection with the above, the question has been raised as to whether in radical existentialism one's choices can be said to form and flow from any established character, or whether each decision must remain not only an undetermined but also a totally unrelated and meaningless leap. If this latter interpretation were true, then the very concept of an established and dependable character and of its meaningful relation to behaviour is questioned. Personal choice or freedom would be meaningless, and that which is chosen could never be identified with or significantly related to the act of choice or the person making it. However, if such an extreme view were to be thought of as 'pure' or 'radical' existentialism (as has been suggested), it would be important to understand how totally alien it is to the outlook of Kierkegaard, the 'father' of existentialism.

To begin to state the issues of existentialism with clarity it has been useful to somewhat distort or even falsify its meaning, so far as Kierkegaard is concerned. For him not only radically free and creative choice, but also that which is chosen, is essential to existence. Further, not only existence but also essence is fundamental to men. For Kierkegaard, 'being there' or existence is always 'before God', although it is true that God's presence does not predetermine one's character and thus one's choice. What this means is that for S.K. quite as much as for Plato and Aristotle, there is a definite and proper whatness for man, an essential humanness which originates in the mind and purposes of God. However, it is also true that for Kierkegaard as for Sartre man finds himself with existence but without an *actual* given proper essence. The reason for this with Kierkegaard is not the non-existence of a proper pattern, as for Sartre, but instead the sin or rebellion by which man rejects the pattern. Yet in a strange fashion although man does not properly manifest the eternal pattern, he cannot succeed in escaping from it and breaks himself upon the eternal in his rebellion. Thus the image of God is implied by and veiled with man's very repudiation of it.

In the light of the above, it becomes clear that many of Kierkegaard's basic tenets are either abandoned or washed very thin by some subsequent existentialisms. Thus for S.K. the 'leap' whereby one gains true selfhood and by which one moves from one sphere or stage to another, and perhaps higher, level of existence is not made in a vacuum; if it were so, then the leap would be really pointless. For S.K. the leap is important because of the direction in which one leaps and moves, or may move, and ultimately this should be in the direction of the holy. Proper existence requires moving away from externality, towards subjectivity and internality, and towards a kind of selfhood which ultimately has meaning only because it is encompassed by the love of God. The contents of experience, the essence of humanness, and the authority of God are the framework within which free choices are made. What the 'leap' signifies is that no matter how important these backgound factors are, a man can still never escape the responsibility for saying 'yes' or 'no'. No one can do another's willing for him, nor another's loving. The insistent voluntarism of Kierkegaard is neither irrationalism nor non-essentialism; it is one key element in the dilemma of human freedom as it relates itself to a causal environment and to divine grace. There is no easy compromise or balance between personal or subjective freedom and external influence in any of life, but above all this is the case with divine influence. Thus for Kierkegaard man is saved without merit by the grace of God. Yet, as for Luther, if man does not himself say 'yes' to the love of God and perform the *works of love* (for a Christian cannot love with the tongue only), then he is not saved. In the thought that faith is responsible obedience to God there is expressed the thought that both free self-expression and the sovereignty of God are required. If for Sartre man 'makes' himself, for Kierkegaard man becomes or is restored to (not makes) his true self by deliberately yielding to God. For Sartre, man *qua* man has only existence and no native essence; in Kierkegaard's case, for man to exist is to responsibly accept the essence which has been bestowed upon him.

Although it is beyond the scope of this discussion to review the full spectrum of existentialisms or even to carefully delineate all of the main types, some brief comment may be made about Kierkegaard's relationship to two chief kinds or aspects of existential position. The one is an existential attitude which does not so much identify itself with a doctrine as express itself as a mood, particularly such a mood as designated by the term 'nausea', or that occasioned by a sense of the absurdity and irrationality of existence.

Kierkegaard would undoubtedly deny that it is genuinely *existential* to say that existence is absurd; that is, he would deny that this is a true reading of existence. An examination of experience simply does not disclose the fact of existence being absurd. Such a notion, in his view, is dogma imposed upon experience. It is true that S.K. used the term 'absurd' and that he recognized that negative emotions may reveal a certain absurdity in the life of an individual—an existential failure or need. However, such negative emotions may indicate one's failure to face reality, to actualize one's true self, to genuinely exist with the meaning and purpose possible in life. That which S.K. is more ready to call absurd is the deed of God in Christ who, from a sinful human perspective, acts in seemingly irrational ways, all in order to help suffering man. Human existence in itself may be relatively rational in spite of its always being subject to both limitations and pathos.

A second existential position of more substance and of greater importance (not necessarily divorced from the first mentioned) is that of the atheistic or perhaps more properly 'secular', existentialists. Kierkegaard's relationship to them is complex and subtle. It is so, first, because it remains unclear whether and in what sense such men as Jaspers, Heidegger and perhaps even Tillich may be called atheists—or theists. The first Christians were also with some point called atheists by pagans whose gods were not transcendent nor so elusive. Second, Kierkegaard would presumably not regard secular existentialism as fundamentally wrong but rather as incomplete. In spite of his reference to a sort of natural religion, Kierkegaard would certainly not charge any atheists with being irrational, for it is Christianity which in his judgment above all violates reason. He could argue and doubtless would argue that Christianity offers man a healed existence in place of a pathetic one. Probably he would agree that only the Christian could know full or completed existence, viewing Christianity not as something added on to life, but rather as such existence before God as brings man to fullness of stature. Yet Kierkegaard would certainly add that the belief that Christian existence is *fulfilled* is not demonstrable, but is instead a *claim* of Christianity and a part of the faith-awareness of the Christian (and only of the Christian).

Zuidema develops the interesting thesis that S.K. is himself responsible for atheistic existentialism, even though he intended to use existential thought in the interest of Christianity. The point is that while he thought of the existential stages as an *ordo salutis* leading to 'religiosity B' (faith in Christ), he actually developed in the theory of stages a non-Biblical anthropology which could be used by Jaspers, Heidegger and others in complete independence of any religious concern, and as a theory of human self-redemption. Zuidema of course grants that S.K. intended the stages to be a stairway in Christian salvation but insists that they are in fact a non-Biblical philosophy illegitimately wedded to Biblical faith.[4] While it is correct that there are such non-Biblical philosophical and even commonsense roots in the theory of the stages, Zuidema overlooks the fact that for S.K. there is no stage of actual experience which is unrelated to a Biblical interpretation of man. The aesthetic and ethical stages are incomplete modes of existence for man who more or less vaguely senses his creaturely status and responsibility, but who is not yet prepared or able to face the pathos of sin and its relation to a gospel of forgiveness. The stages are indeed not simply integral parts of a Christian way to faith, but they are for Kierkegaard impoverished styles of life which can be properly and fully understood only by Christian insight. S.K. would not concede that the stages prior to religiosity B are self-contained or fully immanent and humanistic. They are not Christian, but they are not unrelated to the Christian, for they are the ways in which the child of God tries unsuccessfully to exist apart from Christ, and thus cannot be fully understood without reference to Christianity.

We may now turn to a review and summary statement of the distinctive features of existential thinking in Kierkegaard, and to some extent also consider the roles of these in subsequent existentialism.

Existence. That man has a unique kind of being and that he cannot be essentially defined as a 'rational animal' but rather must be understood in terms of his use of freedom as he responds to the world—this is a basic theme in all existentialism. This places the existentialists in the camp of the voluntarists, except, of course, that choice need not be thought of as a function of 'the will', as a separate faculty, but rather as an act of the total person. Man is most fundamentally not the creature who says 'This I am aware of' but 'Here I stand'. This is not to discount rationality in man; for S.K. even the lowest mode of existence transcends impulsive pleasure-seeking and is an intelligent human art. Nevertheless, reason does not itself establish a kind of existence; it only makes possible a structure or order within it.

Existence is in *time*. Man exists *for* eternity, but will not exist humanly *in* it, for eternity is the state of being in relation to which existence is the period of choice. 'God does not exist, He is eternal.'[5] Existence involves awareness of the future possibilities of life's commitment. One can live as an Epicurean with pleasure as a goal, as a Stoic in a life of confident duty, or as a Christian with faith in divine salvation. Since existence is passionate concern and commitment, the existing person is not a thinker who deals with timeless concepts but a person who in the flux of life continually relates himself to its possible values.

The spheres (stages) of existence—by now very familiar—are three, viz. the aesthetic, ethical, and religious (in its two forms). This specific delineation of the stages is necessarily unacceptable to the atheistic existentialists. and even Christians have not made it so central a matter as did Kierkegaard. With the reminder that by the spheres S.K. himself had in mind not step-ladder progression and no mutual exclusion, his general concept nevertheless seems fruitful.

Full existence, for Kierkegaard, is only *before God*, precisely for the reason that it is only as the self confronts God that it finds its real capacities, finds true freedom, discovers the significance of spirit, and above all gains the possibility of self-fulfilment in a life of action. Yet such Christian existence is profoundly paradoxical in that eternity transforms the instant, as God becomes Jesus, as faith takes the form of passionate need, and as trust in God becomes man's only virtue. Jolivet comments: 'The existent being knows at once both disquietude and peace, infinite terror and infinite confidence: the peace within him is compounded of disquietude itself and the terror of confidence.'[6] For S.K., unlike the atheistic and despairing existentialists, existence is repetition, not simple thing-like self-identity but a continually renewed choice of one's true and identical self as it lives in but frees itself from the process of change.

With reference to existence, later existentialists have differed from S.K. chiefly in two ways. First (as with Heidegger), the interest shifted in emphasis from the kind of being which humans possess to an analysis of all kinds of being. As Regin Prenter notes, the consequence of this is that although 'existence' is determined by acts of free moral choice and thus lacks the logical or causal necessity which are requisite for speculative interpretation, nevertheless Heidegger and Sartre are (like Hegel himself) speculative ontologists. Further, Sartre, by virtue of his definition of existence champions much that S.K. had strenuously and explicitly opposed.

Second, the analysis of existence has been attempted by many later existentialists without reference to God—although retaining some kind of transcendence—whereas S.K. viewed man as truly man (i.e. 'spirit') only when related to God. All agree that the unique feature of man's being is that it is not ready-made, nor does it come about by evolutionary growth, but only by choice. Kierkegaard stresses the positive: man may choose and thereby become himself. Sartre emphasizes the negative: man should be free, yet in freedom he annihilates himself, destroys his *present* being by choosing a future self, and eventually loses even his freedom.

Essence. It is common to say that existentialism insists that man has no essence (proper nature) but possesses only existence, i.e. that he is whatever he makes of himself. Yet such a thinker as Paul Tillich argues that an existential interpretation of man is meaningful only in the light of an understanding of his essence or nature,[7] and if Kierkegaard be accepted as the chief founder of existentialism, then this interpretation is not only false but appalling. S.K. repudiates this notion with directness, clarity, and purpose. In one sense it is true, he says, that the self (*qua* pattern) one chooses to exemplify does not yet exist and comes into being by the choice, viz. when and in so far as one creates a deviant self which is a malformation of his proper nature. It is also true that one's *actual* being as a self (as distinguished from his proper nature) is realized and in a sense created by choices. Thus one's particular selfhood is to an extent one's personal responsibility, but one does not thereby create his nature, or even escape the influence of his essentially human character. Thus Sartre makes an unqualified truth of that which for S.K. is a half-truth, i.e. that man makes himself.

Moreover, for Kierkegaard, it is equally true and certainly equally important that the self or pattern which is chosen (if the choice is godly) already has a divinely authorized status. The godly man is thus *returning to himself*, or, as S.K. puts it, 'repents himself back into himself' and at the same time 'back into the race' until he finds himself in God.[8] Although in existence there is no completely abiding or unmodified being, because in existence 'the temporal disappears' into the past,[9] yet the eternal does make itself evident by evoking an awareness of the self as an individual.[10] The eternal in man enables him to be absorbed in the present where real being is to be found, rather than turning to the past or the future.[11] More specifically, by being contemporaneous with Christ the believer receives the eternal,[12] and through faith is freed to live a proper human existence.

Plainly, existentialism per se is *not* a repudiation of essentialism, for at least in the case of Kierkegaard it is not such. To properly exist is to freely and willingly identify oneself with a divinely established pattern. This not only gives one proper relationship with God and proper identification with one's authentic self but also brings proper identification of the individual with humanity. To be an individual is in one sense to be unique, shaping one's own destiny. Yet for S.K., as for Socrates, to be an individual is to find a universal pattern and meaning in one's life to which one can appropriately commit oneself. In light of the above there is something of an historical tragedy in the fact that Kierkegaard has been frequently misunderstood at this point because of a tendency to interpret him in the light of his followers and deformers. It would be happier if, in proper historical sequence, the influence—either authentic or modified—of the founder were traced in the work of his successors.

Freedom. Implicit in all that has been said is the centrality of freedom. Yet S.K. emphatically denies that the self 'is entirely free and abstract' so that in an absolute choice it could become a different self, containing none of the old finite qualities. Indeed, returning for the moment to the context of S.K.'s stages, it is the 'whole aesthetic self' which one has been which is chosen in the absolute choice. The infinitized free self is 'quite the same self' it was before but at the same time becomes a new self in that the absolute choice 'permeates everything and transforms it'.[13] The absolute choice is not in pure freedom in the sense of abstractness. Man is *not* free to choose to be a kind of God (or lower animal), and one does not even try to do so—contrary to Sartre. Nor does he choose to be other than a man, or even a different man. If one really makes a genuine choice, then he freely chooses himself, the only self he can be, with all its hopes, sufferings, recollections, but he chooses it in its *eternal validity*, i.e. with reference to God's judgment and grace.

Not only is freedom, for Kierkegaard, concrete and circumscribed by at least the limits of his nature, rather than the abstract leap of some atheistic existentialists; it differs also for him in that the freedom of the creature fulfils itself only in a decision to be obedient to the creator. This means that man is properly free only when he chooses the good. For Sartre this would constitute the very nullification of freedom. In Sartre's view of radical or total freedom, man must be absolutely uninfluenced, even by God. There can be no eternal value laying its claim upon existing man. The consequence is that *dread* is for Sartre the very quality of human existence as such, whereas for S.K. dread is a quality of inauthentic—if typical—existence. Regin Prenter argues that whereas the ethical (constant) person alone has chosen himself, that for Sartre the authentic man is the Kierkegaardian 'aesthete', for ever freely changing.[14] Because he views man's freedom as absolute or unconditioned, Sartre views man as a would-be God. To be human is to strive in a quest for absolute freedom, but unfortunately and pathetically to experience progressive loss of freedom.

It might be argued, say by Sartre, that in his doctrine of faith and obedience Kierkegaard repudiates the entire existential outlook of responsible freedom. Whereas the existential goal had been identified as self-realization in an act of free choice, now, under divine judgment, that which for the existential thinker (and idealist) was good becomes branded as evil. Sin is precisely this pretentious attempt at 'making' oneself, and in place of freedom one becomes obedient to the mastery of God. Yet for S.K., faith —freely accepted—is itself the means of self-fulfilment. The only true freedom is obedience to God, and the only way to self-fulfilment—both as creature and as creature-turned-sinner—is through the reconstitutive power and love of God. One does existentially make himself, but not alone.

Finally, since faith is a passionate commitment to a God who remains an objective uncertainty, the free leap of faith is a dangerous adventure. It cannot be secure because there can be no rational certainty in a God-relation which involves trusting and being offended. Rational certainty would remove God from the realm of the holy, the personal and penitential, to the world of things, unflavoured by any values.

Transcendence. Kierkegaard's notion of transcendence is tied to God and the thought of paradox. The very nearness with which God-in-Christ approaches man is the means of making his transcendence secure. The possibility of taking offence at a god who has seemingly 'lost his wits' in incarnation is 'the guarantee whereby God assures Himself that man cannot come too near to Him'. 'So human is His divinity.'[15] Purportedly this basic theme of transcendence is repeated widely in existential thinking. However, there is a great line of division between the Christian and the secular existentialists on the matter. The Christian (and some other religious) existentialists agree with S.K. that God is the transcendent who breaks into man's finitude in order to redeem.

Further, they are inclined to agree that the riddle of existence is (as held not only by Kierkegaard but also by such men as Augustine, Pascal, and in a sense Nietzsche) to be found in his being stretched taut between the finite and the infinite.

The secular existentialists tend to split the concept of transcendence in two. First, there is a kind of absolute over against which they see man compelled to define himself, e.g. death, or the world. This absolute eventually masters man—death is the only inevitability—but to *exist* is to struggle creatively if temporarily against this insurmountable force. For men like Jaspers, to lovingly commit oneself to death, doom, or 'shipwreck' is proper existence, perhaps even constituting an odd kind of redemption. The unlikeness of Kierkegaard to such thinking is dramatic. S.K. would agree that death, among other things, can challenge a man to exist but he would hold that the brave and self-conscious facing of doom is not in itself proper existence but only an intensification of the pathos from which one is to be redeemed, if ever he is to have proper existence. Only God can give the enablement for authentic (redeemed) existence, and God does this, providing the possibilities of a much richer existence than that open to a resigned nihilist.

The other remnant of Kierkegaard's concept of transcendence in secular existentialism is in the notion (cf. Heidegger) that it is man himself who is transcendent. Man goes beyond himself, in a sense also beyond being for he threatens and changes being. By thus reducing the connotation of transcendence to conscious and purposive self-transformation, it is then argued that by definition God could not be transcendent since by supposed definition he is absolute and therefore not subject to change. On this view, only man remains transcendent. Without considering the question of whether God could be in such a sense self-transcendent, it is clear that for Kierkegaard while man does have an element of such transcendence, it is the infinite God that is properly—relative to man—transcendent.

Subjectivity of truth. With considerable vagueness, all existential thinkers stress the subjectivity of truth, that the truth which they seek is a truth to live by and is necessarily related to the self. Yet sharp distinctions need to be made. Frithiof Brandt is guilty of over-simplification when he asserts that all the existentialists agree on a 'subjective, emotional and volative concept of truth'.[16] However far other existential thinkers may have gone in abandoning objective truth, Kierkegaard does not do so, and his approach is not based on emotionality. For him, inwardness, or subjectivity, is the way to gain true objectivity in ethical and religious matters, in that subjective faith (not empirical objectivity) is a response to and the means of apprehension of the objectively real, eternal, and transcendent God.[17] Christianity itself is objectively factual, 'the fact that God has existed' in the world in the person of Christ, even though this fact has certainty only for faith, grasping the truth in an awareness which 'culminates in passion'. The variable intensity of this faith is, moreover, not proportionate to or dependent upon the variable degrees of objective certainty but reflects the personal freedom of religious response.[18] It is therefore not the depth of feeling but the value of the object of feeling which makes passion significant.[19] What is more, Kierkegaard repeatedly and explicitly denies that subjectivity has anything to do with perfectly objective criteria for methods of obtaining the truths of science and practical life.

Paradox. This concept is typical of existentialism. Largely because of its extensive use, and because it may initially and loosely be defined as irrationality, existentialism is often thought of as a cult of irrationality. Nevertheless, to the extent that contemporary existential thought is irrational, it is more frequently than not a deformation of S.K.'s view. Indeed, few men have been more avid intellectuals than he, and he highly honoured even such a rationalist as Hegel in spite of his lampooning of the latter's pretentious 'system'. Moreover, it must not be thought that the notion of paradox originated with Kierkegaard. It is as old as the New Testament doctrine of an eternal logos in the temporal Jesus. What is most distinctive of S.K.'s thought is the subjective significance he makes paradox have for the believer. Fundamentally, it serves as a reminder that there is something in religion which requires faith rather than reason, which can only be trusted or doubted rather than explained and understood, and which is to man a positive but strange fact to be reckoned with instead of a mere unknown temporarily beyond the human ken.

Like innumerable others, Kierkegaard did insist on the limitations of reason. Not so unlike contemporary positivistic thinkers, he pointed out that what reason provides is system, structure, or ideality—not reality. He insisted that reason cannot of itself move one to take decisive personal stands (as for home, work, love or God), which choices really make the self to be what it is. Reason can wonderfully comprehend (see what it accomplished in S.K. himself!); it can give order to life, but it cannot initiate; it cannot will, love, hate, nor have faith.

At one point and only one point does S.K.'s limitation on reason become a principle of absurdity. Existence is not absurd, nor is the world (as some existentialists have held), nor—finally—is God irrational. Nevertheless, God freely and lovingly did the absurd (which then was certainly not rationally required of him, as, for example, by the demanding circumstances of evil), in that he, the Eternal, chose to become a mere moment in the historical person of Jesus. It is, however, not so much the principles of pure logic as it is the norms of common human sensibility which are thereby violated. Christianity is, nevertheless, at least so far as man can comprehend it, absurd, and this precisely is why it remains a dramatic gospel (news) which can neither be fully understood nor made plausible, but only accepted in faith. God's deed in Christ is the supreme paradox and man's response in faith is correspondingly paradoxical. This element of irrationality in Kierkegaard, having nothing to do with the ordinary world of experience, of men or society, but instead being severely confined to Christian experience, is very far removed from a cult of irrationality. It is a bit ironic that in S.K.'s judgment only that is irrational (viz. Christianity) which is so often similarly branded as irrational by his own rationalistic critics.

Connected with the notion of paradox is that of offence, the alternative to faith. This offence is objectively two-fold in that a Jewish carpenter should claim to be God, and that the God-man should come in lowliness rather than in shining splendour. Subjectively, the offence arises over the incomprehensibility and absurdity of God's act.[20] Even though offence is the alternative to faith it also prepares the way for faith by sharpening the understanding of the mystery of divine love and sacrifice. It is 'the repellent force by which faith comes into existence'[21]

Perhaps at no point is the contrast between Kierkegaard and the secular existentialists more striking than in the concept of paradox,

In a sense Sartre would agree that God is absurd but whereas Kierkegaard would in faith accept the absurd, Sartre thereby rejects it. For the secular existentialists the objective 'absurdity' with which man must deal is not lodged in God but in the world. Albert Camus identifies the world itself as 'absurd', as it frustrates human hopes and fails to embody such meanings as man seeks to inject into it. In two important respects this differs from S.K. First, while the 'absurd' in Camus does somewhat relate to the 'Unknown' in S.K., i.e. a perplexing limit to rational understanding, it is not at all *the* Absurd, or Paradox of God, becoming offensive by entering into time and loving unlovely man. Second, Camus rejects S.K.'s 'leap of faith' whereby the absurd element is affirmed and grasped. Camus holds that proper existence is to live resolutely as a rebel, in a state of defiance of the absurd or meaningless world, and with no reconciliation with it. Existence is defiance of the cosmos.

The Individual. To have authentic existence is to be an individual. Jaspers, Marcel, Heidegger, and many others have echoed Kierkegaard's bitter complaint against the levelling effect of mass society which effect hinders a man from being his true self. Enslaved by the ideologies and fashions of the age, by the concern for sheer numbers and what the mass of men believe and do, as well as by one's own 'public', a person is for example tempted to think 'Now I am a man' at the very pathetic moment when he, like other men, yields to the slavery of passion. To personally exist is not to successfully repeat the normal actions and thoughts of the race, still less those of some momentary public. To truly exist is not to be a kind of generalized man but a unique individual, knowingly responsible for the way in which one has dedicated and shaped his life. On this point almost all of existentialism seems to follow in S.K.'s path. Indeed, it is interesting that many who are not existentialists are increasingly impressed by the insistence that any democracy which is not composed of genuine individuals can be only a frightening mobocracy.

However, the very severity of this general complaint against the mass man endangers one's understanding of Kierkegaard. Far from assuming a superior attitude towards ordinary folk, he personally loved the common people and deliberately lived in close touch with them. Most emphatically, he did not withdraw from the large community to a chosen group of companions as did Nietzsche's Zarathrustra, nor did he, after the fashion of a thinker like Jaspers, suggest an elite if austere companionship of an enlightened few. He wrote with touching concern for all, addressing himself in his later and most earnest writings to the 'plain man'. Thus did Kierkegaard forgive the simple people who had cruelly laughed at him and his physical deformity during the attack of the *Corsair*, and he continued to feel the closest affinity with them.

The 'individual' in S.K.'s thought is much the same concept as that of 'the person' in American personalism, except that the stress in Kiergaard is on the responsibility to measure up to one's potentials, rather than on the natural or native qualities of the person. There is no Stoic pride implicit here, but instead humility before God. The true individual is one who reflects and fulfils the common humanity and is as responsibly social as he is genuinely individual. In personal encounters individuals meet one another not as greater or lesser forces to be contended with, and not as mere things or objects, but as subjects who stand for something, committed selves deserving respect. Thus genuine subjectivity leads to the 'thou and I' encounter, which is supremely represented by the God-relation but is present in all social relations.[22] Subjectivity therefore puts individual man in society and in a God-relation rather than in a world of mere things or faceless humans in a crowd. Due to obvious Christian influence, Kierkegaard thought of social responsibility as a concern expressing itself primarily in religious love and only relatively and perhaps derivatively in political life, social action, or even in the fellowship of the church.

Kierkegaard's doctrine of the individual allows for two specialized forms. First, since one becomes authentic only in relation to the will and grace of God which are constant and universal, every man is an individual simply by personally relating himself to the universal and absolute. This in no way requires uniformity, however, and one is unique even in becoming what every other man ought also to be, a child of God.[23] Second, while every man has at least something different in his relation to the absolute, there are a few exceptional persons in history who find themselves set apart and even excluded from many of the normal patterns of the created order. Consequently, every man must at least contemplate the possibility of being called on to be such an exception.[24]

Lacking a divine imperative to love, the doctrine of the individual manifests itself quite differently, socially, for secular existentialists. The contrast appears strikingly in Sartre's view of social relations. For S.K. one's neighbour evokes love and a sense of duty in a Christian concern for the neighbour's true self. For Sartre, other humans evoke suspicion and even hatred as they mutually threaten one another by treating each other as mere things. Other secular existentialists show less harsh negativism in their individualism, but seldom the warmth of social concern manifest in Kierkegaard. For the latter, true individualism and true society are mutually implicative.

In conclusion, the facts here reviewed give some warrant to Cornelio Fabro's strong statement: 'Contemporary existentialists have pillaged Kierkegaard's writings without scruple. They have borrowed themes and terms in order to empty them immediately of their specific content...'[25] Without implying the illegitimacy of rival existentialisms, as Fabro's statement perhaps seems to do, it is at least vividly evident that the fundamental purposes and concepts of Kierkegaard are antithetical to a great deal of more recent existentialism.

NOTES

Chapter I

1. Cf. WALTER LOWRIE, *Kierkegaard*, New York: Harper & Brothers (1962), or (brief) Frithiof Brandt, *Søren Kierkegaard*, Copenhagen: Det Danske Selskab (1963), or (richly sensitive) Johannes Hohlenberg, *Søren Kierkegaard*, New York: Pantheon Books (1954).
2. Cf. REGIS JOLIVET, *Introduction to Kierkegaard*, transl. W. H. Barber, New York: E. P. Dutton, p. 165 f.
3. Cf. T. HAECKER, *Kierkegaard the Cripple*, New York: Philosophical Library (1950), p. 46.
4. Cf. HAECKER, *op. cit.*, p. 32 f.
5. A. USSHER, *Journey Through Dread*, New York: Devin-Adair Co. (1955), p. 38.
6. HOHLENBERG, *op. cit.*, p. 143 f.
7. *Journals*, 53.
8. *Ibid.*, 27.
9. Cf. HAECKER, *op. cit.*, pp. 41 ff.
10. Cf. P. D. LEFEVRE, *The Prayers of Kierkegaard*, Chicago: University of Chicago Press (1956), p. 133.
11. LOUIS DUPRÉ, *Kierkegaard as Theologian*, New York: Sheed and Ward (1963), p. 31.
12. USSHER, *op. cit.*, p. 10.
13. T. S. ELIOT, *The Cocktail Party*, New York: Harcourt, Brace & World (1950), p. 29 f.
14. S. U. ZUIDEMA, *Kierkegaard*, transl. D. F. Freeman. Philadelphia: Presbyterian and Reformed Publishing Co. (1960), p. 25.
15. *Fear and Trembling*, p. 68 f.
16. Cf. *Postscript*, p. 507.
17. *Papirer*, XI^1 A 570.
18. *Papirer*, VII B 235, p. 20; *Postscript*, pp. 347, 494.
19. *Either/Or*, II, p. 10.
20. *Stages on Life's Way*, p. 430.
21. Cf. *Postscript*, pp. 271 f., 99, 109.
22. *Journals*, 1029, 1031.
23. *Papirer*, XI^1 A 131; cf. foreword in *A Kierkegaard Critique*, ed. by H. Johnson and N. Thulstrup, New York: Harper & Brothers (1962).

Chapter II

1. *Diary of Søren Kierkegaard*, ed. P. P. Rohda, New York: Philosophical Library (1960), pp. 124, 121.

2. Cf. T. H. CROXHALL, *Kierkegaard Commentary*, New York: Harper & Brothers (1956), Appendix A, for the list.
3. *Point of View*, p. 39.
4. JOHANNES HOHLENBERG, *Sören Kierkegaard*, New York: Pantheon Books (1954), p. 13 f.
5. *Postscript*, p. 551.
6. Cf. CROXALL, *op. cit.*, pp. 6 ff.
7. *Postscript*, p. 551.
8. LEE M. CAPEL, in introduction to Kierkegaard's *The Concept of Irony* (New York: Harper & Row, 1965), p. 27.
9. *Ibid.*, p. 360.
10. Cf. HENRIETTE LUND's 'Recollections from Home', in T. H. Croxall, *Glimpses and Impressions of Kierkegaard*, Digswell Place: James Nisbet & Co. (1959), pp. 41 f., 52 f., 31, 57, 66, 70.
11. Cf. quoted passages in *The Concept of Irony*, pp. 27–28.
12. Cf. DAVID F. SWENSON, *Something About Kierkegaard* (rev.), Minneapolis: Augsburg Publishing House (1945), p. 12.
13. Cf. HENRIETTE LUND's 'Recollections', in Croxall, *Glimpses*, p. 64.
14. Cf. HOHLENBERG, *op. cit.*, p. 72.
15. Cf. A. DRU, *The Journals of Søren Kierkegaard*, New York: Oxford University Press (1938), p. xxxi f.
16. CAPEL, *op. cit.*, p. 360. S.K. writes a satirical reply which remained unpublished. *Ibid.*
17. *Irony*, pp. 34, 20. On varying interpretation see pp. 8, 428, 351–57.
18. *Papirer*, XI^2 A 108.
19. *Journals*, 149, 150.
20. Cf. DAVID E. SWENSON, *op. cit.*, p. 246 f.; also R. Thomte, *Kierkegaard's Philosophy of Religion*, Princeton: Princeton University Press (1948), p. 99.
21. *Diary of Søren Kierkegaard*, p. 92.
22. SWENSON, *op. cit.*, Chapter II.
23. *Papirer*, XI^2 A 147.
24. *Postscript*, pp. 448, 473 n.
25. *Ibid.*, p. 242 f. On the difficult issues as to whether humour lies between the ethical and religion A or religion B, see Thomte, *op. cit.*, p. 100 f.
26. A. A. KOYRE, *Discovering Plato*, New York: Columbia University Press (1945).
27. M. GRENE, *Dreadful Freedom*, Chicago: University of Chicago Press (1949), pp. 24–26.
28. *Journals*, 468.
29. *Sickness Unto Death*, p. 164 f.
30. *Postscript*, p. 176.
31. *Ibid.*, p. 223.
32. *Stages on Life's Way*, p. 430.
33. *Ibid.*, p. 56; *Either/Or*, II, p. 229.
34. *Journals*, 331.

NOTES

35. Cf. *Papirer*, II A 365.
36. PIERRE MESNARD, 'Is the Category of the Tragic Absent from the Life and Thought of Kierkegaard?' *A Kierkegaard Critique*, ed. by H. Johnson and N. Thulstrup, pp. 102–15.
37. JAMES COLLINS, 'Faith and Reflection in Kierkegaard', *A Kierkegaard Critique*, ed. by H. Johnson and N. Thulstrup, p. 144 f.
38. Cf. *Concept of Irony*, pp. 292 ff.
39. Cf. Introduction, in Eduard Geismar, *Lectures on the Religious Thought of Søren Kierkegaard*, Minneapolis: Augsburg Publishing House (1938), p. xviii f.
40. M. WYSCHOGROD, *Kierkegaard and Heidegger*, London: Routledge & Kegan Paul (1954), p. 30.
41. Cf. *Postscript*, p. 119 f. and *Fear and Trembling*, p. 167, note.
42. DAVID SWENSON, in Geismar, *op. cit.*, p. xviii.
43. *Sickness Unto Death*, p. 162.
44. *Works of Love*, p. 174.
45. LUKE 18:22 f.
46. Cf. *Concept of Dread*, p. 97.
47. HOHLENBERG, *op. cit.*, p. 13; *Point of View*, p. 18 f.
48. Cf. *Papirer*, IV A 112, IV A 116; also Thomte, *op. cit.*, p. 65.
49. *Postscript*, pp. 126, 138.
50. Cf. JOHN WILD, 'Kierkegaard and Contemporary Existentialist Philosophy', *A Kierkegaard Critique*, ed. by H. Johnson and N. Thulstrup, pp. 26 ff.
51. *Papirer*, XI² A 76.
52. Cf. 'The Individual', in *Point of View*, p. 127.
53. *Point of View*, p. 20. Regarding the storm created by the publication of *Either/Or*, see Hohlenberg, *op. cit.*, pp. 12–20.
54. Cf. treatment of *Repetition*.
55. *Papirer*, XI² A 130.
56. *Ibid.*, XI² A 132.
57. T. H. CROXALL, *Kierkegaard Commentary*, p. 129.
58. Passages of a still more scornful nature were deleted from the manuscript. Cf. Hohlenberg, *op. cit.*, p. 124.
59. Cf. *Postscript*, p. 271.
60. Cf. PAUL S. MINEAR, 'Thanksgiving as a Synthesis of the Temporal and the Eternal', *A Kierkegaard Critique*, ed. by H. Johnson and N. Thulstrup, p. 306.
61. Cf. *Dread*, p. 16, ftn.
62. *Works of Love*, pp. 24, 237.
63. *Fragments*, p. 23.
64. Cf. S. U. ZUIDEMA, *Kierkegaard*, p. 24.
65. *Christian Discourses*, p. 146.
66. *Ibid.*, p. 145.
67. *Ibid.*, pp. 143, 151.
68. *Ibid.*, p. 146.

69. Cf. the very brief but helpful chapter on repetition in H. V. Martin, *Kierkegaard, The Melancholy Dane*, New York: Philosophical Press (1950).
70. *Journals*, 444.
71. Introduction, *The Present Age*, p. 27.
72. *Postscript*, p. 412.
73. Cf. T. H. CROXALL, *Kierkegaard Studies*, London: Lutterworth Press (1948), pp. 124 ff.
74. *Either/Or*, II, p. 182; *Postscript*, p. 133.
75. *Journals*, 78.
76. Cf. THOMTE, *op. cit.*, p. 161.
77. Cf. W. LOWRIE, *Kierkegaard*, New York: Harper & Brothers (1962), Vol. I, p. 159.
78. Cf. *Irony*, p. 396 f.
79. *Either/Or*, II, p. 215.
80. *Fragments*, p. 102.
81. Cf. LOUIS DUPRÉ, *Kierkegaard as Theologian*, New York: Sheed and Ward (1963), pp. 116 ff.
82. *Postscript*, p. 281.
83. Cf. T. H. CROXALL, *Kierkegaard Studies*, p. 63.
84. *For Self-Examination*, p. 88; *Works of Love*, p. 192 f.
85. *Journals*, 846.
86. *Sickness*, pp. 46 ff.
87. Cf. T. HAECKER, *Kierkegaard the Cripple*, p. 11.
88. H. BUTTERFIELD, *Christianity and History*, New York: Charles Scribner's Sons (1950), pp. 114 ff.
89. *Christian Discourses*, p. 103 f.; Cf. also *Postscript*, p. 360.
90. *Christian Discourses*, p. 350.
91. *Postscript*, p. 4 f.
92. *Papirer*, XI^1 A 329.
93. M. WYSCHOGROD, *op. cit.*, p. 44.
94. *Either/Or*, II, pp. 252, 217 f.
95. *Irony*, p. 363 f.
96. *Papirer*, XI^2 A 175.
97. *Journals*, 605.
98. JOHN 7:17.
99. *Fragments*, p. 58 f. See also *Postscript*, p. 188.
100. Cf. GEISMAR, *op. cit.*, p. 44.
101. *Journals*, 616.
102. ZUIDEMA, *op. cit.*, p. 44.
103. *Papirer*, V B 151; Malantschuk, *Kierkegaard's Way to the Truth*, Minneapolis: Augsburg Publishing House (1963), p. 102.
104. *Fear and Trembling*, p. 53.
105. Cf. MALANTSCHUK, *op. cit.*, p. 102.
106. WYSCHOGROD, *op. cit.*, p. 34.
107. *Postscript*, p. 182.
108. On the radical blending of contradictories, see Zuidema, *op. cit.*, p. 35.

NOTES

109. *Journals*, 871.
110. Cf. CROXALL, *Kierkegaard Studies*, p. 118.
111. Cf. J. HEYWOOD THOMAS, *Subjectivity and Paradox*, Oxford: Basil Blackwell (1957), pp. 103 ff.
112. Cf. *Sickness*, pp. 133 ff., also the treatment below of *Training in Christianity* where paradox in incarnation is dealt with.
113. Cf. LOWRIE, *op. cit.*, Vol. I, p. 165 f.
114. Cf. N. H. SØE, 'Kierkegaard's Doctrine of the Paradox', *A Kierkegaard Critique*, ed. by H. Johnson and N. Thulstrup, p. 215.
115. *Fragments*, p. 128. Cf. also the commentary on the text by N. Thulstrup, p. 205.
116. SØE, *op. cit.*, p. 224. Cf. also the treatment below of *Reply to Theophilus Nicolaus*.
117. *Papirer*, XI^1 A 427.
118. *Postscript*, p. 514.
119. *Papirer*, XI^2 A 212.
120. *Journals*, 560.
121. *Either/Or*, II, p. 93.
122. *Postscript*, pp. 186 ff.
123. *Stages*, p. 408.
124. *Journals*, 1064.
125. *Ibid.*, 984.
126. *Journals*, 634; cf. Croxall, *Kierkegaard Studies*, p. 215.
127. Cf. MALANTSCHUK, *op. cit.*, pp. 23 ff.
128. Cf. PAUL HOLMER, 'On Understanding Kierkegaard', *A Kierkegaard Critique*, ed. by H. Johnson and N. Thulstrup, p. 51.
129. Cf. *Diary of Søren Kierkegaard*, p. 153 f.
130. *Postscript*, p. 471 f.
131. *Journals*, 967.
132. *Ibid.*, 1061.
133. Cf. N. H. SØE, *op. cit.*, p. 216.
134. Cf. ZUIDEMA, *op. cit.*, p. 21.
135. Cf. W. LOWRIE, *op. cit.*, Vol. I, p. 281.
136. *Repetition*, p. xv.
137. *Fear and Trembling*, p. 13.
138. *Edifying Discourses*, Vol. III, p. 106.
139. *Postscript*, p. 256.
140. DAG HAMMARSKÖLD, *Markings*, New York: Alfred A. Knopf (1964), p. 11.
141. *Journals*, 572.
142. Cf. HANS BRØCHNER's Recollections, in T. H. Croxall, *Glimpses*, pp. 23, 35.
143. *Stages*, p. 457.
144. *Purity of Heart*, p. 49.
145. *Journals*, December 2, 1837, in Lowrie, *op. cit.*, Vol. I, p. 100.
146. *Edifying Discourses*, Vol. III, pp. 63, 84.
147. *Papirer*, V A 25.

148. HAMMARSKJÖLD, *op. cit.*, p. 13.
149. M. GRENE, *op. cit.*, p. 27.
150. F. J. BILLESKOV JANSEN, 'The Literary Art of Kierkegaard', *A Kierkegaard Critique*, ed. by H. Johnson and N. Thulstrup, p. 14 f.
151. Cf. *Postscript*, p. 264.
152. *Either/Or*, II, p. 182.
153. *Postscript*, p. 265.
154. *Either/Or*, I, p. 37.
155. *Ibid.*, p. 357.
156. *Postscript*, p. 256.
157. See treatment of the *Postscript* and of *Gospel of Suffering*.
158. *Papirer*, XI¹ A 2.
159. *Ibid.*, XI¹ A 7.
160. *Ibid.*, XI¹ A 35.
161. 'The Banquet', *Stages*, in *Selections from the Writings of Kierkegaard*, translated by L. M. Hollander, Garden City: Doubleday & Company (1960), p. 64.
162. *Ibid.*, p. 87.
163. *Diary of Søren Kierkegaard*, ed. by P. P. Rohde, p. 95.
164. *Papirer*, XI² A 205.
165. P. 188 f. Cf. also the careful if brief treatment in *Kierkegaard Commentary* (Ch. III), by T. H. Croxall.
166. M. GRENE, *op. cit.*, p. 36.
167. *Journals*, 763.
168. Cf. C. FABRO, 'Faith and Reason in Kierkegaard's Dialectic', *A Kierkegaard Critique*, ed. by H. Johnson and N. Thulstrup, p. 161.
169. *Journals*, 1021.
170. Cf. treatment of *Reply to Theophilus Nicolaus* for S.K.'s later re-evaluation of this.
171. M. GRENE, *op. cit.*, p. 21.
172. Cf. 'The Expectation of Faith', *Edifying Discourses*, Vol. I, pp. 7–33.
173. *Journals*, 1054.
174. *Ibid.*, 605.
175. *Ibid.*, 924.
176. In introduction to Geismar, *op. cit.*, p. xxxix.
177. Cf. 'The Expectation of Faith', *Edifying Discourses*, Vol. I.
178. P. 350. Cf. Lowrie, *op. cit.*, Vol. II, p. 329.
179. *Journals*, 1079.
180. P. 405 f. Cf. also the treatment of *Gospel of Suffering*.
181. M. GRENE, *op. cit.*, p. 38.
182. On the very subtle issue of philosophical and theological influences on S.K., see J. H. Thomas, *op. cit.*, pp. 6–12, 40–44, 48–59.
183. Cf. C. FABRO, *op. cit.*, p. 172 f.
184. Cf. VALTER LINDSTROM, 'The Problem of Objectivity and Subjectivity in Kierkegaard', *A Kierkegaard Critique*, ed. by H. Johnson and N. Thulstrup, pp. 238 ff.
185. Cf. FABRO, *op. cit.*, pp. 160 ff.

NOTES

186. Cf. LINDSTROM, *op. cit.*, pp. 228-43.
187. Cf. *On Authority and Revelation*, p. 168.
188. H. S. BROUDY, 'Kierkegaard on Indirect Communication', *The Journal of Philosophy*, April 27, 1961, pp. 225-33.
189. G. MALANTSCHUK, 'Kierkegaard and Nietzsche', *A Kierkegaard Critique*, ed. by H. Johnson and N. Thulstrup, p. 124.

Chapter III

1. *Postscript*, p. xiii.
2. Cf. P. D. LEFEVRE, *The Prayers of Kierkegaard*, pp. 135, 147.
3. *Journals*, 809.
4. Cf. 'A First and Last Declaration', *Postscript*, pp. 551 ff.
5. A. USSHER, *Journey Through Dread*, p. 22.
6. S. U. ZUIDEMA, *Kierkegaard*, p. 30.
7. *For Self-Examination*, pp. 42-44.
8. *Training in Christianity*, p. 83.
9. *Diary of Søren Kierkegaard*, ed. by P. P. Rohde, p. 90.
10. Cf. J. HOHLENBERG, *Sören Kierkegaard*, p. 160. Cf. unit 53, below.
11. *Ibid.*, p. 169.
12. *Papirer*, VII[1] A 222.
13. *Fragments*, p. 131.
14. *Journals*, 1091.
15. Cf. HERMANN DIEM's difficult but valuable 'Kierkegaard's Bequest to Theology', *A Kierkegaard Critique*, ed. by H. Johnson and N. Thulstrup, pp. 244-65.
16. *Postscript*, p. 317.
17. Cf. Preface No. 3, also the postscript of *On Authority*.
18. *Irony*, pp. 263 f., 268.
19. *Papirer*, XI[1] A 55; XI[2] A 203.
20. *Papirer*, VII[1] A 205, quoted in Liselotte Richter, 'Kierkegaard's Position in his Religio-Sociological Situation', *A Kierkegaard Critique*, ed. by H. Johnson and N. Thulstrup, p. 70.
21. *Papirer*, XI[1] A 227.
22. *Diary of Sören Kierkegaard*, ed. by P. P. Rohde, p. 103.
23. *Papirer*, XI[1] A 51.
24. Cf. *The Individual*, p. 124.
25. *Point of View*, p. 59.
26. Quoted in *Purity*, p. 13.
27. Cf. ZUIDEMA, *op. cit.*, p. 18.
28. I. COR. 7:22.
29. *Papirer*, XI[2] A 8.
30. Cf. A. NYGREN, *Agape and Eros*, London: S.P.C.K. (1953).
31. *Journals*, 769. Cf. L. Richter, *op. cit.*, p. 55.
32. M. GRENE, *Dreadful Freedom*, p. 21.
33. Cf. BASIL MITCHELL, ed., *Faith and Logic*, London: George Allen & Unwin (1958), p. 213.

34. Cf. J. SLØK, 'Kierkegaard and Luther', *A Kierkegaard Critique*, ed. by H. Johnson and N. Thulstrup, pp. 85–101.
35. Cf. W. LOWRIE, *Kierkegaard*, Vol. II, p. 375 f.
36. *Papirer*, X^2 A 644. Cf. C. Fabro, 'Faith and Reason in Kierkegaard's Dialectic', *A Kierkegaard Critique*, ed. by H. Johnson and N. Thulstrup, p. 171.
37. *Papirer*, X^4 A 114. Cf. Fabro, *op. cit.*, p. 170.
38. *Works of Love*, p. 257.
39. Cf. *Postscript*, pp. 73, 137.
40. Cf. also *Point of View*, pp. 22 ff., *Training in Christianity*, pp. 122 ff., and *Postscript*, pp. 67 ff.
41. *Sickness*, p. 161.
42. *Training*, pp. 132, 134.
43. *Christian Discourses*, p. 252.
44. See appendix to treatment of *Gospel of Suffering*.
45. *Diary of Søren Kierkegaard*, ed. by P. P. Rohde, p. 73.
46. On this difficult issue see G. Malantschuk, *Kierkegaard's Way to the Truth*, pp. 89 ff.
47. *For Self-Examination*, p. 9.
48. *Diary of Søren Kierkegaard*, ed. by P. P. Rohde, pp. 94, 93.
49. Cf. T. H. CROXALL, *Kierkegaard Commentary*, pp. 112–14.
50. On Hegel's influence see *The Crisis*, pp. 17–29.
51. F. J. BILLESKOV JANSEN, 'The Literary Art of Kierkegaard', *A Kierkegaard Critique*, ed. by H. Johnson and N. Thulstrup, p. 18.
52. This is commonly regarded as autobiographical.
53. *Diary of Søren Kierkegaard*, ed. by P. P. Rohde, p. 156 f.
54. Cf. J.HOHLENBERG, *op. cit.*, pp. 191 ff.
55. BILLESKOV JANSEN, *op. cit.*, p. 7.
56. *Journals*, in Lowrie, *op. cit.*, Vol. II, p. 392.
57. ZUIDEMA, *op. cit.*, p. 16.
58. *Ibid.*, p. 17.
59. *Postscript*, p. 163.
60. *Works of Love*, p. 27.
61. See treatment of *Dread*.
62. Cf. *Either/Or*, II, pp. 217–20; also *Training*, p. 159.
63. *Journals*, 487; Croxall, *Kierkegaard Commentary*, p. 16.
64. Cf. the treatment in Louis Dupré, *Kierkegaard as Theologian*, pp. 41–43.
65. Cf. *Dread*, p. 123.
66. E. GEISMAR, *Lectures on the Religious Thought of Søren Kierkegaard*, p. 77 f.
67. Cf. MALANTSCHUK, *op. cit.*, p. 104 f.
68. *Dread*, p. 131.
69. Cf. T. H. CROXALL, *Kierkegaard Studies*, section on despair.
70. DAG HAMMARSKJÖLD, *Markings*, p. 197.
71. *Diary of Søren Kierkegaard*, ed. by P. P. Rohde, p. 106.
72. M. GRENE, *op. cit.*, p. 32.

NOTES

73. Cf. *Journals*, 1050.
74. *Papirer*, XI² A 164.
75. *Journals*, 1050.
76. *Sickness*, p. 202 f.
77. *Papirer*, XI¹ A 352.
78. Cf. *Journals*, 1050.
79. Cf. M. CHANING-PEARCE, *The Terrible Crystal*, p. 39 f.
80. HANS BRØCHNER's Recollections of Søren Kierkegaard, in T. H. Croxall, *Glimpses and Impressions of Kierkegaard*, p. 35.
81. *Point of View*, p. 77.
82. *Papirer*, XI² A 426.
83. *Journals*, 887.
84. Cf. treatment of *Reply to Theophilus Nicolaus*.
85. Cf. ZUIDEMA, *op. cit.*, p. 42.
86. Cf. *ibid.*, p. 39.
87. Cf. unit 42.
88. *Papirer*, XI² A 206.
89. Cf. N. H. SØE, 'Kierkegaard's Doctrine of the Paradox', *A Kierkegaard Critique*, ed. by H. Johnson and N. Thulstrup, pp. 207 ff.
90. Cf. FABRO, *op. cit.*, p. 202, note 44.
91. Cf. SØE, *op. cit.*, p. 210.
92. *Papirer*, X² A 594. Cf. Søe, *op. cit.*, p. 208.
93. *Journals*, 1084.
94. *Papirer*, X A 79.
95. *Papirer*, VIII A 672. Cf. Fabro, *op. cit.*, p. 176 f.
96. FABRO, *op. cit.*, p. 186.
97. SØE, *op. cit.*, p. 218.
98. *Postscript*, p. 504.
99. T. HAECKER, *Kierkegaard the Cripple*, p. 28.
100. LOWRIE, *op. cit.*, Vol. II, p. 468.
101. *Journals*, 1337.
102. HAECKER, *op. cit.*, p. 11.
103. *Journals*, 809.
104. *Ibid.*, 1304.
105. *Postscript*, p. 30.
106. Cf. ZUIDEMA, *op. cit.*, p. 41.
107. *Postscript*, p. 324.
108. *Diary of Søren Kierkegaard*, ed. by P. P. Rohde, p. 24.
109. *Journals*, 794, 335, 1181.
110. Cf. MARIE M. THULSTRUP, 'Kierkegaard's Dialectic of Imitation', *A Kierkegaard Critique*, ed. by H. Johnson and N. Thulstrup, p. 272.
111. *Papirer*, XI² A 204.
112. Cf. M. THULSTRUP, *op. cit.*, p. 270.
113. *Journals*, 581.
114. *Fear and Trembling*, pp. 103–11.
115. *Diary of Søren Kierkegaard*, ed. by P. P. Rohde, p. 152.

116. *Ibid.*, p. 166.
117. Cf. SWENSON's introduction to Geismar, *op. cit.*, p. xlvi.
118. Cf. MARIE THULSTRUP, *op. cit.*, p. 271 f.
119. *Ibid.*, p. 267.
120. *Papirer*, XI^1 A 552.
121. *Ibid.*, XI^1 A 63.
122. *Ibid.*, XI^1 A 296.
123. *Present Age*, p. 83.
124. *Postscript*, p. 366.
125. *Judge for Yourselves*, in *For Self-Examination*, p. 202. Cf. also *Papirer*, XI^1 A 572.
126. *Papirer*, XI^1 A 193.
127. *Journals*, 711.
128. *Papirer*, XI^2 A 304, 305.
129. *Ibid.*, XI^2 A 301.
130. *Ibid.*, XI^2 A 80.
131. *Ibid.*, XI^2 A 410.
132. *Ibid.*, XI^1 A 572, XI^2 A 150.
133. *Ibid.*, XI^1 A 193, XI^2 A 150.
134. *Ibid.*, XI^1 A 226.
135. *Ibid.*, XI^1 A 532.
136. L. DUPRÉ, *op. cit.*, pp. 2–21.
137. *Ibid.*, p. 222.
138. *Ibid.*, p. 189 f.
139. H. L. MARTENSEN, *Christian Ethics* (General Part), Edinburgh: T. & T. Clark (1899), p. 226.
140. March 31, 1855. *Attack*, pp. 37 ff.
141. *Papirer*, XI^2 A 19.
142. *Ibid.*, XI^1 A 56.
143. *Ibid.*, XI^2 A 294, XI^1 A 21.
144. *Ibid.*, XI^2 A 253.
145. Cf. J. HOHLENBERG, *op. cit.*, p. 220 f.; also, unit 53, below, letter of January 31, 1851.
146. *Papirer*, XI^2 A 253.
147. *Ibid.*, XI^1 A 208.
148. *Ibid.*, XI^2 A 22.
149. *Journals*, 1407.
150. *Papirer*, XI^2 A 265.
151. *Ibid.*, XI^2 A 30.
152. Cf. DUPRÉ, *op. cit.*, p. 28, ftn. 17.
153. *Training*, pp. 217–18.
154. *Papirer*, XI^1 A 546.
155. *Ibid.*, XI^1 A 556.
156. *Ibid.*, XI^1 A 150.
157. *Ibid.*, XI^2 A 154.
158. *Postscript*, p. 351; *Either/Or*, p. 193; *Postscript*, p. 289.
159. *Ibid.*, XI^1 A 587.

NOTES

160. *Ibid.*, XI¹ A 547; Malantschuk, *op. cit.*, p. 94.
161. *Papirer*, XI² A 244.
162. *Training*, p. 194.
163. *Papirer*, XI¹ A 226.
164. *Papirer*, XI¹ A 149, 150.
165. *Ibid.*, XI¹ A 204.
166. *Ibid.*, XI¹ A 289.
167. *Ibid.*, XI² A 242.
168. *Ibid.*, XI¹ A 157, 313.
169. Cf. GEISMAR, *op. cit.*, p. 91 f.
170. *Journals*, 970. See also the treatment of *What Christ's Judgment is About Official Christianity*.
171. Cf. R. JOLIVET, *Introduction to Kierkegaard*, p. 27 f.; also *Journals*, 1191.
172. *Postscript*, p. 440 f.
173. *Training*, p. 71. Cf. also *Postscript*, p. 424 f.
174. T. H. CROXALL, *Glimpses*, p. 68. However, S.K. was not impoverished, as has been intimated by some. Cf. J. Hohlenberg, *op. cit.*, pp. 152 ff.
175. Cf. R. JOLIVET, *op. cit.*, p. 42, n. 23.
176. *Journals*, p. 549.
177. *Ibid.*, p. 550.
178. M. GRENE, *op. cit.*, p. 39.
179. Letter of February 17, 1856, in T. H. Croxall, *Glimpses*, p. 42.
180. *Ibid.*, p. 102.
181. TROELS LUND's Memoirs, in T. H. Croxall, *Glimpses*, pp. 113 ff.
182. *Ibid.*, pp. 106, 84.
183. Cf. MARIE M. THULSTRUP, *op. cit.*, p. 274 f.
184. *Either/Or*, II, p. 203 f.
185. *Papirer*, XI¹ A 123.
186. *Ibid.*, XI² A 192.
187. *Ibid.*, XI² A 193.
188. *Ibid.*, XI² A 70.
189. *Ibid.*, XI² A 187.
190. *Journals*, p. 548 f.; also T. Haecker, *op. cit.*, p. 43.
191. See the extended and illuminating comments in Karl Jaspers, *Reason and Existence*, New York: Farrar & Straus (1955), pp. 40 ff.

Chapter IV

1. Cf. W. LOWRIE, *Kierkegaard*, Vol. I, p. 91; J. HOHLENBERG, *Sören Kierkegaard*, p. 48 f.
2. Cf. LOWRIE, *op. cit.*, Vol. I, p. 288.
3. Cf. FRITHIOF BRANDT, *Søren Kierkegaard*, pp. 69 ff.
4. LOWRIE, *op. cit.*, Vol. II, p. 350.
5. *Ibid.*, Vol. II, p. 351.
6. *Ibid.*, Vol. II, p. 515.

7. P. S. MINEAR, 'Thanksgiving as a Synthesis of the Temporal and Eternal', *A Kierkegaard Critique*, ed. by H. Johnson and N. Thulstrup, p. 302.
8. *Postscript*, p. 145.
9. *Ibid.*, p. 303.
10. R. JOLIVET, *Introduction to Kierkegaard*, p. 191 f.

Chapter V

1. Cf. FRITHIOF BRANDT, *Søren Kierkegaard*, pp. 104 ff.
2. DAG HAMMARSKJÖLD, *Markings*, p. 165.
3. *Journals*, 583.
4. S. U. ZUIDEMA, *Kierkegaard*, pp. 27, 33.
5. *Postscript*, p. 296.
6. R. JOLIVET, *Introduction to Kierkegaard*, p. 103.
7. P. TILLICH, 'Existentialism, Psychotherapy, and the Nature of Man', *On The Nature of Man*, by Simon Doniger, pp. 42–52.
8. *Either/Or*, Vol. II, p. 220.
9. *Works of Love*, p. 261.
10. *Purity of Heart*, p. 193.
11. *Christian Discourses*, p. 76.
12. *Training*, p. 67.
13. *Either/Or*, II, p. 187.
14. R. PRENTER, 'Sartre's Concept of Freedom Considered in the Light of Kierkegaard's Thought', *A Kierkegaard Critique*, ed. by H. Johnson and N. Thulstrup, pp. 136 ff.
15. Cf. *Sickness*, p. 206; *Training*, p. 81.
16. FRITHIOF BRANDT, *Søren Kierkegaard*, p. 110.
17. Cf. the treatment of the *Postscript*.
18. Cf. *Postscript*, p. 291; *Training*, p. 158.
19. Cf. *Postscript*, pp. 33, 288.
20. Cf. *Training*, p. 84; *Postscript*, p. 188.
21. *Training*, p. 122.
22. Cf. *Training*, p. 228.
23. Cf. *Journals*, 1050.
24. Cf. *Point of View*, p. 131.
25. Cf. C. FABRO, 'Faith and Reason in Kierkegaard's Dialectic', *A Kierkegaard Critique*, ed. by H. Johnson and N. Thulstrup, p. 158.

INDEX

Abraham, faith in the absurd, 107; pre-Christian faith, 115

Absolute, absolute commitment to, 216; *see* Eternal

Absurd, 136; a response to the age, 154; faith which lacks rational support, 155; means incomprehensible, 205; *see* Paradox; *Reply*

Adler, derided, 231; relation to Kierkegaard, 230; revelations, 230

Aesthetes, 38, 185

Aesthetic stage, chaotic, 65; 'choice' in, 47; despair in, 65, 68, 74; ironic treatment, 194; moral awareness in, 64, 78; music in, 67; passive, 64; pathos, 194; redeemed by ethical, 83 f.; refined hedonism, 64; temporal, 77; uncommitted, 195; *see* Natural religion

Aesthetic writings, 40

Andersen, Hans Christian, attack on, 44

Anxiety, *see* Dread

Apostle, authority of, 234, 293; hidden nature of witness, 234; not a genius, 292; right to martyrdom, 291

Aristophanes, on Socrates, 53

Armed Neutrality, 314; purpose of authorship, 314

Art, *see* Crisis

Asceticism, 216; an ideal but impractical norm, 34, 367, 375; opposed, 80; *see* Otherworldliness

Attack Upon Christendom, 352; aim, repentance, 353; polemical tracts, 353; S. K.'s relation to Catholicism, 355; self-criticism of Protestantism, 355

Authority, *see* Apostle

Banquet, 183; aesthetes' view of woman, 184

Bible, *see* Scripture

Boredom, 71

Catholicism, piety in, 222; S. K. and, 355; *see* Monasticism

Change, from possibility to actuality, 150

Children, 66; religion of, 214

Choice, absolute *vs.* relative, 82, 88; aesthetic, 82; danger of evasion of, 82; glory of, 247; historical, 162, 164; *see* Freedom

Christ, died for enemies, not for truth, 291; eternal contemporary, 329; not professor, 349; pattern, 349; servant, 133; tragic, 70

Christian Discourses, 275; Christian experience deepens longing, 281; like birds, a Christian is free from anxiety, but with freedom, 276; nature of, 275; penitential doubt 'Do I love God?' 280; resurrection is not immortality, 278; the eternal enters time to give consolation, 277

Christian writings, 227, 239 f.

Christianity, and natural religion, 31 f.; not subject to proof, 200, 204; objective element in, 233; paradox, 27; *see* Religion 'B'; Church

Church, can never be 'established', 330; can serve if penitent, 332, 348, 358; error of, 232; national, 363; reform of, 361

Churchmen, 38

Concept of Dread, 158; nature of, 158; psychology of anxiety, 159; *see* Dread

Concept of Irony, 47; *see* Irony; Romanticism; Socrates

Consciousness, collision point of ideality and actuality, 120

Contemporaneity, available in faith, 147; rid of historical accretions, 330; makes time and history irrelevant, 148 f., 233; not likemindedness, 149

Corsair, conflict with, 228, 231, 239, 360, 385

Cowardice, 176

Crisis and a Crisis, greatness in any art not hindered by tribulation, 283; shows continuing aesthetic interest, 282; timelessness of art, 284

425

Culture, confused with Christianity, 292, 322, 364

Death, earnestness of, 182; existential view of, 206
Descartes, 121 ff.
Despair, aesthetic, 65, 68; and doubt, 121; and melancholy, 66; cannot destroy the eternal, 305; forms and gradations of, 304; opposite, not of virtue, but of faith, 307; overcome by God, 307; the advantage of the Christian, 303; *see* Dread; *Sickness*
Dialectic of Ethical . . . Communication, 272; on indirect communication, 272; *see* Indirect communication
Diapsalmata, 63; despair in, 65 f.
Diary of the Seducer, 72; shrewdness of, 73
Don Juan (in opera), 68, 284
Doubt, and despair, 121; love a solution for, 123; not a way to truth, 123; overcome by 'following', 345; spiritual nature of, 121
Dread, glory of, in man, 159, 163, 246; in existentialism, 165; mark of spirit, 160; nature of, 161 f.; of 'nothing', 162, 167; personal background for, 160

Edifying Discourses, accompaniments, 90; aesthetic, 40; preparatory, 90 f.; significance of, 90 f.
Edifying Discourses in Various Spirits, 240
Either/Or, 59, 76; a love letter, 59; a philosophical treatise, 60; contents, 62, 79, 86; theory of existence, 61; whimsical, 73
Empiricism, partial agreement with, 81
Essence, 24; *see* Existence
Eternal, an expectation of faith, 92 f.; and the temporal, 32; breaks into time, 136, 153; brings constancy, 377 f.; disclosed only in value experience, 299 f.; enters time to restore the temporal, 217, 277; grasped by love, 103 ff.; has no history, 151; introduces a norm for the temporal, 352; involved in repentance, 242; need for constitutes perfection, 174; not an infinitude of time, 129 f.; paradox of, 205; possibility and necessity in, 308; relation to temporal, 368; role in the 'leap', 30; *see* Infinite; Instant; Resurrection; Transcendent
Eternal life, contrasted with immortality, 53, 278
Ethical stage, despair in, 84 f.; freedom in, 77, 82 f.; incorporates aesthetic, 83; involves religion, 78, 86 f., 201 f.; is unfulfilled, 164; issues in repentance, 83, 85, 86; personal and universal, 87, 189 f.; roots in eternal and universal, 78
Ethics, difference from religion, 57; not mere resignation, 125; not social action, 35; Protestant, 216 f.
Exception, radical, 113 f.; S. K. an exception, 295, 370 ff.; *see* Individuality
Existence, and essence, 24; and eternal, 33; and voluntarism, 25; Christian, 27; distinctive of man, 248; grasps essence by repetition, 152; in time, for eternity, 402; none in heaven, 218; reality, 211; responsible freedom, 402 f.; religion is fulfillment of, 218, 401 f.; spheres of, 401 f.
Existentialism, 38, 394; changes in, 394, 403; freedom in, 405; meaning of, 394 f.; pseudonyms in, 41 f.; role of essence, 398, 404; transcendence, 406; view of individual, 410; *see* Existence

Faith, a gift, 225; a God-relation, 114; accepts forgiveness, 208; accepts Paradox, 141, 208; gives treasure in heaven, 130; is immediacy after reflection, 110 f.; is individuality, 113; is resignation plus trust, 111; leap of, 87; marked by fear and trembling, 208; objectively grounded, 225; of children, 214; paradoxical, 108, 111; paradoxically free, 225; passion for the transcendent, 192; suspends the ethical, 107, 109, 115; that all

INDEX

Faith (*continued*)
things are possible, 110; *see* Leap; Subjectivity
Fatherland, articles in, 357; conflict with church, 358; nature of Christian 'witness', 358
Fear and Trembling, contents, 105 f.; solution of broken love, 106; study of faith, 105; title, 105; view of faith, 107 ff.
Finite, break with, 215 f.; relative commitment to, 215 f.
For Self-Examination, Christ is narrow Way, 341; genius of Protestantism is protest, not reform, 341; initiates attack on Christendom, 341; scripture a mirror, 342; the Spirit gives new but costly life, 346
Freedom, choice in, 75; definitive of ethical, 77; implies the eternal, 162; mark of spirit, 163; only for choice of good, 164; stands for possibility, 308
From the Papers, 43

Genius, without authority, 233; *see* Apostle
God, objective uncertainty grasped in passionate inwardness, 213; only existentially grasped, 308
Gospel of Suffering, nature of, 248; purpose not theodicy but therapy, 249; *see* Suffering

Hegel, and tragedy, 70; appeal to, 44, 48; attack on, 50, 55, 60, 75; mediation of rejected, 74 f.; presuppositionless, 122 f.; treatment of religion opposed, 75
Heiberg, 172, 282
Heracleitus, 105
Herr Phister, 285
High Priest—the Publican—the Woman, Christ a High Priest, 310; publican a model of humility, 311; sinful woman's love, 311
Higher criticism of scripture, irrelevant, 146
Historical, point of departure for eternal, 136; result of choice, 162, 164; *see* Eternal; Instant
History, the realm of freedom, 151
Holy Spirit, gives new life, 346
Humanism, 26
Humility, 220
Humour, an intermediate stage, 51

Idealism, rejected, 136, 137
Image of God, 247, 320
Imitation of Christ, not reduplication, 350
Immediacy, 64, 110
Immortality; *see* Eternal life; Resurrection
Incarnation, hidden God in visible man, 328
Indirect communication, 26 f., 63; instruction from God, not from communicator, 273; is ironic, 274; reflects teaching of Christ, 274, 388; volition cannot be taught, 272 f.
Individual, 317; Christian an individual, 315 ff.; in *From the Papers*, 45; only a few individuals to be exceptions, 295, 370, 371; S. K. an individual, 315; degraded by the crowd, 316
Individuality, does not invalidate universal, 189 f.; image of God, 320; incomplete principle, 115 f.; loss of, 238; of Christian, 235; opposed to universal, 113; relation to eternal and to society, 238 f.; solitary, 238
Infinite, *see* Absolute; Eternal
Instant, 136, 362; is moment of faith, 372; when eternal enters time, 148, 207
Instant, not an attack on Christianity, 364 f.; otherworldliness in, 366; polemical tracts, 363; to separate church from state, 363; to stir up conscience, 363
Irony, an intermediate stage, 51; defined, 48, 51; in Socrates, 47; personal background, 47

Job, problem of, 124
Johannes Climacus, study of doubt, 119; theory of reality and knowledge, 120; *see* Doubt
Journals, 379

Judaism, an optimistic piety, 351, 375; as ethical life, 58, 330
Judge for Yourselves! Christ a pattern, 349; dying to the world, 351; false pretenses, 348; opposed spiritual flabbiness, 347; preacher who did not live as he preached, 347
Judge William, 79; relation to S. K., 81, 86

Kant, and S. K. on moral law, 87, 260
Kierkegaard, anticipated early death, 49; asceticism, 34, 367 ff.; choice of suffering, 231; conversion, 227; crises, 21; death, 371; did not abandon universal, 376; essentially religious, 396; exemplified love, 261; existed as a Christian, 228; fanaticism, 366; genius, 233; humility, 372 f.; love affair, 21, 80, 95, 106, 190 f.; meaning of, 21 ff.; melancholy, 44, 66, 160; parental influence, 19; peril of self-righteousness, 368; personality, 17; plan of authorship, 312, 315, 320 ff., 374; poet, 232, 285 f.; prayer life, 391; pseudonyms of, 41; relation to existentialism, 394, 401 ff.; relation to Judge William, 81, 86; social conservative, 239; Socratic task, 372; tragic, 70; two-fold message, 23; use of indirect communication, 228; wished for martyrdom, 289; a witness, 228

Leap of faith, 30, 75, 87, 199; term borrowed from Lessing, 224
Lessing, 224
Lilies of the Field, parable of lily and bird, 245; parable of wood pigeon, 246; splendour of man, 246 f.
Lilies of the Field and the Birds of the Air, beauty of, 285; repudiates the poetic, 286; silence, obedience and joy, 286
Literary Review, 236
Love, an imperative, 260; agape, 260; how love works, 268; intensely personal, 260; is invisible life of spirit, 258 f.; is neighbour-love, 263; individualistically social, 263; introduces the transcendent, 261 f.; not reformatory, 262 f.; not sentimental, 265
Lutheranism, S. K.'s place in, 354 ff.

Marriage, defense of, in *Stages*, 188 f.; ethical validity, 79; exception to, 106, 189; makes love a duty, 181; not invalidated by exception, 190
Martensen, attacked, 358; on doubt, 119
Meditations from Kierkegaard, 387
Melancholy, 66 f.
Miracles, 334
Monasticism, 216, 219, 257; see Asceticism
Music, immediacy of, 67
My Activity as a Writer, S. K. a reader of his writings, 320; sought attention by aesthetic works, then wrote on religion, 321
Mynster, attack on, 358; S. K.'s relation to, 359

Natural religion, 31 f., 178, 200; ends in despair, 178 f.; is wonder before the Unknown, 152, 178; issues in guilt, 180, 181; see Religion 'A'
Necessity, does not determine actuality or being, 150; identical with meaning or essence, 150
Newspaper articles, 384
Novel, theory of, 45

Objectivity, 233; see Subjectivity
Otherworldliness, 367; called for, 374 f.; qualified, 220; rejected, 53; see Monasticism
Offense, at revelation, 134, 137, 204, 323, 349
Omnipotence, can make anything a perfect gift, 93, 125
On Authority and Revelation, on church, 232; on mass mind, 232; significance of, 230
On the Difference, 236
Opera, 68

Papirer, 11, 379
Paradox, a divine act, 144; ambiguity, 156 f.; as offense, 203; existential meaning, 145; faith and, 141; influenced by Hume, 155; in

INDEX

Paradox (*continued*)
  revelation, 141; lesser paradoxes, 155; positivism akin, 205; relates to faith/offense rather than to bewilderment, 157; result of sin, 144; *see* Absurd
Pastors, guilty of compromise, 360
Patience, 125, 127
Perfect gifts, only from God, 125
Perfection, is need for God, 174
Philosophical Fragments, Christianity, its subject matter, 131; hypothetical, 131; nature of, 131 f.; parable of king and maiden, 132
Plato, analysis of dialogues, 52
Poetry criticized, 286
Point of View, entire authorship was religious, 312; S. K. a poet who was educated by his writings, 313
Positivism, 81, 205, 212
Postscript, existential rather than dogmatic, 198; place in authorship, 227 f.; purpose, 214; title, 199; treats transcendent Christianity, 201
Prayer, denial of is a good gift, 93; gives concord through solitude, 180; is silence, 176, 391; victorious when God conquers, 176
Prayers of Kierkegaard, prayer the epitome of existence, 391; spiritual quality of, 390 f.
Prefaces, attack on Heiberg, 172; nature of a preface, 172; purpose and plan, 171
Present Age, dehumanization of society, 238; significance of, 237
Professor, 37, 330, 349
Protestantism, ethics of, 216; piety, 222; S. K.'s relation to, 355
Pseudonyms, authors, 41; existential, 42; nature of, 43; relation to S. K., 42, 62 f.
Purity of Heart, honest confession, 244; nature of, 241; path to repentance, 241; to be an individual, 243; to will one thing, 243

Quidam's Diary, autobiographical, 191; contents, 190 f.

Regine Olsen, 21

Religion 'A', a pre-Christian quest, 202; an awed response to the Unknown, 153; good but pathetic, 152; only immanent, 202; optimistic and humanistic, 202; is resignation, 112
Religion 'B', by faith recovers what is lost, 112; gives composure in suffering, 192; involves guilt and joy, 193; marked by pessimism and grace, 202; marked by yearning and by tension between time and eternity, 174 f.; reached by leap of faith, 200; transcendent, 202
Repetition, a love letter, 94; autobiographical, 100; plan of, 96 f., 99; purpose, 95
Repetition, aesthetic, 97 f.; attaining the 'impossible', 99; concept of, 96; contrasted with recollection, 103; gaining the eternal, 102 f.; identity of self, 97, 101; in *From the Papers*, 45; religious significance, 97, 100, 103
Repentance, 83; *see* Ethical stage
Reply to Theophilus Nicolaus, 'absurd' means offense to unbelievers, 334; corrected definition of paradox, 334; faith not contrary to reason but above it, 335 f.; paradox is a divine call, 336
Resurrection, unlike immortality which is a sedative, 278; causes fear and trembling, 279; *see* Eternal
Revelation, blocked by sin, 134; discloses the eternal, 137; objectivity of, 233; self-authenticating, 135
Richard III, 115
Romanticism, agreement with, 49; attack on, 49; defective view of self, 56 f.; deformed view of irony, 56
Rotation method, escape from boredom, 72

Schleiermacher, 226
Scripture, a mirror, 342; existential use, 344; S. K.'s reliance on, 342, 344; wrong use, 343; *see* Revelation
Seduction, 72
Self, apprehension of, 75; *see* Soul
Sensuality, attack on, 77

429

Sexuality, 169, 374
Sickness Unto Death, Christian view of existence, 297; greatness of, 296; man an insecure synthesis of temporal and eternal, 298 f.; man is spirit by virtue of duty to eternal, 299; sickness is disorientation to God and inner disproportion, 302; *see* Despair
Sin, 58, 164; absolute guilt, 85, 88; can cause dread or issue from it, 170; distorts finitude, sensuousness and sexuality, 169 f.; is alienation from God, 166; original, 135, 168 f.; paradox of, 85; presupposes itself, 167; *see* Sickness
Society, hides from God, 242; *see Present Age*
Socrates, ethics of, 58; ironist, 47, 52; maieutic, 40, 47; on recollection, 134; presumptuous as a martyr, 290; S. K.'s identification with, 50
Solitude, 238
Soul, a becoming, with Christ as measure, 297 f., 301; acquired in patience, 125, 127; synthesis of finite and infinite, 218; synthesis of time and eternity, 125, 160, 174
Spirit, *see* Soul
Stages, 28; aesthetic, 29; number of, 28 f., 61; philosophies of life, 29; relations, 31; transitions, 30
Stages on Life's Way, aim, 194; autobiographical, 195 f.; nature of, 183; *see* Banquet; Marriage; Quidam's Diary
State, changing view on, 48; state church, 363
Subjectivity, gains objectivity, 209, 224 f.; Hegelian, 210, 223; is free obedience, 209; is truth, 209 f.; kinds of, 224; not arbitrary, 226; Platonic, 210; *see* Faith
Suffering, can be light, 249; caused by man, 175; Christian, 175, 221; gift of God, 93 f.; in S. K.'s last writings, 254; God's way, 251; mark of Christian, 256; mark of fallen world, 255; mark of spirit, 255; mysterious, 193, 250; natural suffering, 255; not all is Christian, 254; peril of pride in, 253; result of sin, 255; to be accepted as instruction, not with apathy, 250; unavoidable for Christian, 249; varied meanings, 221; *see* Religion 'B'

Temporal, 33
This Has to be Said, cease church attendance, 360; reform of church, 361
Thoughts on Crucial Situations, nature of, 177
Time, durational nature, 89, 164
Tragedy, 68 f.
Training in Christianity, attacks church's betrayal of Christianity, 323; Christ the eternal contemporary, 329; church should confess failures, 332; contents, 324 f.; Copenhagen's evasions of Christ, 326
Transcendence, apprehended only by 'expectation', 81, 129, 212, 218; an Unknown, 139; as divine limit, 36; beyond rational demonstration, 145; existential meanings of, 139, 205; God, 138; object of faith, 92; paradoxical, 139; unimaginable, 142; *see* Unknown
Truth, existential, 212; is subjectivity, 210 f., 222; relates to subject, not object, 224; valuational, 225
Twentieth century, 17, 35.
Two Discourses at the Communion, love includes judgment and requires penitence, 339 f.
Two Ethico-Religious Treatises, apostles alone have a right to be martyrs, 291; apostles not men of genius but of authority, 292; exceptions among individuals, 295; importance of book, 288

Unchangeableness of God, always available, 377; changeless love, 377; forgets no sins, 377
Unknown, Christian significance, 139, 144; passion for, 139; *see* Transcendence

Voluntarism, 25, 399, 402

INDEX

Woman, *see* Banquet; Marriage
Woman that was a Sinner, eulogy, 311, 337; trust Christ rather than imitate him, 338
Work, ethical validity of, 81
Works of Love, 258; an ethic, 258; Christian love, 259; identification with Luther, 266; S. K. not Catholic, 266; *see* Love

Xenophon, on Socrates, 53

Youth, naturally religious, 128

For Product Safety Concerns and Information please contact our EU
representative GPSR@taylorandfrancis.com
Taylor & Francis Verlag GmbH, Kaufingerstraße 24, 80331 München, Germany